STATES OF SUBSISTENCE

Diliana,

Hoping this book offers food for thought. Wishing you all the success.

In solidarity,
Jun

Stanford Studies *in* Middle Eastern
and Islamic Societies *and* Cultures

STATES OF SUBSISTENCE

The Politics of Bread in Contemporary Jordan

José Ciro Martínez

STANFORD UNIVERSITY PRESS

Stanford, California

STANFORD UNIVERSITY PRESS

Stanford, California

Printed in the United States of America on acid-free, archival-quality paper

Library of Congress Cataloging-in-Publication Data

Names: Martínez, José Ciro, author.

Title: Performing the state : the politics of bread in Hashemite Jordan / José Ciro Martínez.

Other titles: Stanford studies in Middle Eastern and Islamic societies and cultures.

Description: Stanford, California : Stanford University Press, 2022. | Series: Stanford studies in Middle Eastern and Islamic societies and cultures | Includes bibliographical references and index.

Identifiers: LCCN 2021041612 (print) | LCCN 2021041613 (ebook) | ISBN 9781503630369 (cloth) | ISBN 9781503631328 (paperback) | ISBN 9781503631335 (ebook)

Subjects: LCSH: Bread industry—Political aspects—Jordan. | Bread industry—Subsidies—Jordan. | Bread—Government policy—Jordan. | Public welfare—Jordan. | Jordan—Politics and government.

Classification: LCC HD9058.B743 J653 2022 (print) | LCC HD9058.B743 (ebook) | DDC 338.4/76647523095695—dc23

LC record available at https://lccn.loc.gov/2021041612

LC ebook record available at https://lccn.loc.gov/2021041613

Cover design: Kevin Barrett Kane

Cover image: Adobe Stock

Typeset by Kevin Barrett Kane 10.5/14.4 Brill

اعطي الخباز خبزو لو اكل نصو

Let the baker make bread, even if he eats half.

Levantine proverb

Contents

BREADLINES

On a cold Saturday morning in early November, Zayd and I leave his house, walk a couple of blocks, and join a single-file line. About ten people are ahead of us; another five soon join behind. The queue moves swiftly. It always does. While we wait, an unmistakable aroma wafts through the air. A scent impossible to confuse, and even harder to resist. The local bakery is in full swing, and the breeze carries the distinctive smell of bread. We come here often, and Zayd's order is always the same—three kilograms of bread, fresh out of the oven—what he describes as the vital component of his family's breakfast of hummus, falafel, and *ful* (fava beans).

Across the Hashemite Kingdom of Jordan, variations of this scene occur every day. Families pick up bread to make a speedy breakfast before school. Construction workers briefly pause their labors to collect items for their second meal of the day. Friends gather to eat after football. Office workers descend upon hectic sandwich stands during their breaks and commuters hastily gather supplies for dinner on the way home. More than nine million people reside in Jordan. Each day, they eat approximately ten million loaves of *khubz 'arabi*—the slightly leavened flatbread also known as Arabic or pita bread. Some rely on this bread to avoid starvation, others to help make ends meet. For the more fortunate, it is an occasional pleasure, rather than a gauge of poverty. But inevitably, on all days and at all working hours, someone goes to the bakery, where *khubz 'arabi* sells for the subsidized price of 16 *qirsh*

(US$0.25) per kilogram. Without exception or exclusion. Devoid of doubts or apprehensions, without conditions or prerequisites. So easily accessible that one can forget the many hands that make it. So palpably present that one can overlook the vast array of actions required to provide it. "There's bread," Zayd beams as we wait. "There's always bread."

It took me some time to realize that these scenes and routines would become the indelible heart of this book. I had thought, and was often taught, that politics was entirely distinct from the mundane; that politics was about big institutions and even bigger events: revolutions, coups d'état, wars, elections. It required the detailed study of campaigns and coercion. Data sets were needed, large-scale surveys indispensable, lab experiments highly recommended. There was simply no occasion for the monotonous or humdrum, the dreary or commonplace. The real action happens elsewhere, I was led to believe, far from the tedium of the quotidian. And so I went in search of that "real action," only to realize that the ordinary was more significant. Perhaps we are governed not at the level of the spectacular or the episodic but in the realm of the most mundane: the actions, experiences, and repetitions that make up the everyday.

We have all waited in line for food. Many of us have experienced analogous forms of anticipation or excitement while waiting for bread and baked goods. The familiar monotony of purchasing a basic foodstuff and consuming it among neighbors and co-workers makes such occasions easier to dismiss as having political import of any kind. This book, then, is a call to pause, to consider both the routine practicalities and broader repercussions of these moments. It addresses how subsidized bread is made, moved, and managed as well as the ways in which it is demanded, distributed, and desired. Most centrally, it asks why bread is there and what it is doing. How come bread is never lacking, when so many other things are? Why do so many in Jordan continue to demand that it be made available as a public good? What are the politics of this food?

There are many ways to answer these questions. Several would lend themselves more easily to the comfort of an armchair or the efficiency of a linear regression. I chose another path—to situate myself as deeply and durably as possible in the processes I sought to examine. And to think with, rather than against or without, those from whom I learned and with whom I lived. I eschewed distant observation. Instead, I decided to bake. To blend, beat, dust, fold, knead, mix, mold, proof, punch, score, and soften. Week after week, loaf after loaf, with weak arms and terrible posture but no shortage of enthusiasm, I observed, listened, and participated. To better understand how bread becomes welfare, and how welfare becomes something else entirely.

This book is not a detailed study of Jordanian bakeries. Nor does it offer a social history of bread or bread riots. It is instead an attempt to study the state ethnographically, in places where it is rarely disinterred and displayed. These settings are varied and unevenly examined, but they all seek to illuminate how the state coheres—not as a thing or institution, but as an effect of power that assembles and entangles. My argument here does not just interrogate the state's apparent unity or expose its inconsistencies, but thinks through some of the ways the state maintains its permanence and inevitability—the labors, echoes, and reverberations required to make an unwieldy set of processes transpire in its name. Despite its continual construction, the state appears robust and durable. Notwithstanding its manufacture, it feels and appears perpetually stable. How is this feat achieved?

As it is only through practice that subjects and objects are actualized, this book examines material, bodily, and discursive practices in order to explore how the state becomes a tangible, thinkable entity among Jordanians. I have turned to the bakery and started with bread in order to approach power at its point of generation and consequence rather than the other way around. That is, I look at power where it occurs and see where that leads, rather than automatically attribute agency or actuality to someone or something. Examining bread may seem at first glance an odd way to do this. My own fascination with this foodstuff arose because I very much loved to devour it; only later did its import become discernible. Despite its undeniable ubiquity in accounts of Middle East politics, bread has always functioned as the prompt for a story about social contracts and authoritarianism, a metonym for the exchange of basic goods for acquiescence, sustenance for compliance. As an object of inquiry itself, bread has been all but invisible. We have little sense of how it is prepared and produced, used and consumed, discussed and circulated. Here I want to give a sense of these dynamics while drawing *khubz 'arabi*, and the welfare program that ensures its discounted provision, into a constitutive relationship. Like sugar and oil, bread establishes connections and enacts realities, in careful alliance with people and things.[1]

Foremost among these associations are those with the structure that is imagined and felt to provide the bread. And it is this relationship that I will scrutinize here, in order to explore how one foodstuff both governs and creates the effect of a structure doing the governing. Not to do away with the state, but to pursue more insistently the conditions of its emergence, operation, and reproduction. Without glorifying the ostensibly menial, this book seeks to reinsert the routine and commonplace into our thresholds of visibility and analysis. Perhaps we are formed, acted upon, and dominated—anchored in this world—not by structures that exist outside ourselves but through forms and practices folded within our bodies amid the unglamorous and unspectacular day-to-day. Maybe the forces that govern us do so not from a distance, but through the immediate and immanent—the rhythms and routines, the sociomaterial worlds in which we dwell, subsist, and survive. And yet . . . we do not live on bread alone.

Acknowledgments

This book is mired in debts. Most big, others small, and the majority of them ones I will never be able to fully repay. The earliest ones accrued in the Berkshires. Robyn Marasco pushed me to read and ruminate. She continues to remind me that the study of politics is an art, not a science. Mary Lynn Chick opened new worlds. Ngoni Munemo, James Mahon, and Magnus Bernhardsson were munificent with their knowledge, time, and sense of curiosity. Kiren Chaudhry offered an inimitable primer on serious research. Michael MacDonald remains a valued interlocutor, no longer just an ally or the most generous of mentors but a friend.

In Cambridge, Glen Rangwala provided endless insight and support. Alex Jeffrey offered nourishing advice and stimulating conversation. Too many friends discussed this work with me, offering suggestions and saving me from missteps. For doing so with sympathy, humor, and good cheer, I thank Ana Almuedo Castillo, Arthur Asseraf, Adam Bobbette, Justin Decker, Dima Krayem, Fabrice Langrognet, Sheina Lew-Levy, Eduardo Machicado, Jeff Miley, Lizzie Presser, Ed Pulford, Tom Pye, Ryan Rafaty, Hana Sleiman, Hester van Hensbergen, and Michael Vine.

Houchang Chehabi was an unfailing wellspring of guidance. I am glad he introduced my parents, and that we have developed a friendship all our own. Igor Polesitsky and Jeff Thickman offered food, music, and a respite from work in moments when all three were sorely needed. I have yet to find better hosts. In Puerto Rico, or among its all too rapidly expanding diaspora, Juan Pablo Acosta, Carla Benito, Luis de la Rosa, Cheryl Díaz, Tarek El Gammal, and Ian Lloreda deserve special mention. They may not know it, but our times together always nourished this book. And I am grateful to Lina Nejem and the Eid family in Damascus for spending countless hours teaching me Arabic, long before this project got off the ground.

The Gates Cambridge Scholarship, Trinity College, the Cambridge Humanities Research Grant, the Binational Fulbright Commission in Jordan, the Council of American Overseas Research Centers, and the American Center of Research (ACOR) in Amman all offered generous funding for this project. At ACOR, I thank Barbara Porter for her thoughtful encouragement, and for kindly sharing many contacts. Nisreen Abu al-Shaikh and the librarians Samya Khalaf and Carmen Ayoubi were eager bread tasters and went above and beyond their duties to help me track down sources and organize field research. The Project on Middle East Political Science (POMEPS) and the Middle East Initiative at the Harvard Kennedy School kindly cosponsored a book development workshop that helped me to craft this story. Jillian Schwedler and Erica Simmons offered incisive comments and charitable critiques. So too did Marc Lynch, Daniel Neep, Deen Sharp, and Sean Yom. For charitably reading and commenting upon different parts of this book, I must also thank Alia al-Kadi, Salma al-Shami, Paul Anderson, Thierry Desrues, Veronica Ferreri, Salwa Ismail, Alex Mahoudeau, Zachariah Mampilly, Simon Springer, Tariq Tell, Lewis Turner, and Rami Zurayk. For their feedback on this work at its later and more stressful stages, thank you to Yael Navaro, Mezna Qato, and Sherene Seikaly. All three inspired and encouraged me, and I am grateful for their examples.

In Jordan, I am eternally appreciative of those at the Bakery Owners Association who made my fieldwork possible. Without the kind prodding and support of the many comrades in Amman's bakeries, this book would have been far less interesting. Despite our many disagreements, Mohammad al-Momani, Marwan al-Qasim, Jawad Anani, Mustafa Hamarneh, Hani Mulqi, Omar Razzaz, and Umayya Toukan were all generous with their time, thoughts, and memories. I am sad that I cannot name the many others involved in my research, many of whom have asked not to be identified. Abu Fahed and the enormous Adarbeh family are unidentifiable enough that I can mention them here. I thank them for their hospitality and innumerable conversations over family meals and cups of tea. The rest, I can only hope, find their voices and insights expressed fittingly in this work. They have taught me more about politics, generosity, and friendship than I could have ever imagined. Their wisdom I hope to carry with me, for as long as I can.

For offering healthy distraction and friendship while in the field, I thank Ayman Adarbeh, Zied Adarbeh, Matt Demaio, Khaled Elkouz, Zainab Hasan, Ayman Hassouneh, Ahmad Hourani, Marwan Kardoosh, Hani Khouri, Eda Pepi, Christine Sargent, and Steven Schaaf. I am grateful to Estee Ward for long walks, as well as many other occasions, during which she let me talk endlessly about bread. Abdul Qader Dali taught me about courage and patience, and preserving both with a smile. Nadine Fattaleh offered stellar research assistance. This book is better because of her attention to detail. I was lucky enough to coincide with Ali Nehmé Hamdan at ACOR. Conversations there proved crucial to the development of this work. Fernando Tormos-Aponte has been there from the beginning. I thank him for many things, most crucially for constantly reminding me of what is truly at stake in what we try to do, even though we often fail. We have been in continuous conversation for twenty years. I can only hope we get at least twenty more.

Two friends lie at the core of this book. They have read every word, improved every sentence. Omar Sirri I met by good fortune in a sweaty basement in Fairfax, Virginia. His dazzling prose has stimulated my own. His big heart and warm smile made the hard days easier. Brent Eng has been and remains a crucial interlocutor. He is a giving reader, an inspiring thinker, and the most wonderful of friends. From Skopje to Second Circle, Córdoba, Thessaloniki, and Queens, he has always brought me insight, laughter, and optimism. Aside from his questionable taste in sports teams, I hope he never changes.

Lastly, but no less important, my family. Mohammed El-Bachouti and Danielle Martínez Tully persistently offered support, as did Shirin and Mina Milantchi. So too did Amir and Sussan Ameri. José Roberto Martínez Ramírez patiently taught me to read and write. And to cultivate affections for both of these fundamental tasks across the languages that he also made come alive. My sister, Mercedes, was an endless source of enthusiasm and camaraderie. Without her, this book would have taken far longer than it did. I had the good fortune of living with my brother, Darío, during nine months of fieldwork. I thank him for looking at innumerable drafts of this work in its early stages, and for always pushing me to do better. His modesty and acute sense of solidarity are traits I seek to emulate. Camille Ortega Rodríguez entered my life towards the end of this project. I am glad she did. The final push would have been far more onerous without her encouragement. On bad days, her love gives me hope. On the good ones, her laugh makes me smile. My world is irrevocably and beautifully different because she arrived. Finally, I thank my best friend and mother, Setare Milantchi. The time, effort, and zeal that went into this project are all a testament to her own resolve, resilience, and strength of character. Without her love and unending sacrifice, this book would simply not have been possible. And so I dedicate this work to her. For believing in me when, rather simply, even I no longer did.

Notes on Translation and Transliteration

I have transliterated most Arabic terms using the simplified system recommended by the *International Journal of Middle East Studies*. When transliterating words and phrases from Jordanian spoken Arabic, I have done my utmost to retain the language in its original form. Long vowels and diacritics have been left out in order to make the text more fluid and to minimize confusion for non-Arabic speakers. Names and surnames have been rendered according to the preference of those cited or interviewed.

STATES OF SUBSISTENCE

INTRODUCTION

HANI PAUSED TO REFILL HIS GLASS, asking for the sugar as he complained, one last time, about my recurring failure to make the tea sweet enough. I started to offer my usual response—I prefer tea with sugar, not sugar with tea—but he cut me off. Though convivial and kind, Hani was not one to digress. Business was his creed, bakeries and restaurants the pillars of his conversation. The rest was futile chitchat.

Today was different, though. I had only a few hours left before my noon flight. I knew the last people I wanted to see. At nine in the morning, the bakery was sweltering—muggy, damp, and stifling. The oven's flame had just been turned down. The morning rush hour had given way to a brief lull, and everyone's exhaustion was palpable. The bakers behind Hani scarcely managed a tired wave as I yelled my greetings to those inside the life-giving crypt. Already, these bakers were sweating, dripping, and steaming. The workday here had started four hours earlier, and they had at least another ten hours to go. I had made the tea, as had once been my charge, in an effort to prevent sadness from enveloping our farewells. The bakers must have sensed my unease. They swiftly downed tools and joined Hani and me at the storefront, smoking in unison. Outside, cars and trucks passed by in a storm of noise and a relentless honking that somehow never became drab.

Hani's blue shirt was coated with flour—a thin, off-white dusting that suggested he had been required to bake that day, an increasingly uncommon occurrence, given his age and station. A bakery owner for the past twenty years, and a salaried baker for twenty before that, he has seen Jordan's commercial bread industry be born, rise, and ripen. His bulging neck and barrel chest speak of a life of exacting manual labor; he owes his protruding forearms, lower back pains, and disjointed but nimble wrists to incalculable hours spent making bread. Hani describes himself as a *khabbaz* (baker): he bakes and sells *khubz* (bread) for a living.

The Jordanian government began subsidizing the price of this foodstuff in 1974. Ever since, bakers like Hani have worked with government regulations and ministerial inspections, alongside flour and yeast, to provide what has become the country's most important staple. Hani often reminded me that, in the early years, this bread was a novelty, something that only the displaced and destitute ate. Others still grew and milled wheat and made their own dough, which they then baked in a village or neighborhood oven. Fairly quickly, however, population growth and foreign cereals undercut these practices. Soon, everyone found it easier, and cheaper, to swing by the bakery and purchase what had once been disparagingly called *khubz al-suq* (bread from the market). By 2013, the year I first came to Hani's, there were more than 1,500 bakeries operating across Jordan. The vast majority were small, unassuming establishments, with at most six or seven employees. Profits were consistent but not particularly abundant. The bakery is a volume business, one that is enhanced if the owner can buy the ingredients and machinery necessary to make more profitable cookies and pastries. Hani did neither. His bakery made subsidized bread, nothing more, nothing less. And it did this well. "If one has bread, one has life, and what better than to give life?" Hani was fond of asking after a strenuous day. "We give life."

On this last day, Hani reached over my shoulder to grab the small carton of sugar from the nearby counter, then waited while I served the others tea. Before I finished, I heard his gruff voice behind me, calling my name.

"So, what will you tell the world you've learned," he asked, "besides how to mess up a cup of tea?"

Enveloped in clouds of flour, I thought about operating the mixer and working the oven. I remembered days spent shaping unformed dough and rolling it into temporary submission. But I knew this was one of those questions that Hani asked only to answer it himself before anyone else could chime in.

"That we live only for bread? That we exchange it for freedom?" he probed, as he grabbed the back of my neck affectionately. "No," he chuckled.

We had discussed overtly political topics on only a few occasions. It was usually late at night, after some of the workers had left and in response to a particular news story or personal travail. Discerning and caustic in equal measure, Hani did not particularly resent the Jordanian king, although he found the entire premise of monarchy baffling. His critiques of US empire were cutting, but not particularly aggrieved. It was the impulse to govern, to rule and exercise power over others, that troubled him.

"No, there is no exchange," Hani stated, as the rest of us listened. "They give us bread and nothing more. We have no say, no escape, because we are part of the same system we oppose. Sometimes we forget, but because we are used to it."

"Used to what?" one of the bakers shouted.

Hani gave a knowing smile, the whole room silent at his feet: "Used to being governed, used to feeling that way every single day."

The somber tone quickly subsided, the serious subject matter as well. Two of the bakers mocked my somewhat formal attire. "Are you going to propose to someone? Is there a wedding when you return to England?"

These men had only ever seen me in run-down work apparel: track bottoms and faded T-shirts. Two others asked if I had gotten to eat my favorite foods in the past few days, whether I would try to smuggle some falafel through customs control—my complaints about English cuisine had been profuse. I glanced at my phone. It was almost ten. The traffic and the lines at the airport were unpredictable. I had to go. After bidding each baker adieu, I saw Hani quickly bag a couple of kilos of bread and generously toss them on top of my travel bag.

"So you remember us," he whispered, as he wrapped me in his arms. I waved good-bye to the others. Hani ambled uphill with me to my rental car. "Be humble. Be kind. Be generous," he counseled, as I bundled my things into the vehicle. "And don't forget. We are governed through bread, but this is not the whole story."

As I drove to the airport and boarded my flight, I thought back to my very first conversation with Hani, on a similarly unclouded September day. I had arrived at his bakery more than a year earlier, with nothing more than a hasty introduction via telephone from a prominent member of the Bakery Owners Association. Bewildered by my request to bake without compensation (his first response was to ask whether the CIA didn't have better ways to spend its time), Hani had asked what my research was really about. Why, given my stated lack of interest in opening a bakery, did I want to study bread, and in this unusual fashion?

Anxious and hesitant, I decided to come clean. "There is this debate that I have come across, which revolves around a concept—the democracy of bread (*dimuqratiyyat al-khubz*). It says that in the Middle East, citizens exchange bread for freedom. I want to know if this is accurate, and working here might help me figure it out."

Hani's eyes widened, and an ironic grin appeared as he nodded his head. "So . . . There is a big question here, a complicated one," he granted, as he sized me up.

Although it had long been a matter of concern, since 2010 bread had become an increasingly palpable and debated symbol. Hoisted aloft at any number of protests, it stood alongside freedom (*huriyya*) and social justice (*a'dala ijtema'i-iyya*) in countless chants intoned during the Arab uprisings. In a related set of debates, bread came to be positioned as an icon of subsistence and well-being, a symbol of stability that was impossible to achieve alongside public participation. Bread or democracy (*khubz am al-dimuqratiyya*) was the central question, suggesting that one had to choose. Bread *and* democracy was the most frequent and emphatic answer. Hani, I would later learn, was unsatisfied by these arguments. They assumed outcomes, as if bread or democracy came fully formed and one could simply choose between the two.

"All right. Come back tomorrow at four thirty in the morning and we will see what you can do," he told me, skeptical that I would last more than a couple of days (as he later confessed). I awkwardly mumbled a hurried thank-you, fearful that he might regret his decision and rescind the offer. "Listen," Hani bellowed as I started to walk away. "Lesson one. Bread is never the beginning or the end. It's always the middle."

To my mind, Hani's account is illuminating in its sensibility: it is colored by shrewd discontent but unmarred by embittered doctrines or naïve reductionism. Hani is alert to the contradictions that characterize political action and the conundrums that come with being governed by something we can feel, hear, smell, and discuss, but never see. He knows that while he may act and achieve, he is also always and inevitably being acted upon. He can discern the lineaments of the script that both empowers and disempowers him, circumstances that are familiar but hardly reassuring. Conscripted into a world not of his own choosing, Hani seeks no easy escape from tragedy, knowing full well that he is obliged to live amid the violences, exclusions, and inequalities that compose modern mechanisms of rule—the state foremost among them. Like most of us, he has nowhere to go.

BEYOND BREAD AS WELFARE

My focus on subsidized *khubz 'arabi* as both an ethnographic object and an analytic vantage point is driven by its omnipresence in Jordan. One can stumble upon this bread, or on something made with it, on almost any block of the country's cities and towns. It is the crucial base for a wide array of sandwiches and an ingredient in dishes such as *fatoush* (salad) and *fetteh* (thick yogurt with soft chickpeas). In other meals, subsidized bread functions as both a utensil (for dipping) and a vessel (for filling). Without it, one cannot fathom eating other dishes. It is regularly the only foodstuff at a meal that is touched by each diner and passed around among all of them. It makes eating "family style" both convenient and easy and helps obviate the need for individual portions. The amount of subsidized bread present does tend to index the class position of diners, of course. The more *upscale* the meal, the more numerous the dips and salads (*mezze*) as well as grilled meats (*mashawi*), and the less central the main carbohydrate. Yet no matter how many other dishes are served, a meal is not complete without bread. It is the cornerstone of almost every repast, the linchpin of daily cuisine.

Bread's political importance can be explained, in part, by its centrality to the diets of Jordan's poor and working classes. Residents of the Hashemite Kingdom are estimated to consume a loaf of this bread per day, averaging around ninety kilograms of bread per person annually.[1] Reliance on subsidized bread is most pronounced in Jordan's poverty pockets, where average monthly food expenditures go almost entirely to cereals; some residents consume *khubz 'arabi* at every meal of the day.[2] Support for this welfare program, however, is not limited to the Jordanian poor nor the marginalized areas where they live.

Cheap bread functions as an emergency relief program for Syrian refugees. It also feeds low-salaried and migrant workers, underwriting the labor costs of small and large businesses. Lastly, the bread subsidy facilitates a certain quality of life among Jordan's lower middle class, which helps explain why support for the policy defies a simple class logic. But subsidized bread does more than nourish, nurture, and sustain; it generates effects in excess of its obdurately alimentary ones. The recurring provision of *khubz 'arabi* engenders a relationship to political authority, to the structures and sovereigns deemed accountable for its presence. And while the provision of food by the powerful has a long and variable history in the Middle East, it is only over the past hundred years, as a result of the encounter with European colonialism, that such allocations have begotten patterns of rule that appear fixed and enduring rather than temporary and ephemeral.[3]

Khubz 'arabi's price is fixed, its distribution closely regulated and consumption heavily underwritten. In this sense, it functions as a mechanism for the provision of social welfare—a service, infrastructure, and/or program intended to promote the well-being and security of recipients.[4] Considered in this way, the bread subsidy appears deceptively simple. Analyzing it seems easy, using verifiable outputs and consequent conclusions—how much bread is provided, who consumes it, what social classes benefit from its provision. Alternatively, one could ask why this welfare program exists, what struggles explain its emergence, and whose interests it serves. Still, in these formulations, welfare assumes purely static properties. It is the product of key variables—class struggle, regime type, administrative capacity, cultural proclivities—or the backdrop through which other dynamics—patronage, corruption, sectarianism, good governance—are elucidated.[5] I went to Jordan to explore precisely these conundrums, in order to scrutinize what scholars term the welfare state. Although they have not been as rigorously studied as examples in Europe and the United States, an increasing number of political scientists have set out to study the programs through which governments in the Global South protect and promote the well-being of citizens.[6] But in most accounts, welfare stands in for something else; it is either the beginning or end but never what Hani taught me: the middle. As a result, we have little sense of how welfare programs are built, maintained, used, and perceived. More troublingly, welfare's relationship to political authority lies obscured.

Like other welfare programs, subsidized bread is composed from a wide array of people, processes, and things. Jordan's Ministry of Finance purchases wheat through public tenders that invite bids from competing suppliers. Once a price is agreed on with a qualified bidder, the cereal is sourced from a variety of countries, increasingly Romania, Russia, and Ukraine. It arrives in the southern port of Aqaba, where it is examined by officials of both the Jordan Food and Drug Administration and the Ministry of Industry, Trade, and Supply (MOITS). These officers test the wheat for contaminants hazardous to plants, people, or animals. If it is deemed acceptable, which it is in the overwhelming majority of cases, discharge begins. Following approval, the wheat is transported to several storage facilities, the largest and most important of which are operated by the government-owned Jordan Silos and Supply General Company. The cereal is then stored according to the tender in which it arrived, as well as its country of origin. Around one million metric tons of wheat enter the country annually in this fashion.

Then, anywhere from three to nine months later, a unit within MOITS's storage division blends different shipments in order to obtain ideal protein levels. The resulting wheat mixtures are transported to one of fourteen privately owned flour mills, where they are made into several types of flour. Only one of these varieties (colloquially referred to as *muwwahad*), milled at a 78% extraction rate and sold below market price and financed by the government, can be used for the production of subsidized bread. Each sack of this discounted flour is endorsed by a ministry official before departing the flour mill. It is then shipped through a network of sanctioned distributors to privately owned bakeries scattered across the Hashemite Kingdom. Each of these bread-makers receives an allocation of *muwwahad* that depends on the number of customers they serve. At the bakery, the discounted flour allocations are mixed with water, salt, sugar, and yeast. The resulting dough is deposited in a bakery owner's oven of choice and then withdrawn as *khubz 'arabi*, a flat, round loaf about sixteen inches in diameter. This bread must be sold at the discounted price of 16 *qirsh* (US$0.25) per kilogram to any and all consumers, irrespective of age, income, or nationality. MOITS officials regularly inspect bakeries to ensure that this is the case.

The exertions, expertise, and know-how required to provide bread should probably have come as no surprise to me, but they did, precisely because the study of welfare services in political science tends to elide the objects, people, and ideas that compose such services, as well as their productive effects. Welfare is a completed process or one that fails to be completed; it is never an ongoing action. But what becomes apparent at the bakery is that subsidized bread is a living and lively thing. As we will see, ambiguous regulations, haphazard standardizations, convoluted decisions, and fluctuating ingredients permeate this welfare service. Subsidized bread is the contingent outcome of humans and nonhumans working together and in cooperation, a marshaling of agencies that coalesce to make *khubz 'arabi* not only cheap and accessible but edible and appetizing. And while this welfare program is composed of nothing but an amalgam of sociomaterial practices, its regularity, uniformity, and arrangement create the effect of a structure—the state—that seems to exist outside this world of practice, separate from the society it organizes, manages, and dominates.[7] That is to say, welfare has performative dimensions. It is not simply a reflection or result but a congealing that acts and does, authorizes and renews a set of relations that produce an effect.

PERFORMING THE STATE

My approach to the study of the state is to view it as an achievement, an effect always in formation, not an axiomatic structure that is. In doing so, I draw on a host of thinkers inclined to disavow the premises of representationalism, in which there are ontologically discrete entities that exist prior to and separate from their representation. The state is there, representationalist works posit, it has discernible boundaries and properties that need simply to be identified and measured. Friedrich Nietzsche, a precursor of the performative, posits that no such prior entities exist: "there is no 'being' behind the doing, acting, becoming; the 'doer' has simply been added by the imagination—the doing is everything."[8] In this spirit, I want to do more than simply contend that the state is a construction, an assertion broadly accepted in most social scientific circles. Instead, this book explores some of the ways in which the state is performatively constituted and how, in turn, this edifice subsists.

Judith Butler, who popularized the term "performativity," wrestles with readings that claim that sexuality is either biologically determined or socially constructed. These oppositions can never fully capture the complexity of what is at stake, Butler argues, for they assume either a fixed entity or an acting subject.[9] Alternatively, they divide the world into representations and the world they represent, instead of troubling the distinction between the two. *States of Subsistence* accepts, as a point of departure, that there are neither pre-existing subjects nor institutions, but rather processes of reiteration by which both subjects and institutions come to appear at all.[10] Working in Butler's wake, I want to build upon and extend their insights to upend the presumption that the state is a metaphysical substance that precedes its instantiation. Instead, the state requires, indeed relies upon, iterative practices. It is an effect of power rather than its source. Performativity captures precisely the repetitiveness and flux of this process, the constrained and ritualized actions that engender onto-logical effects. To be clear, these acts are a matter neither of self-presentation nor of theatrical performance, frameworks that reinscribe the willful liberal subject that Butler rejects. Performativity denotes less a doer than a doing, an effecting by a collection of forces and things that precede, compel, and exceed any one performance.

This book lavishes attention on precisely these doings, and on the ways in which the state is performed in and through them. It does so in contra-distinction to much of comparative political science, which conceptualizes the state as a delimited institutional actor, separate from the citizens it acts upon, governs, and controls. The state's capacity or power is then condensed to what can be observed or quantified: the ability of government institutions to extract revenue,[11] exercise legitimate violence,[12] or provide public goods.[13] Observations at these levels or in some amalgam of sectors are then made to represent the state as a whole, by analogy or extension.[14] An epistemological project of creation, patently in need of explanation, is granted ontological status as a given.

In his influential essay "The Limits of the State," Timothy Mitchell con-tests precisely this given-ness, along with the state–society distinction upon which it relies. Rather than state and society being two discrete entities, he posits that the threshold between them is a line drawn through and within the very practices by which a political order is maintained. That this distinction appears as a boundary between separate spheres is not only an aberration manufactured by scholars but the product of modern mechanisms of power and the varying ways they enable ordinary practices to take on the appearance of an abstract form, what Mitchell terms, in an earlier book, the "peculiar metaphysic of modernity."[15] Structure is divorced from content, action from intention, meaning from materiality, representation from reality, society from the ostensibly autonomous state. Crucial here is Mitchell's reading of Michel Foucault, who furnishes him with the notion of disciplines, microphysical methods of order that do not work as an exterior force or prohibition but operate from within, producing subjects rather than simply repressing them. He adds that just as these disciplinary mechanisms—the way space is partitioned, bodies distributed, and movements coordinated—"become internal in this way, and by the same methods, they now appear to take the novel form of external structures."[16]

It is here that I want to depart from Mitchell, and in a way that mirrors a shift in Foucault's own thinking. In his analysis of the French physiocrat Louis-Paul Abeille, which appears at the beginning of his 1978 lectures, Foucault finds a modification in governmental thinking in response to problems—food scarcity, demographic explosion, industrialization—that could not be managed through extant tools.[17] Whereas disciplinary power seeks to control and possess bodies, managing the grain trade is impossible through such mechanisms. Instead, government requires restrained interventions into processes that can never be fully proscribed. Farmers, bakers, consumers, and traders do not allow straightforward command and control. Disciplinary mechanisms that must constantly intervene become uneconomical, exacerbating the problems (scarcity and famine) they were meant to resolve. Other modes of governing are required. Abeille's appraisal offers an "irruptive moment of critical reflection"[18] and marks a turn essential to Foucault's theorization of government. Vital to this shift is the concept of biopolitics, not as a global diagnosis of power relations but as a configuration of rule that targets the population through the management of its biological life.[19] Faced with processes they can never fully contain (shortages of wheat, for example), governmental techniques aspire instead to shape conduct, using regulatory instruments that can better respond to population growth, urbanization, and increased exchange. There are, of course, important differences between Foucault's dissection of (neo) liberalism as a form of political reason and governing emergent in the Global North, and the very different set of historical circumstances that obtained in the Hashemite Kingdom. And while the grain trade will prove crucial to my own story, what I want to foreground here is how the productivity of power extends beyond the disciplinary, operating through regulatory mechanisms that manage life at the level of the population, not just the individual. Mitchell himself gestures towards these regulatory mechanisms, contrasting them with earlier, less synchronized forms of domination. Whereas imprinting political authority once required periodic acts of violence and countless techniques of euphemization, new mechanisms make patterns of rule seem both settled and permanent.[20] Yet Mitchell never fleshes out how exactly routinized practices enable these patterns of rule to reproduce themselves.[21] Here, then, is the aporia that interests me. The objective of this book is to specify the mechanisms by which the state is materially and discursively rendered; to scrutinize how welfare services instantiate in subjects and subjectivities this structural effect; to examine the modes of agency that occur amid these processes; and equally, to gauge the impact of these dynamics on the modes of compliance, defiance, and struggle that traverse Jordanian political life. Throughout, I exhibit how a theory of the performative not only disrupts but can also enrich political analysis.

First formulated by the English philosopher J. L. Austin, the performative has a long and checkered history; it has been regularly invoked in cursory and incompatible ways.[22] In its initial form, Austin deployed the term to distinguish between constative utterances such as the "cat sat on the mat," which can be assessed as true or false, and performative ones, such as "I name this ship King Edward," in which the utterance itself carries out the action. Austin's fundamental point was that language is not solely an instrument used to represent the world it describes, but also works to change it by generating meaning through linguistic utterances. In the case of performatives, he surmised that their "success" was always circumstantial, their uptake dependent on conventions and conditions being in place when they were uttered.[23] Austin's vocabulary was soon adopted by others, who rarely agreed about what the performative meant or the possibilities it afforded for understanding social phenomena.

In a generative engagement with the work of Pierre Bourdieu and Jacques Derrida, Butler gives the performative a Foucauldian gloss. Through their critique of metaphysical presumptions linked to the category of gender, Butler displaces the notion of a stable ontological subject that prefigures action and language. They do so through an elaborate notion of performativity, one that emphasizes "embodied rituals of everydayness" and "social iterability," the norms, forces, and repetitions through which the body is composed.[24] Performative acts are thus not reducible to verbal utterances spoken by an established subject; their force is that of a "citational chain lived and believed at the level of the body."[25] This is why the domain of performativity both includes and exceeds the verbal and written. In other words, the model of the speaking subject that usually works as the paradigm for theorizing performativity cannot fully capture how the latter works. Instead of discrete verbal enunciations or speech acts, it is a set of relations and practices that must be constantly renewed, in domains that traverse the human and nonhuman.[26] Gender ceases to be the product of an identity ascribed at birth and becomes the result of performative acts that, through regularized and constrained repetition, work to forge us as gendered subjects. Butler forces us to question the ontological status that pre-given entities, already knowable, identifiable, and bounded, occupy within the social sciences more generally. But how are these ontological effects produced?

Karen Barad's posthuman feminism offers perhaps the most productive reworking of Butler's oeuvre in this regard. Through close engagement with the work of the Danish physicist Niels Bohr and his philosophical reflections on quantum mechanics, Barad arrives at an agential realist elaboration of performativity, one that accounts for the fact that "forces at work in the materialization of bodies are not only social, and the bodies produced are not all human."[27] Crucial here is her account of how materiality and discourse are constituted by and through each other, sutured together in a constant exchange.[28] Matter and humans, like the atomic entities Bohr examines, are considered not independent objects with determinate boundaries but the provisional result of intra-action (rather than inter-action, which would presume their prior existence). In drawing attention to the role of boundary-making practices in quantum experiments, Barad pushes us to ask not what structures are, but how certain phenomena come to be, to consider them as practical accomplishments that transpire through the reiterated materializations of bodies that are not exclusively human. Freed from anthropocentric limitations, performativity is no longer understood "as iterative citationality (Butler) but rather iterative intra-activity."[29]

The performative has been taken up in a number of fields, notably in science and technology studies and its most influential theoretical strand, actor network theory.[30] The latter has proven especially adept at identifying how amalgams of humans and nonhumans "take their form and acquire their attributes as a result of their relations with other entities, the actor is generated *in* and *by* these relationships."[31] The economy, as Michel Callon and Donald MacKenzie's powerful set of works demonstrate, does not exist in the abstract but is produced on the ground by an elaborate set of framing efforts aligning a variety of agencies and forces, practices and technologies that repeatedly work to stabilize its coordinates.[32] These alignments can succeed in instantiating the economy, just as they can fail if certain objects or actors jeopardize their coherence.[33] The performative has also proven useful to students of nationalism. Lisa Wedeen's formidable work on national identity in Yemen has illustrated some of the ways in which a theory of politics as performative helps denaturalize "political identification," drawing attention to the "mechanisms that make identity categories seem fixed."[34] Despite several important differences, all these theorists share a critique of representationalism—the belief in the metaphysical distinction between representations and that which they claim to represent. All challenge the capacity of words to stand in for pre-existing things and reject the bracketing out of practices, particularly those through which representations are produced. The concept of performativity, as I will use it here, echoes these aversions and pushes against continued attempts to study politics by capturing properties of an observation-independent reality that scholars merely uncover. I will suggest, and seek to demonstrate, that the state too is performed, sidestepping its deconstruction in order to attend to its dubious solidity.

The bread subsidy is a particularly rewarding site in which to follow the work of performativity because it allows us to denaturalize the state as a pre-given structure and focus instead on one of the recurring processes through which it is produced. While these practices may be most obvious during violent conflict or liberation struggles, as in wartime Syria or the Tibetan government-in-exile,[35] they are always present, often sustained and frequently enhanced by people and practices outside the centers of officialdom.[36] The ministry official who allocates wheat to certain bakeries, the citizen who purchases subsidized bread, the petitioner who denounces corruption in the bread sector, and the baker who produces his wares from discounted flour all participate in intra-actions through which the state is performed. To emphasize a point made earlier, intentions need not dictate these practices. They need only re-peat, echo, or reiterate a set of relations that prime citizens to inhabit and act in a world in which the state reigns supreme, "as if there was such a thing *sui generis*."[37] And it is in the everyday lives of Jordanian citizens that such uptake is best assessed. For it is an empirical question whether, where, and when a particular welfare service comes to be considered as the bearer of the state's imprint.

METHODS AND ORGANIZATION

States of Subsistence is based on ethnographic fieldwork conducted over a total of nearly two years in Jordan, most of which was completed during four-teen uninterrupted months (August 2013 to October 2014). During this time, I spent sixty days learning from and accompanying officials of the Ministry of Industry, Trade, and Supply (MOITS), rejoining them occasionally in sub-sequent months. I followed them as they inspected bakeries, discussed flour allocations, and dealt with petitioners in the bread industry who sought to curry their favor. I also interviewed key intermediaries in the bread subsidy system—millers, transporters, silo personnel—and explored how their work and outlooks shaped this welfare program. Twelve months were spent working in three different bakeries in the Jordanian capital, during which I observed and participated in the daily labors of bakery workers and owners. This ap-prenticeship was made possible by several verbal introductions and a generous letter written by the Bakery Owners Association, the professional body that represents Jordan's bakery proprietors. My goal was to invert, to some extent, the logic of participant observation, and to become instead an observing par-ticipant.[38] Various factors facilitated my ability to do so—gender, funding, connections, some baking experience—but most crucial was the fact that I entered all three bakeries as a conventional apprentice, subject to the controls, requisites, and reprimands that fall upon anyone who is learning to bake.

Later, an additional four months (September 2015 to January 2016) were spent living between the capital and the southern cities of Ma'an and Aqaba, mainly conducting open-ended interviews, while also visiting and occasionally working in bakeries. I also observed and frequently took part in activities (com-munity meetings, protests, celebratory meals) at and around these and other bread-makers. Then, in addition to several briefer visits, I spent two further months (July to September of 2019) in the country to reacquaint myself with life and bread in the neighborhoods I had lived in during my previous stays. I use unspecified designations for some of these districts (Jabal B, C, and D), as well as aliases for several bakeries and bakers, because I describe a set of illegal practices that, although widely acknowledged and discussed, could have acute repercussions for those involved if they were identified. I use pseudonyms for each and every person who asked that I do so, or when I concluded that any sort of harm could result from not doing so. From the beginning of the project to its end, I conducted interviews with policy makers, politicians, journalists, and diplomats, mainly in Arabic but occasionally in English. Undoubtedly, some of the more revealing insights into the bread subsidy came during unexpected encounters and informal conversations on buses or over meals or coffee, often simply because I mentioned my research to people who were puzzled by my project or presence. These less formalized observations were particularly revealing about the centrality of *khubz 'arabi* to subsistence, ritual, and routine. They also made eminently clear the political salience of subsidized bread. In addition, my fieldwork was conducted at the same time as various projects of subsidy reform were being considered. This augmented and enriched my work, as debates around bread and welfare sporadically erupted in the news and offered an easy avenue through which I could introduce my research. I combine these ethnographic insights with careful readings of texts, mainly of government documents and newspapers located in archives in Washington, DC; London; Oxford; Amman; Beirut; and online. These materials allowed me to understand the development of Jordanian welfare policy as well as the ways in which the government of subsistence has been conceptualized and implemented. Throughout, I center subsidized bread, positioning it in the middle not once and definitively but continuously and repeatedly.

These methods depart from those that now dominate the field of comparative politics, where both quantitative methods and a certain "methodological elitism" increasingly reign supreme.[39] The latter tendency also troubles the study of Jordanian history and politics, where an inordinate amount of attention has been paid to the tenacity of the country's monarchs,[40] the exertions of its elites and political parties,[41] as well as the nature of Jordan's geopolitical alignments and revenue streams.[42] In contrast, I borrow techniques largely from anthropology and geography to produce a political ethnography of the state by way of the ordinary and mundane.[43] And I do so without remorse, because everyday life does not just make for interesting stories—it is precisely where political authority is made and unmade. This banality is not a barrier to critical engagement with powers that govern but one of its most fundamental conditions.

States of Subsistence is divided into two parts, which register certain affinities between chapters rather than defining a sharp analytical distinction between matter and meaning. In the first half, I examine processes of assemblage, what Anna Tsing terms "open-ended gatherings," that make the state both possible and persistent.[44] Chapter 1 sets the scene, focusing on sweeping changes in welfare policy following an under-examined mutiny in the Jordanian army in February 1974. If the next chapters turn to ethnography, in this first one I seek to offer a clear portrayal of what those at the helm of government understood their priorities to be, how these were refashioned in response to one landmark event, and why these changes transformed patterns of rule. Because bread is never entirely exhausted by its symbolism or semiotics, chapters 2 and 3 continue to unpack the bread subsidy's conditions of possibility while analyzing its operation and impact. In particular, I explore how a divergent set of people and things (bakers and bureaucrats, wheat and flour) associates and combines, entrenching an embodied relationship to the state.

The second half of the book turns from the tenuous work of assemblage to the ways in which the state effect transpires through entanglement, a term I take from Karen Barad and her illuminating work on quantum mechanics. Just as atoms do not exist prior to their measurement and observation, so too the state lacks an independent, self-contained existence with determinate boundaries. It is produced and reproduced through intra-relations, "the entanglement of the 'object' and the 'agencies of observation.'"[45] In chapters 4 through 6, I observe and converse with a variety of observers, interrogating "situated knowledges" and the use of the concept of *al-dawla* (the state), while asking how its ongoing materialization makes a difference to these representations.[46] It is worth noting that contemporary use of this term is a dramatic departure from earlier deployments, where it denoted an ephemeral mode of dynastic rule that was neither territorially fixed nor sovereign.[47] While its etymology and historical usage remind us of the very different iterations of political authority in the precolonial Middle East, today *al-dawla* has become the most common Arabic term for the state, even as the translation is not exact and its utilization varies.

Rather than disencumber the subsidy of local histories, contexts, and sociomaterial arrangements so that it can function as an indicator, I explore the political possibilities this welfare policy both opens up and narrows down, the different ways it engenders forms of rule and arranges subjects in relation to that rule. The point of each chapter is not to draw attention away from the state or replace it with a more appropriate concept. Instead, the burden of this book will be to home in on those mechanisms that are constitutive of the state effect, neatly summarized as "practices or performances of representing, as well as the productive effects of those practices and the conditions for their efficacy."[48] *States of Subsistence* tries to make a meal, or at least a humble snack, out of bread. And out of all that is left unexplored when the state is assumed and measured rather than softened and sifted through.

THE VIEW FROM THE BAKERY

Not one careless word, not a single furtive glance. An unplanned cadence saturated the bakery. Nothing seemed fixed, motionless, or easy. Movement was constant, draining exertions relentless. I tried to remain calm but was edgy and uneasy. It was mid-December and a snowstorm had been forecast for the following day. Hani's bakery was packed. No one knew for certain whether the roads would be traversable tomorrow, or the next day. Everyone, or so it seemed to me, was rushing out to make sure they had enough *khubz 'arabi* to ride out the storm. This bread was insurance, protection against deprivation. Many in the neighborhood could afford little else. Inside, the oven pulsated, trays filled with rising dough were continuously stacked.

Hani yelled to the bakers behind him, frantically trying to transmit vigor and verve: "Bake, guys, bake! And then after, bake more."

No one could leave empty-handed. Not a soul could be left without nourishment. Seven hours later, at ten in the evening, the work abated as the bakery shut its doors. On this day, twice the usual amount of subsidized bread had been sold. Many customers thanked Hani as they departed, relieved that someone, something, had summoned the resolve to ensure their subsistence. Here, no one can live without bread.

During the next forty-eight hours, the streets were covered in slick ice. Only a few brave denizens ventured outside to face the cold. In East Amman, it is the responsibility of residents to remove the snow. No organization or institution arrives to assist them or make certain that they have endured. For two full days, Hani's bakery, *al-Khalil*, was closed.

The following day, the bakers and the bakery owner returned. I arrived half an hour late; buses had been scarce and taxis unwilling to negotiate the deceptive, uphill pathways covered in slush. I apologized, set my things down in the backroom, and got to work. I was visibly irritated by the commute, and my now-soaked shoes; Hani jokingly asked whether I had been inconvenienced by the winter chill.

"No," I responded. "By the icy streets, by the lack of central heating, by the unending stream of grimy water that has inundated my street."

Everyone stopped. They all began to laugh. "What do you want? What did you expect?" one of the bakers asked. "A radiator in your kitchen and a jacuzzi instead of a bath?"

Flummoxed, I had no idea how to respond. And so, eventually, after I had complained about slippery roads and frozen pipes, electricity blackouts and flooded alleyways, I asked, "Well, who is responsible for the mess? Why doesn't someone deal with this? Where is the state?"

Hani scanned my face and gave me a wistful look, as the others groaned at my privilege. I waited, and wasn't sure what to expect. "Where is the state?" he muttered back, jaded. "Here. At the bakery. In every loaf of bread."

*   *   *

To speak of the presence of the state, a state linked to the availability of bread and the sensations emanating from the bakery, takes us in a very different direction than the sort of instrumentalism implied in terms such as bread riots or bread revolutions. This is not to say, however, that political concerns are not integral to such a perspective. Inasmuch as the hold that states have on us is shaped by our experience of particular governmental programs, the political and institutional conditions within which our subjectivities are formed will play a key role in determining how and when revolutions form and detonate. But to assume that hunger and deprivation, or the price of bread, are the straightforward drivers of dissent does a disservice to the ways in which people encounter and respond to their historical emplacement.

Undoubtedly, bread has been at the center of a wide array of contentious episodes in the Middle East. Following painful cuts to food subsidies, affordable bread became a central demand in Egypt's 1977 intifada, appearing again in the 1984 uprising in Kafr al-Dawwar. Inflation and rising food prices instigated by IMF-backed measures in Morocco led many to march while hoisting loaves of bread in 1981 and 1984. Other examples abound, ranging from Tunisia in 1983–84 to Jordan in 1996 and, most recently, the Arab uprisings of 2011. Yet in no instance was bread a passive symbol or facile evidence of anger, indignation, and rage. As an emblem, it enjoys both universal and immediate recognition, yet its meaning and magnitude vary individually and collectively. What is clear, however, is how easily bread tugs at the strings of subjective experience because of how intimately and repeatedly it connects people's lives to the authorities that govern them. In the contexts above, and in so many more, bread's force derives not just from how it feeds people, but from its central position in a charged force field of experiences, promises, and obligations.

By foregrounding the Jordanian bread subsidy and attending to the routine practices that surround it, this book provides the context needed to investigate how welfare programs operate in relation to the hegemonic orders they frequently enshrine. A corollary of such an approach is to interrogate not only how our oppositional stances and actions are formed but to consider anew what they target and seek to achieve. The question becomes, how are the forces that govern us produced and reproduced? My argument is that performativity deserves our attention because it brings light to this crucial question. It forces us to consider whether the state is the product of a natural or transcendent truth or just the pragmatics of its recurring generation. More importantly, the horizons of thought and life it opens may be vital to the task of finding our way beyond modes of government that have repeatedly failed us, yet continue to loom large over our collective existence.

Part 1

ASSEMBLY

Chapter 1

A NEW STYLE OF ADMINISTRATION

HANI SPOKE OFTEN ABOUT THE EARLY 1970S, but not for the reasons I expected. In a period often described as politically tumultuous, it was the more ordinary struggles that he always recalled. Hani had already embarked on his career as a bread-maker by then, but it was long before he had opened his own bakery. He had apprenticed in several locales. Still, work was hard to come by. Commercial bread-makers were not yet common, and most people preferred making *khubz* at home. More troubling was the rapid rise in living costs, which made even stable employment an insecure basis for life. "One week bread would be cheap and easily available. The next it would be a luxury you had to contemplate," Hani recalled. That was how he often explained the importance of the bread subsidy—the foodstuff should be affordable, an expense you need not chew over or premeditate. This had not always been the case.

In Hani's teenage years, welfare services and nutritional assistance were provisional and *ad hoc*. United Nations agencies occasionally provided free bread, as did various tribal elites and political groups. Sometimes help would arrive; other times it would not. Jordan was a fragile kingdom, its government unable to consistently provide for those it sought to rule. But things changed swiftly and suddenly, Hani often told me. By the time inflation definitively reared its head, the energies of revolution and war had dissipated, as had the anxieties and opportunities they brought with them. It was the struggle for subsistence that most concerned Hani and those around him. Rapid price increases meant that, by the end of 1973, it was harder and harder to make do. Within months, the subsistence of the population had become a matter of governmental reflection. Price controls and subsidies were instituted; the hold on basic foodstuffs would no longer be so tenuous. "Things became easier," Hani remembered, "even if more boring." Life as a foot soldier in the Hashemite Kingdom's army of subsidized bread-makers beckoned. The state apparatus would no longer just repress and discipline Jordanians. It would seek to feed them too.

On February 3, 1974, members of Jordan's elite 40th Armored Brigade, stationed at a military camp in the al-Khaw district, took to the streets to express their frustration over dramatic increases in the prices of basic goods. The mutiny is said to have involved more than a hundred Bedouin troops who paraded in trucks and armored personnel carriers around the nearby city of Zarqa. Because King Hussein was abroad, Crown Prince Hassan was immediately dispatched to the barracks to persuade the mutineers to stand down.[1] The Jordanian government prohibited news outlets from covering or publishing reports of the event, and Prime Minister Zaid al-Rifa'i went so far as to deny that it had even occurred.[2] While press reports issued in Beirut pointed to politically motivated insubordination related to the king's relations with the Palestine Liberation Organization (PLO), diplomatic cables and interviews with government officials serving at the time confirm the principal complaint of the mutineers: inequities in military pay scales, along with rising prices, were undermining morale among mid-level Jordanian officers and enlisted personnel.[3] A now-retired member of the armed forces who was present at the mutiny confirms this assessment: "We thought we deserved better pay. The conflict with the PLO was very difficult and many of us felt our efforts were not being appreciated. Sugar prices triggered the unrest but the cost of everything was going up. We could barely afford bread and rice for our families."[4]

The mutiny was unprecedented. For the first time in the history of the Jordanian Arab Army, its brigades had left a military camp and taken to the streets to publicly convey dissatisfaction with their living standards. According to one declassified CIA document, the mutineers announced their readiness to march the twenty miles southwest to the capital, Amman, if their demands were not met.[5] To make things worse, King Hussein was on a diplomatic mission in London and had scheduled a meeting with President Nixon in the United States for the following Tuesday.[6] According to Jawad Anani, a researcher at Jordan's Central Bank at the time, "The king came back in a hurry, for this was an unprecedented move. To have the army express itself in this fashion, this was a source of alarm for the king, so he rushed back, motivated by crucial security considerations."[7] Anani and others also confirm that the immediate spark for the mutiny was indeed the upsurge in sugar prices, which had risen threefold over the previous year. This hit army members particularly hard, as many of them drank sweetened tea in the morning and snacked on sugary biscuits during afternoon breaks. Although the mutiny was limited to the 40th Armored Brigade, there is said to have been "considerable sympathy for the demands of the mutineers throughout the armed forces and in the civilian population."[8]

Beginning in 1971, the Hashemite Kingdom witnessed several bouts of inflation. Over the next two years, a devaluation of Jordan's currency against the dollar and the rising costs of imports led to a dramatic fall in the purchasing power of the citizenry. Drought and adverse weather conditions in 1973 further drove up the cost of fruits and vegetables. A precipitous jump in international commodity prices, partly driven by the 1973–74 oil shock, combined with growing remittances and large increases in foreign aid to fuel an inflationary upsurge. Prices that had been increasing at a rate of 4.7% in 1971 grew by 19.2% in 1974.[9] Inflation disproportionately affected bureaucrats and members of the armed forces on fixed salaries, but its consequences were wide-ranging. Marwan al-Qasim, a future head of the Royal Court, summarized the moment in this way: "Everyone was angry in 1974, not just the military. All sorts of consumer products were rising in price. It was becoming harder and harder to get by."[10] In response, the government granted public sector workers a salary increase of 10% in late 1973. But this proved more a temporary bandage than a lasting solution. Already some years earlier, the Palace had concluded that a more centralized process of economic decision-making was required. Empowered by martial law, in late 1970 King Hussein had created an Economic Security Committee (ESC) to ban currency flight and sequester private property and insolvent investments.[11] First headed by

Crown Prince Hassan, this body sought to insulate technocrats from private sector pressures and systematize economic policies across the boundaries of the newly created Ministry of Commerce and Industry (previously the Ministry of National Economy) and the Ministry of Finance.[12] Members of the ESC had discussed how to combat price gouging and the rising cost of key dietary staples in the aftermath of the conflict with the PLO and the world food crisis of 1972,[13] after which the price of wheat increased by nearly 400%.[14] The Zarqa mutiny hastened these deliberations, laying bare the government's inability to address the scourge of inflation. As one soldier told a reporter just days after the mutiny, "It's not over, because tomorrow the prices will be just as high as they were today."[15]

But prices did come down; if not the next day, then within a matter of weeks, as Hani often recalled. The Zarqa mutiny engendered a moment of reflection, followed by a hurried set of deliberations on how to prevent similar unrest in the future. Inflation had made painfully obvious the need for a set of mechanisms to regulate prices and ensure that they never again threatened the population's subsistence. Whereas previous crises had been ameliorated through *ad hoc* measures, a more permanent solution was now required. And so, by the end of 1974, the Hashemite regime extensively reorganized the mechanisms through which it governed. Fiscal and bureaucratic capacities were developed and linked in novel ways, shifting the emphasis of government from individuals and territory to the management of life. Subjects would increasingly be administered through regulatory mechanisms targeting the population as a living body.

This chapter traces this shift, and the edifice of government through which the Hashemite regime sought to rule the citizenry. It does so by examining the provision of social welfare in the country's post-independence history, focusing specifically on the creation of the Ministry of Supply and the welfare program commonly known as the bread subsidy (*da'am al-khubz*). I concentrate on this ministry and its trademark policy because their advent, implementation, and evolution are emblematic of a shift in political reasoning and administration that resembles what Foucault terms "the governmentalization of the state,"[16] or the "process by which the juridical and administrative apparatus of the state come to incorporate the disparate arenas of rule concerned with the government of the population."[17] These measures connect the designs, calculations, and strategies that are developed in institutional centers to the scattered locations in which the habits and health of the population are managed.[18] The foundation of the Ministry of Supply in 1974 marked the onset of an increasingly elaborate set of governmental practices that would target the country's residents. These expanded dramatically over the next fifteen years. Centralized institutions became the primary source of social insurance and basic goods, slowly replacing kinship groups. State power would become inextricably linked to the everyday life of the Jordanian population and the policies shaping its conduct.

This dramatic transformation has been under-studied, both in the Hashemite Kingdom and the broader Middle East. While various authors have pointed to the emergence of a post-independence social pact between authoritarian elites and the citizenry,[19] these accounts are mostly limited to Egypt and Syria, and often simply generalize across the region. More importantly, they are limited by an instrumental logic that equates the expansion of social protection with the purchase of political acquiescence.[20] Yet as Salwa Ismail argues, the provision of welfare goes beyond simple "exchanges between rulers and ruled."[21] Rather, it comprises broader reflections on how to administer a population, the delineation of a sphere of legitimate governmental intervention, and, crucially, routine actions through which political authority is reproduced. Key to the Jordanian variant of this process is how inflation was "discovered" and translated into a social problem requiring precise remedies, what one could term the bread subsidy's historical conditions of possibility. Of course, the price and availability of subsistence goods were not a novel challenge in Jordan. Drought and war had previously threatened their accessibility. But post-Zarqa, inflation was problematized and acted upon in radically new ways. The Hashemite regime's response to an outburst of frustration in the armed forces fostered a rethinking and reworking of what was, at the time, a rudimentary system of welfare provision, one whose novelty I will emphasize by briefly tracing the logics of rule that preceded it. As will become clear, novel techniques struggled to make the population legible through measures that could prevent the scourge of inflation and potential corollaries, especially social unrest. A new constellation of governmental practices targeted "the complex unit constituted by men and things," with concrete effects.[22] This amounted to nothing short of a new formation of biopolitical government.

At its heart lay the bakery, and the subsidized bread it would soon indiscriminately provide to all residents of the Hashemite Kingdom.

THE PRINCE AND HIS TERRITORY

The government of residents and resources predates Transjordan's nationalization in the form of a British mandate in 1921 under the ostensible rule of Hijazi Amir Abdullah.[23] The Ottoman Empire's Vilayet Law of 1864 was vital in this regard, as it established a set of mechanisms through which the imperial administration sought to extend the empire's reach into the periphery of its domain.[24] It did so by integrating frontier districts (Ajlun, Karak, Salt) into a growing bureaucratic network that sought to foster linkages between major regional markets. Notwithstanding several failures,[25] the Ottomans slowly established administrative outposts and military bases throughout what would become the Hashemite Kingdom of Jordan by the end of the nineteenth century. Top-down administrative reforms were reinforced through a robust martial presence that was occasionally called upon to quash local rebellions animated by extractive decrees from the imperial center.[26] Vital to Ottoman expansion was the stimulus of commerce in wheat. The territories on the East Bank of the Jordan River offered a "new granary" for merchants from Nablus, Damascus, and Jerusalem, many of whom came to trade, lend money, and, eventually, acquire land.[27] Their efforts were incentivized by the settlement of new villages, the extension of titled parcels under cultivation, and the establishment of a permanent Ottoman military presence that enhanced the security of commerce.[28] Not for the last time, wheat became central to how Jordan's inhabitants were ruled.[29]

The first decade of the twentieth century proved a tumultuous period, especially in the southern outposts of Karak and Ma'an, where local rebellions sought to avert the Ottoman administration's extractive measures.[30] Following the well-chronicled Great Arab Revolt and colonial machinations linked to the Sykes-Picot Agreement of 1916, various regional governments fleetingly emerged (August 1920 to April 1921). They soon gave way to the establishment of the Transjordanian mandate with Abdullah, the second son of the *sharif* of Mecca, as ruling amir, and British authorities as his overlords. Popular opposition to the mandatory regime was rampant, as Tariq Tell's work powerfully demonstrates.[31] Despite these antagonisms, however, institutional development proceeded as a thoroughly colonial enterprise, building upon Ottoman foundations. Crucial to this endeavor were the arrival of John Bagot Glubb and the establishment of the Desert Patrol (later Desert Mechanized Force), as well as the integration of Transjordan's security forces into a system of aerial control under British command.[32] Aided by drought, famine, and the opening up of Transjordan to the world economy, Glubb's "disciplinary mechanisms of surveillance and education" drove more and more Bedouin into the Arab Legion.[33] It also transformed their political organization and way of life in ways that were amenable to the British imperial project. Soldiering and subsidies for grain and feed, along with occasional relief work, slowly "replaced the claims on clan and sheikh that had guaranteed survival in the past," further binding the tribes to the mandatory regime.[34] Fashioning the Bedouin into Hashemite subjects, either by integrating them into the army or turning them into agriculturalists with stakes in immovable property, was a central pillar of the British colonial project.[35]

Government expenditures during the mandate period sought, above all, to ensure local allegiance to the colonial regime. The reform of landholding and the channeling of outside funds to sympathetic tribal elites were fundamental in this regard.[36] Despite regular calls for increased spending on social welfare, the vast majority of British aid not spent on administrative costs was allocated towards two key military considerations: strategic road building and defense.[37] Martial concerns took precedence over the transportation, manufacturing, and educational sectors, as British officials were not particularly interested in the everyday conduct of colonial subjects. The result was something Tell describes as a "military bureaucratic 'enclave economy,'"[38] in which British spending financed an import surplus consumed in towns around military bases. Throughout the colonial period (1921–46), concerns with social welfare amounted to little more than guaranteeing a sufficient level of subsistence for the Bedouin tribes embedded in the military and the villagers who labored on mandatory infrastructures. There was very limited promotion of health, education, or well-being. And while a land registration program designed by the British dramatically increased interactions with officialdom,[39] for the vast majority of the kingdom's inhabitants, government interference in every-day life was minimal.[40] British investments and aid overwhelmingly focused on providing colonial authorities with the tools to ensure that control over

Transjordanian territory was not endangered. While discipline functioned as a key mechanism of power in certain circumscribed spaces, such as the army, military schools, and the bureaucracy,[41] the logic of sovereignty reigned supreme. Colonial authorities and their sharifian ally exercised political power not over citizens but first and foremost in relation to subjects of a colonized terrain. As Foucault would put it, the problem government sought to address was "the safety of the Prince and his territory."[42]

Notwithstanding League of Nations obligations, the few welfare measures that were enacted during the mandate took the form of makeshift responses to particular events and problems (diseases, food shortages, overcrowding) as they occurred.[43] These provisions were largely improvised, limited to what the British could afford in order to maintain the colonial status quo. The exigencies of conflict quickly transformed this approach. Following the outbreak of World War II, Britain and the United States established the Middle East Supply Center (MESC)—a regional body granted the authority to regulate the entire region's trade arrangements to minimize wartime shortages and save shipping space. Allied forces sought to prevent an expansion of the food riots that were seen in Cairo, Beirut, and Damascus after the onset of conflict in Europe.[44] The subsistence of city dwellers became an important concern, if only to ward off an Axis advance. To prevent unrest, the MESC collected intelligence on patterns of agricultural production and consumption in the region and established import allocations for countries under British control.[45] And while the "diversity of people and practices confounded and resisted these attempts at every turn,"[46] the MESC soon became the most powerful institution regulating economic activity in the region, forcibly "imposing its views and wishes on the production and consumption of nearly 100 million people toiling in a vast subcontinent."[47]

The MESC proved highly beneficial to Jordan's cereal merchants, who profited from the higher prices paid by the British army. Ties to the Hashemite monarchy resulted in favorable or semi-monopolistic import licenses for many of these well-connected traders, quotas through which they grew their fortunes, frequently through smuggling to nearby Syria and Lebanon.[48] The inflow of aid to the Arab Legion, coupled with Amman's favored position in the Anglo-American wartime supply chain, produced previously unseen levels of affluence, especially for the so-called "quota coterie."[49] Critical for the purposes of this chapter, however, is how the MESC's links with certain merchants, as well as its intervention in local markets, mark a subtle shift in governmental practice. As in neighboring Palestine, supply shortages and a fear of unrest pushed colonial institutions to gauge bodies and determine their needs through indices such as the calorie and the cost of living.[50] Key measures in this respect included import permits that protected merchants from competition and the discounted distribution of basic foodstuffs.[51] For reasons to be discussed below, Jordan did not adopt MESC-inspired policies as quickly as Syria or Egypt. The country's first decade after independence came close to but did not witness the revolutionary upheavals that transformed welfare policies in those two countries. Nevertheless, measures enacted during World War II can be said to have transformed perceptions among rulers and ruled regarding the role of the state apparatus—seen no longer as simply a repressive colonial tool but as an amorphous set of institutions that could also work as an agent of public welfare.[52] By Jordan's independence in 1946, the relations underpinning political authority had been substantially transformed. Clan and shaykh no longer held as much sway, government was centralized in Amman, and political decision-making had been severed from any semblance of local control.[53] The collapse of nomadism, a revolution in land tenure that all but eliminated communal holdings, and the growth of urban enclaves alongside military outposts all increasingly tied a broad swath of inhabitants to the mandatory regime. Still, Jordan lacked a coherent planning regime through which its rulers could both contemplate and enact more expansive interventions in the daily life of the citizenry.

INDEPENDENCE, DISASTER, AND UNCERTAINTY

Far from being a robust engine for development or a munificent distributor of imperial largesse, the mandatory regime was run on a paltry budget that was overwhelmingly spent on military concerns. British officials showed little interest in measures aimed at improving the lives of the population. But just a few years after independence in 1946, Jordanian policy makers were forced to reflect on the challenges related to ensuring a basic level of subsistence for the country's residents. This pivot was provoked by events in Palestine in 1948, both the forced displacement of Palestinians to the now Hashemite-controlled West Bank and the arrival of others in the East Bank, many of whom settled in and around refugee camps.[54] The creation of the United Nations Relief and Works Agency for Palestine Refugees in the Near East (UNRWA) in 1949 was decisive in this respect. The refugee influx, coupled with the new body's task of providing jobs and direct relief to displaced Palestinians, required a local partner with far more elaborate planning capacities than the Jordanian government had at the time. Housing and public service facilities were totally incapable of shouldering the unexpected burden now placed upon them. Where surplus cereals had once been exported to Palestine and Syria, now there was not even enough to meet demand among the rapidly expanding urban population.[55] Had foreign aid not been forthcoming, the standard of living of between one third to one half of the population would have dropped below subsistence level.[56] A decade later, the UNRWA continued to provide basic necessities to nearly one third of the Hashemite Kingdom's population.[57] Welfare measures under the purview of the Jordanian government remained tentative, unreliable, and makeshift.

The first fifteen years after independence (1946–61) were a period of chronic political instability. Scholarly accounts have focused on the brief interregnum of King Talal (1951–52) and the role of the "King's men" in ushering in an orderly transition following the assassination of King Abdullah I in 1951.[58] Others have analyzed the Jordanian monarchy's confrontation with "the challenge of Arab radicalism" following the Free Officers' coup d'état in Egypt (July 1952) and the stern test posed by the Jordanian National Movement to a young King Hussein, who formally ascended the throne in May 1953.[59] Attention has also been given to the Hashemite regime's attempt to mold a pan-Jordanian identity that could somehow preempt the establishment of a separate Palestinian entity after Jordan's annexation of the West Bank in 1948.[60] Scholars and historians of international relations have examined the attempted shift from the long-standing reliance on British subsidies to Arab solidarity, which eventually gave way to the rise of the Eisenhower Doctrine and the United States' ascendance as Jordan's foremost foreign patron.[61] Yet as Paul Kingston rightly notes, comparatively little has been written about the Hashemite regime's parallel efforts to ensure Jordan's economic viability during the country's early post-independence history.[62]

In a matter of years, the Jordanian government spearheaded several new large-scale infrastructural and industrial ventures, all while leaving commerce largely to the private sector. The 1955 Law of Encouragement of Investment and the creation of the Industrial Development Board in 1957 formally established this nascent form of import-substitution-industrialization. These initial steps were supplemented by government investments in newly created semi-public (or shareholding) companies in what became known as the Big 5 (the national airline, cement, phosphates, potash, and petroleum), four of which were established in the 1950s. The dismissal of Parliament in 1957 and the suppression of an ostensible coup in the same year further dampened enthusiasm for risky ventures among investors. Large industrial projects remained extremely difficult to finance, unless the government was willing to facilitate private capital.[63] Yet unlike its regional counterparts, Jordan's embrace of interventionist measures was neither instigated by revolutionary upheaval nor inspired by socialist ideology or a coherent development model. Instead, it was the weakness of the private sector, an unstable business environment, coupled with tactical political considerations, that shaped policy. The latter was always subject to the calculus of the monarchical regime, which sought to promote economic growth but, critically, without disrupting the tenuous matrix on which its authority rested. Joint ventures, the conferral of licenses, and import controls sought to make the monarchy's overthrow inimical to the financial interests of key commercial actors. Public expenditures "often served the political exigencies of coalition building . . . loyalty was exchanged for profit," working to bind the largely Amman-based merchant class to what remained a persistently unstable Hashemite regime.[64]

Notwithstanding a slow expansion of the civilian bureaucracy, the majority of external assistance continued to find its way into the hands of the military, which grew dramatically following the dismissal of Glubb Pasha in 1956 and the replacement of British aid with American support towards the end of the decade.[65] Given the paucity of jobs in the private sector, military service now appealed not only to the sedentarized Bedouin population but also to Jordanians from small towns and rural outposts. With army salaries bringing steady income and access to health care and small loans, military service replaced other modes of employment, including seasonal work on the Palestinian coastal plain.[66] Slowly, the Jordanian Arab Army became as crucial to the livelihoods of Jordanian villagers as it had been to the previously nomadic Bedouin.[67] Its members, along with employees of the burgeoning bureaucracy, were the targets of what few social policies existed at the time. With no autonomous bourgeois sector of note, a peasantry divided through land registration, a military freshly purged of leftist currents, and a small working class split along sectoral and national lines, Jordan lacked the conditions that fostered more expansive social policies in other countries of the region. Schools lacked teachers and classrooms; no national university had yet been established.[68] Government interventions in housing and facilities for water supply, power distribution, and sewage were minimal, shortcomings that an International Bank for Reconstruction and Development (IRBD) team, sent to assess the country's economic situation, described as "one of the most striking features of the Jordanian economy."[69] The government had not yet established the infrastructures or institutions capable of administering the conduct of the population as a whole.[70]

WASFI AL-TAL AND THE BUDDING GOVERNMENT OF THE SOCIAL

After a decade of political uncertainty, the monarchy embarked in the 1960s on a far more aggressive pursuit of development. Faced with decreasing aid from Washington, King Hussein turned to Wasfi al-Tal (1919–1971). An eager reformer from the northern city of Irbid, al-Tal was first appointed prime minister in 1962, and given a technocratic brief. His cabinet appointments emphasized professional expertise over and above ideological attachments.[71] Al-Tal's first government prioritized economic growth, which both the prime minister and the king saw as crucial to binding together the diverse constituents of the country while disincentivizing any reemergence of the political opposition that had been seen in the 1950s. The primary goal of new policy measures was "to broaden the domestic basis of support for and the legitimacy of the Hashemite state."[72] The main tool through which al-Tal's government sought to achieve this objective was the implementation of the country's first five-year plan for economic development (1962–67).[73] Drafted by a team of young technocrats in the recently created planning division of Jordan's Development Board (JDB),[74] the blueprint looked to expand GDP, rationalize government expenditures, and reduce unemployment, which in 1962 was estimated at around one third of the workforce, or 120,000 people.[75] With the elaboration of this plan, government officials began not only to reflect upon the sociopolitical problems engendered by poverty and unemployment but also to address them through premeditated measures.[76] These conceptual developments, drawing on minority currents of thought that had been present in Jordan since the mid-1950s, were matched by incremental expansions in the bureaucracy.[77] A budget bureau was established within the Ministry of National Economy to aid the JDB in fiscal deliberations and the planning process. In 1964, the Central Bank of Jordan was created to further assist in this undertaking.[78] Both worked extensively with the Ford Foundation[79] and soon became hubs of Jordan's slowly expanding planning apparatus.[80]

Although it initially gained broad-based popular support, al-Tal's first government quickly collapsed. Upon returning to office two years later (1965–67), he fully embraced the pursuit of economic growth as laid out in the relaunched seven-year plan (1964–70).[81] This was the mission set out for al-Tal by King Hussein when he reappointed him in 1965: to design efficient mechanisms through which to "deepen national consciousness" and attachments to the Hashemite regime among the country's diverse constituents.[82] In addition to promoting greater reliance on local income sources for recurrent expenditures, al-Tal was especially keen on boosting development in Jordan's small towns and villages. He attempted to do so by laying a more extensive road network and building elementary schools and healthcare facilities in parts of the country previously neglected by centralized institutions. Although his successes in this regard proved modest, al-Tal instigated a campaign of village electrification aimed at improving the lot of the rural poor.[83] The prime minister was especially interested in boosting the viability of agricultural activity so as to keep rural communities on the land. He intended not only to prepare for armed confrontation with Israel[84] but also to foster economic growth, dissipate the pressures of urbanization, and avoid popular unrest. Concerns over sedition, poverty, and discontent meant that the well-being of Jordanian citizens was slowly becoming a crucial element in political reflection.

Al-Tal's ambitions define this interstitial period. Before his appointment as prime minister, the well-being of Jordanians not linked to the military or bureaucracy had been largely secured through tribes and family networks. Social policies were considered largely redundant, as work-based remunerations were supposed to meet the citizenry's material needs, while extended families were expected to fulfill care-related welfare functions. Following al-Tal's appointment, an integrated approach to economic planning was put in place for the first time in Jordan's post-independence history. The prime minister's development drive certainly attempted to boost macroeconomic indicators and better incorporate the West Bank.[85] But for the first time, government policies also strove to improve collective life through direct measures, with the ultimate purpose of boosting support for the Hashemite regime. In contrast to the process traced by Foucault, al-Tal's planning propositions were biopolitical but illiberal; the Jordanian economy was not conceived as an autonomous realm governed by the natural laws of the market. Nor was it envisaged in ways analogous to Soviet modernization strategies, in which society was conceptualized as a realm of physical resources and persons susceptible to management and planning "as a whole."[86] Al-Tal's political ontology lay somewhere in a hazy in-between. Influenced by experiments in Egypt, Syria, and Yugoslavia and shaped by the paradigm of state-led development that emerged after World War II, the prime minister saw Jordan's pathway to modernity as requiring far different measures from those taken in advanced industrialized countries.[87] Al-Tal saw government investments as a necessary encouragement for development that he believed would ultimately be led by the private sector; as an initial stimulus that could be removed once Jordan had broken patterns of dependency. Whereas the socialist and *étatist* strategies of Egypt and Syria had led to repressive dictatorship, economic crisis, and class confrontation, al-Tal spoke proudly of Jordan's commitment to a mixed-market economy that could ensure the citizenry's well-being.[88] Without undermining the authoritarian political order, government institutions would act as the primary motor of development and the main avenue for wealth redistribution. In macroeconomic terms, al-Tal's policies were a success. Buoyed by American fiscal support and increasing investments by Jordan's budding bourgeoisie, the country's growth rate averaged around 7% throughout the 1960s.[89]

Although al-Tal did not achieve all he set out to do, his reformist impulses eventually led to a clash with entrenched interests, which partly explains the downfall of his second government. Merchants profiting from government contracts resented increases in taxes and customs duties as well as his anti-corruption initiatives. Members of the security forces feared his budget-conscious measures would alienate traditional bases of support in the armed forces. As Paul Kingston argues, "While al-Tal was able to block the expansion of the patrimonial system of government, he was unable to institutionalize the kind of mechanisms needed to transform it."[90] But in pondering a different pathway to modernity, and reflecting upon the role of government in doing so, al-Tal's tenure as prime minister marks the beginning of a drastic shift, one that had to be "thought" before it could be fully implemented. The population as a collective subject and society as a distinct body that could be acted upon had not yet been envisaged; planning documents at the time still portray the economy as a sphere of sovereign action amenable to monarchical designs.[91] Instead, al-Tal's time in government marks a transitional phase, not quite a new formation of biopolitical government but a subtle harbinger of its impending arrival. But wholesale transformation would have to wait.

MAKING SOCIETY INTELLIGIBLE: WAR AND STATE FORMATION

Opposition in Parliament and among elites stymied many of al-Tal's initiatives. Further complications came from regional developments. The creation of the PLO and the decision to establish a unified Arab military command, with Egypt as its nominal head, marked an important turning point. These decisions fostered a crescendo of aggressive rhetoric regarding the confrontation with Israel. They also built momentum for an independent Palestinian national movement that would eventually confront the Hashemite regime. By February of 1967, al-Tal's position had become untenable. He resigned, as King Hussein sought a rapprochement with Egyptian President Nasser, which would accelerate over the next three months. On June 5th, Jordanian forces under Egyptian command attacked Israeli positions. Six days later, the conflict was over, and Jordan's military was decimated. The conflict, extensively analyzed elsewhere,[92] drastically altered Jordanian politics, geography, and demography. Some 300,000 Palestinian refugees entered the East Bank, triggering a humanitarian crisis. The loss of the West Bank also resulted in reductions of 40% of GDP, 50% of industrial capacity, 25% of Jordan's arable land, and more than one third of grain production and livestock.[93] Reconciliation with Egypt and a short-lived entente with the PLO soon gave way to the next major challenge to the monarchy.

The War of 1967 convinced many supporters of the Palestinian cause that the Hashemite monarchy did not have their best interests at heart, and that its subservience to the United States was not the path towards the liberation of occupied territory. Criticism of the Palace increased dramatically. Negotiations between King Hussein and the PLO head Ahmed Shuqairi, replaced by Yasser Arafat in February, 1969, in what amounted to a seismic shift, did little to decrease tensions between Jordanian authorities and the reenergized *fedayeen*. Confrontations between Palestinian guerrillas and Jordanian security forces increased over the next months, inflamed by restless elements on both sides.[94] Equally if not more troubling to the Palace was the PLO's increasing assertiveness in the realms of taxation and policing, which threatened the monarchy's monopoly on key governmental practices. In spite of various attempts to avoid a violent confrontation, the Hashemite regime soon faced its most decisive challenge, a convoluted conflict ostensibly fought between the PLO and the Jordanian armed forces.[95] On September 15, 1970 King Hussein declared martial law and set about destroying the *fedayeen*. A ceasefire reached with the help of President Nasser on September 27th offered a brief reprieve, but the monarchy was now set on its path: to systematically eliminate the PLO's military presence in the country. Fortified by American military assistance, the Jordanian army spent the months between March and July of 1971 pursuing the PLO's guerrilla forces. On July 15th of that year, the *fedayeen* surrendered or absconded to Syria and Israel, eventually moving their operations to Lebanon. This conflict, known by many as Black September, had an array of short and long-term effects on the country. The human costs were colossal, especially in those districts and neighborhoods that had offered support to the PLO. The conflict also inaugurated the ascendance of an exclusivist Jordanian nationalism, one that no longer sought to blur the distinctions between West Bank and East, preferring to erect Jordanian-ness on the basis of the latter, drizzled with a large dose of adulation for the monarchy.[96]

For the purposes of this book, the conflict marks a critical juncture, after which the Hashemite regime's hold on power was no longer under direct military threat and its control over the population could thus be consolidated.[97] Following Black September, the enemy no longer took the form of external forces nor armed militias that imperiled the monarchy's existence.[98] More salient now was the potential threat of local opposition. Tools had to be fashioned with which to wage "an internal war that defend[ed] society against threats born of and in its own body."[99] A radical transformation in governing strategies beckoned. The conflict with the *fedayeen* had laid bare the disdain with which many citizens viewed the Hashemite regime. It also made eminently clear that a minimalist approach to social welfare could severely undermine support for the monarchy. What approach would the Hashemite regime adopt in order to turn the tide? With a few small exceptions, including land registration and irrigation schemes, previous measures had been erratic and piecemeal; they sought, above all else, to strengthen the monarchy's control over individuals and territory. But with al-Tal's ascent to power, policy makers' concerns slowly began to shift, from the safeguarding of Hashemite supremacy over subjects through coercive and disciplinary instruments to the problem of maximizing the well-being of citizens in order to maintain the authoritarian status quo. Government was no longer to be exercised over territory but in relation to the population and to the forces that shaped its habits, health, and subsistence. It would take rampant inflation and a far-reaching but under-analyzed event in Jordanian history to see novel techniques of governance fully implemented. Nevertheless, without the conflict with the PLO, the subsequent shift to the management of the population as the Jordanian government's primary modus operandi could never have occurred.[100] The expansion of welfare policy required social peace. Soon-to-be-privileged mechanisms of rule would target Jordan's population: a living body in need of management, measurement, and administration.

THE ZARQA MUTINY: A MOMENT OF PROBLEMATIZATION

Surprised by the scope of discontent expressed by the most loyal of troops, King Hussein immediately cancelled his trip to the United States upon hearing of the mutiny at al-Khaw in February, 1974. Over the following days, the monarch made several trips to this and other military outposts. Although the press was not allowed to attend any of these events, it was reported that the king arrived in al-Khaw dressed in military uniform, pistol strapped to his waist, and answered soldiers' questions for around an hour.[101] But more important than his personal advances were the king's prompt royal decrees in which he pledged to review the status and pay scales of army personnel and the police, measures amply publicized in the local press.[102] The king confided to those present at a ministerial-level meeting that a more comprehensive approach was needed to prevent similar unrest in the future.[103] The monarch had been "greatly disturbed" by the mutiny, "bitterly disappointed in the army," and "determined to deal with profiteering merchants" who, he felt, were exacerbating price rises.[104] Never otherwise known for his interest in economic matters, the king participated in breakneck deliberations over the next week.

On February 13th, King Hussein met with members of Parliament and other notables in a closed session of Parliament to discuss how to prevent further unrest. A day later, he addressed the nation via radio. In his remarks, the king made indirect references to the mutiny while assuring citizens that the Jordanian Army's loyalty was above suspicion.[105] He then addressed the rising cost of living. After describing inflation as a worldwide phenomenon and threatening monopolist merchants with severe punishments for hoarding, King Hussein announced the creation of the Ministry of Supply (MOS), a centralized body that would oversee the pricing and distribution of basic goods.[106] In the king's speech and subsequent pronouncements, one can detect a dramatically different conceptualization of the economy compared to the one that had prevailed in previous policy plans and official pronouncements. For example, while declaring his unchanging desire to "increase production, doubling it time and again," the monarch acknowledged that the country "still imports most of our consumer products and cannot avoid being affected by the waves of inflation and high prices that are sweeping the world."[107] Differentiating the approach of the Jordanian government apparatus from the variants of Arab socialism that were dominant at the time, King Hussein now spoke of the economy as an apolitical realm, a specific level of reality constituted by autonomous processes not amenable to sovereign action.[108] While he did not subscribe to the juridical categories of liberalism, be they in the form of individual rights or a social contract, the king's newfound conception of government shared liberalism's recognition of the reality of the economy as an independent sphere.[109] The global market was conceived as a site of spontaneous forces that had to be acknowledged, observed, and remedied. Inflation was especially important in this respect. As a "worldwide phenomenon" over which the monarchy could exert only minimal influence, the inflationary spiral led the monarch to break with views of the economy as a sphere that could be readily controlled by the Palace's initiatives.[110] The huge increase in commodity prices had posed a disquieting conundrum: How could the Hashemite regime regulate the effects of inflation given this independent "economic reality" over which it could exert little control? The answer was to design new welfare programs and price controls that could mitigate the impact of unpredictable threats caused by market forces; government had to take on a "social vocation."[111]

I find the king's speech to mark a drastic modification in governmental thinking, one that underpins the institutional and policy changes that quickly followed it. While various scholars identify the post-1973 period in Jordan as one of planned economic development,[112] none mentions the fundamental transformation in how the economy was "thought" among Jordanian policy makers. Clearly, modes of governing were subjected to a series of reflections and critiques in closed-door meetings. A far different path forward was chosen, one that required a dramatic expansion of regulatory tools. Of course, sovereign instruments of repression remained, as did the disciplinary techniques that worked to produce Jordanian subjects. But decisive as well was how subsistence was rendered administrable in relation to a specific theoretical discourse on the economy.[113] A brief spark of anger in the army, the disciplinary institution *par excellence*, forced the double entry of population into political reflection, both as a field of knowledge and as an explicit target of government.[114] Policy measures ranging from the discounted provision of bread to the subsidy of water for agriculture addressed citizens and sought to safeguard their well-being.[115] In this respect, the Zarqa mutiny marks a crucial moment of problematization in which a form of governing is called into question, when various actors pose the question of how exactly the conduct of a more clearly defined citizenry could be managed.

Until the mutiny, government interventions in local markets were more "a case of complementarity imposed by unanticipated circumstances," such as war and regional instability, than expressions of any coherent approach.[116] After it, the task of government was no longer to organize and control an economy subject to its strictures but to engage in the sagacious management of economic processes external to itself. By articulating an image of a managerial state that could intervene to combat the instabilities of capitalism, King Hussein's public pronouncements, as well as those of government ministers, argued for a middle way somewhere between the nationalization of the means of production and the unregulated free market. There was a tacit acknowledgment that price fluctuations would be a permanent feature of capitalism, and that a set of measures would be required to manage their corollaries and consequences. In his first press conference, the newly appointed minister of supply reiterated this stance: "The problem [inflation] will not be solved with the press of a button, as prices will not go down that way. . . . But there is no doubt that the state will spend large amounts, in the millions, to decrease prices for consumers, primarily on basic foodstuffs."[117] The negative consequences of a worldwide economy prone to challenging fluctuations had to be combated in order to secure the citizenry's well-being. Public policies now had to be preventative, concerned with the preclusion of events and modes of existence that could threaten the political status quo. Overnight, the prices of consumer goods, the consumption patterns of citizens, the health of male breadwinners became problems in the eyes of policy makers and the target of systematic interventions. The massive uptick in budgetary assistance from the Gulf,[118] increased wheat shipments from the United States,[119] and the political calm that came with martial law made this interventionist turn possible. But crucial as well was the drastic shift in thinking that had taken place. Attitudes regarding the volatility of free markets and the usefulness of government intercession in certain sectors became important pillars of a burgeoning policy consensus: to ameliorate both inflation and social instability through active measures, without ever abandoning the principles of private ownership. Policy measures would seek not to direct the economic sphere but to actively manage its oscillations. After the Zarqa mutiny, the Hashemite regime crossed the threshold to an entirely new mode of government: administering everyday life.

A NEW FORMATION OF BIOPOLITICAL GOVERNMENT

The campaign against inflation is the fulcrum of a dual transformation: one concerning the various ways in which the Jordanian population, and the factors upholding its subsistence, are theorized, classified, and observed; the other related to administrative measures intended to combat inflation and bolster the citizenry's standard of living. The former, which I will address first, required dramatic changes in the types of information, knowledge, and data produced by official institutions. As Nikolas Rose and Peter Miller argue, "Knowledges of the economy, or of the nature of health, or of the problem of poverty are essential elements in programmes that seek to exercise legitimate and calculated power over them."[120] In Jordan's 1976–80 economic development plan, published less than a year after the Zarqa mutiny, the Hashemite regime's concern with these knowledges is quite clear. Given the new mission of the MOS, the "lack of precise information on the number and geographical distribution of the Jordanian population" was seen as highly problematic. In response, the policy plan outlines various measures meant to "expand statistical coverage to include the various fields of social and economic activity in the country," so as to remedy a "dearth of comparable time series data" and the "lack of comparable time series statistics for various social and economic indicators."[121] The document describes data gathering, over and over again, as a basic requirement for development planning. The new concern for the population required not only the financial means to improve the citizenry's well-being but also forms of knowledge that could help carry out the task.[122] An arena of intervention had to be mapped, documented, and studied and forms of knowledge had to be devised to connect new interventions to the problems they would solve.

The task of statistical compilation was taken up with vigor. The production of reliable data on unemployment, food consumption, and agricultural production quickly became vital.[123] Quantitative measures offered technical supports for new modes of administration housed in centralized ministries, making "government at a distance" increasingly feasible.[124] While gaps in information and failures in collection inevitably occurred, this accumulation of data rendered visible a particular domain, giving the social body both external boundaries and a certain internal homogeneity, one that policy makers could target with strategic interventions. A vast array of scattered governmental actions could now be imagined as part of a unified whole: the "state" was acting on "society."

Still, the impact of statistical compilation went beyond simply documenting the dietary habits and consumption patterns of the Jordanian population. As James Scott argues in his assessment of state apparatuses' information-gathering strategies, such pursuits do not merely monitor or map so as to increase visibility. They shape a people and a landscape to fit the state's techniques of observation and control.[125] One now-retired employee of the MOS details how this process transpired, at least as it related to bread:

> We began by surveying the neighborhoods of every city in the country and determining their needs. We then examined local bakeries to verify their production capacity. Then we gathered at the ministry for a full day and determined

flour allotments for the following month. These calculations also depended on what the Minister [of Supply] heard from his counterpart in Finance, who was the one that purchased wheat on international markets. This was all new to us at the time. We had to devise methods, create documents, and establish procedures to make sure no one in the country lacked for bread. It was a huge undertaking.[126]

MOS's statistical compiling procedures strove not only to organize the field of observation in abstract terms, but also to gain as much control as possible over the life processes they sought to encapsulate, to both know and (re)order social reality according to certain precepts.[127] Neighborhoods, towns, and cities previously viewed through the prism of agricultural production or political loyalty were now surveyed in terms of their nutritional requirements. The quote above reveals some aspects of how this process unfolded, the ways in which the MOS sought to know the Jordanian social body and increase its legibility in order to better administer it. While the expansion of the state apparatus's ability to name, locate, and track its subjects is typically linked to expanding extraction in the form of taxes, in post-1974 Jordan, this process was inverted. Distribution was the activity that drove the efforts to "see like a state."[128] New institutions were needed in order to act like one.

The second axis of the transformation initiated in 1974 regards the multiplication of administrative agencies and regulatory measures targeting the population. Following the 1973 war, foreign assistance, principally from Gulf countries, Iraq, and the United States, constituted almost 50% of total government revenue; from 1970 through 1980 it averaged 30% of Jordan's GDP.[129] In the Hashemite Kingdom, as in the rest of the Middle East, this jump in government revenues contributed to a dramatic growth in public expenditure.[130] The Jordanian government now had the financial means to adopt measures that King Hussein's newfound conception of the economy deemed imperative. In this endeavor, policy makers borrowed from the interventionist toolkit of the outwardly more socialist regime in Egypt, just at the time when that neighboring republic was about to embark on a process of economic liberalization.[131] Although not a direct copy of Egyptian food-subsidy programs, Jordan's anti-inflationary measures did borrow from the former's conceptual delimitation of the legitimate field of action.[132] New welfare policies did not seek to threaten private property or the inviolability of contracts, focusing instead on subsistence and a certain quality of life within the strictures of capitalism. Central to this process was the foundation of the MOS, charged with "providing essential foodstuffs in reasonable quantity and good quality and at reasonable prices,"[133] so as to produce a "financially and psychologically secured community, in addition to creating more jobs."[134] Given vague but broad powers to meet this objective, the MOS expanded rapidly and soon became one of the country's "most important ministries."[135]

With the rationale of consumer protection, the MOS established a monopoly over the import of a number of items, including wheat, flour, sugar, rice, meat, and frozen poultry. It also fixed their wholesale and retail prices. In the space of a fortnight, the government prohibited merchants from importing these "essentials."[136] The ambiguous responsibilities it was tasked with meant that the ministry had ample room to widen its brief.[137] Jawad Anani, who became the minister of supply in 1979, describes the expansionary logic: "The ministry was created and had to find itself a job, so it found itself doing a number of very unexpected things."[138] Its portfolio, on the grounds of "consumer protection," eventually grew to over forty items.[139] Those items not defined by decree were subject to changes of interpretation by ministers, which gave the more activist among them leeway to extend the ministry's purview. Despite constant complaints from businessmen, often lodged through the Amman Chamber of Commerce, interventionist ministers repeatedly expanded the list of price-controlled goods. Ministry officials became notorious for their frequent attacks on merchants for "stockpiling goods" and "price gouging" at the expense of lower-income citizens.[140] In 1975, the MOS created the Civil Consumer Corporation, "to provide civil servants (and military personnel) with durable and non-durable consumer goods at cost price, duty free in respect of imported items."[141] This led to the establishment of retail outlets throughout the country where MOS sold items that it now imported or regulated. Although these outlets were initially intended only for members of the bureaucracy and armed forces, "informal reciprocal mechanisms" meant that they acted as price suppressors, thus boosting the real income of the populace as a whole.[142] These policies were part and parcel of an "income policy approach," carefully calibrated to minimize discontent among both business and labor.[143] This was done by augmenting the citizenry's purchasing power at the government's expense, rather than through negotiated wage increases.

For the decade following the establishment of the MOS, foreign funds made fiscal prudence seem superfluous. Jawad Anani recalls the dizzying financial heights: "Those were great times for the economy. Our five-year plans were fully funded, everyone had a job, remittances were high and foreign aid seemed unending." With government coffers filled to the brim, spending on universal subsidies for a growing array of goods was a minor concern: "When I arrived at the Ministry [of Supply] in 1979, the government was pushing us to spend more and more. No one questioned the logic of subsidizing individual consumption. Wheat prices at the time were going up, but we had the money, and could afford to spend more."[144] No proponent of government intervention in local markets, Anani was discomfited by the negative effects of such outlays:

> By the time I became minister [of supply], a disproportionate amount of an average family's expenditure was subject to government regulation. We were creating all sorts of distortions in the market. For example, we helped expand consumerism because merchants were forced to import anything whose prices were not controlled by the ministry. They were not making enough profit on regulated goods so started bringing in chips and chocolate and all sorts of unnecessary things that we still over-consume today. The national airlines, the airport, all sorts of prestige projects went over-budget. We were all too eager to spend the money. We were transforming the relationship of the economy and citizens to the state without thinking through the consequences.[145]

When Anani became minister of supply (1979), some 80% of an average family's expenditure was subject to direct government decrees and regulations.[146] In the words of one Jordanian senator, "Jordan's economy in those days was as socialist as those of the Soviet bloc. The government monitored and controlled the price of nearly all important consumer items."[147] Unsurprisingly, many merchants came to see the government as a direct competitor rather than a facilitator. Until the creation of the MOS, local businessman had had an almost totally free hand in importing and distributing commodities, with the exception of cereals. Even in the case of wheat, the Grain Office that was established in July of 1954 limited its remit to occasionally buying stocks on the international market and storing PL 480 contributions from the United States food-for-aid program in order to avoid price increases during drought years.[148]

After the 1967 war, the refugee influx and high rate of population growth expanded total wheat consumption by nearly 10,000 tons a year. For more than a decade, national consumption had been exceeding production levels even in the most productive years, as the country faced increasing demand and declining domestic output, triggered by urbanization and repeated floods of American wheat.[149] Many farmers had shifted from self-provisioning to the production of animal products and non-regulated agricultural goods in the preceding decade, as customary subsistence practices gave way to the logic of the market. Previously, makeshift solutions to the occasional shortages of wheat had sufficed. Following the Zarqa mutiny, and the dramatic increase in global food prices with which it coincided, a more lasting solution to combating inflation and safeguarding subsistence was deemed necessary. The MOS was at the heart of this adminis- trative expansion, and the bread subsidy would become its keystone policy. As key nodes in a set of increasingly integrated infrastructures that traversed the entire country, bread-makers became crucial points of articulation between the management of needs in Jordan's cities and towns, on the one hand, and the countrywide distribution of resources, on the other. Yet unlike with the Soviet heating systems analyzed by Stephen Collier, the MOS did not plug populations and food provision into minutely detailed master plans for urban development.[150] Rather, regulating bread production was about responding to market instability and failure, fine tuning the MOS's ability to ameliorate the negative repercussions of an independent economic realm—an important parallel between the monar- chy's approach to government and the liberal variant analyzed by Foucault. The bakeries that the MOS regulated and the bread these outlets provided allowed the population to be administered as an object of government.

The next fifteen years (1974–89) saw an unprecedented intensity in the regulation of intimate matters of subsistence. In addition to increasing public employment, the oil boom fostered rapid growth in spending on housing for the poor, as well as the extension of water and electricity grids throughout the coun- try.[151] Health and education spending grew apace, reaching levels significantly higher than in other developing countries.[152] Military service provided a further layer of social benefits, including subsidized housing and higher education. Of course, it is important not to depict this period as a golden age of Jordanian welfare.[153] The system was bedeviled by a number of exclusions. Social security and health care benefits were circumscribed to those employed in government agencies. Efforts to "Transjordanize" the bureaucracy and armed forces after Black September worked to exclude most Palestinians, who overwhelmingly were not privy to the benefits that came with government employ. Like the systems in Pahlavi Iran, Greece, Italy, and several countries in Latin America at the time, this highly fragmented system offered generous benefits to those in the public sector and very little to those outside it.[154] Additionally, an urban bias that favored the "modern capitalized sector" meant that public invest-ments were overwhelmingly channeled towards Amman, largely excluding small towns and rural areas from government outlays.[155] The arid and semi-arid Jordanian steppe was especially underserved. Yet, for all its problems and exclusions, social policy, coupled with severe limits on political activity and real GNP growth between 7 and 11%, underpinned the relative calm seen throughout the 1970s and 1980s.[156] Critical also were changes in inter-Arab politics, the truce with Israel, the suspension of Parliament, and the oil boom in the Arab Gulf, which filtered through to Jordan in the form of remittances and geopolitical aid, allowing taxation to be kept at a minimum. Unemployment reached historic lows, while quality-of-life indicators increased. Slowly, "economic prosperity offered citizens a stake in Jordan's welfare and allowed governing bodies to increase their relevance to the population."[157] By taming (though hardly elim-inating) economic insecurity, new welfare measures helped to entrench both the political status quo and the ability of families to survive through wage labor. The MOS was central to this endeavor. Price controls and subsidies for fuel, water, and bread quickly became pillars of Hashemite authoritarianism. The ground upon which citizens lived their lives had transformed. The break with previous forms of government was definitive. What had once been a distant, amorphous body became crucial to Jordanians' subsistence. The state became, quite literally, their "bread and butter."[158]

CONCLUSION

The dramatic escalation of inflation, the brief army mutiny it sparked, and the radical rethinking of welfare policy it produced began a fundamental trans-formation in the way Jordanians were governed. The mutiny in Zarqa marks a turning point after which certain phenomena were observed, analyzed, and acted upon through an entirely different way of seeing the world. These developments fostered a new style of administration, a redefinition of the field of state action. This shift grew out of the Hashemite regime's concern with maintaining social cohesion and political order in the context of new forms of inequality and mobilization among key constituencies. These grievances were only able to emerge following the conflicts of 1967 and 1970–71, after which there were no more active threats to the continuity of the Hashemite monarchy.[159] The grievances coalesced around the price of key subsistence goods. The regime's response to an outburst of frustration in the armed forces fostered a rethinking and reworking of what was, at the time, a rudimentary system of welfare provision. New policies sought to make the population legible and manageable through measures that could better shape its conduct. Changed forever was the disciplinary-juridical dyad so meticulously analyzed in Joseph Massad's *Colonial Effects*. Disciplinary and sovereign logics were not replaced but recast within biopolitical measures concerned with the health, well-being, and productivity of the citizenry. What would emerge was a contingent, unstable triangle, composed of "sovereignty, discipline, governmental management," with the Jordanian population "as its main target" and "apparatuses of security as its essential mechanism."[160]

This shift entailed a wholesale expansion of centralized intervention in areas previously deemed familial or tribal responsibilities, consolidating a transformation begun under the prime minister Wasfi al-Tal, who began to carve out a new field of political concern. After Black September, governmental practices took an interventionist turn, not only in organizing a market economy but also in remedying its negative effects, evincing concern for the citizenry as a whole. An array of measures targeting Jordanians as a complex biological body were devised to manage the citizenry's existence, exchange, and circulation. Rather than attributing this transformation to elite machinations, strategies enacted by an autonomous institution, or a social pact entered into by volitional individuals, this chapter has attempted to trace the emergence of new welfare programs through forms of knowledge that provide the "very possibility of appearing to set apart from society the free-standing object of the state."[161] Methods of distribution and regulation internal to the social body produced the effect of an external structure. Bakeries and subsidies not only ensured subsistence and helped contain dissidence. They also operated at less instrumental registers, productive and performative of a state that now worked at the level of the sensory and mundane.

Chapter 2

SENSING THE STATE

AT THE JUNCTION NEAR HIS JOB in Tal'a-l-Ali, we would always stop. Every time, for ten or fifteen seconds, Ibrahim would pause. Perplexed by the routine, I asked about it and was told to shut up. "Attune your senses (*dawazin hawasik*)," he barked; "the bread speaks (*al-khubz byahki*)." My puzzlement at the sudden halt during our otherwise hurried walks gave way to a realization that Ibrahim had devised his own method for determining which bakery was producing bread at that moment. Four bakeries competed for the favor of local residents and workers in this middle-class neighborhood in Amman. Driven largely by demand, as well as the whims of their respective owners, any one of these bakeries could be making fresh *khubz* when I met Ibrahim at his workplace before our weekly football match. The bread, our contribution to the post-game meal, would not be consumed until eight in the evening. The fresher the better—our senses had to be attuned. What I felt as a fog of commotion, sounds, and smells was, for Ibrahim, something more coherent. His sensibilities had been formed by far different forces than my own.

I want to take Ibrahim's routine and remarks as a starting point for pondering the ways in which particular sites and welfare services shape sensory engagements and bodily dispositions that, in turn, generate the state effect. Crucial here are the aromas, tastes, and timbres that emanate from the bakery and how these orient citizens vis-à-vis the state, which does not pre-exist such encounters but is reproduced in and through them. That is, the bakery works to distribute the sensible, molding subjects that make the state become common sense, a relationship that is embodied before it is grasped through reflection and representation. Welfare services act on bodies. They configure experience and generate sensations through which political authority circulates in the world.

Why consider sensation? Since Benedict Anderson's influential *Imagined Communities*, scholars have acknowledged the centrality of print, language, and imaginaries in cultivating national sensibilities.[1] The familiar figure of the newspaper reader, immersed in a "secular ritual" that is replicated by anonymous others, has become a well-worn trope among students of nationalism.[2] Print capitalism, in this reading, pushes readers to transcend the confines of face-to-face solidarities through an act of imagination, as they slowly congeal into a broader national public. More recently, an array of works has delved into how the state is imagined and represented among citizens.[3] The influential edited volume *States of Imagination* marked the definitive arrival of this approach, as it emphasized the need to study "how the state tries to make itself real and tangible through symbols, texts and iconography."[4] While the detailed ethnographies included in the volume pay close attention to governmental practices and citizens' encounters with public institutions, the overarching emphasis on "languages of stateness" leads many to overlook how newspapers and traffic signs, documents and roads, act on the body.[5] Particularly unheeded are the myriad ways in which aesthetic experience—both perception and cognition—relates to the subtle dissemination of the state in everyday life. Without diminishing the importance of practices of representation, I am interested here less in the productive properties of discussions about the state than in the conditions that make them possible. Pivotal among these are sensations and bodily dispositions. For how can the state appear, persist, and survive if it is not somehow embodied within those who produce it?

Maurice Merleau-Ponty argues that social theory errs when it divorces the body from the mind and presumes that the production of subjectivity is not somehow entangled with bodily experience. Building on this fundamental insight, this chapter argues that, when assessing welfare services, we must attend to the ways they work upon the embodied dispositions of those they target. By inducing particular modes of experience, "felt" individually but produced socially, the bread subsidy and the bakery play a key part in what I will term *stately sensations*. Such sensations, what Davide Panagia terms "the heterology of impulses that register on our bodies," are both objects of and conditions for the generation of the state effect.[6] In what follows I want to home in on these sensations via the bakery, so as to explore how this site anchors perception, contours sensory experience, and shapes the aesthetics of political authority in Jordan. The bakery does not just distribute a basic foodstuff or prevent social unrest. Equally important, if not even more so, are the sensations that surround the provision of bread itself.

Tacking back and forth between interviews and ethnography, this chapter argues these points in two parts. First, it will detail how the bread subsidy reconfigured the habits and practices through which people fed themselves and their families, altering social relations and implementing an entirely different aesthetic regime of ordering. The set of transformations I describe not only modified gastronomic routines and patterns of subsistence; it also introduced new modes of sensorial engagement with conduits of state power. Here I will emphasize the centrality of bakeries, as crucial nodes in Jordan's welfare infrastructure, in fashioning the sensations through which a heterogeneous Jordanian public was fostered. While in 1970 blunt force was used to repress potential opponents, after the 1974 Zarqa mutiny the Hashemite regime increasingly deployed regulatory measures that could configure a compliant public and entrench the political order. Cognizant that the citizenry's reception of political authority could not be cultivated through coercion or ideology alone, elites deployed a host of policies that they believed would, over time, develop more lasting, intimate modes of attachment between citizens and the structures that ostensibly ruled them. Yet the impact of these measures went far beyond their designs and intentions. The bakery not only changed people's relationship to bread and the institutions seen to provide it. It also worked to instill ways of inhabiting political authority crucial to the state's reception. Like roads and electricity, bakeries took root in the corporeal immediacies of individuals and neighborhoods while also linking them to a broader public, what Jacques Rancière terms a "community of sense."[7] By carving out space and time and fusing daily routines under a particular rubric of intelligibility, the bakery molded embodied attributes crucial to Jordanian political subjectivity. The result was a citizenry not interpellated by nationalism or monarchical ideology but conjoined by quite tangible patterns of consumption and commensality.

In the second half of the chapter, I will focus more intently on the bakery as an aesthetic ensemble. As several recent works in anthropology and history have demonstrated,[8] infrastructures shape bodily engagements and modes of emplacement. In other words, they transpire through "a certain kind of aesthetic experience."[9] My understanding of aesthetics here refers not to the common use of the term in reference to the disinterested observation of high art, but to the broader Aristotelian sense of *aesthesis*, the capacity of embodied beings to sensorially apprehend the world.[10] In this respect, I am hardly alone in trying to rescue the aesthetic from its Kantian imprint. I depart, like many others, from definitions that drain the concept of its sensory plenitude; instead, I attempt to explore a more immediately corporeal politics. I will use the term, as in its original formulation by the German philosopher Alexander Baumgarten, to explore the realm of sensation, the frequently overlooked yet incontestably palpable dimensions of everyday life, in order to consider embodiment along with the more traditionally "political" topic of the state.[11] I contend that this more capacious understanding of aesthetics can help us account for the impact of welfare services and the sites and infrastructures through which they circulate. While Rancière's foundational work on the aesthetics of politics is limited in its examination of the force of common objects or governmental practices, I will draw on his corpus here to see the bakery, and the welfare infrastructure of which it is a part, as "sharing with works of art the similar role of producing sensory experience and through that experience constituting political life."[12] In sum, the bakery does more than ensure subsistence. It works to naturalize the state by making it seem part and parcel of everyday life, cultivating stately sensations, and through rather delectable means.

FROM THE HOME TO THE BAKERY

"We used to feed ourselves," an elderly farmer near the border town of Ramtha told me. "Now we grow olives for the rich and eat bread that tastes like shit." While I did my best to defend the quality of some of the bakeries I had come across during my fieldwork, Othman steadfastly disagreed. Happy to reminisce about the *khubz tabun* of his youth,[13] he could not understand how I could prefer the industrially produced breads made in automated machines (*afran*) to the kind of dense loaves his mother had baked in a clay oven outside the family's modest rural home. What he resented was not so much the state's provision of cheap bread as the disruption of the agricultural practices and household routines he held dear. Although he himself resisted the onslaught of stately sensations, his sons preferred city life. Subsistence agriculture had ceased to be the family's way of life, or even a viable option: "Growing wheat was harder than olives, and less profitable. My sons wanted to study and live in Amman. So, I gave up too. Now we all go to the bakery and buy *khubz mad'aum* (subsidized bread)."

As outlined in the previous chapter, the creation of the Ministry of Supply (MOS) and the implementation of the bread subsidy radically altered the imbrication of state institutions with everyday life. This change was linked to the rise of "population" as a category of concern for the Jordanian government. Along with a dramatic expansion in water and electricity provision, bakeries became a crucial site not just for intervention in a pre-constituted "social,"[14] but also for the Jordanian citizenry's very materialization. Antina von Schnitzler points to similar developments in apartheid South Africa, where municipal infrastructures "mediated a biopolitical relation between state and population through which the latter was rendered both measurable and subject to regulation."[15] But while her excellent work focuses on infrastructures as both symbol and conduit of state power, I want to explore here a more embodied habituation to the state effect, its naturalization through corporeal means.

As Othman's recollections indicate, one of the primary avenues through which this occurred were changes in bread production and consumption.[16] Following the institution of the bread subsidy in 1974, there was a rapid decline in dry-land wheat production in Jordan's northern governorates.[17] Before the establishment of the MOS in 1974, flour mills obtained approximately 40% of their wheat from local producers.[18] After the MOS was created, the government became the sole purchaser and distributor of wheat from abroad in the country. Local production declined rapidly. The MOS now provided the country's six main flour mills with the overwhelming majority of their wheat requirements, obtained from donations by USAID and the European Economic Community or purchases from other foreign markets. Villages throughout northern Jordan that had once been self-sufficient in cereals saw their agricultural practices and alimentary routines transformed.[19] Wheat was previously one of the region's primary crops.[20] It was converted into flour throughout the year in the household, in mechanized village mills, or in water mills in nearby *wadis*.[21] Bread was then baked at home or in a neighborhood oven where families took their proofed dough. Bakers were paid "either in bread or in dough."[22] But after 1974, foreign wheat imported by the government flooded the local market. Silos allowed policy makers to preserve these shipments and manage the life of grains, storing and discharging them when necessary.[23] Flour now appeared in closely measured sacks standardized by the MOS. In the north, where barley and wheat had been the two agricultural mainstays, this shift altered which crops were grown and the temporal patterns that accompanied them. As farming plots were shifted towards other crops (mainly olives) or sold to make way for rapid urbanization, purchased bread became the most practical option for many residents.[24] In areas where subsistence agriculture was prevalent, bread slowly became divorced from the temporal rhythms of harvest and milling that had previously defined its production. This transition was neither uniform nor wholly negative. Several female farmers, for example, spoke to me of how the subsidy freed many of them from the onerous, and gendered, work of milling flour and making bread, giving them time that could now be spent on other tasks. Although it did not liberate women from the toils of unpaid labor, the proliferation of commercial bakeries led to a gradual decline in the number of self-sufficient households, driving a broader integration of villages and towns into a seemingly unitary social body.[25]

The bread subsidy and the rapid proliferation of bakeries radically altered consumption habits as well. Previously, the purchase of bread for sale had been a primarily urban phenomenon, confined mainly to the capital, where a few European ovens fed with wood (rather than dried dung, brush, and straw) had started to appear.[26] Abd al-Rahman Munif's memoir of childhood in Amman, *Story of a City*, briefly reminisces about one of these bread-makers, which unsuccessfully attempted to popularize "Western bread."[27] He recalls how, during the 1940s, "Ovens in residential neighborhoods did not sell ready-made bread because no one was used to buying it." It was inedible within hours; the capital's residents believed that "'bread from the souk does not go a long way.' Only strangers bought it, or those who had no choice."[28] At the time, most families had a *tabun* oven or *saj*, a convex metal baking sheet with which they baked bread at home. After the creation of the MOS in 1974, commercial bakeries selling ready-made bread quickly spread throughout the country.[29] One resident of a village near the city of Irbid, a wheat-growing hub in the north of the country, makes clear the far-reaching nature of these changes:

> When I was young, my family would always make bread at home. The commercial bakery was something you only saw in Amman, we had no use for it. Then in the 1970s everything changed. Very quickly, it became cheaper and easier to just buy bread outside the home. We were not allowed to sell wheat to anyone except the government. My neighbors stopped caring where the wheat came from, or how the flour was made, as long as bread was cheap. Soon, every little village had a bakery with subsidized bread. My mother still made bread on special occasions, but this tradition has slowly died out as well. Why spend time milling flour or baking when you could buy subsidized bread so easily? The state became the one who fed us.

These remarks indicate the extent to which the bread subsidy penetrated dietary habits and gastronomic routines. In the southern regions of Jordan, where wheat was sparsely grown, eating patterns began to resemble diets that were previously associated with urban life, driven by the uptick in bread consumption. Carol Palmer has traced this shift, in which the availability of "inexpensive imported flour" gave bread a much more prominent place in the Bedouin diet than the coarsely ground grains that were previously their culinary mainstay.[30]

Citizens slowly wove the bakery into the very fabric of their quotidian rhythms and routines. While commercial bread producers allowed people to save time and decrease certain types of fatigue, it also mutated the ways people engaged with each other in and around mealtimes. Carole Counihan finds a similar transformation in the town of Bosa in Sardinia. Whereas the wheat–bread life cycle was once pivotal to local economies and subsistence, consuming much time and effort, villagers began to "buy bakery bread" and consume it in ways "increasingly divorced from earthly rhythms."[31] Similarly in Jordan, where bread had once been either absent or enmeshed in the patterns of household and communal life, it was now wrapped up in the welfare provisions of the Hashemite regime. Driven by the replacement of seasonal agricultural cadences and the alteration of food consumption patterns, subsidized bread soon became a primary source of daily calories. These shifts were not immediate;

some families held steadfast to previous alimentary practices. Yet over time, the introduction of subsidized bread generated a slow but steady bodily habituation, synchronizing "a heterogeneous population through the attunement of bodies at a distance."[32] The bread subsidy transformed *khubz 'arabi* from a novelty sold in a few urban bakeries into an essential foodstuff consumed by almost the entirety of the citizenry, converting inhabitants of the smallest of towns and most rural of villages into members of a commensal community.

Changes to agrarian and alimentary practices were not the only channel through which people's relationship to political authority was transformed. The slow homogenization of gustatory tastes also worked to produce sensations that coalesced in moments of ingestion. After establishing the bread subsidy, the MOS established detailed production guidelines, flour allocations, and price controls to manage the output of bakeries. Extensive guidelines now covered how flour was to be produced and for which breads it could be used. A retired baker succinctly described the changes to business practices prompted by the establishment of the ministry: "Before [the Ministry of Supply] we had a free hand in production. This changed drastically in the space of a few months. All of a sudden, every aspect of our production was put under total supervision."[33] Another change that was repeatedly referred to, to my initial surprise, was a sensorial one—subsidized bread tasted different. Whereas *khubz* was previously "pungent," "dense," or "delicious," with the subsidy it became "dull," "tasteless," and "bland." One lifelong baker, now installed in a supervisory role in one of Amman's most famous bread outlets, detailed some of the changes:

> The job of bakers and bakery owners used to be much more difficult. We would do the same things we do now—accounting, servicing customers, managing employees. But then [before 1974], we would have to buy wheat on the free market, figure out which varieties made the best flour, and how we could then bake the best bread. Each sack of flour and loaf of bread was unique. No two bakeries tasted alike.

Asked how the subsidy had altered the bread business, he summed up changes to commerce but dwelled just as long on taste:

> Bakeries became like factories. Making bread involved uniform inputs, similar outputs, predictable profits. What we have lost because of the subsidy is the

taste of bread. Ovens make a difference, bakers can make minor improvements, but most loaves taste the same. The flour all comes from the same wheat, and it is industrially produced. The bread is dull. It is not from the baker's hands.

Prior to the establishment of the bread subsidy, bakers had to distinguish between wheat varieties and milling techniques, adjusting their recipes and methods depending on a flour's qualities. Variability in breads was inevitable. After 1974, bakers received a steady supply of comparatively uniform flour. Loaves gradually became more similar. Needless to say, attempts to harness bakers to the task of state-building ran into numerous obstacles, some of which I will discuss later. What I wish to dwell on here is how bread-making was once grounded in the temporalities and dexterities of households and local communities, passed down and shared informally. With the establishment of the MOS, baking became a governmental practice, increasingly bereft of the distinctive traits of those who made *khubz*.

Another retired bread-maker, who had worked in the Ashrafiyeh district of Amman for over forty years, similarly emphasized how the welfare policy catalyzed the homogeneity of the citizenry's palette: "All the *khubz 'arabi* tastes like paper. Whereas before there were so many differences, the bread subsidy made uniformity. The taste is gone. The Ministry [of Supply] wanted everyone to eat the same bread." These recollections both mourn lost tastes and identify how they were transformed. Alongside *khubz 'arabi*'s governmentalization came substantive changes to the product itself—a countrywide consolidation that decreased the importance of region and topography to the taste of bread.[34] Neither sweeping moral verdicts nor wholesale condemnations, these descriptions of the alteration of *khubz 'arabi* register how Jordanians' sensibilities jostled uneasily against the state's intrusion onto their palettes. By the late 1970s, as economies of scale in flour milling, transportation, and production made the bread industry more and more attractive to investment, *khubz 'arabi* increasingly came to resemble a mass-produced industrial product. The taste of bread, according to many, was never quite the same after it entered into the governmental networks that now provisioned the Jordanian populace: "*t'amu kan ahsan* (its taste was better)" was a lament I heard often when I talked to people over sixty about their favorite bakeries and breads.[35] But the homogenization of previously plural flavors did not just worsen the taste of bread. Equally important was the fact that this process fostered "palatable lines of attachment" among the population, all while excluding other possibilities, now frozen in the memories and flavors of a bygone era.[36] If television and radio were important mediums through which the Jordanian population was imagined,[37] one avenue through which it was materialized was the shared consumption of subsidized bread. As a standardized loaf produced according to strictures set at the MOS replaced the diverse breads consumed in rural and urban areas, the taste of *khubz* slipped from being a taste associated with place to a sensation managed by the state. Something new was felt with every bite.

It was not just the taste of bread that evoked the state, but the smells and sounds that emanated from the bakery as well. As commercial bread outlets began to spread outside the capital, loud, fragrant ovens releasing aromas from small chimneys and storefronts became a key feature of urban neighborhoods and market centers across the Hashemite Kingdom. Their reverberations worked as both acoustic and aromatic reminders of the state presence for citizens living within their sonic and olfactory range.[38] "The first bakery was down that street," one resident of the northern town of Ramtha told me, pointing down an alleyway in the *souk* near his vegetable stand. "We'd always walk by it on the way home after school. The smell of fresh bread was exhilarating." Another shopkeeper fondly remembered an outlet that opened near his childhood home in 1978: "My brother and I would run to get bread every morning before school. Our mother would send us when she heard the oven firing up. We'd get excited just on the walk over, just from hearing the bakers at work." Smells and sounds were recurrent themes in recollections of the advent of commercial bakeries among those who remembered a time before their extension throughout the country. Residents of the wheat-growing hubs around the cities of Irbid and Ramtha emphasized the impact of newly established bakeries on their diets, yes. But their most evocative remarks were usually rooted firmly in modes of sensorial experience. Particular streets and specific buildings served as powerful mnemonic cues. Whether their assessments were positive or negative depended on whom you asked, but their memories were consistently called up through what Ann Laura Stoler terms the "sensory recall of the unremarkable."[39] Tastes, smells, and sounds were summoned not because my questions were directed at bodily engagements with the bakery but because interlocutors so insistently held me there. For Abu Amjad, a bakery owner in the city of Irbid: "The sounds of flour mixers and the oven firing up with diesel were, for us, the sound of bread. The vibrations and echoes meant there would be food, that you would not go hungry, that the state was taking care of us." These recollections do not simply trace the centrality of the newly arrived bakeries to culinary or social practices, but also track the dramatic intrusion of stately sensations into everyday life.

The bakery instantiated this change, in part, by sculpting a temporal rhythm at the level of bodily dispositions. In her work on socialist Romania, Katherine Verdery discusses the ways in which citizens' temporal cadences were transformed by governmental practices.[40] While temporality is frequently noted as a social construction, Verdery goes to great lengths to demonstrate the political corollaries of its configuration, the ways in which actors and institutions shape temporal disciplines that contour daily life. She carefully traces how the Romanian state apparatus, through its control over the distribution of basic goods, fashioned time in ways that ramified throughout the social order. By instigating shortages and forcing citizens to queue for key provisions, Communist Party leaders not only "produced incapacity" but also flattened the time of citizens across the country.[41] Although Jordan's bread subsidy did not occasion long lines at bakeries nor seek to intentionally incapacitate citizens or capture their labor as in the Romanian case, it did entail important shifts in people's relationship to time.[42] Abu Amjad points to some of these reverberations: "Making bread was no longer an arduous task or something the family needed to plan. You could stop by the bakery in the morning or on the way home after school." The source of compulsion was both the flooding of the Jordanian wheat market with American aid and the discounted price at which bread was now sold.

As citizens were pushed towards the bakery and bread production was further decoupled from erstwhile agricultural and culinary rhythms, the state insinuated itself into people's experience of time, shifting daily routines, from Ramtha in the north to Aqaba in the south. "Families in my neighborhood would go to the bakery at least once a day," Abu Amjad stressed. "Very few people did not rely on it for their subsistence. It changed the way we ate and lived." Experiences of and negotiations with political authority were geographically variable; much depended on where one worked and lived. But for the vast majority who came to rely on subsidized bread, bakeries worked to group, calibrate, and synchronize. Citizens were "made to feel coherently collective through particular orchestrations of time."[43] More than just being hardwired into Jordanian cities and towns, commercial bread outlets altered the way people perceived and traversed the world around them. With every purchase of *khubz 'arabi*, a "community of sense" was being produced among strangers. The state became part of these rhythms, a looming figure on their horizons of expectation. Now everyone went to the bakery.

Through recurring exposure to and reliance on the bakery, Jordanian citizens developed a certain *"corporeal knowledge"* of the state, something very different from the modes of cognition that are generally subsumed under theories of interpellation or ideology.[44] It is these modes of perception and bodily engagement, in all respects divergent from those of an explicit social contract, that make it possible to submit to an established order in which the state intuitively makes sense. It is why, at the bakery, the state becomes present in the manner of an obvious object rather than as an unceasingly oppressive entity. As a new set of sounds, smells, and tastes entered the sensuous immediacies of everyday life, the state became sensible, "both 'what makes sense' and what can be 'sensed.'"[45] It was narratable because it was felt, representable because it was lived through the body. If post-representationalist accounts building on the work of Michel Foucault have positioned the body as the ground of productive forces, "the site where the large-scale organization of power links up with local practices,"[46] then any robust consideration of the state should consider how deployments of power connect to the body and how such processes actively shape the constitution of subjects.[47] Not how bodies "have been perceived and given meaning and value," but the "manner in which what is most material and most vital in them has been invested."[48] To a certain extent, people's political views about the Hashemite regime or the authoritarian nature of government were secondary. Jordanians were connected to each other insofar as they were deeply imbricated with the performative force of the state, as enacted through the provision of subsidized bread.

DISTRIBUTING THE SENSIBLE

In Jordan, stately sensations played an important role at a time when efforts were being made to tie together the heterogeneous population, now free of the conflicts and social unrest of the preceding decades. The bread subsidy, along with the creation of a network of discounted retail cooperatives for those in the military and the bureaucracy, was a carefully crafted response to an array of challenges that had coalesced around the time of the mutiny at Zarqa in 1974. As the avowed free marketeer and one-time minister of supply Jawad Anani summarized it:

> The country and the economy were changing quickly, there was lots of migration to the cities, farming was not as profitable, inflation was skyrocketing because of the oil crisis. We knew we would have to increase food imports dramatically. This gave us the chance to rethink the entire retail system, especially in regards to food.[49]

In various interviews with those involved in the bread subsidy's design, government officials rarely justified the policy in commercial or economic terms but yoked it instead to a set of political concerns—it targeted citizens, rather than consumers. The welfare program's aim went far beyond macroeconomic considerations, even for those suspicious of regulating prices and intervening in the "free market." According to Anani, "the goal was to provide people with sufficient basic goods at just prices. We did not want only to subsidize consumption but to ensure that everyone had enough to eat, to guarantee the subsistence of every citizen." For Marwan al-Qasim, a future head of the Royal Court who became the minister of supply in 1976, the point was never just to feed people: "yes, we wanted to tie people to the bakery, and via the bakery to the state. Bread seemed an obvious way to do so. It was a policy that would touch every house." The calibration of the citizenry's sympathies was linked to considerations of statecraft. As al-Qasim put it, "We aimed to secure citizens' well-being, to make sure everyone knew they could afford a loaf of bread. Food availability was not an economic issue, it was a security concern." Unlike Anani, al-Qasim embraced close regulation of the private sector during his time in government. Proud of the political and redistributive outcomes the bread subsidy helped stimulate, al-Qasim was also cognizant of the dependencies and societal transformations that the welfare policy engendered:

> Of course we considered how receiving subsidized foods would change people's relationship to the state. We knew it might create a form of dependency but, for many of us, that was all right. We thought the state should work as a vehicle for development and redistribution and that having bakeries

throughout the country would aid these goals. At a time of rampant inflation, what better way to show the state's commitment to citizens than through their daily bread? [50]

For al-Qasim, as for some of his counterparts, subsidies targeting subsistence made the utmost sense. These policy makers recognized the challenges that accompanied rapid urbanization, shifting demographics, and new modes of sociability, all of which could threaten monarchical rule. Subsidies of basic goods sought to harness these challenges and turn them into an opportunity. In addition to averting hunger, the bakery was valorized because of the immediacy through which it could communicate the Hashemite project of rule. Integral to the bakery's promise in this respect was its potential to address citizens in sites crucial to their subsistence, all while cementing popular dependence on monarchical munificence. In a context where bread was semiotically inflected as a source of life, its discounted provision could symbolically index the Hashemite regime's commitment and capacity to care for its subjects. The bakery would act as a key vehicle for the amplification of this message.

As the remarks of the ministers Anani and al-Qasim make clear, the bread subsidy sought to foster conditions upon which a sustainable political order could be built. That these two ministers, so diametrically opposed in their visions of public policy, could both embrace the bread subsidy points to the centrality of the welfare service in forming Jordanian citizens. In his exploration of the Islamic regime in Sudan, Noah Salomon finds a similar focus on modes of "citizen-making" among those charged with forming a population congenial to a political project. [51] Through the use of reconfigured artistic forms such as *madih* (traditionally Sufi chanted poetry with religious content), Sudanese political elites sought to make people not "only tolerate an Islamic state but desire one" as well. [52] Previously, *madih* was just one component in broader ritual contexts, achieving its spiritual effects within the sacred spaces of Sufism. The contemporary version, aimed at urban audiences, sought to target citizens regardless of their religious affiliation or piety, emphasizing their ties to the Sudanese state over and above other bonds. While in Sudan it was radio that bureaucrats deployed to transform the urban soundscape and foster pious citizens, the bakery was the means by which the Jordanian government sought to nudge citizens in the state's direction. Through the infiltration of gastronomic routine, the bread subsidy sought to harness the exigencies of subsistence faced by families and turn them into an opportunity to cultivate attachments to political authority—a craving for the state.

Political elites embraced bakeries as a crucial means through which to shape a coherent Jordanian public. Why? In a country where nationalism could never aspire to interpellate all, where most citizens had strong identifications with either North or South, urban or rural, settled or nomadic, descent from the East Bank or West Bank, bakeries could conjure attachments that would span the Hashemite Kingdom. They were an effective tool precisely because they exercised power in such seemingly benevolent ways, outside the patron-client ties and kinship relations that drove so many of Jordan's other public services. Yet my argument is that the bakery did far more. It instated what Catherine Fennell aptly terms, in a different context, a form of "sensory politics," interventions that shape affectual experiences and routine engagements that are generative of political feelings and outlooks among citizens.[53] By slowly untethering Jordanians from their reliance on alternative sources of staple foods, the bakery gradually incorporated them into a shared corporeal circuit, braiding together their dietary habits and daily routines. That is, the bakery worked to gradually reframe and distribute the sensible, the "system of self-evident facts of sense perception that simultaneously discloses the existence of something in common and the delimitations that define the respective parts and positions within it."[54] And while many of Jordan's citizens did not necessarily think of themselves as part of a cohesive "imagined community," they could, at the very least, come to recognize one another through their shared consumption of tasteless *khubz 'arabi*.[55] Subsidized bread not only worked to contain the threats that came with hunger and poverty, as policy makers intended. The policy also transformed the very dispositions that produced those threats in the first place.

Over time, village and city came to embrace the bakery. Much like the gas lamp and the electric grid in other locales,[56] the bakery played a central role in how people perceived the world around them. Other services, such as the extension of the water and electricity supply, produced similar effects, enabling citizens to both imagine and inhabit their connections to people beyond their places of residence. Together, these interventions worked to reconfigure space and time, shaping what Wael Hallaq describes as a "cohesive system of doing and ordering things, all of which culminated in the production of new identities and subjects, and a new regime of truth."[57] Patterns of rule that were once capricious and variable were now implanted in the warp and weft of Jordanians' everyday lives. Bakeries worked to give the state "an effect of fixity and permanence."[58] Commercial bread production also worked to displace rich food-making customs and local agriculture, only some of which are now being rescued. It also, as many state theorists and parts of this chapter have emphasized, brought new imaginaries into play. And while I agree with Patrick Joyce, whose excellent analysis of the post office in 19th-century England illuminates how certain governmental practices can reorder "social life irrevocably, and with it the daily experience of the state,"[59] what I have sought to illuminate here is more than an expansion of visible and physical connections between the state apparatus and the citizenry. I emphasize instead the ways in which bakeries and the bread subsidy worked to tie Jordanians together through a "certain sensory fabric, a certain distribution of the sensible, which defines their way of being together."[60] What this reading proposes is that the state is not just "engineered into the lives of its citizens,"[61] as if some institutional substratum pre-existed this engineering. Rather, the state effect is inextricable from the bodies of subjects, the locus through which power prompts productive effects. As the bakery became imbricated with habit and routine, the state became a principle of unspoken consensus within social life, continuous with the rhythms and routines of everyday life. It was not given; it was learned.

NAVIGATING SENSATION

In the following pages, I will focus on the Jabal Nadhif neighborhood in Amman to elucidate and expand upon arguments made in the previous section. Specifically, I trace the role of sensations at the bakery to the present day, locating the immanence of the state in the midst of things and relations, governmental practices and bodily dispositions that work to circulate political authority. Crucial here will be my own entanglements with aesthetic experience, what Terry Eagleton describes as "the business of affections and aversions, of how the world strikes the body on its sensory surfaces, of that which takes root in the gaze and the guts and all that arises from our most banal, biological insertion into the world."[62] My ethnographic rendering here "reads" the environment by attempting to be attuned to it, what the anthropologist Yael Navaro describes as an "analytical approach that allows sensing as a method to understand and conceptualize one's surroundings."[63] If sensations have a part to play in the sociality and political outcomes of those who inhabit a place, then it seems only reasonable that they play a part in my analysis.

What is also key is that I followed routes and attuned my body to the rhythms and dispositions of people in a particular place. Jabal Nadhif is a densely populated neighborhood in Amman's poorer eastern quarter. Palestinians who had been violently expelled from their lands informally settled in the area in 1948, gradually building homes over the decades that followed, long before the government, in the late 1970s, provided electricity and water to the area. Today Nadhif suffers, like most of East Amman, from poverty and unemployment, high building density and overcrowding, as well as a distinct lack of public services. While the neighborhood has never been economically prosperous, the acceleration of neoliberal economic reforms over the past twenty years has left an increasing number of residents in a condition of precarity. Erratic and informal employment was common among those with whom I sometimes lived and often conversed. Most have been trying for some time to gain a foothold, to beget modes of composure through which to navigate the city they inhabit. Amid capital accumulation and radically unequal patterns of wealth distribution, the bakery, and the bread it provides, are notable both for their comparative stability and the aesthetic engagements they foreground. Because of its centrality to alimentary routines and neighborhood life, as well as its status as one of the few reliable interactions many of Nadhif's residents have with the state apparatus, I suggest that the bakery molds bodies to apprehend and inhabit the world selectively. It cultivates a particular distribution of the sensible, one in which the state becomes and remains common sense. In doing so, the bakery not only shapes what citizens can feel, smell, and hear but also garners "embodied attachments to historically specific forms of belonging,"[64] thus disposing Jordanians towards certain political arrangements rather than others. If the state is commonly associated with institutions or coercive powers, in Nadhif it is reproduced through sensations, not least of which are those forged at the bakery.

Thursday evenings were usually fun. Bilal and I would meet after he finished his shift as a fixer at a store in a large shopping mall in West Amman. We would then begin the heavily trafficked route east, starting with two minibuses before taking a shared taxi to his family's home in Jabal Nadhif. Along the way, we would usually stop at a butcher he knew well, purchasing a few discounted scraps of meat the butcher had held for Bilal beneath the counter, just outside of his boss's line of sight. Bread was the other critical component of the meal we could never forget. We'd order five or six kilos at least, the purchase at the bakery next door often accompanied by a wry smile from the perspiring bread-maker, who could guess our evening plans. "Smell the bread," Bilal would whisper excitedly while in line. "Tonight we'll eat well." Those evenings were a heady mix of charcoal and lamb, grilled chicken and sugary tea. Bilal was the sole member of his seven-member household who was gainfully employed. Thursday nights marked the beginning of the weekend, a brief coming together when neighbors, brothers, and cousins would unwind and enjoy a communal meal. The grilled meats were often paltry or insubstantial, but fresh bread meant food was never lacking. Everyone, somehow, had enough to eat.

Notwithstanding the delights of the barbeque, I preferred Friday mornings. The tight quarters led to odd sleeping arrangements. In the summers, we would doze outside in the small courtyard area between roofed home and external gate. Old mattresses and restless mosquitoes meant sleep was intermittent. In winter, it was the movement of bodies in seek of warmth that did me in. Five of us would huddle under a set of blankets to escape the cold, with at least two of the five suffering from what I later diagnosed as a rather severe case of restless leg syndrome. Sunrise, at least for some of us, brought a return to movement, the end of unrewarding rest. It also meant breakfast—falafel, hummus, fava beans, a bit of olive oil, maybe some cheese, and a heap of fresh bread. Bilal would hand everyone some cash. We would divvy up responsibilities and set out to pick up ingredients.

I always accompanied whoever was going to the bakery. On Fridays, it was buzzing. Clusters of children and their parents streamed toward the outlet from a wide radius of labyrinthine streets and hastily paved paths. Some came empty-handed; others carried produce, or bags already teeming with breakfast items. A few drank coffee or tea; many wore tousled hair and a sleepy smile. Something about the aroma, the commotion of moving bodies and murmuring voices, always made me cheerful. Amused by my delight, Bilal would often expound upon his own attachments to the bakery, mentioning any number of sensations, along with the qualified feelings they engendered. Calm (*hud'u*) and relief (*raha*) came to the fore most often in his descriptions. In one case, he expanded upon his bodily experience at the bakery, and then compared it to bodily shifts undergone at the mosque:

> When I approach the bakery, something happens. I become relaxed, peaceful. My mind is undisturbed. You know what the price will be. There is something about the price being fixed, the smell of bread, the sounds of the ovens that produces a feeling of relief. Do you feel it? It's similar to what I experience at the mosque. I become relaxed and peaceful. Something happens when you are inside, about to pray or buy bread. Both are atypical spaces where I feel like I can escape my troubles and my worries. Life seems different.

Bilal was hardly alone in relating such sensations. Unlike the experience they had at other food retailers, many in Nadhif portrayed the bakery as disrupting, for a moment, the hassle and anguish that often accompanied the purchase of foodstuffs. There was little need to calculate how many mouths to feed or stomachs to fill, no anxious weighing of products to ensure they could be paid for. Again, in Bilal's words:

> Prices are going up and new taxes are always being decreed. For fruits and vegetables you have to arrive early or you are left with the worst. Restaurants we do not even step into, the cost is always too high. The bakery is different. The same line, the same price, the same product for everyone. For us here in the neighborhood, it is peaceful.

This contrast with other food outlets reappeared constantly, as the bakery fostered otherwise uncommon assessments of urban life: discontent or displeasure, cynicism and anger, were replaced by approval or satisfaction.

The bakery's efficacy and force can also be gauged by the ways in which residents worked to distinguish it from other public services. When I asked Bilal's brother Ahmed to compare the experience of buying subsidized bread with that of receiving electricity, he explained:

> The electricity here comes and goes. Some people steal it and others pay for it when they can. Even when we have it we know it might be temporary, that it is a luxury we have to pay the state for dearly. The bakery is different. We don't have to worry about anything when we are buying bread; the place induces calm and happiness. The smell, the sound, the entire bakery is soothing.

Ahmed contrasts two opposing relationships to infrastructure here. While electricity engenders anxiety about payment and transience, the bakery does something far different. Something better, noticeably uncommon, is briefly disclosed. This is not an alternative social project fully formed but a mode of shared experience, stimulating modes of "sensory and emotional gratification" that briefly shimmer, before fading again before the onslaught of everyday life.[65] And if the latter is unforgiving, residents of Nadhif have at least one enduring and collectively binding source of occasional relief, moments that become all the more important in a neighborhood where these are usually hard to come by. "Running water, we get it two, maybe three times a week," Ahmed explained. "Not the bakery, it's always working." As on other occasions, I could not help but ask "Why?" Why did these other infrastructures and services work so poorly, when the bakery appears to never fail? "The state is strong but gives us little," Ahmed surmised. "We can live without some of the other things or figure out a way to find them. Not bread. The bakery is our reprieve (*istirahatna*). It is the one place everyone can afford and enjoy." Everyday practices of bread procurement and consumption were powerful because they were comforting. They eased, or seemed to alleviate, the toils of labor and subsistence, while making certain modes of inhabiting the world possible. Attachments to the bakery among my interlocutors confirmed my social distance from them and the contrast in our bodily training and in what our bodies have been coached to respond to—subsidized bread never fostered such peace and relaxation in me. Nevertheless, the calm and relief that the bakery produced in them were evident.

In some instances, it was the commensality fostered by the subsidized bread that was most remarked upon. Adnan, another one of Bilal's brothers, noted: "The bakery makes bread so we can eat together and share our food. That is why going to the bakery is so agreeable. You know you'll come back with the key ingredient for sharing a meal." And so it was, the vast majority of the times we dined together. Alone, of course, bread could not constitute a meal, but it was always more indispensable than the rest of the menu. It made eating family-style both convenient and easy. Its discounted price allowed for practices of generosity and hospitality that fostered relationships with others, ties expressed in phrases such as *"baynuna khubz wa meleh"* (there is bread and salt between us).[66] "This is why the bakery matters," Adnan would often remind me as we gathered at mealtimes, "so that we and others can eat like this, in every house." Bread here gives weight to the table; it provides feelings of fullness and togetherness, an assurance that life together is possible.

Food, of course, is often a source of connection between individuals and among communities.[67] Its centrality to daily life, the socialities and rituals it can shape and foster, have been widely commented upon. But what I want to accentuate here are the ways in which the bakery fosters certain sensations that travel far beyond the locales where bread is produced. Certain people may transport bread, others may produce it, some buy it, while others mainly eat. Yet subsidized bread continues to leave traces upon people's lives, extending well past those involved in production or purchase. It generates sensations that connect people to each other and to the authority seen to provide bread, with its specific expectations, practices, and modes of practical reasoning. Take, for example, the moments when I found myself with friends or acquaintances in a city or district with which we were not familiar. On such occasions, the bakery acted as a haven, a surefire retreat, where bread could be purchased at exactly the same price as in the outlets my companions frequented in Jabal Nadhif. No one needed to ask if bread was available, or whether we could rustle up enough money to eat. The bakery was ever-present, simply a matter of asking for the nearest outlet and completing a hasty purchase. In such moments, Jordanian citizens participate in what Kathleen Stewart terms "a world of shared banalities,"[68] generating proximities and intimacies across difference. The public produced is, of course, fragile and contingent, but it congeals not because of modes of critical reasoning enacted by a bourgeois public, but rather through styles of exhortation that have honed and continue to hone the sensibilities of citizens. In this respect, subsidized bread underpins modes of embodiment through which political authority is inhabited. The bakery's potency is at once individual and collective, its allure as much "a social relationship as it is a form of experience."[69] The bread-maker offers reiterative modes of aesthetic experience that produce sustaining links between citizens and structures of rule, just one of the ways in which "the state incorporates by being incorporated."[70] While government officials would often present the bread subsidy as a mechanism ensuring that no one lacked for food, the program's bearing on everyday life exceeded such concerns. Welfare services address an audience, cultivate subjects, and bind citizens into a broader collectivity. Of course, subsidized bread reinforces a common experience of rule, but it also instantiates a crucial "moment of capture in the political life of sensation."[71]

In the *Politics of Aesthetics*, Rancière defines politics as consisting of a set of actions that transform the coordinates of the prevalent order, practices that can alter the communal distribution of the sensible. More important than the objectives or content of such practices is their trajectory, the cascading effects they can spawn in people's engagements with the world. And while Rancière awakens us to the centrality of sensation for political life, he never unpacks how routine practices relate to, even underpin, the status quo.[72] It is precisely at this level that I find the bakery to be at its most potent. Just as certain actions and forms can transform sensibilities in ways that subvert the social order, as Rancière's conception of political action surmises, there are others that work to shape perception and inscribe certain truths, thereby partitioning the sensible. Drawing on Rancière's work on aesthetics, Birgit Meyer dissects how bodily engagements reproduce feelings of collective belonging among Pentecostal Christians in Ghana. Much as with contemporary ethnographies of the state, she finds, in the ways that pious subjects are studied, a lack of engagement with the body and the senses to be a key shortcoming. In contrast, Meyer closely examines the forms and practices that inculcate Christian sensibilities in her informants. She terms the broader modalities that bind believers an "aesthetics of persuasion": a set of forms that appeal to the body and through which the "divine transcendental presence is to be perceived as real and powerful."[73] And while I disagree with the strict correspondences she posits among form, sensation, and persuasion, Meyer does elegantly point out the significance of aesthetic experience to rendering certain things sensible. In doing so, she grounds Rancière's abstract theorizations in her informants' experiential modes of worship, foregrounding the body as a site central to the production of Pentecostalism. But forms of sensation are not only important to the production of (religious) subjects, they are also vital to the cultivation of (political) subjectivities and the ontological truths to which these must subscribe. The bakery surely "evokes a multiplicity of embodied sensations across the human sensorium."[74] For some, subsidized bread was far less important, signifying little more than a passing curiosity or a very occasional acquisition. Still, discounted bread generates the possibility, indeed it presupposes the existence, of a collectivity defined by the entity seen to distribute it, whether one relies on it or not. Without implementing a functionally integrated totality that espouses a single, overarching logic, bakeries attune citizens to political authority so that the state never seems out of place, rooted as it is in the historically tempered modalities of the body in its entirety.[75] It is here, I posit, far from the realms of consciousness and representation, that the state becomes "commonsense," where what Rancière terms "consensus as a mode of government"[76]—an ordered social universe rather than a polemic about common ways of being—transpires. Jordanians are certainly molded through social categories and norms that include questions of nationality, gender, and class. Yet equally powerful, if not more so, is the repetition of certain practices through which subjects are both activated and acted upon. If the state is an effect of power, it is a power that marks, trains, and transmits by and through the body.

THE BAKERY IS DIFFERENT

When in Nadhif, I spent most weekday mornings with Sa'id, Bilal's youngest brother. Infrequently employed, he was often charged with household errands, which would consume most of his mornings. I would often tag along, to practice my Arabic or better observe the neighborhood while alongside a recognized local. Sa'id had little time for politics. Annoyed by my dogged questions about the monarchy and Parliament, or the drama surrounding some recent protest, he would dismiss my queries with a sigh. More important were the prices at the butcher's and the produce stand. I remember inflated falafel and shawarma prices causing far more ire than Saudi profligacy or Israeli apartheid. Wealthier households are relatively unaffected by small price increases on such staple goods. Yet in large and modest families like Sa'id's, they can make the difference between a simple meal and going to bed hungry. Actions that many others might take for granted—hurriedly buying a cheap sandwich, a cup of coffee, or a handful of tea leaves—were an explicit object of considerable deliberation for Sa'id during his daily rounds. But bread and the bakery were different.

As we moved between run-down streets and decaying buildings, marked up with tasteful graffiti, colorful advertisements, and sarcastic scribblings, Sa'id's and my own sense of the neighborhood formed through a host of sensory stimuli. At times we were pressed up against redolent pedestrians, waiting to cross a street. At others, we were forced to inhale the exhaust fumes emanating from a nearby mechanic. I realized that Saʿid's maps of sensory classification were far different from my own, and I began to learn which places we could enter and which we had to do our best to avoid, especially when we had some of the family's younger members in tow.[77] On the fringes of Jabal Nadhif, the more expensive butcher, the coffeeshop with juice for one dinar, and the sweetshop selling baklava were all "bad." Saʿid recognized them through sight and smell as places that were outside his financial grasp. On one of our first walks together, the embarrassment caused by my own curiosity quickly became palpable. "Not there," he howled, "very expensive, don't even smell it," as we walked past a pastry shop gleaming with enticing cakes. Saʿid knows the layout of Jabal Nadhif well, but what counts here is what Lauren Berlant terms the "affectsphere," organized, in part, "by the sensory pressures of the biopolitical."[78]

Jordan's capital is not cheap. Average salaries in East Amman hover between 320 and 400 Jordanian dinars (JD) (US$450–565) a month. Rent ranges from 175 to 225 JD (US$245–320). Faced with overcrowded public transportation, crumbling streets, and sporadic electricity, Saʿid knows how to manage, or at least defer, feeling overwhelmed—to use what is at hand in order to ensure his subsistence. Like urban dwellers around the world, he has learned to identify and categorize retail outlets in and around his residential quarter through certain markers. He relies on these markers to ensure that he avoids discomfort and does not exceed his daily budget or spend money he does not currently have and would later need to repay. During our walks, it was impossible not to detect his unease. Following one of our many strolls together, the shift in his gestures and temperament around the bakery suddenly became obvious. When I asked about this shift, Saʿid shrugged; the relief triggered by the bakery hardly required explanation. On several occasions, when I asked him to explain, he described the smell of his local bread outlet as "producing sensations of relief." The aroma, along with the jumble of movement that accompanied purchase, he said, both "whet the appetite (*taftah shahiyati*)" and "relax me" (*bitarihni*). This experience of relief, a certain easing up in the burdens and hassles that troubled him, was, of course, partly a question of price. Financial worries seemed less pressing when bread cost 0.16 JD (US$0.23) per kilo. If some bread was left over, eventually it would be eaten or added to a separate dish; if there was not enough, a few more kilograms could quickly be purchased.

The pursuit of increased consumption was impossible for most in Jabal Nadhif. So too were the cultivated desires of Amman's small but growing upper middle class—cars, clothes, and fancy kicks. Food has very much been woven into the construction of lifestyles and used as an indicator of social position. What made the bakery different was its more inclusive character. In a neighborhood characterized by the absence or breakdown of so many infrastructures (roads, electric wiring, water lines), life may very well require endless improvisation, "quiet modes of encroachment" through which the urban subaltern survive.[79] But it may also, at the same time, foster attachments to those places that do seem to function in the interests of the poor, or at least offer them a moment of respite. The bakery is vital in this respect. It allows Sa'id to ease up, to relax. In conjunction, his gestures, movements, and descriptions provide critical indicators of why the bakery matters to those who must traverse the city with little in the way of financial leeway. Fatigue and exasperation could dissipate, if only momentarily.[80] "Everyone is welcome here," Sa'id would often remark while inhaling the bakery's unmistakable odor. "We can all afford bread. We all eat it. It feels good." It may seem like an overstatement to suggest that the state effect occurs through such encounters and routines. Nevertheless, the fact that so many in the neighborhood not only ate bread every day but also expressed their "messy dynamics of attachment" to the bread-maker makes me think otherwise.[81]

At the bakery, it was hard not to feel overwhelmed. The built environment was "anything but inanimate."[82] Heat, sweat, diesel, flour, dough, and dirt—an indescribable mix. It was not people *or* things, neighbors *or* bread, friends *or* appealing smells, but people *and* things that mattered here, their sum somehow adding up to much more than their constituent parts. "The smell of flour, touching the warm bread, the heat from the oven, they all make the bakery special," Sa'id remarked. "It is the one place where you don't need to rush, where you can take in the smells and sounds without hurrying." Although ministerial officials often measured the success of the bread subsidy by the lack of unrest in marginalized areas, for many in Nadhif its "success" could be felt in the instances of relaxation and comfort it permitted. There is no operative ideological consensus or straightforward interpellation, grounded in the tenets of Jordanian nationalism, to be found in this neighborhood nor in many others. Nor are the flows and energies at the bakery generative of nationhood among residents, who are unwilling or quite hesitant to describe themselves as Jordanian (as opposed to Palestinian). Instead, what slowly became clear to me was that Nadhif's bakeries allow the state to be sensed in ways that travel through but surpass any individual body. Amid the uncertainties and difficulties of daily life and the almost complete absence of welfare services, one could witness at the bakery moments of responsiveness and embodied aptitudes that captured subjects in different relations to political authority, without the necessary scaffolding of interpretation. What was interesting about the gestures and movements of my interlocutors during innumerable trips to the bakery was precisely the ways in which bakeries seemed to both soothe and seduce, animating sensory sediments that are integral to the Jordanian state's reception. This is not a social pact entered into through contract. Nor is it a frank exchange of bread for political acquiescence, as so much of the literature on authoritarianism in the Middle East hypothesizes. We might say that the bakery does not elicit unanimous affects or political preferences but rather works to performatively engender a shared sensibility on which the state effect relies. Few in Nadhif are invested in the state because of any traceable series of choices or willful commitment to institutions; more often, they "ride the wave of the forms they know, even when there is no water beneath them nor air to float them."[83]

An occasional companion on our daily walks, Ayman was more suspicious of the sensations engendered by the bakery. During one of our conversations, he surmised that bread provision was hardly a benevolent act. Politically astute and distrustful of the powers that be, he saw the bakery as a clever ruse. Its effectiveness lay precisely in how it redirected anger or frustration that might otherwise easily lead to social unrest:

> I remember going to the bakery as a child with my grandmother. The smell, the heat, it was always so pleasant. She would give me a coin to pay and the baker would always warn me to be cautious: "Hot bread!" he'd scream. "Be careful!" But now I don't like going as much, even though I have to so I can eat. Too many people act like the bakery and subsidized bread are some sort of gift. We all pay taxes here, on our other foods and phones, on the internet and gasoline. The state gives us bread just to keep us quiet. They don't care if we are hungry or

unemployed, just that we don't revolt or cause disorder. Why do we have subsidized bread? The relief and gratification you get from stepping inside the bakery is a veil. Take all these people who thank God when they buy bread or pick
it up off the floor and kiss it. I always say: "Don't do that. Bread is like any other
food. It's the least we should have." This other time I was at this bakery and saw
a picture on the wall of the king handing out food. I started to tell the owner,
"Oh that's nice, so we must beg while he gives us what is our right." And he said:
"Bread is a gift from God and the king." No one understands. Bakeries work to
fool us. It's been the same since the Romans and the French. We eat bread. It's
all we can afford. Our only moment in the day to feel content. The state makes
sure to provide it. All while the rich stuff their pockets and eat cake.

Several threads run through Ayman's scathing account. It is spiked with
emotion, peppered with feelings, denunciations, and political observations
furiously knotted together. At its most straightforward, the depiction relays
the views of a dissatisfied citizen, contemptuous of the Hashemite regime's
welfare policy. There is a fair dose of animosity, though there is clearly also
a recognition of the bakery's role in ensuring subsistence, interlaced with
childhood recollections.

Ayman's account highlights both the particular role of the bakery as a
service provider and the significance of this welfare program in shaping the
relation between Jordanians and political authority. It hints at the ways in
which past histories of provision remain active in the bodily dispositions
they worked to produce, and how these bind citizens to each other, regardless of the very different political positions they may espouse. In *The Ethical
Soundscape*, Charles Hirschkind traces the role of embodied sensibilities in
the construction of what he terms an "ethical counterpublic" in Egypt.[84] He
examines the role of mnemonic listening in facilitating the development and
practice of Islamic ethical comportment, dissecting how the soundscape produces attachments to a sense of social mutuality, one reinforced in moments
and practices of collective audition. Although the community and practices
he examines are far different, I consider Hirschkind's work instructive in its
focus on the social circulation of noise, its modes of affective binding, and the
role of such processes in the making of a (counter)public. But I want to take his
provocations further, to suggest that the affects and embodied dispositions

fostered by the bakery tie Jordanians not just to a collectivity, but to political authority. Apart from the claims and demands that Jordanians might later bring to the world, the bakery, much like the cassette sermon, does not cease to produce aesthetic engagements, allowing subjects to cultivate the embodied attributes of a Jordanian citizen. Even in Ayman's critical account, the bakery plays a role in tuning and retuning both individuals and the social body in the direction of the state, channeling affective flows and bodily dispositions that could otherwise very well assume different potentials. In this respect, what the bakery produces is less a fully fledged or unanimous imaginary of the state or its failings than the potentialities from which such ideas and opinions draw nourishment.

I encountered enough people who voiced views similar to Ayman's to make me suspicious of portraying the bakery as a site of unalloyed comfort and positive affection. That the bakery induces both cynicism and relaxation, both ambivalence and contentment, should not come as a surprise, enmeshed as it is in relations of domination, dependence, and subordination.[85] My point in relating Ayman's comments is to make clear that even when it provokes anger or fury, and irrespective of the critiques and appraisals of it that citizens might later voice, the bakery does not cease to foster a set of conditions that make Ayman's statement possible and comprehensible. And it is only because his body has been primed and his senses cultivated, in ways that have become sedimented in his knowledge of the world, that Ayman can formulate the critiques of the state that he does. The bakery's force lies in the way it builds on and melds with social relations, culinary preferences, and alimentary needs to distribute stately sensations that are "anything but momentary or ephemeral."[86] It trains and retrains subjects in a particular relationship to political authority, cultivating bodily dispositions on which the state effect relies, carved out as it is in the realms of action, practice, and routine.

CONCLUSION

In the absence of political rights or representative institutions throughout the 1970s and 1980s, Jordanians engaged regularly with political authority through bread provision and a handful of other governmental services. Over time, bakeries became part of a "broadly shared sensory regime,"[87] subtly rearranging the aesthetic coordinates of the citizenry. Of course, ideological modes of interpellation and coercion permeated the polity. But political authority in Jordan's specificity lay in its intricate ability to form the bodies of citizens through aesthetic means.[88] The bread subsidy was crucial in this respect, transformative because it cultivated bodies in subtle yet comforting ways. The policy did not rely on patron-client ties or public employment, as did so many of Jordan's other welfare provisions. Instead, the bakery silently and subtly changed everyday life, generating forms of experience that worked, in turn, to induce novel forms of political subjectivity. The state apparatus penetrated individual households, tying them into a countrywide system in which gastronomic routines were yoked to a set of centralized institutions. But arguably more important were the ways in which citizens' bodies became attuned to the state via the bakery. Jordan's newfound culinary order worked most profoundly at the level of the "human sensorium, on the affects, sensibilities and perceptual habits of its vast audience."[89]

In contemporary Jordan, bakeries are both a place that most citizens enter and a site of address through which political authority circulates. Far from being confined to a personal encounter, the bakery reinforces a particular distribution of the sensible, shaping what makes sense and what can be sensed. Ethnographic attention to such sites allows us to rethink the state not as some secluded institution that governs at a distance but as an assemblage of forms and practices that require certain conditions of felicity to take hold, bodily dispositions foremost among them. In foregrounding the latter, I have chosen to rely on Rancière's theorization of aesthetics, in a broader attempt to remove the realm of sensation from depoliticized isolation. I have preferred not to begin here with an analysis of the state through language or as a product of representation (efforts I will undertake in the chapters to come), so as to center at the outset the centrality of the body to the state effect. In other words, I have been concerned less with practices of representing or their productive effects than with what makes them possible. Bread provision shapes the fabric of experience within which the state is produced, not just as idea or external imposition but as bodily inclination.

Chapter 3

STATECRAFT

THE WORKDAY STARTS WELL BEFORE DAWN. Nearby, a handful of residents drowsily make their way downtown to take a bus towards school or work. A bit farther along, a stray taxi sets out for an early shift. It is just after four thirty in the morning. Bakers and bakery owner arrive to unfurl the shutters at *al-Khalil*, welcoming the breeze on what will soon become a warm September day. Across Amman, hundreds of these "white miners"[1] traverse dark city streets. Soon they will be consumed by the demanding task of making bread, the lifeblood of Jordan's rapidly growing metropolis. On a normal day of fieldwork, I too get up before sunrise, hurriedly putting on some clothes before rambling down Jabal B's undulating streets. Detached observation is not feasible; I have to bake. After unlocking the doors and putting away their belongings in the backroom, *al-Khalil's* six employees begin moving sacks of flour and sugar. During the next fifteen minutes, and over a hurried cup of tea, they fire up the mixer, thankful that they spent a few extra minutes cleaning the machinery before closing last night. Soon they will feed this appliance with flour, water, sugar, yeast, and a few generous pinches of salt. The same six men will work until nine at night, with their long workday broken up by a two-hour lunch break in the middle. The first hours of the workday are crucial. Dough needs time to rest. The oven requires time to concentrate heat. By six thirty, sparks begin to fly. The bakery comes alive with laughter and light. With the oven now at full tilt, I begin to sweat profusely. Today I huddle over dough, trying to knead the pliable substance into something that will eventually resemble bread. "Concentrate, José," someone screams amid the hubbub. "Move your hands, not your body (*harrak iyydak mash jismak*)." I am unaccustomed to kneading at such a pace, and exasperation is never far away. For the first weeks at *al-Khalil*, I feel both physically defeated and mentally overwhelmed. I had expected the former, but not the latter. My mind and body turn out not to be discrete wholes, amenable to easy manipulation. Operating tools, working with materials, and adjusting my bodily techniques demand time, practice, and repetition. Making bread is harder than I expected.

Some weeks after that beginning, I accompanied two members of the Division for Monitoring Markets (*qism muraqabat al-aswaq*) at the Ministry of Industry, Trade, and Supply on impromptu inspections of several bakeries. It was three in the afternoon, a lull for most bread-makers. On our final visit of the day, the ministerial team needed to determine whether one particular bakery was using its discounted flour quota to make items other than subsidized *khubz ʿarabi*, a practice prohibited by law. The bakery owner knew the inspectors from previous visits and greeted them amicably; the inspectors then started scrutinizing flour sacks and yeast packets. But after a few minutes, the two inspectors began to confer, just out of earshot. Something was not right.

The inspectors turned to the biscuits and cookies displayed prominently in the storefront windows, smelling and touching the goods. Still in hushed tones, they spoke with the owner, who did not seem happy with their observations. When the ministry employees finished their report and asked the bakery's proprietor to sign the official form, he began to complain, energetically waving a packet of receipts. The inspectors were unconvinced.

Back in their vehicle after we had left the bakery, the inspectors explained to me that this bakery produced a considerable amount of sweet Arabic pastries but did not have the requisite amount of nonsubsidized flour necessary for their production.

"But I saw Zero," I declared (Zero being a variety of nonsubsidized flour used to make the Arabic sweets). "Isn't that what he should be using?"

"There was Zero but it's an old sack; it has probably been sitting there for months," one inspector replied. "We asked him to produce a receipt for it but the one he showed us was six months old. The numbers didn't add up."

"Maybe he lost the receipt, or the flour dealer never gave him one," I proposed timidly.

"We see this all the time. The Zero is just there for when we come to inspect the bakery," his counterpart clarified. "He was using some *muwwahad* [subsidized flour] for the sweets. They seemed odd when we smelled them as well." Seemed odd, I wondered. How can sweets seem odd? In the coming days, the ministry would reduce this bakery's subsidized flour quota and an investigatory committee would rule on the inspectors' findings. The owner would be given the opportunity to present any exonerating evidence before possibly being issued a substantial fine.

Both bakers and inspectors are involved here in what Ash Amin has termed a "process of infrastructural crafting," one crucial to the provision of bread in the Hashemite Kingdom.[2] Their labors shape the flow of energy, people, and goods across the country. And while it is easier to imagine bakers as craftsmen, given the common associations between them and artisanal bread, the inspectors operate according to a parallel set of principles that can also usefully be thought through as craft. Unlike baking, the labor of inspection does not require waking before daybreak or maintaining very specific modes of physical fitness. Nor does it demand coaching the body to manage sweltering heat or the congestion of a stifling bake-room. Inspection does, however, involve similar forms of ingenuity and improvisation, tacit modes of knowledge that are not easily communicated or standardized. Regulating bread-makers also requires social, technical, and manual dexterity: an ability to navigate materials and individuals, machinery and temperament, the human and nonhuman, and the various ways in which the latter two can associate.

In his expansive corpus, AbdouMaliq Simone has drawn attention to the centrality of social relations and bodies to the process of making materials move. In doing so, he extends "the notion of infrastructure directly to people's activities in the city."[3] We also know that infrastructures are not static objects but a gathering of institutional actors, public policies, legal systems, knowledges, materials, and human dexterities.[4] Much like welfare services, they are not built, nor do they function according to the plans of policy makers, engineers, or designers. They are not enacted through technical operations alone. Instead, both welfare services and the infrastructures that are central to their delivery "work" and "endure" through recurring practices of maintenance and repair that entangle humans and nonhumans in relations of cohabitation and collaboration.[5] On paper, we do not see how such collaborations occur; superficially, the bread subsidy has a beguiling simplicity. The welfare program floats in a realm of abstraction, carefully delineated in ministerial documents and made legible by way of calculative practices. Yet the welfare program's enactment, the provision of bread to Jordan's residents, relies less on abstract calculation or mechanical expertise than on what the Greeks termed *metis*. Whereas technical knowledge can be expressed in universal rules, principles, and propositions, *metis* is the realm of the contextual, of skills and practices not easily codified.[6] The term captures forms of knowledge grounded in experience and attentiveness, cunning and alertness, honed and expressed in particular circumstances and spheres of activity. I argue that this know-how illustrates something crucial about the craft-like nature of welfare provision. Jordan's bread subsidy is the messy outcome of skills and proficiencies distributed throughout a rather diverse set of individuals who together construct, maintain, and bring this welfare service to fruition. *Metis* is key.

How, then, is this "know-how" learned and applied? And why does it matter? These questions, and provisional answers to them, emerged from the time that I spent with bakers and bakery inspectors. In the case of the former, my apprenticeship was both eye-opening and painful, requiring a laborious retraining of the body in order to engage with what I felt were a rather intractable set of materialities. Flour, yeast, water, and diesel ceased to be the static inputs I had encountered during my first trips to the Ministry of Industry, Trade, and Supply (MOITS). But then, they were never static materials for the ministry's employees either, despite the best attempts of those higher up in the institutional hierarchy to calibrate and quantify, calculate and measure what exactly went on at the bakery. Efforts to capture bread production in statistics and numerical indicators were always partial and uncertain, subject to the whims of fire and dough, yeast and water, or the machinations of a shrewd miller or mischievous bread-maker. Frictions were omnipresent. Cognizant of such difficulties, inspectors did not seek to record or produce robust truths. Their labors, much like those of the bakers, were oriented towards more pragmatic ends. Taming materials to make them congenial to the needs of government takes a great deal of shrewd maneuvering. It requires craft.

The word *craft* tends to carry romantic overtones. Advertisers and business owners often exploit the term's wistful associations, keen to market their products as anything but the result of assembly-line production. In using the term here, however, I seek not to evoke such fanciful connotations but rather to foreground what I find to be the salient modes of labor deployed by those who ensure the availability of subsidized bread. Baking and bakery inspection require skills learned and relearned through experience, repetition, and training. Brute strength and abstract precision are of little use and can even be actively counterproductive. Creativity and resourcefulness, restrained force and improvisation are far more important. So too is responding nimbly to a host of sensory stimuli. Neither bakers nor bureaucrats can impose their will on materials. Instead, they must engage and join with them, following and rearranging the forces, flows, and machines that together bake bread. In addition, both labors rely on modes of "corporeal comprehension" that cannot be acquired solely through mental schemata.[7] Baking and inspection demand a familiarity with tools, materials, and movements achieved over time and sustained acquaintance, a fluency not easily summarized or conveyed in words. The limits of language, as Richard Sennett points out, are "only overcome through active involvement in practice."[8]

And who exactly are these laborers? Bread provision is very much a "gendered production."[9] Both baking and bakery inspection are the exclusive domain of male bakers and ministerial employees, as well as their salaried male assistants. The negligible role accorded to women in this chapter, as well as in much of this book, is not a thoughtless omission but a poignant reflection of how infrequently women appear in the process of bread production as currently organized. The scope and kinds of social relations that I developed and was allowed to pursue with friends, acquaintances, and co-workers were not the result of an unreflective "methodological androcentrism" on my part, or at least so I hope.[10] They were the product of employment practices, masculine control, and broader power dynamics built into the very makeup of work at the ministry and at various bakeries. As at the boxing gyms so gracefully dissected by Loïc Wacquant, the female lovers, friends, mothers, and sisters of bakers and inspectors are, for a broad array of reasons, "kept to the wings and the backstage of the craft."[11] They enter its foreground through connections and absent presences (packed lunches, phone calls, text messages, an array of exertions crucial to everyday survival) to which I was not privy. Of course, those I observed had rich private lives filled with family duties and romantic ties, oppressive patterns of patriarchy and subversive forms of household relation. Yet the bonds and friendships I developed were tilted far away from these spheres. While I grew close enough to some at the bakery to occasionally become apprised of monetary challenges or tumultuous domestic lives, there was a recognition among all these men that intimate lives outside the bakery, beyond a few generic questions, were out of bounds. Familiarity and friendship "at work" very much "militated against trespassing onto intimate terrains outside of it."[12]

This chapter attempts to understand the labors crucial to the enactment of Jordan's bread subsidy. I forefront the skills, practices, and dexterities exercised by people to coax and tame a variety of things into a form congenial to human consumption. I do so because the stabilizations achieved so frequently conceal the conditions of their own assembly—not just from the citizenry, but from the political scientists who address the outcomes that result as the product of a singular entity. Only as the filaments and threads become unwoven does it become clear that the state effect is held together at particular sites and nodes, through the practices of key actors and processes, both human and nonhuman. And while we tend to think of statecraft as the art of conducting political affairs by a country's elite, our analyses might be improved by considering the skills and dexterities that make it possible for the state to become both tangible and thinkable in the first place: the embodied knowledges that allow it to cohere.

How is the state's coherence achieved? What forces contribute to its stabilization? I ponder these questions by considering baking and bakery inspection through my own eyes and ears, forearms and fingers. In this respect, I am inspired by Wacquant's methodology of carnal enactive ethnography, a distinctive mode of apprenticeship-based social inquiry I find aptly suited to unraveling the labors crucial to welfare provision. Further time (and more stable employment) would have been needed to become a recognized member of the craft, at both bakery and ministry. Nevertheless, participating in long-standing modes of knowledge transmission did allow for a very different model of engagement with the bread subsidy. This brand of immersive field-work made clear to me the sensorimotor and social aptitudes that allow bakers and bureaucrats to navigate the web of forces crucial to their work.[13] In foregrounding their labor, this chapter spotlights the routine exertions through which the bakery's main product takes form. For subsidized bread is not possible without animation, toil, and effort, the "collaborative craftwork of hands, eyes and signs," through which humans make *khubz*.[14] Materials and machinery are surely crucial, but I prefer to center the role of embodied labor in their assemblage.[15] Vibrant matter abounds, yet gluten and gliadin require careful work and manipulation in order to bind, stick, and pulsate. If *aesthesis* designates the fabric of experience through which the state is made sensible, then it seems equally important to unpack *poiesis*, the routine practices through which bakers and bureaucrats make the state possible—day after day, loaf after loaf.

ROUTES, RULES, AND REGULATIONS

MOITS closely regulates subsidized bread provision, intervening in every link of the supply chain. The Jordanian government imports approximately 97% of the wheat consumed by its citizens, and oversight and management are crucial. Upon arrival at the southern port of Aqaba, the cereal is tested for live insects, weevils, larvae, and other "impurities." If it is admitted into the country, the wheat immediately enters the realm of bureaucratic knowledge. Each approved shipment is registered before being transported to one of five silos operated by the government-owned Jordan Silos and Supply General Company, where it is stored according to its country of origin. Then, after anywhere from three to nine months, the storage division (*mudiriyyat adarat al-makhzun*) "makes percentages and mixes wheat."[16] This process entails blending different shipments of wheat to obtain ideal protein levels (between 12 and 16%).[17] After the wheat has been mixed, transportation contractors distribute the hybrid cereal to privately owned flour mills around the country, based on demand. Every flour mill has a "capped guarantee" of wheat per month, which is agreed on with the ministry and for which it has to provide a monetary guarantee. Although they will not be my focus, the material qualities of wheat are crucial to this process, as are the frameworks and categories through which the cereal's "purity" is assessed and ideal protein levels determined.

Flour mills in Jordan are privately owned businesses. Most engage in a broad array of cereal-related trades, ranging from the manufacturing of wheat flour to the production of pasta, breakfast cereals, and snack foods. Many have countrywide transport fleets, and a few dabble in the reexportation of some of their products. However, the majority of their commerce relates to milling wheat for the purposes of the bread subsidy. And for this, the flour mills must deal with MOITS. At the time of my fieldwork, this ministry was the sole legal distributor of wheat to be consumed inside the country.[18] No flour could be sold without its permission. This edict was implemented to monitor the amount of both nonsubsidized flour (*Zero, Zahara, and Baladi*) and subsidized flour (*muwwahad*) being purchased by retailers large and small.[19] It also allowed MOITS to monitor how much bread Jordan's residents were eating and ensure that strategic wheat stocks were kept at preferred levels. Although the trade in nonsubsidized flour was left to the mills and their customers (pastry shops, biscuit factories, makers of Arabic sweets, and bakeries making nonsubsidized bread), with MOITS acting as a straightforward wholesaler, the sale of discounted flour intended for the production of subsidized bread was closely regulated by the ministry. Each flour mill was provided with wheat allocations that were required to be used for discounted flour, depending on the number of subsidized bread providers they served. To monitor these transactions, a ministerial official placed at every flour mill approved each dispatch of discounted flour.

Flour mills are allowed to compete openly and ruthlessly for the business of Jordan's more than 1,500 bakeries, each of which registers its preferred purveyor with MOITS. While bakeries are free to purchase as much nonsubsidized flour as they like, each outlet that produces subsidized bread is given quotas of discounted flour that must, by law, be used exclusively for the production of standard *khubz 'arabi*. These quotas, set by ministry officials, guarantee a 7% profit for bakery owners through a complex and confidential formula based on a bakery's potential output, the fluctuating cost of an array of inputs (salt, yeast, labor, electricity), and, most crucially, local demand. The quotas are contentious, and rarely agreed upon swiftly or amicably. Bakeries often claim that their discounted flour allocations do not suffice and that they are not able to meet consumer demand for subsidized bread, putting both their business and their customers at risk. MOITS employees, distraught at the statistical anomalies and blossoming black market, suspect bakery owners of reselling their discounted flour to other shops or using it to make legally prohibited cakes, Arabic sweets, and fancier varieties of bread. To prevent such "leakages" of discounted flour and make the welfare program legible to those tasked with its regulation, the ministry attempts to stabilize the people, materials, and practices required to bake bread.

TENUOUS STABILIZATIONS

The documentary regime through which MOITS administers the bread subsidy aspires to generate what James Scott terms "an overall, aggregate, synoptic view" of the bakery.[20] Codification and homogenization seek to bring order and clarity, and make the welfare program decipherable to the employees who sit at their desks at the ministry and the policy makers who determine the bread subsidy's annual budget. At any time of the day, those working on the "bread file" can quickly find how much wheat is stored in a given silo, the sum of discounted flour a bakery has been allocated, and a given bread-maker's average production, as well as the approximate number of customers it serves. These statistics make bread production and consumption appear both knowable and quantifiable, the goal being to "render visible the space over which government is to be exercised."[21] Yet their solidity, the ability of these numbers to portray an objective reality, belies the uncertainty that permeates how ministerial employees engage with them. Inspectors know that this data is far more vulnerable and uncertain than their superiors would admit. But it is not technical incompetence or corruption that makes it difficult to measure bread output, as the people I spoke with so often stressed. Even when the artifacts upon which the ministry relies for measurement (maps, files, computers, surveys) seem to be working,[22] the unstable and processual nature of bread production itself makes accuracy difficult. *Khubz 'arabi* could never be fully captured by the categories upon which the ministry relied. Materials, humans, and baking practices are not easily stabilized.

I spent most of my time at the ministry with Hazem, an experienced employee who had slowly ascended the hierarchy of the branch charged with administering the bread subsidy. He had held posts in most of its subdivisions, starting with wheat quality control and later moving to mill regulation, then bakery inspection, and, more recently, strategic planning and storage. Hazem loved his job. He never tired of going over the intricacies of bread or the subsidy with me, hastily whipping out some report on ash content in flour varieties or patiently unraveling how gluten in the endosperm of a wheat berry impacts a dough's elasticity. He regarded the bread subsidy with the utmost esteem, and often reminded me why the ministry's efforts mattered so much: "Take clothes. If you have no money, you stop buying. You only purchase what you need. But bread, it is indispensable. Meat consumption I can reduce, chicken too. But bread, I can't give up. Jordan, Palestine, Syria, the entire Levant is like this. Bread is the father of the table. Everyone needs it, no one will give it up."

Trained as an industrial engineer, Hazem was at ease with the operating system that tracked the subsidy and with the countless graphs and tables he would print out for me with barely contained glee. "We have data for every single bakery in Jordan," he would proudly declare. "We have their addresses, their baking capacities and production averages. We monitor them closely. If there is any problem, we try to solve it quickly."

And what sorts of problems arise, I asked, having been told by bakers about just some of the complexities that came with overseeing the subsidy.

He responded, "Look, our objective at the ministry is for every citizen to be able, if they so wish, to purchase bread in sufficient quantity and quality, and at an affordable price. This is our goal. To do so we have to buy wheat on international markets, take care of storage, regulate mills. But the really crucial and difficult part of the job is deciding where bakeries should open, how much discounted flour they should receive, and assessing whether they are offering customers the appropriate amount of subsidized bread. Corruption, graft, and fraud are the main complicating factors. They are the source of most flour leakage."

I was intrigued by his statement, and I wondered how the ministry employees could detect these "complicating factors" and prevent the leakages of discounted flour. I had assumed that regulating the subsidy program was straightforward, that it was composed of elements (flour, water, labor, electricity) with little variation, which could easily be measured and surveyed. "Does the data compiled by the ministry illuminate where the fraud occurs?" I asked.

"The numbers are no use for that," Hazem chuckled. "We have some vague idea of leakage from studies we've compiled over the years, but implementing the subsidy and detecting problems requires going to the bakery. You have to see it at work."

The data compiled by MOITS makes production at the bakery seem ordered, manageable, even predictable. Yet as Hazem's comments indicate, through the eyes of certain bureaucrats, the bakery is a continual source of unsolvable problems. Discounted flour can easily be used to make biscuits or mixed with more costly varieties to produce sweet Arabic pastries. Bakery owners could also resell their flour quotas to factories or restaurants; sometimes with good reason, other times less justifiably. At the same time, Hazem was telling me to see the numbers the ministry compiles not as "verifiable quantities" depicting some independent reality, but as "approximations."[23] "Measuring production and demand is always fraught with uncertainty," he confessed. "Inspectors depend on a host of imprecise tools and personal appraisals. They uncover what they see fit."

Time and experience had taught Hazem two things that ethnographers of infrastructure have only recently begun to theorize. First, technologies of measurement are dependent on the "deployment of a particular series of mediating artifacts."[24] They configure practices in certain ways and shape modes of calculation among bakers and inspectors. Just as importantly, mediation makes any depiction more vulnerable and compromised than we tend to assume. Reliance on computers, surveys, and ordinary members of the bureaucratic collective ensures that the data compiled by the ministry is not an accurate set of representations but a copiously mediated depiction of reality. Second, technologies of measurement are implicated in the very object of knowledge they seek to apprehend. They participate in cutting up the world to make it appear *as if* water, yeast, or flour can be portrayed in fixed form.[25] I was surprised by the willingness with which these uncertainties were acknowledged by those I spoke with at MOITS. Of course, when necessary, especially in public forums and in interactions with international financial institutions and elected figures, ministry officials would claim objective measurement. In order to avoid intense scrutiny of the bread subsidy and the proposals for elimination that often came with such scrutiny, they could not openly disavow the quantification and measurement of the resources entrusted to them and the good management that these practices seemed to demonstrate. However, as routine inspections quickly made clear, compiling data so as to administer the bread subsidy was more a matter of engaged conjecture than detached calculation. Certain materials, processes, and practices were particularly difficult to capture and quantify. But such difficulties did not bedevil the ministry in the ways I expected. Considerable scope for imprecision was afforded during inspection precisely because flour, diesel, and yeast were so easily disordered by machinery, weather, and skill. More worrying was whether the humans crucial to making bread were manipulating the subsidy.

CAUTIOUS APPROXIMATIONS

After I had spent a few weeks shadowing employees at the ministry, Hazem arranged for me to tag along on different rounds of bakery inspection in Amman. I followed inspectors, quietly jotting down my observations and their answers to my rudimentary questions. My first three forays all transpired without incident. Then, late one afternoon, I was informed that I would be accompanying the inspectors to one of East Amman's more marginalized neighborhoods the following day. Hazem thought this field trip would be especially illuminating, as the inspectors were not only going to conduct their routine checkups, which usually took a couple of hours, but were also meeting with a prospective bakery owner who was hoping to open a new business in the district. The applicant had already passed the first stage of the licensing process, in which he had to prove his identity, demonstrate the necessary funds, and certify through the Public Security Directorate that he was an upstanding citizen. The inspectors were now tasked with interviewing the candidate to determine whether he was well-suited to the bread business and with assessing whether there was enough demand in the neighborhood to sustain a new bakery.

In approving licenses, the ministry's goal is to avoid flour leakage and unnecessary competition while ensuring that local demand for bread is being met. "We don't like having more than four or five bakeries in any one neighborhood," the more senior inspector, Fadi, told me as we left the ministry that morning. "If there is more supply than what customers require, this negatively affects the business of those bakeries already present and lots of bread goes to waste, which worries the ministry."

Estimates of subsidized bread demand are crucial here. Inspectors compile them by gathering an array of data, mostly furnished by Jordan's Department of Statistics, regarding the local resident population. They then gauge business activity and commercial foot traffic at the time of application. Demand is important, but so too are the prospects and preparation of the applicant—hence the interview. Fadi explained: "We are expected to make sure they [the prospective owners] are honest and have adequate knowledge of the bread business. We hate giving licenses to people who close down in a few months or to those who don't have good intentions. You have to remember that bread is a sensitive material and that the subsidy can be manipulated to make illegal profits. Opening a bakery isn't like opening a corner store."

There were certain parameters that guided the inspectors' decisions—for example, bakeries should be at least one kilometer apart, and prospective owners should be well-versed in the industry—but these were easy enough to ignore, if they saw fit. The inspectors could use the presence of people such as construction workers, refugees, informal renters, and others not included in the Department of Statistics' calculations to manipulate the population numbers and produce a greater or lesser demand for bread in their reports. Personalities and intentions were also hard to surmise; applicants could be portrayed in any light. A bakery's viability, the granting of a license to open for business and receive discounted flour, depended on how the inspectors evaluated the tempos and demands of urban life, as well as the character of the aspiring bakery owner. Inspectorial acumen was vital.

On an unseasonably warm December morning, Fadi, his partner Faris, and I departed from the ministry at nine thirty. Twenty minutes later, Fadi parked his vehicle on an inconspicuous corner of the neighborhood's primary thoroughfare, roughly half a block from the largest bakery. Faris purchased some coffee for the three of us from a nearby stand, around which we attempted to position ourselves discreetly. The goal, from what I could tell, was to assess this bakery's work patterns in order to determine whether it was producing enough *khubz 'arabi* for those who lived and worked near it. After almost an hour of observation, aided by more coffee and cigarettes, the inspectors decided to walk along the main street and survey pedestrians and business owners. Did they think the neighborhood needed another bakery? Were the opening hours of this bread outlet sufficient? Was there ever a lack of *khubz 'arabi*? These were the main questions that they posed during our stroll. Initially hesitant, the vast majority of residents, once the inspectors had explained their objective, gave positive reviews, extolling the bakery's qualities. "It works well (*shughlu kuwayis*)," one interviewee answered. "There is always subsidized bread, even when they run out of sweets or other breads." Accessibility was a key area of concern. As profits on *khubz ʿarabi* were far lower than on other breads, some bakeries produced a minimal amount of it, nudging their hurried customers to purchase more expensive products. "The bread could taste better," another resident relayed, eager to demonstrate his familiarity with the baking process. "I don't think they are letting the dough rise long enough. The bread does not last as long as it should. But yes, there is always subsidized bread, the bakery works well." Occasional disparagements of quality aside, most of those queried seemed satisfied, and expressed no desire for another bread-maker in the district when asked. Popular opinion is not the only diagnostic measure of bread demand that matters, but it is one of the things that is important to inspection work. Conscious that public approval of the bread subsidy was crucial to the policy's continuation, Fadi and Faris sought out complaints or approbation "on people's tongues (*ʿala alsinat al-nas*)."[26] This was hardly a straightforward process, of course, since bakers are vulnerable to false accusations of corruption or malfeasance from competitors. And yet, while the inspectors knew that talk on the street was not always precise, optics counted, as I was frequently reminded. How things seemed was often more important than how they actually were.

After thirty more minutes talking with local residents, we met with the prospective bakery owner, just outside the location he was proposing to rent for his operations. Fadi and Faris asked about the machinery he intended to purchase, the number of workers he would employ, and what his proposed subsidized bread output would be. The conversation seemed amicable enough; the applicant was eager to please the inspectors with spreadsheets, organizational charts, and even a brief slide presentation hurriedly displayed on his laptop. Fadi inquired as to whether the applicant planned to make sweets. Faris asked for any experience the candidate might have in the bread industry. Both probed for potential connections with other bakery owners, each of whom is technically only allowed to have a proprietary interest in three bakeries, in order to promote competition and avoid any type of collusion. The meeting lasted nearly forty-five minutes, after which we left the neighborhood for lunch. The applicant had seemed well-prepared and his business plan innocuous enough, although the neighborhood did not seem to lack for bread. "I don't think it should open," Fadi declared swiftly after we got in his car. "The other bakeries are working well and there is even some bread that is not being sold. The new one would be bad for their business." Faris nodded, quickly jotting down some observations on his notepad.

The case seemed straightforward. Not much unmet demand, no reason for a new bakery. Yet as I learned over lunch—shawarma sandwiches wrapped in *khubz 'arabi*—this particular application had some added complications. The aspiring bakery owner was well-connected. Faris relayed that two separate members of Parliament had called the ministry over the past week, ostensibly to corroborate the applicant's good standing in the community. The two inspectors did not know the true nature of their intentions. Neither member of Parliament represented the area, so it was probably not a matter of requesting improved services to bolster their reputation in an electoral constituency. They could have been doing someone a favor, or simply, as they themselves said, vouching for a person they thought worthy of the ministry's trust. Neither Faris nor Fadi knew with any certainty; Hazem had simply told them about the calls and their content. The inspectors recognized that their decision was complicated by the applicant's relationships, as the ministry relied on the support of parliamentary figures in order to avoid cuts to its operating budget. While they did not reveal the exact ways in which members of Parliament or their own superiors at the ministry exerted pressure on their verdicts, I was struck by the influence such endorsements could have, and the time and positioning that went into tackling them. In the following months, I would witness several occasions during which elected officials and influential figures arrived unannounced at MOITS, their bakery-related petitions courteously listened to over tea and sweets. Hazem would usually do his best to offer assurances that their appeals would be noted, but he would never fail to emphasize that the ministry's verdicts were "scientific, not political." The inspectors, too, complained when the bread subsidy became a question of "politics." They resented such infringements not just because they impinged upon their areas of influence or autonomy but because of what Bernardo Zacka terms a "bureaucratic disposition."[27] For Fadi and Faris, as well as most of their colleagues, the welfare program was a point of pride, a source of identification with a state apparatus whose remits had drastically decreased. These men did not see themselves as impassive administrators or corruptible service providers. They were watchful guardians of public resources, cognizant that their decisions adjudicated the value of neighborhoods and residents every time they resolved to increase a flour quota or grant a bakery license. "Many politicians exploit their access to the ministry and use the bread subsidy to further their own ends," Fadi remarked. "They don't understand the subsidy system, and why giving anyone a discounted flour quota can present a serious problem." Faced with such intrusions, most at the ministry argued that the discretionary remit of inspectors was best left unspoken.

Such "official secrets," what Max Weber terms "the specific invention of bureaucracy," are often considered a source of power and clout. Bureaucrats conceal their knowledge and the ways in which it is produced to maintain the authority of the professionally informed and prevent outside scrutiny and interference. "Nothing is as fanatically defended," Weber tells us, as these official secrets.[28] Yet emphasizing that their verdicts were "scientific" and not "political" was not just a way for those at MOITS to avoid oversight or criticism; inspectors also recognized that they could not escape the potential fallout from the faulty distribution of the resources they managed. Local residents and politicians held the ministry accountable, sometimes vociferously so, if bread was deficient, lacking, or absent. A scarcity of bread often translated to palpable anger on the street. So the "official secret" here was not strictly about preventing oversight. It did not appear to function as a way to slyly de-politicize questions of resource allocation in order to bolster an "anti-politics machine"[29] or a seamless "rule of experts."[30] Rather, concealing uncertainties in the production of knowledge and discretion in decision-making was a way for these officials to prevent what they saw as unsavory forces from impinging upon their work. This was a delimiting of the technical, of course, one that muffled and silenced alternative forms of knowledge, as all such delimitations do.[31] But it did so in the service of bureaucratic discretion that pursued a (political) goal, not depoliticized expertise. Officials at the ministry understood that their reputations and possibilities for promotion would be in danger if their judgments were hasty or their flour allocations incorrect. Their success, Fadi and Faris told me, depended on their ability to quickly determine the needs of a neighborhood, the real output of the current baker-ies, and the intentions of the applicants seeking to join the industry. None of these phenomena was easily captured or quantified in a survey or chart; the inspectors readily acknowledged that their decisions were based on pragmatic abstractions that they constructed rather than accurate portrayals of reality. Yet, to those outside the tightly woven MOITS bureaucracy, such uncertainties could not be revealed.

In its planning documents, press conferences, and interactions with elected figures, MOITS said little about its ample room for maneuver. It fully embraced a rational-legal depiction of bureaucracy that so many suggest does not exist in the Hashemite Kingdom.[32] Individual inspectors were but insensitive cogs in a rule-worshiping system with little leeway, they emphasized. Through official surveys and other documentary appraisals, they made their inspections appear as if there were no illegibilities or uncertainties in the ministerial data and decision-making. Those "in the know" were very conscious that surveys and statistics could never be the sole, or even primary, basis upon which a flour allocation or bakery license was given. Nevertheless, these documents continued to conjure the ministry as a particular kind of entity, one that relied on objective quantitative data and technical expertise to make decisions about Jordan's most widely consumed foodstuff. In a context where a general skepticism about government decisions was pervasive, the appearance of objectivity was key.

Despite efforts to avoid outside interference, appeals and entreaties were habitually relayed to the inspectors in charge of a particular district or neighborhood, their importance deduced from the forcefulness with which they were conveyed. Inspectors routinely complained about such petitions, grumbling about how they compromised their work. "We're supposed to be concerned only with citizens' needs and the provision of bread," Faris said during this particular round of inspections. "People see the bakery as a source of profit, they think if they do a favor for someone then they will be in his debt. Sometimes these petitions will be genuine; some neighborhoods really could use another bakery. But most of the time, it's a question of self-interest." Fadi nodded, before narrating a series of what seemed like hyperbolic anecdotes: "One time we found out a member of Parliament was exchanging discounted flour allocations for 10,000 dinars [US$14,104] per ton," he stated. "Another time we found an inspector colluding with a parliamentary staffer for payments of 500 dinar [US$705] a week." Allocating flour quotas or bakery licenses would be difficult in any context, but these inspectors had to fulfill their duties in a particularly challenging setting—one that forced them to navigate scarce resources, external pressures, incompatible objectives, and a regular stream of emotionally trying confrontations with bakery owners and citizens. As they made subsidized bread available, these inspectors knew that they were bringing the state to bear not just on where and when people buy and consume bread but also on the vast array of other businesses that tend to pop up around bakeries (restaurants, grocery stores, sandwich shops). Their goal in speaking of "science" in contrast to "politics" was not to thwart oversight or stockpile influence but to build and maintain a welfare infrastructure that required, indeed depended on, discretion. Bernardo Zacka has explored the difference "between the formal discretion to which officials are entitled 'on paper' and the real discretion they actually wielded on the ground" in an American welfare agency.[33] Much like bakery inspectors, the bureaucrats he works with constantly confront questions that cannot be settled except through contextual judgment. Rules and procedures eliminate certain options, yet "street-level bureaucrats"[34] still have alternatives to choose from; they inhabit a realm of what he terms "bounded discretion."[35] MOITS's forms and surveys helped to maintain this prerogative. They were "useful fictions," which bureaucrats could deploy and broadcast strategically in the face of omnipresent skepticism about government decisions.[36]

On this occasion, as it happened, the external endorsements did not succeed. "His store would be too close to the others," Fadi concluded in reference to the applicant's proposal. "There are a lot of Syrians now in the area, but most people leave the area for work, they eat their lunch elsewhere." Faris concurred: "You are right, but let's keep him on file, he's well prepared. If an opportunity opens up in another area, we can see if he's interested."

To be an effective inspector required detailed knowledge of the rules, regulations, and administrative decrees that governed the bread subsidy. That said, the job required other skills as well, an amorphous combination of cultural competency, social intuition, and poise, all of which worked to soften the encounter between the rules and the fluid realities of everyday life. As most inspectors openly admitted, the administrative directives and operating procedures outlined by the ministry were of little use once they hit the street. Most of the factors they were asked to consider when granting a bakery license were impossible to know or measure in reliable ways. Residency in East

Amman's neighborhoods was always in flux, as were the commercial patterns and pedestrian routines that drove bread demand at any given moment. At the same time, and to complicate things further, inspectors had to navigate people with access to political figures, or an ability to grease the palms of those well-connected at the ministry. Much like the "artisans of Mumbai's water system" explored by Nikhil Anand, bakery inspectors were exposed to an array of political pressures from elected figures and community leaders they tended to complain about.[37] Yet they could not completely disavow or ignore such intrusions, dependent as they were on parliamentarians to approve their budget, adopt occasional recommendations, and refrain from publicly protesting their decisions.

As Fadi and Faris struggled to decide when and where to approve a bakery opening, they had to calculate demand and discern production as well as approximate need. And in order to do that they had to survey the public, consider current bread-making patterns, and consult a variety of empirical indicators. They also had to determine the integrity of applicants. Equally important were the ways in which they dealt with impatient and influential petitioners. While bakery licenses were ultimately granted through a central-ized decision-making committee at the ministry, this crucial step in bread provision was no simple feat of detached projection made in an air-conditioned office. It was, as I would learn, the result of bureaucrats exercising discretion on a daily basis, striving to ensure that the bread subsidy was implemented in accordance with certain conceptions of human responsibility. The approval of bakery licenses made visible the resourcefulness and creativity required to assess people and demand. It would be difficult if not impossible to parse out and codify what exactly went into each such determination. Soft evidence reigned supreme.[38] Inspectors did not just implement preordained policies and guidelines. Discretion permeates their craft.

IMPOSSIBLE STABILIZATIONS

After lunch, Faris, Fadi, and I returned to the neighborhood. As we arrived, they told me to prepare for heated arguments. Some of the neighborhood's bread-makers had garnered a reputation as being particularly inclined to flout the law. The plan was to conduct a routine inspection of three more bakeries. Each received an allocation of discounted flour, which was only allowed to be used for the production of *khubz 'arabi*. However, the fact that most bakeries produce other wheat-based goods makes this decree vulnerable to manipulation. Inspectors struggle to measure and prevent such leakages. Discounted flour is hard to track and identify once the baking process begins. As a result, indeterminacy textures the inspection. "Understanding the varieties of flour and how they shape the baking process isn't easy," Faris explained. "Even for us it's difficult to know what type of flour is being used in any one piece of bread or pastry." Bakers are at a distinct advantage in this respect. They can distinguish the flour's properties with a quick glance or, failing that, swiftly run their hands through the material. Crucial in this respect is ash content (*al-rumad*), the percentage of mineral material contained in any wheat flour, primarily determined by the extraction rate at which wheat is milled. An ash content of about 55% was the average in the nonsubsidized Zero variety of flour; in *muwwahad* it was 65%. The 10% difference is far from obvious to the naked eye, but it does affect the baking performance of the flour, and the quality of the baked goods depends on it. For the inspectors, determining which flour was being used in any one product was not straightforward, especially when different varieties were mixed together to further conceal their origin. They recognized that they would only sporadically be able to identify the leakages in ways that would be upheld by the investigatory committee charged with issuing fines. The ministry deemed the necessary laboratory tests for accurately determining ash content or extraction rate to be too costly and too time-consuming to be worthwhile, and the inspectors therefore had to take bakers at their word. If the flour sack they were using said *muwwahad* (subsidized flour) and came from a ministry-approved miller, with the appropriate approvals and paperwork, inspectors were told not to quarrel with the owner. Other methods would be used to untangle what exactly was going on at the bakery.

When conducting routine inspections, ministry employees were equipped with an official inspection form (see figure 1). Here, they recorded the name of the bakery, its owner, address, flour provider, and other identifying details, as well as various figures related to the bakery's production: flour allocation, subsidized bread output, yeast consumption, production of nonsubsidized goods, number of workers, and opening hours, as well as the amounts of different flours present at the time of inspection. These categories worked as

وزارة الصناعة والتجارة والتموين
مديرية إدارة المخزون
نموذج كشف مخابز

التاريخ: / / 2018

اليوم ::

رقم الزيارة

رقم المخبز :		اسم المخبز :	
الناقل المعتمد :		اسم صاحب المخبز:	
المطحنه:		نوع المخبز:	
وقت الزيارة :		عنوان المخبز:	
كمية الطحين الموحد الموجود : ( )		المخصصات اليومية: ( )	
كمية طحين الزبرو الموجود : ( )		عدد العمال : ( ) ( )	
كمية الطحين الموحد المستخدم :( )		عدد خطوط الإنتاج العربي ( ) ( )	
ساعة بدء الإنتاج: ( )		عدد العيون : ( ) ( )	
ساعة الاغلاق: ( )		استهلاك الخميرة حسب الفواتير كل أسبوع ( )	
عدد خطوط الافرنجي(الدوار) ( )		عدد العجانات العربي ( )	
		عدد العجانان الافرنجي ( )	

● نتائج الكشف :

١. تم صرف كمية ( ) الساعة ( ) بتاريخ / / 2018 لمدة ....

٢. واصل مخصصاته من الطحين المدعوم الموحد لغاية : / / 2018 ....

٣. مسحوباته من الطحين الزبرو خلال شهر .... 2018 ( ) نسبة سحب الزبرو (%)

٤. تاريخ اخر زيادة :( ) ومقدارها( ) ( ) .

ملاحظات: ....

....

....

....

....

التنسيبات: ....

....

....

صاحب المخبز   عضو اللجنة   عضو اللجنة   رئيس اللجنة

FIGURE 1. Official inspection form.

"inscription devices": they transformed vibrant matter and a set of practices into a figure, which became usable in the construction of facts.[39] Among inspectors, the numbers produced were known to be rough estimates, jotted down hurriedly while ambling about the bakery, which was often in the midst of baking. But when amassed with other documents, these cautious approximations were indicative.

A few weeks earlier, I had entered Hazem's office as he was going over a bakery inspection form and the importance of yeast quantities with a new inspector under his supervision. In an awkward attempt to make conversation, I asked Hazem why yeast mattered. He laughed and explained that computing yeast consumption was one of the primary methods through which the ministry detected leakage. The logic was simple. Every batch of dough requires yeast, roughly ten kilograms per ton of flour, with slight variations in summer and winter. Not enough yeast consumption in proportion to the bakery's flour allocation was a red flag. It usually meant that discounted flour was being used to make something other than subsidized bread. Gathering receipts was therefore crucial to establishing yeast consumption, and Hazem was reproaching his subordinate for having overlooked exactly that. This particular bakery had been caught selling its discounted flour to nearby pastry shops in the past, Hazem told me. Its production numbers were a little off this time, hence the need to check whether its yeast purchases were up-to-date. "The inspector forgot to ask for the receipt, so we can't accuse the bakery owner of anything; the investigatory committee will not uphold any penalty without paperwork."

"But what if they forge an invoice?" I asked, "Or just buy yeast for the receipt and then resell the product?"

"Look, the numbers are never precise," Hazem answered. "You check on yeast purchases, look at electricity consumption and production capacity, maybe talk to the workers and a few customers. You want as comprehensive a picture as possible."

For a bakery to be accused of fraud, certain types of evidence were required, ones that could at least appear to be reliable and objective in front of an investigative committee. Time, cost, and efficiency meant that more verifiable modes of scrutiny, where matter could be stabilized and studied, were simply not feasible. Still, compiling data for these forms was not a hopeless bureaucratic task either. In addition to portraying the ministry as an objective decision-maker, these documents assisted inspectors in their attempts to achieve the best understanding possible of a particular bakery, from which they could deduce whether other documents or information might be of assistance. If the form prompted uncertainty, the inspectors had to think on their feet, quickly determining what other types of evidence might either bolster or allay their suspicions. The data compiled was suggestive without being conclusive. Effective inspection entailed going beyond the collation of statistics; it required improvisation, creativity, and something else: "The problem is that this guy [the new inspector] is not yet *mudaqdaq* (clever)," Hazem said, half-jokingly. "He needs more time on the street to develop his skills."

The afternoon that I was accompanying Faris and Fadi on their inspections, the inspection of the first bakery was swift and problem-free. The inspectors greeted the employee at the cash register, who called on an assistant to take us to the bake-room. The room looked more like a factory than a bread-making shop. Several large ovens manufactured in Italy were making European breads and pastries. These ran on timers and required little in the way of human intervention. On the other side of the bake-room, a steady trickle of dough was being deposited onto a three-level machine with a conveyor belt. In three minutes, the dough was flattened, shaped, baked, and briefly rested. *Khubz 'arabi* emerged, descending a slide to the section of the storefront where it was packaged. (This bakery received 22 tons of discounted flour a month—around three quarters of a ton per day—a comparatively large allocation reserved mainly for large, mechanized outlets where most of the baking was automated. Only the more expensive sweet Arabic pastries were produced by hand.) The yeast and electricity receipts were in order. The bakery's manager had recently implemented an auditing system to preclude potential problems with inspectors.

"This bakery works well," Faris told me as we left. "The bakery owner put his son in charge a few months ago and the kid knows what he's doing. Before we would always have problems with this place. The managers were crooked, and we thought some of the employees were taking advantage of the absentee owner." Fadi agreed: "Yes, the kid is doing a good job. He's finally gotten that place in order."

Bakery number two proved more eventful. With an allocation of a quarter ton of discounted flour a day, the setting was far smaller. It had a mechanized flour mixer, but all other processes were completed manually. Only a few stale loaves were available for sale when we arrived. Fadi and Faris asked the owner for the necessary information for their inspection form, and took a closer look at the baking equipment. Most of it was old and rundown, but that on its own was not meaningful or disconcerting. What prompted their suspicion was the dust that had accumulated on the mechanized mixer and on the counters where the dough was ostensibly shaped and formed.

"How much bread have you produced today?" Faris asked the man in charge.

"About 175 kilos. We'll start making more in the late afternoon, when the children get out of school."

With a discounted flour allocation of a quarter ton, the bakery should have been producing somewhere in the vicinity of 375 kilograms of *khubz 'arabi* per day, with around 20 kilograms given over to errors and mishaps, whether human, material, or some combination of the two. As Fadi and Faris strolled around the bakery, exasperation surfaced on their faces. The inspectors requested the bakery's electricity bills. After some delay and protestation, the owner produced one. The information was clearly alarming. Large fluctuations in monthly electricity consumption were evident, I later learned. The bakery owner was not using his discounted flour allocation to produce subsidized bread, at least not every day. He was reselling his allocation, to pastry makers or households, maybe a biscuit factory. The owner's fraud was not egregious, but it was noticeable. Fadi and Faris decided to temporarily decrease this bakery's flour quota, which would then undergo further review at the ministry.

"How did you realize it?" I asked Fadi at the end of the day.

Plenty of bakeries have downtimes, he explained, and many have days where they do more business than others, but none that are baking consistently have dust and grime on their machinery and on their counters like that bakery did. Forming dough on such a surface is not only more difficult, it would also produce filthy bread. The customers would never return. Fadi summarized: "The guy had clearly not baked anything in at least three days."

"He's clever (*mudaqdaq huwe*)," Faris remarked with a playful smile.

Adroitness at inspection is largely transmitted through apprenticeship. Acquiring the skills needed does not occur via a discrete training course at the ministry, just as determining compliance with regulations is not simply a reflection of the inspection form. Know-how only accumulates through repeated visits and observation. Skills learned at the office must be refined and nurtured on the street. Those who had acquired those refinements, over time and through repetition, were frequently described as *mudaqdaq*. Typically used to refer to a wily shop owner or cunning drug dealer, not quite malicious but far from harmless, the term *mudaqdaq* was deployed at the ministry to portray those inspectors who had gained a detailed familiarity with the bread industry and were thus less liable to be fooled by devious bakery owners.

When I asked how one became *mudaqdaq*, no one clear explanation was given. For Hazem, it involved some combination of previous involvement in the bread business, repeated bakery visits, and an intangible ingenuity. To recognize how others were cheating the system, you had to be able to imagine cheating it yourself. In her exploration of tacit knowledge in Cairo, Julia Elyachar unpacks a similar term, *fahlawah*. Usually used to describe the poor masses of the Egyptian capital, the phrase is often translated as "cleverness" or "sharpness," a type of street smarts that only comes with experience, rather than formal education. Like Fadi, Elyachar's informant Mr. Amir depends on his "sense (*hiss*) of the market,"[40] as well as impressions and past experiences, to preserve the state's resources in his work at a public-sector bank. Just as the inspectors do, Mr. Amir gathers, filters, and processes information via methods he has honed over the years. Preformatted technical expertise is of little use in either job, incapable of unraveling the always-changing secrets of the trade that characterize each context.

Various ministry employees had been fired or taken to court for colluding with bakers and millers over the previous decade. In response, several initiatives had been undertaken to better codify the procedures through which routine inspections occurred. Forms and modes of documentation had been altered, as had the process for issuing fines, all in an attempt to make the flows of flour and bread more visible and leakage less likely. At the higher echelons of the ministry, many assumed that, since the process had now been codified in this way, the bread subsidy would be easier to monitor. But the inspectors knew that much of what went on at the bakery escaped such measurement devices. Some important pieces of information were not accessible via forms and surveys, no matter how often those documents were revised. The sheer variety of the bakeries made easy replication impossible; formulas and fixed instructions were of little use. Hazem organized his inspection teams so that the skills required of them could be transmitted and learned. Only by observing senior inspectors and participating in routine processes could new ministerial employees become adept at the distinctive ways of seeing, acting, and reacting that would enable them to develop a knack for the job.[41] This knack was vital precisely because the settings in which it was applied were so mutable. Codified forms could never account for the innumerable possibilities that emerged in the day-to-day.

To be described as *mudaqdaq*, then, an inspector had to shrewdly maneuver an array of situations. How to disentangle the accounts of a factory-like bakery run by an owner with an MBA, when to ask for receipts from bakers who used a cigarette carton as a cash register, or whether to look into the yeast purchases of a bread-maker who claimed never to make sweets. "One time we visited a small bakery that someone reported as not using its flour allocation," Faris recalled. "But the bakery was producing the expected amount of bread, and it had plenty of customers. I just could not figure it out. It was a small, run-down place in a very poor neighborhood. The guy didn't have any sort of accounting system or much in the way of receipts."

Both inspectors smiled as they remembered the story.

"Then Fadi stepped outside and looked at the electricity lines. I was sure he suspected something. He came back in and asked the owner for the electricity bill," Faris continued. "It was 2JD (US$2.80) for an entire month," he said with a smile. "We asked him how it was possible to bake all that bread with such a low bill. We accused him of selling some of his flour quota and pocketing the profit. We were ready to report his infraction. He yelled and complained a little, but then he just looked at us and said: 'No, it's simple. I steal the electricity.'"

The inspectors speculated that a nearby restaurant owner, on discovering a surge in his own bill, had probably called the ministry, aware of the fact that bread issues would be dealt with far more quickly than electricity provision, at least in the more marginalized parts of East Amman. But local residents relied upon this particular bakery, and a fine or suspension of discounted flour deliveries could very well have put it out of business. The inspectors decided that no penalty would be issued, nor the flour allocation decreased; an informal warning would suffice. "We told him to get the electricity in order," Fadi recalled. "We didn't get into this job to punish bakers or make their lives difficult, just to make sure citizens have access to a loaf of bread."

David Graeber posits that "in practice, bureaucratic procedure invariably means ignoring all the subtleties of real social existence and reducing everything to preconceived mechanical or statistical formulae."[42] But while forms, questionnaires, and statistics do indeed simplify and schematize, as Graeber argues, what he overlooks is the ways in which bureaucrats deploy and work with these documents and the varying ambiguities that color their engagements. Bakeries and bread provision offer challenges that can only really be solved once inspectors are on the ground, working in direct relation with the materials they regulate and the people they serve. Sometimes this requires overlooking the theft of electricity. Other times it means ignoring dubious yeast amounts or threatening future fines while colluding with bakery owners out of compassion or to benefit the poor. It is impossible to ignore the subtleties of social existence; it is unsustainable to disregard the complexities of baking bread in favor of abstract standards.

Our last inspection was briefly recounted in the introduction to this chapter. The third bakery, somewhere between the first and second in terms of size and production, was accused of using discounted flour to produce sweets, thus substantially augmenting its profits. Although the amount of subsidized bread that it produced, as well as its electricity and yeast bills, were all aboveboard, I was told that the bakery did not have the necessary evidence of non-*muwwahad* flour purchases. There was nonsubsidized flour present, but the receipt for it was old. After a cursory touch and a close glance, Fadi deemed the sweets to be of poor quality, the mix of flour varieties giving them what was to me an almost undetectable yellowish hue that, Fadi claimed, affected their taste. Identifying the leakage here required an acute sensory knowledge that was attentive to contingent combinations of flour, water, and yeast. It also involved thinking with and beyond the official inspection form to determine which of these ingredients were not present at the appropriate amounts. On this occasion, the inspectors informed the bakery owner that they would be reducing his discounted flour allocation and that he could be issued a fine if he did not mend his ways. Both of them later told me that the reduction would almost surely not hold up after the formal investigation. Receipts for nonsub-sidized flour were easy enough to fabricate, with the help of the transporters who dominated the flour trade for small and medium-sized bakeries. More important, at least in this case, was cautioning the owner, tying him up in the inevitable paperwork that would accompany the forthcoming investigation, in the hopes of dissuading him from persisting with his unlawful practices. Effective regulation of the bread subsidy required far more than complying with or fulfilling hierarchical directives. It demanded street-level bureaucrats who could give prudent content to imprecise mandates and make judicious compromises between conflicting demands. Jordan's bakery inspectors had to improvise and accommodate, occasionally remain ignorant or turn a blind eye, deliver a warning or issue a fine, if it meant that bread would be provided to those who needed it.

In exercising discretion and assessing the people and materials at the heart of the bread industry, these bakery inspectors followed in a long line of government officials in the Islamic world. Paulina Lewicka has explored the role of state-appointed *muhtasib* (those who bring to account) in medieval Cairo, deftly tracing the different aspects of city life with which these officials were concerned.[43] The *muhtasib*'s responsibilities were vast, as was the scope of their activities.[44] These officials checked scales and weights at wholesalers and supervised mills, butcheries, and slaughterhouses. The grain trade and bakeries, and the numerous intermediaries involved, were foremost among their concerns.[45] Bread's centrality to urban life meant that the *muhtasib* were under constant pressures from rulers. The latter knew well that public dis-content could emerge "if any irregularity adversely affected, or could affect, the population's access to bread."[46] Then, as now, making bread offered an array of possibilities for manipulation.[47] Just as bakers used an endless bag of tricks to adulterate their product, so too did the *muhtasib* use any number of "counter-methods to expose their deceit"[48] and enforce *hisba* (bring people to account). Today, Amman's inspectors follow government edicts rather than the injunctions of shari'a law. Yet what strikes me is not only that their work remains crucial to maintaining public order and preventing hunger, but the extent to which their labor continues to depend on their ability to negotiate the vibrancy of human and nonhuman, and the various ways they can combine. As in medieval Cairo, handbooks and surveys cannot contain all the possible abuses and scams in the bread industry. What was and remains crucial is how the inspectors move between probabilities and positivistic evidence, between what can be known and what can be proven, between abstract regulations they are keen to uphold and an equally keen awareness that what matters is that bread is provided regularly and that fraud does not become widespread. The task is difficult because bread is never static. The vagaries of humidity, temperature, machinery, and skill are hard to control or map; manipulation is easy, while adulteration is hard to detect. Cleverness requires wrestling with these contingent relations between human and nonhuman, not pretending that they do not exist.

MOITS's main objective is to guarantee that every Jordanian resident can purchase subsidized bread in sufficient quantity and quality. This requires controlling the daily provision of the foodstuff through a number of administrative and regulatory practices—keeping track of wheat quality, setting milling standards, determining flour quotas, and verifying bread accessibility. Dexterity, care, and judgment are crucial to every part of this process. Challenges abound; matter and materials essential to the bread subsidy rarely stand still. Too often, we assume that welfare programs such as this one work through calculative techniques that render outcomes predictable: implementation via bureaucracy either works in a relatively straightforward fashion or is bedeviled by corruption and malfeasance. Yet as the above-documented inspections indicate, leakages and malfunctions do not necessarily mark a failure. Nor do they compromise the tall task of governance. Rather, bureaucratic practices range over and attempt to navigate an ever-changing sociomaterial terrain, one that inspectors seek to manage but can never completely control. Those in Parliament could actively ignore such contingencies, portraying the bread subsidy as legible and quantifiable through the ostensibly accurate statistics upon which they rely. The inspectors, in contrast, work in a far more direct relation with the policy they are charged with monitoring. Regulating the bread subsidy becomes far more of a "craft practice" at the stage at which they enter the scene.[49] Despite the inspectors' detailed knowledge of labor decrees, health codes, and baking regulations, bakeries offer challenges they can only really solve once they are on the street. We can shed light on such encounters only when we stop privileging governmental representations and the static certainties they espouse. Inspectors do not search for, nor do they produce, robust truths. They do not relate to numbers as unmediated portrayals of reality. Nor do they regulate bakeries through codified standards. Tools and techniques are employed to pursue a specific, pragmatic end: making materials move so as to provide subsidized bread. Their labors make clear the centrality of tacit, uncodifiable knowledge to the realm most associated with its erasure—bureaucracy. Fadi and Faris must combine a *metis* for maintenance and repair with an understanding of how *khubz 'arabi* is made and its ingredients potentially manipulated. People and things both present obstacles. That few in Amman lack for bread speaks not only to the efficacy of the subsidy system, but to the reliability, discernment, and acumen of these ministerial employees.

CRAFTWORK AT THE BAKERY

Almost everyone in Jabal B knew Hani by name. Endlesssly good-humored and gregarious, he had been making bread in this neighborhood for more than twenty years. His bakery enjoyed the patronage of almost all those who lived nearby. The bakery's hours, open from early to late, boosted its popularity. So too did the quality of Hani's bread: fluffy but robust, supple without being feeble. Eaten warm, it was pure delight. A few hours, or even a day later, it was still satisfying.

Hani's bakery, *al-Khalil,* was small. The storefront measured two feet by six, with just enough space for a wooden table, on top of which sat a makeshift cash register and a scale. Here, Hani took orders and dispatched the subsidized bread after it was weighed. Just behind this small entryway was a long wooden table where freshly prepared *khubz arabi* was placed beneath a cloth to protect it against humidity and dust. And further back, behind that table, was the main bake-room. It contained one large, diesel-fired oven; a refrigerator; an oblique mixer; and a larger, marble-top table where dough was formed and shaped after being kneaded. Long, low-sided wooden trays were stacked in every corner of *al-Khalil.* On top of these trays, ball-sized slivers of dough rested and rose before eventually going into the oven. There was a small, narrow storeroom to the side of this bake-room where large flour sacks were kept, along with a few other baking supplies, tools, and the employees' personal belongings. The surface area of the entire bakery was 110 square meters, a stark contrast to larger outlets in the city, which could range anywhere from 250 to 500 square meters. The amount of capital invested was minimal. Tools were sparse—a rolling pin, flour scoop, dough scraper, and several knives. Electricity, Hani told me, had brought a few changes to the craft of baking he learned growing up: an oven powered by diesel, rather than wood, as well as the mechanized mixer.[50] He preferred the old days, when dough was kneaded by hand and yeast was not of the instant, commercial variety. Despite those few concessions to mechanization, he insisted that most processes be done manually. Machine-made bread was deemed inferior to loaves made with a baker's hands.

Hani spent most of the day on a swivel chair next to the cash register. He faced outwards and took charge of customer relations. The chair was also an observation tower, from which he could quickly pivot and appraise the bake-room in a single glance, barking out directions to his employees. After twenty years as an operator-owner, following an earlier twenty working in bakeries around the city during his youth, he no longer felt the need to make bread. Age had taken its toll. Hani's time and efforts were best spent elsewhere.

Al-Khalil sold only subsidized *khubz 'arabi*. Hani had neither the space required for nor any interest in preparing other, nonsubsidized wheat-based products. Local residents rarely purchased sweets, he had found. "And people like real bread in this neighborhood," he proudly declared, "none of that mech-anized garbage you see in West Amman" (the wealthier side of the capital). Producing handmade bread rather than the automated variety sold by an increasing number of Jordan's bakeries was not a maneuver meant to improve his market position. Nor was it a way of boosting revenues. Subsidized bread had to be sold at exactly the same price no matter how you made it; less labor, fewer errors, and more profit came with mechanization, once you had made back your initial investment. Hani preferred handmade bread because he be-lieved in a praxis contrary to that of industrial production, one generated by a distinct set of values and epitomized in the material qualities of his bread. "The loaf has to have a bit of fluff but not become doughy," he relayed. "Good bread is soft and slightly chewy, strong enough for a sandwich but also light enough to use for *mezze*" (appetizers, usually in the form of dips). A fluffy interior and a slightly charred crust were also key, a clear contrast to the thinner, more paper-like versions rolled out and baked by machines.

Converted, committed, or coerced, Hani's employees had imbibed his ap-preciation for non-mechanized bread. They saw subsidized bread as far more than just fuel for the body; taste and enjoyment mattered. The division of labor at the bakery further fueled such attachments. Unlike at larger, mechanized bakeries, all six employees "baked." That is to say, there was no rigid division of responsibilities. All laborers rotated through different tasks during the workday. While there was some flexibility in response to illness, fatigue, or emergency, the bakery was much more like a workshop than like Amman's larger bakeries. In those bakeries, each employee had circumscribed tasks. There tended to be a strict chain of command, where authority was based on employment status rather than skill. At *al-Khalil*, authority was not set down on paper. The "right to command" was established "in the flesh," afforded to those whose skills were recognized by all, rather than by a rigid organizational hierarchy.[51] Three of the bakers, the *mu'allimin* (masters, or senior craftsmen), had been at Hani's for more than a decade. Their orders were not questioned; their advice was always heeded. Three others had been at the bakery for shorter lengths of time, but none of them for less than a year when I arrived. Hani agreed to let me join the bakery as an observer under the condition that I work like everyone else, an "exchange of toil for ethnographic knowledge."[52] This was not as odd as it might seem, given how learning at these non-mechanized bakeries tended to function. Apprentices often provided heavily discounted labor during their training period, which could last anywhere from a week to a year, depending on prior experience.

Hussein was assigned to be my tutor. We would share shifts during my entire three months working at *al-Khalil*. His family is from Nablus, but he was born in Amman and has worked with Hani for nearly fifteen years. At about six foot three, Hussein towered over me. He had impressive biceps and triceps, honed from years of kneading and working the peel with which we inserted dough into the oven. He also had large breasts and a protruding belly, nurtured by his love of chocolate and sugary tea.

Apprentices, as I would soon learn, usually worked with master bakers and completed the same assignments. Occasionally, the easier but more physically onerous tasks (cleaning, stacking, transferring) were given to the recent arrivals, but for the most part, apprenticeship was rather literally a trial by fire. There were practical considerations that made it so: a small bake-room meant that there was no ancillary space for onlookers—present bodies had to be laboring ones. But more important were pedagogical concerns. Immersion was key. Working with a specific baker and rotating among different tasks plunged the novice into the craft. In the short term, it allowed the tutor to demonstrate the proper preparation and handling of materials and machinery. Mistakes could be rapidly corrected; none would become so large or consequential that it affected the bakery's operations or profit margin. In the long run, it was hoped, apprenticeship would instill a certain rhythm into the new baker's movements, along with a respect for the tempos and disciplines of life as a baker. The latter two were important, for to become a bread-maker at an outlet such as Hani's required a certain regularity of life. Except for Fridays, work started every day at four thirty in the morning, only ending at nine at night. Replacements were not readily available, so absenteeism, which Hani did not tolerate for very long in any case, punctured the entire flow of the workplace. Employment at this bakery required chronic stability and temporal balance, conditions that could rarely take root among those at the threshold of secure socioeconomic integration. Without exception, bakers at *al-Khalil* earned slightly more than the vast majority of the precarious customers they served. To be sure, the jobs were low-paying and offered little in the way of formal security. Many of the bakers had spouses who also worked. Others "hustled" in different ways to make ends meet. Yet theirs was not the insecurity of the new capitalism of flexible workers, nor was it the precarity of Amman's swelling un- or underemployed masses. These bakers made reliable wages that placed them in a position just above poverty. Nevertheless, if it had only been about financial remuneration, my workmates often told me defiantly, they would have gone to work in a five-star hotel. For these men, baking was a vocation in which they took pride, confident that they were meant to do this, and nothing else, with their lives.

LABORING WITH INGREDIENTS

Khubz 'arabi is made from a mixture of flour, water, salt, sugar, and yeast. Every day, the dough was made almost immediately upon the employees' arrival. First, they proofed the instant yeast by mixing it with a cup of warm water and sugar. In ten to fifteen minutes, the yeast would begin to foam and bubble. At the same time, flour and water were added into the mechanized mixer. After these were briefly mixed in, it was time to scoop in some salt and another pinch of sugar. Then the proofed yeast and a bit more water were added to the mixer. The ingredients were kneaded at a low speed for five minutes, then at medium-high for another ten to fifteen. The speed and duration of this process were a bone of contention among connoisseurs; haste and the wrong pace can destroy the dough. At *al-Khalil*, a vague recipe existed, taped to the wall in the storeroom. I studied it attentively during my first week, but quickly realized that no one heeded what was written on this piece of paper. More important than the recipe was a grasp of how the dough should look and feel. Despite MOITS's attempts to standardize the flour, different kinds of wheat have different qualities, even when milled at the same extraction rate. The "better" the wheat, for example, the more absorbent and permeable the flour, so that slightly less yeast is necessary. In response to this variation, bakers must adjust their recipes ever so slightly, usually by adding or subtracting water. Too much water and the dough becomes soggy and sticky; too little and it becomes compact and inelastic. The dough has to be resistant to separation; it should not stick to your hands. Temperature also makes a difference. It takes longer for the dough to rise in cold weather, so a bit more yeast is added in winter than in summer. I found all of this frustrating, expecting the recipe to offer precise instructions rather than a vague outline. But the people around me, in contrast, embraced this uncertainty and even celebrated it. Sure, there were scales and measuring cups somewhere in the storage room, but these tools were viewed with disdain. Good dough, I was told any number of times, was not the result of the mechanical implementation of a recipe. That would require inert substances.

At *al-Khalil,* dough is made three or four times per day, depending on demand. Two bakers complete the procedure, once just before five in the morning and once again at nine, then again at one and five in the afternoon. An "experienced hand" (*il-iyyd libta'rif*) is crucial. The more experienced baker always takes the lead in making the mixture. Day after day, for almost my entire three-month stay, Hussein would unendingly repeat the same mantra when we turned off the flour mixer: "Touch the dough, feel the dough." The ideal dough (see figure 2) was pliable, moist without being wet, so that it "kneads well" (*ya'ajn mnih*). Sometimes this was visible to the eye, but on plenty of occasions I was fooled. Dough preparation tests the baker's sense of touch, his ability to "read" with his hands. The bakers knew that the properties of flour and yeast change as they interact. Timing was also crucial. If the mix was not corrected quickly and the mixer continued to do its work, the dough would

FIGURE 2. Dough, minutes before it is ready.

FIGURE 3. My first attempts at shaping dough.

weaken as the fermentation lost its force. Flour and yeast, water and salt, are dynamic, unstable ingredients in constant motion. The bakers always had to remain attentive to the multiple ways they could combine and associate in the mixer, because their agency could only be determined through their "intra-action."[53] An apprentice had to gain a "feeling for the dough, as if it were a living creature," Hussein told me, only then could "one develop the ability to speak with the dough." To make dough, one had to understand what the ingredients could *do*, rather than determining what they *are*, in order to be able to collaborate more productively with them.

I struggled throughout my first weeks of work, sluggishly making it through the most basic set of tasks—stacking flour sacks, amassing ingredients, and then operating the mixer. I nodded when told what amounts of the different ingredients to collect, and agreed when told never to make dough without someone else nearby. By six thirty in the morning, the dough had completed its first fermentation. The bake-room was sweltering. I was not yet used to the heat generated by the oven, whose flame had to be lit twenty to thirty minutes ahead of time so that it could gather warmth. Six of us were inside the bake-room, while one worker helped Hani dispatch bread at the storefront. After the dough had rested, the first fermentation being vital to the development of aroma and dough elasticity, two bakers would shape and form it. One worker was charged with preparing and moving around the trays onto which the dough was placed. One worked the oven. Another moved the prepared *khubz 'arabi* from oven to storefront, shuffling back and forth. After our shift making dough, which was then given time to ferment and rise, Hussein and I formed it into balls, a procedure that is now mechanized in most bakeries. Before we began, we washed our hands, after which Hussein called upon God for his blessing (*bismAllah*). Then we dried our hands, took a pinch of flour between a thumb and two fingers, and flicked it across the counter, using our wrists. We needed just the right amount: too much flour and the dough would toughen, too little and it would stick to the surface. After this dusting of flour, we each took portions of dough from the large bowl attached to the flour mixer, using a dough scraper, and placed them on a marble tabletop. Then, we pinched out fifteen small pieces of dough and formed each piece into a tight ball, slightly larger than an apricot. We shaped the balls with our palms by rolling the unformed dough against the marble counter in a circular

FIGURE 4. Hussein shaping dough and having a laugh at my shoddy work.

FIGURE 5. Improvements.

motion, using a cupped hand. This process was supposed to take a matter of seconds, the size of each dough ball gauged by using one's hand as a measure. My first attempts were an abject failure, recorded by Hussein for comic relief (see figure 3). After I had completed several unsuccessful rounds, Hussein cheerfully pointed out the flaws in my form and described the deformations they would inevitably cause (see figure 4). Indicating that I should observe, he then rolled the dough into balls over and over again, patiently demonstrating how I should position my palms. I continued to make misshapen balls for my entire first week, using my fingers to shape the dough rather than letting my palms do the work. Hussein adjusted my hands on several occasions, and over the course of the following weeks, I slowly developed a "feel for the game."[54] By the end of the month, my dough balls start to look decent. Hussein no longer needed to reshape them (figure 5).

The fifteen equally sized pieces were then placed on a wooden tray, where they were allowed to rise for anywhere from twenty to thirty minutes—a second fermentation that was vital to the bread's volume. We filled two trays per minute, so that between forty and sixty trays were stacked in the various corners of the bakery by the time the first dough balls had doubled in size. Next, we had to flatten the dough balls in preparation for their time in the oven. To flatten, fold, and form them, you had to use back, shoulders, fingers, and wrists. Hussein, again, demonstrated. The thumb supported the dough ball while the other fingertips flattened its edges in nine or ten quick vertical, downward movements. Then we flipped the dough and did the same to the other side. The dough had to be uniformly flat and thin; thick edges would result in a chunky texture. A rolling pin was rarely used. Hands were the tool of choice. Once it was flattened, we passed the resulting disk from one hand to another to stretch and squeeze the dough further. On more than one occasion, my dough completely fell apart because I underestimated how pliable it had become. My hands were not literate. The art of stopping at the right moment eluded me. This step was difficult and taxing: arms and shoulders had to repeatedly stretch forward and move back, with little pause. Good posture was key; a sunken chest would only cause further fatigue. Hussein told me to use my hands, to focus on my hands. It was not that the rest of the body was completely static, but that it acted as a platform. "Move your hands, not your body" (*harrak iyydak mash jismak*), he repeated, so that I could maintain good posture and focus my attention on the rolling and stretching. But my hands lacked dexterity; they were not as agile as Hussein's. I also was not sure when the dough was at the appropriate thickness. I messed this step up often, and the results were disastrous. The dough needed to be almost paper-thin, its surface smooth and continuous, so that the oven's heat could quickly penetrate its center. My dough was almost always too thick. In the oven, these loaves got firm before heat reached their center. The resulting *khubz ʿarabi* lacked the characteristic puff: the core was far too chewy, almost inedible. On more than a few occasions, I paid Hani for the thirty to forty loaves we had to throw away because of my mistakes.

Once the dough was stretched appropriately, the soon-to-be loaves were placed first on another set of trays to rest, and then on the wooden peel that was used to insert and withdraw them from the oven. Timing was key. If the dough was not put in the oven within half an hour, it would over-ripen, resulting in slightly sour loaves. The optimum temperature of the oven is somewhere between 425 and 450 degrees Celsius. To determine when it was ready, Hussein would take a pinch of flour and fling it onto the floor of the oven. If the flour stayed white, the over was not hot enough. If it darkened and burned, the oven was already too hot, meaning that the diesel-powered flame needed to be turned down. Only when the sprinkle of flour turned golden, darkening very slowly, was the oven just right. The first round of baking, when the first loaves entered the oven in the morning, was the most chaotic moment of the day. There was minimal time for deliberation. The first customers would arrive soon, and many more were on the way.

After checking the temperature, the baker inserted the dormant loaves into the oven, where they only needed a short blast before they rose. The wooden peel held six disks of what would soon become *khubz ʿarabi*. Insertion required lifting the peel and holding it at a proper height, introducing it into the oven slowly but with a steady hand. Then, you released the six disks of dough onto the oven floor with a quick jerk, placing them strategically so as to take best advantage of the heat.

I had been instructed on how to complete each of these steps before my first attempts, undertaken at night so as to avoid causing a morning logjam. But the wooden peel was thick and heavy. My triceps and wrists were not quite strong enough to manage it deftly. I lifted the peel sluggishly and moved it towards the oven awkwardly. I was too slow. The dough stuck to the peel because I took too long to insert it into the oven, as the flour used for dusting had absorbed some of the dough's water content. Another time, I shook the dough off the end of the peel, rather than giving it a skillful jerk. Only the ends of the dough caught the oven floor, so what when I pulled the peel back, other bits and pieces fell to the floor, permanently separated from the disheveled loaves now baking at high heat. For about twenty days, my stints at the oven were consistently a disaster. Thankfully, the stakes were low; the evening rush hour had already passed. On most nights, when there was a spare moment, Hussein watched my mishaps and then took the peel from my hand. He grunted, indicating that I should watch. Hussein placed six disks of dough onto the peel, with barely a centimeter between them but ensuring they did not touch. He inserted the wooden tool into the oven, jerking precisely using triceps and wrists, and depositing the bread. I watched as the dough puffed up. Less than two minutes later, he reinserted the peel, scooped up the bread, and gave it a quick final whirl around the oven to add a touch of crispness, before removing the loaves, all in one graceful movement. Hussein did this again and again, with dexterity and elegance. He offered very little in the way of verbal instruction. *"Bas shuf kayf,"* (just watch how), he would repeat, *"bas shuf"* (just watch).

About two weeks and many destroyed loaves into my apprenticeship, I took the peel and tried to lift it just above my belly button, the ideal position given my height. I then tried jerking, over and over again, for a good ten minutes, with no dough on the peel, just as practice. Hussein watched and then ambled over. His burly arms grabbed mine and he guided me through the process quickly, four or five times. We then put dough on the peel. He made minor adjustments to my movements, motioned to jerk quicker or ensure that my torso was rigid, but he always returned to the process as whole. "Feel the peel, concentrate on the peel," Hussein repeated.

Sure enough, a brief glance at my fingers to confirm they were correctly placed or a quick shift to ensure my abdomen was properly squared would inevitably lead to failure. My focus had to be on the peel. Hussein's instructions aimed to bring certain tools into my "focal awareness" to improve my use of them.[55] But then, I was always urged to focus on the larger process at hand, to allow tools and techniques to return to the background of my conscious. Arms and posture were not important, the peel was. In her evocative ethnography of glassblowing, Erin O'Connor terms this process of learning by watching and doing the "defining exercise of apprenticeship," where the trainee fashions their practices by explicitly considering the bodily techniques of the trainer.[56]

After watching Hussein, I improved and realigned, learning through guided rediscovery, before these lessons could recede into their proper place in the unconscious, forever influencing my still nascent baking habitus.[57] I improved once I realized that strict imitation always failed, because our bodies were different. Our strengths and weaknesses were not the same. I could not mechanically reproduce Hussein's gestures but had to work instead to inculcate myself with and incorporate a set of skills, a "practical mimesis" rather than the reproduction of gestures "explicitly constituted as a model."[58] Language was rarely of use in this learning process, as Hussein steered me through the entire bread-making cycle with barely a word, relying on gestures and nods, grunts and shrugs. It was only through repetition that I began to fine-tune my own movements, to develop a "corporeal comprehension" that allowed me to approach the rhythmic fluency of the accomplished craftsman who taught me.[59]

I never did become adroit at using the peel. Hussein could talk, smoke a cigarette, and send a humorous text message while he worked the oven. But over the following weeks, I became proficient. My triceps and wrist became stronger, as did my torso. Crucially, I learned how to incorporate the tool into a regular pattern of bodily movement. The peel was heavy, and my initial inclination was to hold it tightly to prevent it from falling or escaping my grasp. But I learned to loosen my grip and let the weight of the wooden tool guide me. I established a silent complicity with the peel, slowly grasping the combination of force and release required to insert the dough adeptly—and I lost fewer and fewer loaves because of overly brusque motions. The peel stopped being an inert tool that I manipulated and became instead an extension of my body, or "sensori-motor apparatus."[60] Phenomenologists have long spoken about this process of mutual incorporation, where an instrument comes to be felt as part of the body, blurring the distinction between the two. In reference to a blind person who uses a stick to navigate his local surroundings, Merleau-Ponty notes that over time, the instrument "has ceased to be an object for him, and is no longer perceived for itself; its point has become an arena of sensitivity, extending the scope and active radius of touch, and providing a parallel to sight."[61] It is only when this affiliation had occurred that I began to handle the peel properly, assimilating it to my body so that we became entwined, our boundaries permeable and enmeshed.

Loaves had to be removed from the oven just as carefully. Failure to scoop them up correctly would result in splitting or burning them on account of the additional time spent in the oven. While I had less trouble with the peel during this step, since the loaves were now robust and easier to gather, I could never quite tell when they were done. The color of the bread had to be just right, its crust exposed to the fire for just enough time to have become ever so slightly charred. Baking here was treacherous mainly because one could not remove the bread to check on its progress. Once withdrawn, the bread could not be reinserted without causing damage to its crumb and crust. This happened occasionally, a bad set of loaves mixed in with good ones, but it could not be allowed to occur often. Working the oven during rush hour was almost always the responsibility of one of the three *mu'allimin*, while those with less experience were relegated to times when there was less at stake. It was during these latter times that I got the most instruction. As with the other steps, Hussein would demonstrate and observe, rarely speaking, more often simply displaying how to remove loaves from the oven in one fell swoop. He reminded me to focus on the peel, before returning to the larger task at hand—gathering the loaves of bread. It was only when I stopped thinking of these tasks as a set of successive stages while helming the oven that I became adept, if only barely. Hands and eyes, as well as peel, had to be incorporated into a regular pattern of nimble actions. I realized that baking proficiently was not a matter of linking together a series of actions. Whereas the novice tended to proceed step by step, the experienced baker always worked through the process as a whole: steps were never just an end in themselves. It was only when I stopped pondering each single step that the transfer of dough from peel to oven and its subsequent withdrawal ceased to look funny and feel clumsy. The practice took on a *"lived* character"; it became a "graceful extended movement, an arc of embodied techniques."[62] Well, maybe not graceful, but proficient enough that my workmates no longer laughed or became palpably nervous when it was my turn at the oven. And this took time and repetition. To my chagrin, successful baking was not the result of an isolated mind, slowly thinking through and remembering each step of the process. Theoretical mastery of instructions or recipes was considered of such little use that they were barely employed by those who taught me. Much like inspection, the craft of baking can never be fully captured through a set of rules or instructions. Proficiency only occurs when the apprentice baker begins to acclimate his movements to the tools and materials around him, anticipating perturbations without disrupting the steady flow of action.[63]

To learn how to bake, like learning to box, is to "imperceptibly modify one's bodily schema" so that it becomes accustomed to a different set of uses, postures, and gestures, which slowly become crystallized in fragile but embodied forms of knowledge.[64] Like inspection, it is a craft, and one best learned through apprenticeship, where rules and recipes matter far less than learning how to see, smell, touch, and move. By busying myself with daily activities at the bakery—learning how to add just enough cold water to make the dough soft but not soggy, rolling and stretching it so it would be pliable but not defeated, removing the bread just before its edges became scorched rather than charred—I ascertained how to use my body in ways that were previously unfamiliar yet slowly became habitual. But (state)craft at the bakery was not just about developing proficiency in certain bodily techniques. It also required attuning oneself to the ingredients, tools, and machinery that make bread, and the innumerable ways they can intra-act. Learning the fixed properties of independent objects was of little use. Because recipes and instructions were "at best a faint map of the process," visual, auditory, and tactile cues were vital.[65] The bakers at *al-Khalil* coupled their movements and gestures to anticipate, extemporize, and manage the whims of fire and flour, diesel and dough. They did not stand outside the world, as experts or technicians, but were imbricated with the world's becoming, their dexterity emerging out of many years of sensory engagement with materials and tools.[66]

The craftwork crucial to assembling the state requires bodily training; this seems obvious enough. But it does not end there. It also demands adeptness with and respect for vibrant matter—laborers with an ability to negotiate and work alongside the vast array of nonhumans that contribute to baking bread.

OF MACHINES AND MEN

Al-Rif was a large bakery, almost 300 square meters, about triple the size of *al-Khalil*. Upon entering the bakery, one would find biscuits and Arabic sweets amassed on several shelves to the right. On the left were various racks holding different varieties of nonsubsidized bread. A counter with a cash register and scale lay straight ahead, at the far end of the retail space. The counter was positioned about two feet in front of an eight-foot-high partition, which did not reach the ceiling. Just above this partition there was a metal slide, from which *khubz 'arabi* descended to the storefront at various times of the day. Either Hamza, the owner, or one of his two managers operated the cash register, while another employee bagged the newly baked subsidized bread and weighed out customer orders. Behind the partition lay the bake-room, up half a floor. Here one could find five employees, each at a particular station in the production line. One man worked primarily with flour, moving sacks and feeding the mixer that makes dough for different products. Two workers made sweets or different types of nonsubsidized bread, sculpting dough into a variety of shapes and sizes. Another supervised the automated oven in which nonsubsidized products were baked, lending a hand at other stations when needed. The fifth oversaw the automated bread machine that pumped out *khubz 'arabi* at a pace of thirty loaves, or five kilograms, a minute. The machine was mesmerizing. It had been made to order for *al-Rif* by a local manufacturer based in the outskirts of Amman and measured some twenty feet long and eight feet high. Its dimensions exploited every last bit of space in the bake-room. Similar contraptions populate most of the country's larger bakeries. At first they were imported from Lebanon, Greece, and the Gulf, but in the past twenty years a handful of Jordanian manufacturers have emerged. Because they are closer at hand, they can custom-make their wares and service them much more rapidly than foreign manufacturers could. Ranging in cost anywhere from five to fifty thousand dollars, the machines bring obvious advantages. More bread can be produced in a shorter time span, as the owners are no longer hostages to lengthy fermentation. No employees are required to stretch, shape, or fold the dough. Mistakes made by bakers manning the oven are minimized. Overall, mechanized bread-makers bring lower labor costs, increased production, and more time to spend on products with higher margins. They aid intensification, allowing capital to enter the labor process far more pervasively than it could in bakeries that make bread mostly by hand.

Al-Rif was emblematic of shifts in Jordan's bakery business, many of which began in the mid-1990s. An influx of capital from Palestinians who had been expelled from Kuwait at the beginning of the decade quickly trickled down from real estate into consumer services. Amman saw an expansion in shopping malls and clothing stores, restaurants and cafés. Jabal C, where *al-Rif* is located, was witness to these trends. The district began as an extension of a nearby Palestinian refugee camp in the 1950s, but in the past thirty years, it has steadily expanded, becoming a bustling commercial hub populated by mostly middle-class residents.

Al-Rif's owner, Hamza, was born and went to school in the district. He opened the bakery in 2000 with the aid of an investment from his brother, an engineer who had returned from Kuwait nearly ten years earlier. Hamza was more businessman than baker. He had a degree in accounting and had tried his hand at several businesses, ranging from corner store to fruit stand and mobile phone shop, before opening *al-Rif.* Like other large bakery owners, he purchased an automated bread-maker to ensure consistency and boost profits. Yet Hamza had come to appreciate the bread business for reasons beyond mere earnings. He acknowledged the sustenance that subsidized bread provided and the socialities it undergirded. He frequently used the Egyptian term for bread, *'ayish* (life), to emphasize how the foodstuff both represents life and gives it. The bakery was simply not like other businesses, Hamza would emphasize, because bread was an anchor of subsistence for the resident community. While *al-Rif*'s profits were largely driven by the trade in sweets, subsidized bread still needed to be appetizing, if not exactly delicious. Commodification had not diminished bread's material or social significance. If anything, that significance had deepened because of bread's relatively low price in comparison to other goods. As one of the managers of *al-Rif* explained, "Bread is not like other foods; people eat it with every meal. In this neighborhood, there are many places people can choose to buy bread. If our product is not good, most people will go elsewhere. We try to keep our standards high, so that people know they can rely on our product, so they know we care for our customers."

Machine-made *khubz 'arabi* is rarely as good as the handmade version, though; it lacks that pillowy fluff in the center; the crust is never charred; and it is far too thin, almost paper-like. The crust and crumb are white, and aromas and flavors are almost nonexistent. Quantity and yield take precedence over quality. But what it lacks in taste and texture it makes up for in uniformity and consistency, or so many bakery owners argue. In addition, advances in the past decade mean that the differences between handmade and mechanized bread are becoming harder to detect. Craftsmen always know the difference, as do certain lovers and cognoscenti of bread, but bread made with good machinery can come increasingly close. At *al-Rif*, quality bread did not emerge from hands-on apprenticeship. New employees required little in the way of training or instruction. Instead, quality assurance required nurturing, nourishing, and repairing the machines.

The bake-room was hot, but the heat was not sweltering. There was no open flame, just a contained steam oven and the larger automated *khubz 'arabi* machine. Yet the bakery lacked adequate ventilation, and the air was thick with a distinct perfume—flour and dust, a tinge of diesel. Banter abounded, and the younger workers were subject to a fair share of derision, mostly playful. The jokes and chitchat were routinely punctuated with orders and instructions. On my first day, just like on every other day for the next three months, each laborer dutifully played his part in the production line. The work itself was as cheerless as the choking humidity that consumed the bake-room.

Al-Rif's employees were a mix of new and old, including a few migrants from Egypt and a handful of Jordanians from poorer parts of East Amman. There was substantial turnover because the job paid little and the competencies required were quickly learned; the capacity to work hard and obey authority was what Hamza, the owner, valued most. Salaries were the same for all—low. The division of labor was strict and uncompromising. Every worker in the bake-room was an equal; each had a circumscribed task, repeated *ad nauseam* during his eight-hour shift. On good days, we reached a working consensus whereby each employee shifted and responded to the machines and humans that surrounded him. What seemed at first a random jumble of activities I later realized to be, on a good day, a synchronized set of collaborations. The instant a particular step was finished, the following one was already being taken up. When one person accelerated or slowed down, everyone else had to respond. Soon, discrete tasks in the bake-room dissolved into a routinized, mirage-like blur.

My job at al-Rif, most days, was to move flour sacks to the mixer and then feed the *khubz 'arabi* machine with the prepared dough. Occasionally, I got to oversee the automated bread-maker. The size and weight of each loaf were determined with a touch of the button at the control board. After the measurements were set, the prepared dough was fed into a funnel, which descended into the forming section of the machine. Here the dough was divided into

FIGURE 6. Formed dough heading towards the preliminary proofer.

equally rounded disks. The dough then went to a preliminary proofer (see figure 6): the disks arriving from the divider on a conveyor belt traveled swiftly through a plastic-sided tunnel, where the fermentation action of the yeast was accelerated. The dough was then formed by two rolling contraptions that quickly flattened the portioned pieces by trundling them rapidly in perpendicular directions. Once flattened, the loaves were ready for a last proof, the final step in the accelerated fermentation process. It was here that most of the flavor disappeared, as the machine hastily recreated the folding, rolling, stretching, and resting of the dough that took nearly an hour at *al-Khalil*. Next, the bread traveled through a tunnel oven, which radiated heat evenly. The baked loaves then went onto a multi-tiered cooling conveyor belt, which rapidly reduced their temperature (see figure 7). After two minutes of this re-sweating, where the bread released water vapor, the loaves descended a stainless-steel slide and arrived just behind *al-Rif*'s cash register, where they were packed and prepared for sale (see figure 8).

On almost all of my shifts, Adnan oversaw the *khubz 'arabi* machine. His responsibilities were numerous. The most important ones, he told me, were

FIGURE 7. Baked loaves on the multi-tiered cooling conveyor belt.

aimed at what he described as "keeping the machine happy." Adnan relentlessly walked around the contraption and barely ever stood still (see figure 9). He was on the constant lookout for logjams caused by remnants of dough that had not been fully proofed or flattened. He also had to oversee the diesel-powered tunnel oven, keeping it well-fueled and ensuring that it was ready to go when the dough entered the machine. But most of his time was spent pacing around the conveyor cooling system, where prepared loaves rested and diminished in temperature before descending to the storefront. Besides ensuring that the contraption did not get jammed, Adnan functioned as the last line of quality assurance. He quickly picked out loaves he deemed inferior due to discoloration, burns, or condensation and put them into a separate pile

FIGURE 8. Bread descending from a stainless-steel slide, being packed and prepared for sale.

that would eventually become animal feed. After my time at *al-Khalil*, however, I was amazed at how circumscribed Adnan's responsibilities and skills were. He could not operate the flour mixer and struggled to make biscuits and baguettes on the few occasions he was given this job. The mechanization of tools and processes had introduced a division of tasks more reminiscent of a Fordist factory.

Frequently flushed and sweaty, Adnan tended to look forlorn, like a pale mannequin covered with flour and sweat. Like his colleagues, he was not particularly invested in the craft of baking. The job seemed to have chosen the workers at *al-Rif*, rather than the other way around. I was particularly struck by Adnan's indifference to and lack of familiarity with the baking process. He could not explain how either the automated oven or the proofing worked, nor was he interested. Adnan simply fed the appliance with the necessary ingredients, which were then transformed by the push of a button. He seemed to understand what made the machine "angry," and had devised various strategies to prevent

FIGURE 9. Adnan monitoring the automatic bread-maker.

mishaps and shutdowns—keep the conveyor belt oiled, the rolling machine greased, the entire contraption clean and dust-free. But even when it was I who on occasion oversaw the automated bread-maker, its consistency was impressive. Only rarely did I pick out a loaf that had been burnt or misshapen. I was, like those around me, a largely unskilled bystander, superseded by a machine that had taken the place of embodied knowledges. The very ease with which Adnan or I could be replaced points to the anonymity of the bread production at *al-Rif*. As I was told by the owner when I first began my apprenticeship, "Anyone can do the job; you just need to pay attention and work hard." Training was uneven and staff turnover comparatively high. Replacements, whether permanent or just for a day, were pretty easy to find. Yet still, the baking process did not always proceed as planned. The automated oven, rollers, and proofing machines had their own "agency of material things."[67]

Al-Rif's *khubz 'arabi* maker was fifteen years old, built when Hamza first opened the bakery in 2000. On two occasions during my apprenticeship, different parts of the device complained loudly and then shut off entirely. Each time, minutes before this occurred, Adnan knew something was wrong, as did the shift manager. Yet neither had any idea how to ameliorate the problem, despite their ability to anticipate it.

"The machine has a mind of its own," Adnan told me after the contraption had croaked one afternoon. "I try to keep it happy, but it doesn't always listen."

Each time, repairmen arrived swiftly the same evening. They offered little in the way of explanation; I assumed that the demands of a sixteen-hour workday took their toll on human and machine alike. But slowly they brought the automated bread-maker back to life, prodding, pushing, and oiling different parts until the machine eventually revived. When only one or two separate components of this bread-maker worked, it was useless. Much like the electrical power grid explored by Jane Bennett, the bread maker was "a material cluster of charged parts that have indeed affiliated."[68] It was only when the entire machine was mended, when humans and nonhumans worked in sufficient proximity and coordination, that subsidized bread could be made again. The workers at *al-Rif* were powerless to submit the world to their intentions; they remained reliant on a set of interactions that exceeded their grasp. Through sporadic interventions in an overwhelmingly automated process, they strove to guarantee that their subsidized bread would be neither mushy nor moist, neither misshapen nor burnt. Aside from those who made the sweet Arabic pastries, which remained the jurisdiction of highly specialized practitioners, electric appliances had imposed their logic on these bakers' bodily techniques, the ways in which their labor was organized and executed. While at *al-Khalil*, embodied knowledge prevailed, at *al-Rif* this know-how had been supplanted. The rules, techniques, and formulas required to operate the different appliances reigned supreme. Detailed recipes had largely replaced a feel for the dough; automated proofing had superseded stretching and forming with one's hands; an eye for the oven had been swapped out for fully automated cooking times and temperatures, lest any errors be made. Baking procedures were handed down by way of written axioms and verbal instructions, rather than time-consuming apprenticeships. Capital and equipment were crucial to *al-Rif*'s operations, apprenticeship and skilled labor less so. Only the owner and two managers attended to the whole baking process, and that tenuously. Everyone else was a component, a cog in the machine.

It would be easy to mourn this shift, and I often did, irritated that so many bakery owners were choosing the ease and profits of automation over the joys and exigencies of handmade *khubz 'arabi*. But then, maybe baking is not, nor was it ever, a fixed craft. Perhaps humans are simply moving from the center to the periphery of the bread-making process. Yes, automation works to decrease errors and fatigue, even as it devours the exquisite and the ethereal. But then maybe toil and imprecision are the deities of those like myself who are privileged enough to labor only occasionally and to choose when and what they wish to eat. Whereas handmade *khubz 'arabi* relies on the magnetism of its freshness and flavor, industrialized versions of the staple entice through their claim to reliability and uniformity. The skills required at the two different bakeries vary, but in neither of them do bakers labor in isolation from matter or machines. While bread outlets differ dramatically depending on their investment and affluence, praxis and procedure, baking is everywhere a dynamic practice in which diverse types of bodily techniques, tacit knowledges, and fluency with technologies prove crucial to making bread. Facility with automated bread-makers matters more in some bakeries; the capacity to stretch, fold, and knead more in others. But baking is everywhere a collective action, one distributed among several people and things, in sequences of ordered acts that shape what bread comes to be. At *al-Khalil*, the size, burns, and texture of each loaf bore testimony to a set of individuals and to the skills and rhythms that characterized their work. At *al-Rif*, by contrast, each loaf demonstrated the commingled activities of designer, manufacturer, overseer, and machine, a "turbulent river of agencies" in which bakers were less central, but still key.[69] In neither bakery was agency an attribute of human beings alone. Matter, no less than men, could fail to act in the ways expected. Somewhere between symmetrical attachments to frenetic over-mechanization and purposeful deceleration lay the vast majority of Jordan's bread-makers, constantly wrestling with the bittersweet obstinance of men and machines, bakers and dough, flour and fire: day by day, loaf by loaf.

CONCLUSION

Bread in the Middle East is ascribed importance during moments of unrest, when it is adopted in slogans at a protest or amid the commotion of an uprising.

Surely, these moments of upheaval can tell us much about the dissatisfaction of citizens with the people and powers who rule them. They can also, for those looking closely, shed some light on the varied symbolisms of bread. But they cannot tell us about the day-to-day operations and alignments through which subsidized bread comes to be. And these processes matter, for performing the state is not a theatrical deed undertaken by a willful set of leaders, bakers, or bureaucrats. A reading that ignores these processes reintroduces the given-ness of the state (as well as of the liberal humanist subject) and seeks merely to unpack its construction. I refuse this prior existence and have therefore followed the flows of flour, wheat, and yeast to better explore just some of the practices through which the state, by way of bread, is assembled as a coherent entity. Statistics and data sets do a disservice to such dynamics; they reify unstable worlds and obviate the intra-actions required to make them congeal, if only briefly. Moreover, they erase precisely what is interesting about people and things: their lively, agentive nature. The consistent availability and uniform price of subsidized bread across the Hashemite Kingdom of Jordan conceals an extraordinary process of coordination, the result of ordinary people exercising practical skills and tacit knowledges so as to coax and tame a variety of things and processes into a form amenable to consumption. The state is not possible without them.

Much like water in Egypt, bread in Jordan is not "a given object of management" but is "made as a resource through daily practices."[70] As should be clear from the empirical focus of this chapter, I do not wish to supersede human actors entirely, nor portray the bread subsidy as the product of an interchangeable throng of actants, working as a machine. There are identifiable protagonists in this story. And while vibrant matter has a place in this account, I am hesitant to distract critical attention by positing a flattened cohabitation of all things. Without being completely determined by them, the government of matter does rely on humans, who retain a disproportionate ability to make, move, and manipulate things. Bread production and regulation can and occasionally do escape human control. But *khubz 'arabi* simply cannot be disaggregated from the people who maintain, manage, and enable its provision. Without collective intelligence, tacit knowledge, and embodied skill, subsidized bread would never come to be. Welfare provision requires not "enculturation but enskillment," gained through the active socialization of people in contexts of shared practice.[71] If we wish to explain the routine realization of certain welfare policies, we must home in on the efforts and exertions upon which all such services are built. Not just outcomes and results, which enter the fray far too late in the game, but the people and things at the heart of statecraft. For it is only when they affiliate that such associations produce the state as a palpable actor—and make it possible for it to be addressed as a coherent entity.

Part 2

ENTANGLEMENT

Chapter 4

ECHOES, ABSENCES, AND REACH

THE DAYS IN AMMAN were getting warmer, and my friend Basel told me we needed to stock up. Ramadan was not far off. The three bars we frequented would close down for a full month. You would still usually be able to find alcohol, but prices would be steep, and five-star hotels and illicit transactions were outside our price range. Basel was fond of a cold beer, a weakness I shared. That evening, he declared that we needed to go to Aqaba, and soon. "Aqaba," he giggled again and again with a smile, "Aqaba!"

I had been to Aqaba before, just for its beach and seafood, a relaxing few days away from the bustle of Amman. But I had missed out, Basel insisted. What was I doing in the port city without taking advantage of duty-free alcohol? Taxed at 180–200%, drinking in Amman was expensive. A six-pack cost the same as a week's worth of produce. But in Aqaba, cans of Jordanian-made Amstel beer were half-price, exempt from almost all of the excise duties collected elsewhere in the country. Between the two of us we could bring back twenty-four beers, Basel informed me—perhaps more, if we could convince others to tag along.

A few days later, we rented a car. The plan was to drive down and spend the weekend in Aqaba with two of Basel's childhood friends, who had recently moved there to work at one of the city's new luxury resorts. We both took Thursday off, I from the bakery, Basel from his office job, and left Amman early to allow for some stops along the way. Basel had grown up in the city of Karak. Most of his family had moved to Amman in the late 1990s, but some relatives still lived in Karak, unconvinced by the commotion of the capital. We stopped in to see some of his cousins around lunchtime. We exchanged pleasantries and gifts—Basel's mom had sent some homemade date cookies—and then sat down to a generous meal of *maqluba*, a heavy rice dish made with fried cauliflower, eggplant, poached chicken, and toasted pine nuts. The day was hot, lunch was overwhelming, and as our post-meal lethargy set in, the din of the electric fans soon became the only sound.

Later, once everyone was awake again, tea was served. The conversation soon turned, as it often did with Basel, to politics. His cousins said that a small protest was being planned to follow the next Friday prayer. The causes: unemployment, poverty, and a lack of government investment—themes that would inform the rest of our conversation. The cousins' grievances were quite different from those I was accustomed to hearing in Amman from Basel and his work colleagues at a foreign-funded NGO. Those professionals grumbled about high taxes, excessive regulations, and a repressive security apparatus. In Karak, however, it was not a surplus of state power, but rather its absence, that concerned the people I spoke with. The streets outside Karak's historic city center were riddled with potholes. The public schools were in shambles. There was nothing in Karak like Amman's vast third sector of international NGOs, UN agencies, and government subsidiaries. Finding employment, especially for those under thirty, was a constant struggle. Those who did have jobs in the public sector had not seen salary increases in any way commensurate with rises in the cost of living. Basel's cousins seemed to be able to cobble an income together, but the state did nowhere near enough. "We want more state, not less," one of the older cousins concluded. "We miss the days when the state cared for the people." To be cared for: an invocation, a plea, even a longing.

Back on the road, after that conversation, Basel and I still had a second stop to make. He had college classmates living in the city of Ma'an, and they had asked us to bring some books down from Amman. While we were driving, they called us to recommend that we avoid entering town. Instead, we agreed to meet at a roadside coffeeshop just past the city. As we passed the exit to Ma'an, Basel slowed. He was curious, as was I: why had his friends warned us away from the city center? We approached and saw two imposing tanks and several police cars. They seemed to be randomly stopping vehicles taking the exit for the city. "Tomorrow is Friday," Basel said, harkening back to our conversation in Karak—protests would fill Ma'an's main square following the weekly prayer.

A month earlier, the city had witnessed a week of violent clashes. While Jordan's security services, searched for wanted persons hiding out in Ma'an's Iskan neighborhood, local residents allegedly blocked their path, and then torched several government buildings. In response, the security services fired tear gas and made several arrests. Gunfire was exchanged. One civilian was allegedly shot and killed.[1] That April raid had been one of many over the preceding months, the resulting casualties (estimates ranged from five to ten) a carefully guarded secret the Hashemite regime has yet to acknowledge.

"They don't want anyone coming in with arms or fireworks or extremist paraphernalia," Basel told me as we drove by, "anything that could make the protest turn violent or cause it to appear in the news."

A few miles on, we arrived at the coffeeshop and waited for Basel's friends to arrive. Three of them arrived separately at the café, where we lingered. They had been hesitant to leave the city center in the same car. Young men in groups draw the police's attention, one of them told me uneasily. After greetings and life updates were exchanged, Basel asked if recent developments in Ma'an were as bad as the national news had portrayed. The town was a hub of extremism and criminality, the media often claimed. Ma'anis were consistently characterized as people of ill repute.[2]

"That's all bullshit" (*kulu haki fadi*), one of Basel's friends bellowed. "They make it seem like we are outlaws and drug traffickers, but every protest is about unemployment and police repression. All we ask for is jobs and opportunities, the same things they get in the capital."

More government, not less; attentiveness and care, rather than neglect and abandonment, they all seemed to say they wanted. "The problem is the state," another friend added, as the others nodded. "It wants to impose its authority but only through force. Where are the jobs and the services? All we want is to live a dignified life."

After a few more questions, Basel demurred, eager to get back on the road. "Ma'an is poor and ignored," he told me as we got into his car. "The rich can't make money there so the state doesn't give a shit about it, except when it [the city] revolts. Otherwise, they are happy to let Ma'an rot."

An hour later, still on the road, Basel woke me up from another nap. The drive that day had been long, and I had not drunk enough coffee. We were on the highway through Wadi al-Yatim, the principal route to the sea through Jordan's desert. "Get out your passport," Basel hollered, "and my car registration from the glove compartment. The checkpoint is coming up."

"Really?" I stammered, still unsure of how I had slept through the last portion of the drive.

"Yes, yes, we're almost in Aqaba," he cackled. "Get excited!"

The stop at the customs checkpoint was perfunctory. Basel smiled at the policeman, animatedly explaining that we were there for the weekend and eager to relax at the beach and swim in the Red Sea. The officer took a cursory look inside Basel's 2001 Toyota Camry, then quickly flicked through his car registration and my passport. "Welcome to Jordan," he declared in English, as he handed me back the documents and waved us through, gleefully uttering one of the Tourism Board's often-parroted slogans.

As I put my passport away and we began the descent to Aqaba's waterfront, I asked Basel why this checkpoint differed so much from the one we had driven past earlier, just outside Ma'an. He had seemed far less nervous, and I had not sensed any of the indignation that had poured out of him as we drove past the *Darak* (General Directorate of Gendarmerie) post on the Desert Highway. "That last checkpoint was about customs," he told me. "They're not worried about protest and extremism in Aqaba, just things like smuggling."

Skeptical, I brought up a few protests that acquaintances had mentioned, along with the threatened strikes by stevedores at the container terminals that had been headline news some months earlier. "That stuff always gets resolved quickly," Basel responded. "Aqaba is important, it's a tourist zone and has industry. There is money in the city. The state has to be kind here, it can't afford to be mean."

Many Aqabawis would probably disagree. The odd amalgam of police, gendarmerie, customs personnel, and Special Economic Zone Authority that governs city residents here has consistently demonstrated a willingness to be unpleasant, if not actively mean. However, I found Basel's observations illuminating because of how tersely they captured the varied interactions Jordanians have with state power, and the impressions and analyses that emerge in the process. Like his fellow citizens, Basel encounters the state through a variety of sites and practices[3]: hospitals and bakeries, checkpoints and customs checks, taxation and policing. Some work as expected; others do not; and a few arouse suspicion. But crucially and constantly, these encounters are a central means through which citizens imagine and evaluate the abstract body that ostensibly governs them.

Of course, such encounters vary; experiences are multiple and incongruous. The state may seem distant or nearby, effortful or effortless. Yet despite such diversity, or perhaps because of it, the state is still portrayed as "having a reality beyond its incoherence."[4] It is described and depicted as a tangible thing, one that *echoes* far beyond the centers of officialdom. As we purchased our first beers before setting off for the apartment where we were going to stay, Basel shot me a knowing smile. "Cheap, right?" He grinned. "The state does not tax us here. We can drink as much as we like."

TOPOLOGICAL TWISTS

In this chapter I leave the capital in order to consider how subsidized bread *echoes* in places where centralized institutions do not uniformly *reach*. After tracing transformations in Jordan's architecture of governance, I explore why bread matters amid this ever-shifting morass. Despite their many differences, Aqaba and Ma'an make plain how state power in Jordan does not function equally nor coherently across an even landscape. Instead, there are sporadic assertions of authority, planned exceptions to government regulations, and countless sites where the Jordanian state apparatus simply does not extend, or where it prefers not to appear. Sometimes, far-reaching goals confront limited means. Other times, the humans and things upon which governmental practices rely do not act as expected. Occasionally, everything goes to plan. Nevertheless, no matter the case, state power is an intermittent force. For the most part, however, the subfield of comparative politics lacks the tools through which to examine these prosaic geographies of presence and absence, and the routine interactions that illuminate them. Far too often, the state is portrayed as a static spatial entity, a self-enclosed unit with sovereign power that hovers above national territory as a behemoth.[5] On the rare occasions when the state is disaggregated, it is to focus on organizations, institutions, and structures that operate below the national level.[6] Such works have recently unearthed the uneven capacities of state institutions and have delved into some of the substantive outcomes that emerge due to such spatial disjunctures.[7] Yet the overwhelmingly positivist bent of this literature leads it to assume the state. It does not set out to explain it. Whatever the pro forma contentions to the contrary, the objective of such scholarship is to find the best ways to measure the state's power, to calculate its ability to implement policy or determine whether it is weak or strong, failing or collapsed. More than just uninteresting, such questions distract from more penetrating considerations of how political authority forms and echoes with, through, and throughout space.

States come with territory. They strive to dominate it, control it, extend their power over it—or so we are told. In order for that to happen successfully, political authority is frequently delegated or disseminated, flowing down from a central institution to regional, municipal, and other governmental bodies. Sometimes these scales are rigid, their boundaries fixed, the precise extension of authority within and between them easily drawn. Other times, the scales are slightly relaxed, usually when their mutability becomes undeniable— multi-scalar, interdependent, or multicentric tend to be the keywords here.[8] But in either case, state power travels upwards or downwards, maybe even sideways. It is exercised in deceptively coherent ways, over and through spaces that are nothing but surface, in what John Allen describes as an all-too-easy geometry.[9] Yet if we can acknowledge proliferating sites of authority, shifting boundaries of influence, and fluctuating governance regimes, then maybe the state is not a hierarchical entity whose power spreads (or fails to do so) over a static national territory. Perhaps we should examine how the state "comes to assume its vertical position as the supreme authority"[10] and do so without assuming fixed distances, nested hierarchies, or static territorial boundaries, as a topographical mapping would suggest. For state power does not travel smoothly across space. Rather, it hops, skips, and assembles, composing the very spaces of which it is a part and from which it stems.[11]

This chapter thinks with subsidized bread to show what analyses might look like if we stopped assuming the state to be a static object that towers over national territory. Pushing past a Euclidean spatial imaginary, I sift through just some of the "mediated and real-time connections, some direct, others more distanciated," through which the state effect transpires in two very different Jordanian cities, where socioeconomic dynamics differ dramatically, notwithstanding their comparative physical proximity.[12] I do not focus here on governmental hierarchies or institutional realignments, as much of the literature on political topologies tends to do.[13] Instead, I unpack the state effect by way of the quotidian discussions and conversations through which subjects give the state life: the ways in which Jordanians talk about the state, criticize it, mourn it, invoke it, imagine it, and make claims upon it, all in a landscape where the *reach* of government institutions is intensive and strategic, but highly uneven.[14] Perhaps the state effect is composed and brought to bear through "a more *transverse* set of political interactions" than the static conceptions of space with which we operate tend to allow.[15] And it is precisely these more oblique, seemingly askew connections that thinking topologically allows me to foreground: the places where state power assembles, or fails to do so, as well as the entanglements through which the state is invoked and implored, decried and disparaged; how it is represented and performed into being.

SHIFTING ARCHITECTURES OF AUTHORITY

In Jordan, the global decline in oil prices that began in 1982 slowly translated into sizable reductions in foreign aid and worker remittances. With little in the way of direct taxation, the steady reduction in these income sources eventually led to a drastic reduction in government revenue. As a result, spending on subsidies, government employment, and publicly owned enterprises was increasingly financed through rapidly growing levels of debt.[16] In 1989, currency devaluations hastened an unprecedented fiscal crisis. No longer able to service its foreign debt obligations, Jordan's government turned to the International Monetary Fund (IMF) for assistance. Their negotiations resulted in a structural adjustment program (1989) that sought to curtail government spending while reshaping public policy in ways more amenable to capital, although the latter took some time. Anne Mariel Peters and Pete W. Moore term the IMF's arrival in Jordan "the end of an era."[17] Jordan's access to bountiful external aid was curtailed. The Hashemite regime was forced to pursue a far different set of governing strategies than those that had characterized the period following the establishment of the Ministry of Supply in 1974.

Economic reforms fostered a radical transformation in the geography of governmental intervention. Although Amman had always received disproportionate public funding, uneven development throughout the country had previously been addressed through welfare provisions, public employment, and investment measures meant to improve living standards and bolster growth in rural areas and small cities. After the IMF's arrival, austerity and privatization were eventually followed by policies that are best described as "arrangements that articulate incumbent elite power to wider networks of finance and technocratic expertise."[18] Administering the national economy as a whole gave way to managing particular zones linked to economic circuits that flowed between regions and across national boundaries, as specific cities and business hubs were systematically favored over others. Adam Hanieh has traced how these measures spread throughout the Middle East, lubricated and accelerated by Gulf capital, American encouragement, and their joint push to loosen barriers to investment in the built environment.[19] Critical in Jordan were Qualifying Industrial Zones (QIZs), urban regeneration schemes, and other enclaves heavily incentivized by tax breaks and lax labor regulations meant to encourage private-sector growth. And while these tend to sound innocuous, their consequences in the Hashemite Kingdom have been profound. Attracting perpetual flows of investment and enabling a regulatory environment amenable to the interests of capital became the foremost goal of novel government agencies, as a combination of real estate developers, financial institutions, foreign donors, and local elites worked to transform the architecture of authority in the country.[20] Over time, they produced what Aihwa Ong terms "distinct governing regimes within the broader landscape of normalized rule."[21] Market-friendly sites where populations are managed according to a different set of rules and regulations are often located next to towns and villages where long-standing administrative strategies continue to hold sway. Jillian Schwedler, Christopher Parker, and Najib Hourani adeptly follow the impact of such dynamics on infrastructure, wealth accumulation, and protest patterns in Amman, where public policies that seek to facilitate foreign investment and prevent social unrest have transformed spatial dynamics in the capital city.[22] But these processes remain under-explored in the rest of the country, which has also witnessed dramatic transformations.

In southern Jordan, shifts in the spatiality of state power must be set against histories of a very different sort of governmental presence. Before 1989, state institutions had a nearly ubiquitous presence in the citizenry's everyday lives, mainly through the provision of basic necessities and employment.[23] In Karak, 92% of the labor force worked in the public sector, and in Ma'an some

90%; these numbers stand in contrast to Amman, where the rate was more than a third lower than those, at 58%.[24] Citizens' purchasing power was also supported through price fixing and subsidies. Always less dependent on government expenditures, Amman and other cities in the north were therefore also less vulnerable to the vagaries of structural adjustment, although they suffered as well. But in the south, where employment in the private sector was minimal and access to remittances was far less pervasive, structural adjustment was felt as a profound betrayal of promises made; economic reforms worked to "dismantle the social provisioning upon which the state of Jordan had been built."[25] As these distributive measures were scaled back, public unrest became a more frequent occurrence in the Jordanian south.[26] Accustomed to assorted practices of reach through which government agencies promoted local development and human welfare, citizens faced dramatic reconfigurations in the forces that governed them. Charting how institutions achieve presence in this tangled landscape is one of two main things a topological redescription of power sets out to accomplish, to understand the practices and policies through which proximate relationships of authority are realized. But it is the second objective that I wish to advance more consistently here: to look less at "spatial processes of folding and stretching"[27] themselves than at the impact these processes have on relationships of power, and the different ways in which those are reproduced. At a time when the forces that govern us appear so mutable, as people and places are channeled into governing arrangements over which they have little control, through what practices is state power exercised? Where and how does the state become tangible and representable when so many of its former responsibilities have been abandoned, devolved, or contracted out? In Jordan, political authority and leverage over peoples' lives is today more dispersed and imprecise in its boundaries vis-à-vis regional bodies, public-private hybrids, NGOs, and private sector groups than ever before. But somehow, some way, the state remains.

THE AQABA SPECIAL ECONOMIC ZONE (ASEZ)

The accelerated implementation of market-friendly economic policies under King Abdullah II fostered the emergence of an archipelago of specialized economic enclaves scattered throughout the country. The Aqaba governorate's conversion into a decentralized hub for direct foreign investment and luxury tourism is a key example, the centerpiece in a series of initiatives aimed at attracting capital and boosting growth throughout the Hashemite Kingdom.[28] USAID, the World Bank, and the Economic Consultative Council, an unelected technocratic body given unprecedented sway under King Abdullah II, began designing the Special Economic Zone just after the new monarch's ascent to the throne in February of 1999.[29] Initial proposals raised controversy in the Lower House of Parliament, as members of Parliament worried about the collapse of national sovereignty and economic cooperation with Israel inside the proposed zone. Despite the lack of enthusiasm among Jordan's elected representatives, however, the project received strong external backing, especially from the United States and the European Union, and was eventually ushered through Parliament. Efforts in the national legislature were led by the Parliament member Ali Abu al-Ragheb, whose success in getting the controversial project approved would subsequently earn him an appointment as prime minister. King Abdullah II formally launched the Aqaba Special Economic Zone (ASEZ, henceforth "the Zone") on May 17, 2001. Aqaba was to become an "extra-territorial city," a shining "symbol of a forward looking country that wants to play a role in the new global economy."[30] Incentives for the private sector included a host of typical measures, including a flat 5% income tax on net profit, exemptions on property taxes, and the elimination of foreign equity restrictions on investments, all enabled by a streamlined bureaucracy.[31] Overnight, the governorate became an administratively autonomous entity under the aegis of the Aqaba Special Economic Zone Authority (ASEZA), which was tasked with "Turning Sand into Gold."[32]

Since its establishment, ASEZA has been closely connected to an array of physically distant governmental bodies and agencies. The European Union's Euro-Mediterranean Partnership supports various privatization projects in the Zone, while USAID is closely involved through technical assistance and community development.[33] ASEZA has signed agreements with Turkish Free Zones (TFZ) to foster the exchange of expertise and a twin-city agreement with Shizuishan, a city located in a Chinese Free Zone, to enhance cooperation and business ties. ASEZA is also subject to more conventional maneuvers that subvert, or at least reshape, the exercise of state power. Multinational security companies safeguard the gates of privileged development projects. Investors in real-estate mega-schemes, largely from the Gulf, frequently call upon their allies in Amman to cut across decision-making hierarchies and fast-track their business ventures, over which the similarly unelected Aqaba Development Corporation (ADC) holds sway. These relations are facilitated by Jordanian business elites, who use their clout on consultative bodies and executive boards to push semi-public agencies to support large projects that investors cannot or prefer not to fully fund. To ameliorate the unsettling impact of it all, because growth has been unequal and the ostensibly frictionless flow of investments has led to far less prosperity than planned, an array of NGOs and corporate social responsibility units have taken over services that were once the responsibility of the central government or municipality, ranging from employment generation to education and neighborhood enhancement. With the collusion if not active assistance of USAID, local residents have lived through what Benjamin Schuetze describes as a "gradual transformation of socio-economic rights into matters of charity and corporate social responsibility."[34] Clearly, state power has not simply been devolved downwards to ASEZA. Rather, political authority in Aqaba is produced through continuing interplays among all sorts of institutions, organizations, and political and economic interests, some distant and others more proximate.

ASEZA is headed by a six-member team of political appointees. It consists of five delegates and a chief commissioner, who report directly to the national cabinet. To achieve growth, ASEZA was given control over a broad array of responsibilities including financial regulations, attracting investment, labor issues, environmental protection, health inspection, social development, and municipal affairs. In 2004, these responsibilities were divided and the Aqaba Development Corporation (ADC) was assigned "all for-profit activities," while ASEZA maintained responsibility for governance.[35] At the time and to this day, this devolution of authority was seen as vital both for attracting global capital flows and for steering citizens towards self-government in a market environment. Within a year of ASEZA's founding, the elected municipality of the city had been eliminated. In addition, its board of commissioners finalized Memoranda of Understanding (MOU) with 18 national ministries based in Amman to avoid redundancies and delineate responsibilities. With astonishing speed, an unelected technocratic body became responsible for a wide range of activities within ASEZA's nearly four-hundred-square-kilometer purview. These changes dramatically disrupted long-standing patterns through which

Aqaba's residents had been governed. As of 2020, ASEZA remains in charge of regulatory issues and most everyday services, although who exactly governs the Zone's more than 120,000 residents is not always clear.

Known by locals as *al-mufawwadiyya* (the delegated ones), ASEZA is frequently accused of corruption and mismanagement. Common complaints include the unequal distribution of growth, forced relocations from poor but potentially profitable neighborhoods, the dissemination of practices regarded as culturally inappropriate, and severe shortcomings in public services, especially health care and education.[36] This is hardly surprising, as ASEZA is judged not by its ability to ensure the well-being of local residents but by its dexterity in attracting investment, enhancing economic growth, and integrating the Zone into global capitalist networks. However, there are important exceptions to the delegation of responsibilities to this autonomous body, as certain tasks were considered too sensitive for transferal. Unsurprisingly, "foreign and defense affairs" are located outside ASEZA's remit.[37] Perhaps more unexpectedly, the provision of discounted flour and the regulation of subsidized bread production were, and continue to be, deemed a crucial governing practice not suitable for devolution.

As of August, 2015, Aqaba was home to nineteen bakeries. MOITS oversees and regulates these outlets from its headquarters in Amman, aided by a local annex based in the city of Aqaba. In September of 2015, I accompanied Fadi and Faris, the MOITS inspectors introduced in the previous chapter, on a review of Aqaba's bread producers. This particular trip was arranged both to inspect the bakeries and to get a sense of how well the local annex was operating. Over the previous months, several complaints that should have been dealt with locally had reached the ministry's central offices in Amman. The first bakery we were to visit had been reported by citizens for allegedly using subsidized flour in their sweets and more expensive varieties of bread, but had never received a fine from Aqaba-based inspectors. The second bakery's owner had complained repeatedly about the local inspectors because of their unwillingness to increase his discounted flour quota. The local annex was admittedly understaffed, but higher-ups in Amman also implied that its functionaries were not being as diligent or assiduous as they were supposed to be—graft was suspected, although never openly acknowledged. On the ride down from Amman, I asked Faris why the ministry was concerned with the bakery and the potentially fraudulent practices therein. He responded diplomatically: "Bread is the most essential good for many citizens. Corruption at the bakery not only hurts them, it also generates a negative image of the state." I pushed him on this claim, mentioning the frequent accusations of government corruption in the press. "Bread is different," he responded, as Faris nodded. "People depend on the ministry to eat, to feed their families. The bakery is not like other businesses and so corruption in this sector is more sensitive."

"Is this why responsibility for the provision of bread has not been given to *al-mufawwadiyya*?" I asked, eager to compare bread provision in Aqaba to Amman, where I had spent far more time. The inspectors chuckled in unison, amused by my naïveté. Fadi, the more experienced of the two, stepped in to explain: "I would not put *al-mufawwadiyya* in charge of cooking my lunch," he snickered, before adopting a more serious tone and expounding at length:

> Look, the regime knows the red lines. Bread is one of them. When it is lacking, protests occur. Anger boils to the surface when people are hungry. Our job is to avoid this. To make sure everyone has enough to eat, especially the poor. This is why the ministry regulates bakeries so closely: because citizens care, and so does the regime.

If bread was lacking, social order could be in peril, Fadi reckoned. Notwithstanding the triumph of market logics in the Zone, the inspectors recognized that certain services should not be delegated or privatized. Successful subsidized bread provision remained, for them, a key diagnostic of the state's commitment to citizens. They were hardly alone.

After the four-hour drive down from Amman, we grabbed some sandwiches and headed off for the first bakery, just after noon. We parked, ate, and then ambled around outside for about fifteen minutes, attentive to the bakery's rhythms and tempos. Fadi and Faris then conducted a standard inspection, jotting down the bakery's discounted flour quota, examining various goods, and asking for receipts. Everything appeared to be in order, they told me, but they also thought it prudent to talk to a few more people before heading to the next stop. The two inspectors decided to station themselves outside the business to converse with local residents and inquire into the outlet's reputation. A few Aqabawis strolled on, without the time or interest to engage with the officials, but more than half of those who were purchasing bread relayed their opinions.

Unlike in both public debates and private conversations regarding the monarchy's legitimacy or autocratic rule, here few had compunctions about airing their views. Accusations of corruption (*fasad*) and illegal profits (*ribah*) were the most frequent. Fathers and mothers with children in tow were the most emphatic. They accused the bakery owner of misusing his discounted flour quota, probably using it on sweets. This resulted in bread shortages by three or four every afternoon, they told the inspectors. Unable to purchase their daily bread at the outlet after work, customers were forced to travel to more distant bakeries, wasting valuable time, or to go without the foodstuff altogether.

Some of these respondents thanked the MOITS officials. They expressed an eagerness to see the bakery owner penalized, and commended the bureaucrats for exerting their regulatory prerogative. Among those who detailed their grievances, the responsibilities of the state were persistently invoked. "Why have you done nothing? We have complained about this bakery many times," insisted one local resident. "Is it not the state's responsibility to supervise them?" he asked. Taking the inspectors' appearance as an opportunity to air a broader set of grievances, another resident began lobbing complaints related to trash collection and the high price of fuel. The flooding of city blocks during wintertime was another major grievance. He eventually ended up back at the bakery, echoing the allegations of those who had preceded him. He finished rhetorically: "Isn't providing bread a responsibility of the state?" Fadi and Faris grimaced. ASEZA was in charge of other things but not bread, not the bakery. They were responsible, or at least the ministry they worked for was.

We tend to think of market-friendly spaces such as the Aqaba Special Economic Zone as relieving governments of the onerous and costly obligations that supposedly drain national finances, inhibit entrepreneurship, and encourage dependency. Instead, citizens are pushed to manage risk and promote their own well-being through sensible self-government, achieved through what Nikolas Rose describes as technologies of responsibilization.[38] Yet as the remarks above make clear, it is not just subjects who are made responsible through market-friendly policies. The citizens above certainly voice a rather transactional understanding of state responsibility, framed around critical and life-sustaining services. But in a context where political deliberation has never been participatory, and opportunities to decry governmental failures are few and far between, the encounter with inspectors is one of a handful of moments where the ruled, rather than rulers, can hold those who govern to account. Inspections allow Aqabawis to gather as a public and to demand improved service delivery. But they do even more than that. Complaints, objections, and criticisms also hail the state and ask more of it—to erase distance, to be less detached. "Isn't providing bread a responsibility of the state?" These citizens insist that it is, and demand that it remain so.

The most extensive conversation outside this bakery took place between Inspector Fadi and Amira, who identified herself as a mother, as well as a nurse at a nearby hospital. Her criticisms centered on the strains caused by the bakery's fraudulent practices. She mentioned the dearth of *khubz 'arabi* if she arrived at the bakery after work, which meant that she had to either buy more expensive breads or leave her kids without sandwiches for school the next day. Amira had come earlier than she would have liked that day precisely to avoid such an outcome. She continually described *khubz 'arabi* as central to her family and the neighborhood's survival, as onlookers nodded in agreement. "How are we supposed to survive if there is no bread?" Amira asked. "What are we supposed to do if the bakery has no *khubz 'arabi*? We all rely on it. Most of us visit this bakery every day. How do you expect us to live without the bread it is supposed to provide?"

I found Amira's descriptions of the bakery, along with those of so many others, to be evocative of what Bonnie Honig calls, in a different context, "public things."[39] Bakeries are not publicly owned, but outlets such as the one near Amira's work are public insofar as they are subject to governmental oversight and popular accountability. And they matter not only because they provide bread or fulfill subsistence needs but because bakeries allow people to achieve a certain stability. They provide fixed points of reference, elicit affects, and press people into relations with others in a world where little is certain. And while Aqaba's bread outlets do not function as the "holding environment of democratic citizenship,"[40] as in Honig's examples, they do similar work as nodes around which collectivities can occasionally constellate and which they, in turn, help generate.

Since the city's conversion into a Special Economic Zone, there are fewer and fewer sites where Aqabawis are treated equally and as citizens. Rapidly proliferating consumption cultures aimed at tourists, both foreign and domestic, offer little to local residents—a stroll on the ever-more-commodified *corniche*, a picnic on one of the last remaining public beaches—most of whom lack the funds to engage in burgeoning consumer identifications. Amid such flux, in a landscape where civil society organizations must compete to gain grants in order to provide social services, should we be surprised that there remains "a craving for the public thing, the thing that hides in plain sight, but when you need it, it's there"?[41] It is precisely this craving that scholars, policy makers, and politicians overlook when they discuss welfare services through the prism of efficiency or added value. In my reading, Amira is demanding that the bakery be maintained, and be maintained as a public thing, as a site of attachment and meaning that gives life to the neighborhood and allows collectivities to form around it, however fleeting these may be. Those present at this bakery know well that they are not a governmental priority. Yet they constantly evaluate and respond to the uneven provision of public services in the Zone, cognizant that complaints are sometimes the only way to gain access to services that only just make life bearable. As with those who spoke before her, it was when Amira's remarks called the state to account for its regulatory failure that she most roused the small crowd's ire. One of the state's crucial responsibilities had gone unfulfilled, a haunting reminder of how tenuous the hold on public things can be. Although I never found out what came of this particular probe, it became clear that, rather than rejecting the state, Amira was seeking to shape its practices of reach, to prevent the disappearance of bread as a public thing.

RESPONSIBILITY TALK

Our next stop was nearby. We walked the handful of blocks to the next bakery. Faris and Fadi had been asked by their superiors to scrutinize the accuracy of the complaints made by the bakery owner, who had been grumbling to the MOITS central office about his bakery's discounted flour allocation. This bakery was less than a five-minute drive from the imposing offices of ASEZA, and I found it strange that inspectors had been called in from Amman to sort out issues that were happening a stone's throw from the institution charged with governing Aqaba. "They probably don't care," Faris shrugged, as he pointed towards the commanding ASEZA building in the distance. "There is no money in bread. They probably blame any problems on us."

Anwar welcomed us to his bakery eagerly. He could barely contain himself as we stepped into his locale. Relieved that the inspectors had arrived, he began to catalogue his complaints with the ministry's local annex the moment we sat down in his office, situated just through the bakery's storefront. The problem centered around his discounted flour quota, which had not been increased in two years, despite a number of requests. In addition to having grown his customer base through the quality of his product, Anwar now provided two midsize hotels with the entirety of their subsidized bread needs. While he claimed to do his best to bake enough *khubz 'arabi* for everyone, he had been forced to purchase from a competitor to meet demand. Not having *khubz 'arabi* would have been a death sentence for his business, he told us; everyone purchases it, irrespective of whether they go on to buy other goods. He had no choice but to source subsidized bread from elsewhere, which he then sold without making any profit. As I watched in silence, Fadi and Faris trod lightly, cognizant that Anwar was making some rather serious accusations. They asked for the name of the employees in the local annex whom he dealt with and why this baker thought his requests had not been passed on to the head office in Amman. "No one wants to take responsibility for any decisions," he told them. *"Al-mufawwadiyya* tells me to talk to MOITS. The employees at the MOITS annex are overworked and spend all their time inspecting the main market. They tell me to call Amman. I call Amman and they tell me to deal with the local annex. No one wants to take responsibility." Together, Fadi and Faris tried to assuage Anwar. They engaged prudently, conscious that the texture of such encounters impacts what kind of a thing the state comes to be in the minds of citizens. The two inspectors carefully went over his production numbers, the alleged consumer demand, and his discounted flour quota. After a few minutes, Faris squinted sullenly at the paperwork laid out on Anwar's desk and, with a quick, silent look, sought his colleague's opinion. Fadi offered a nod in tired assent. They had reached the same conclusion Anwar had been positing from the outset. He needed more discounted flour, so as to bake more subsidized bread. "So you are the ones responsible for bread in Aqaba?" Anwar asked, exasperated. "Can you help me with this flour quota business? Are you the ones responsible?"

Responsibility talk, like corruption talk elsewhere,[42] mediates Anwar's relationship with the state, his routine encounters with illegible and unpredictable government bodies that seem to purposely prevent the flow of flour to his bakery. While his questions may appear formulaic, they conjure relationships of authority out of routine governing dynamics. Despite the cold comfort it offers in navigating the bureaucracy, talking about responsibility (*masuliyye*) is the means by which Anwar, like Amira, reflects upon and represents the Jordanian state's erratic presence at the bakery. Sophia Stamatopoulou-Robbins has explored similar pleas and negotiations in the West Bank village of Shuqba. Although for far different reasons, the governmental landscape in Shuqba is also made up of "contrasting, competing and fragmented practices."[43] Like her, I find that the significance of Anwar and Amira's statements lies less in how those statements express belief in the legitimacy of governing arrangements than in how they act as what J. L. Austin terms a "performative utterance," shaping social reality rather than merely describing it. Encounters with inspectors, and the discussions of responsibility that result, are instances when the boundaries around addresser and addressees are established. For Stamatopoulou-Robbins, they "occasion the articulation of what constitutes an actor."[44] Responsibility talk is one way in which this occurs, a crucial vector through which Aqabawis both demand accountability and represent the state as a coherent entity.[45] It also illustrates how, amid inescapable failures and yearnings for competence, the state takes on "the appearance of an abstract, nonmaterial form," one that should provide, and that falls short when subsidized bread does not arrive.[46]

Complaints such as the ones I heard at these two bakeries were common among those I spoke to in Aqaba. The citizenry was unsure who exactly was in charge and never quite able to pinpoint which regulatory body was accountable for what; responsibility for their well-being was opaque. Of course, there were some who exploited this indeterminacy, laboring and improvising along the edges of the law in order to survive or thrive. But for others, the uncertain architectures of authority created complex and often convoluted dilemmas about responsibility and its displacement. The juxtaposition of lavish tourist resorts and residential enclaves paid for by the very funds that could not, supposedly, be used to improve the livelihoods of local residents made such questions rather inevitable. So too did the statements and comportment of ASEZA's upper echelon.

"We don't have enough funding to offer the full set of social services," one senior member of ASEZA told me in an interview. "The Development Corporation takes most of the revenues and we get left with nothing. This is how the state designed Aqaba. What are we supposed to do? It is not our responsibility to give people jobs, and we don't have the funds to offer quality education or health services."[47] One of his deputies, charged with coordinating NGO activities in the Zone, was similarly sanguine: "We rely on these organizations to provide the services we cannot offer. We wish we could do more, but this is how Aqaba was designed: it's a place to do business. Low taxes mean the state can't do as much; it acts differently here."[48]

These officials bemoaned their lack of resources and responsibilities, all while the agency that employed them contributed to that very lack. They seemed to suspect that local residents wished to be entangled in a different set of relations with the state apparatus, but knew that ASEZA had been created, in part, as a "separation," established to escape the web of relations and obligations that tugged the state into costly provisions elsewhere.[49] Ordinary Aqabawis who spoke of their longing for reliable interactions with state authorities, in contrast, were not only rejecting this separation. They were representing the state, and seeking to fashion its spatial contours.

Provided with the opportunity to register their complaints, Aqabawis made appeals to the MOITS officials charged with protecting the people's daily bread. When pushed on why they had not approached local authorities earlier, most petitioners told the MOITS officials that the ASEZA's employees were sluggish or altogether uninterested, busy as they were making Aqaba into a tourist haven and entrepreneurial hub. Frequently described as unresponsive and aloof, *al-mufawwadiyya*'s disinterest in welfare services and local grievances fosters popular distrust in its bureaucracy. Failed expropriation of poor neighborhoods, low educational standards, and rampant healthcare shortcomings mean that its interventions in local affairs are fragmentary, ineffective, and widely deplored. In contrast, ordinary citizens approached the MOITS inspectors with hope (tempered though it may have been) that rectifications might be garnered through their intervention, that different forms of connection with political authority were possible, that at least when it came to bread, the state had to be *present*, not *absent*. And while there is little doubt that any number of measures implemented over recent years, such as the elimination of the municipality, the outsourcing of various public services, the delegation of decision-making to a body composed of technocratic elites, seek to distance the state apparatus from the need to meet particular demands, appeals made during inspection seek to do the opposite—"to *fold in* claims for justice and fairness"[50]—as a way of collapsing the distance between the state apparatus and local residents. Petitioning the MOITS officials does not just recognize their ability to do something about bread shortages. Considered topologically, it is about establishing a relationship with one node in a bureaucratic structure so as to gain access to state institutions that, for all intents and purposes, are usually beyond ordinary citizens' grasp, stretched out to such an extent that they seem unbearably far away. By rendering subsidized bread as one among a host of "problems of collective existence,"[51] Aqabawis seek to dissolve a gap, to establish a relation across distance. For the state is diffuse in the Special Economic Zone—its echoes hard to glean, its presence hard to pin down.

As a biopolitical endeavor, inspections seek to manage the conduct of the population, all in the name of national well-being. Yet encounters such as the ones I witnessed in Aqaba are not just pretexts for monitoring health standards or the proficient distribution of public goods. They also serve as everyday occasions that punctuate the lives of Aqabawis with the state's presence. Although far from all-encompassing, inspections bring to life a distinctive form of state power, not one that is based on repression or control at a distance but a visible and proximate form of co-presence with the governed.[52] These inspections reveal not only the very sporadic practices through which the Jordanian state apparatus reaches into Aqaba, but also the "immense popular investment" citizens have in assigning responsibilities to the state.[53] Residents of Aqaba have learned that public services do not come as an "indivisible package of rights, born out of formal legal status."[54] Instead, they must tug, plead, jerk, and pull. For nothing comes easy; little in the Zone beyond low taxes and cheap beer is guaranteed. Faced with abandonment and varying levels of ruination, local residents use the bakery, along with a host of other infrastructures, as sites to make political claims, to identify those responsible for their well-being.[55] Yet one must wonder whether it is the Aqabawis themselves who, by ascribing a set of responsibilities to the state, as if it were a coherent thing, represent and thereby work to reproduce the very state they call to account.

Aqaba was and remains the most important of Jordan's growth-boosting clusters scattered throughout the country. In an attempt to build an internationally competitive city, the ruling elite has transformed the urban landscape into a bid to attract global investment. ASEZA has been tasked with administering daily life, but has been given little in the way of fiscal and managerial resources with which to do so. As a result, NGOs with royal patronage take charge of educational tasks, real-estate developers contract private companies to secure certain neighborhoods, and foreign agencies care for "community development." All these tasks were once the responsibility of the central government or the elected municipality; today they are carried out by a diverse group of actors. For all intents and purposes, an unelected regional body linked to global markets, Gulf capital, USAID, and various NGOs now governs the citizenry, even though the lines between these forces are often hard to distinguish. This is neither a simple process of decentralization nor a straightforward administrative reorganization; it is a mode of government characterized by dispersed centers of power, which are increasingly hard to identify or locate. And yet, as the tasks and responsibilities once fused in centralized institutions are pulled apart, certain practices that serve to reinscribe the state, to perform its authority over the people, to reach into their daily lives, become all the more salient. Such performances are more easily recognized when it comes to coercion or surveillance. The policing of borders or public protests, the presence of security forces—these practices make palpable the repressive power of the state apparatus. Yet there is far more to state spatialization than coercion: "state benevolence . . . also makes its spatial rounds."[56] And it is here that the bakery comes to matter. With every purchase of subsidized bread, with every complaint lodged about the bread subsidy, with every plea for improved service delivery, residents of the Special Economic Zone are reminded of themselves as citizens governed by an abstract body. They not only sense the state but represent it back to themselves. Amid the inordinately dispersed architecture of authority through which local residents are governed, it is at Aqaba's bakeries that the ostensibly distant Jordanian state is lived close up and in concrete form.

MERCURIAL AMBIGUITIES

The city of Ma'an, 216 kilometers south of the capital, Amman, and 116 kilometers northeast of Aqaba, suffers some of the highest unemployment and poverty rates in Jordan. In the most recent assessment, 26.9% of its households were classified as deprived, while another 28.4% were branded "vulnerable," sitting immediately above the poverty line.[57] Despite a variety of statistical indicators that signal Ma'an's dire position, the city's history of public unrest has engendered negative portrayals. Political elites deem it disorderly and rebellious. The government-owned media tend to echo this depiction. They portray Ma'an as a backwater filled with troublemakers (*mashkaljiyye*), where drug trafficking, gun running, and petty crime run rampant.[58] Since September 11th, 2001, Ma'an has also frequently been portrayed as the center of Islamist extremism in Jordan.[59] The city has recently garnered media attention as a supposed "hotbed of terrorist sympathizers," with affiliations to the Islamic State.[60] Ma'anis resent such characterizations. They emphasize instead the shortcomings in public services and the lack of economic opportunities, which have left few prospects for local residents. Both government expenditures and the vagaries of geopolitics were more munificent in the past.

Between 1970 and 1985, the Jordanian bureaucracy more than tripled in size, with many of the new recruits coming from Jordan's southern towns and villages. During the same period, and just as subsistence agriculture was declining due to land fragmentation and desertification, Ma'an became a major transportation hub. Many residents made their living moving goods between Iraq and the port of Aqaba. The success of this sector relied on business acumen and proximity to the seaport and border, but it also relied heavily on the Jordanian government's subvention of fuel. The removal of fuel subsidies, part of the government's package with the IMF in 1989, hit the transportation sector particularly hard, as did rising inflation. The 1990–91 Gulf War and subsequent sanctions on Iraq only exacerbated these trends. This economic decline troubled the monarchy, which had initiated a strategic political opening up in 1989, combining shrewdly designed elections with new forms of patronage, largely in response to countrywide protests that began in Ma'an.[61] In much of southern Jordan, this involved delegating authority and resources to local auxiliaries, usually members of Parliament and tribal leaders. In exchange for their loyalty, prominent Ma'anis were furnished with the means to offer public employment and grants for education and health care, all part of a process that Ellen Lust terms "competitive clientelism."[62] But over the last fifteen years, market-friendly policies and reductions in nonmilitary expenditures have curtailed, though not eliminated, these relationships. This has fueled a dramatic increase in NGOs and kin associations that now provide a wide range of welfare services.[63] Young entrepreneurs with access to these bodies and their pools of funds compete with traditional elites. Both aim to enhance their electoral possibilities, as politicians are judged not by ideological position or party affiliation but by their tribal ties and ability to intervene in the bureaucracy on behalf of voters, "to set the apparatus of the state in motion."[64] These clientelist networks, and the *mafatih* (key figures) who lubricate them, are crucial to the survival of local residents, who repeatedly emphasized their reliance on prominent figures to obtain a share of public goods and services.[65] Unsurprisingly then, discontent and disturbances in Maʿan (e.g. 1989, 1996, 2012) have reliably developed in response to the reform or removal of what few welfare programs had survived structural adjustment.[66]

Following the most recent wave of social unrest in the city, in 2014, Maʿan has been intermittently subject to a heavy security presence, an approach repeatedly employed by the Hashemite regime following bouts of strife.[67] In a ham-fisted demonstration of state power, the Palace deploys an imposing fleet of armored vehicles that stand guard right outside the entrance and exit to Maʿan on the Desert Highway. All traffic into the city is subject to random inspection. On occasion, entry and exit are heavily curtailed. These checkpoints do not seek to secure geopolitical sovereignty; Jordan's borders here are sufficiently secure. They are internally oriented, visibly manifesting political authority in a purportedly rebellious outpost. In stark contrast to the heavy presence of security on the highway, however, there were no police or military officers present inside the city center on my first visit to Maʿan, in September of 2015. They had stopped entering because of sporadic clashes with local residents, which had further cemented a long-standing "environment of mistrust and hostility."[68] Nevertheless, political authority is not absent, nor is Maʿan lawless; instead, the capacity of state institutions simply varies across different dimensions. Although the state apparatus retains *de jure* sovereignty over the city, police incursions into Maʿan are preceded by negotiations with powerful local actors, who exert *de facto* control over those areas deemed inaccessible or dangerous. Informal economic activities are structured by well-known rules. Notables arrange neighborhood watches, well-known communal customs help oversee occasional arms markets, and groups of tribal representatives debate and punish actions deemed inappropriate.[69] The capacity to make and enforce rules is not solely the preserve of state institutions; the fragmented nature of governance simply indicates the geographical unevenness of state power.

Comparative political scientists tend to overlook such disjunctures by defining statehood or state capacity restrictively: the monopoly over the use of legitimate violence, the ability to extract taxes, or the quality of a bureaucracy.[70] Such operationalizations miss out on almost all of the countries in the Middle East and would have little to say about a place like Maʿan, where deficiencies in public services and the lack of police would surely be pegged as evidence of state weakness, incapacity, or failure. I want to push back against such assertions and the modes of data that underpin them, because they flatten out precisely what is interesting about the textures and forms through which people are governed. In Maʿan, as elsewhere, practices of government are multiple and do not reside solely in formal institutions. Nor are they easily gleaned from quantifiable indicators, which tell us little about how people live alongside, respond to, and grapple with political authority. Maʿanis are no longer governed by a unitary entity that is uniformly sovereign over the population; they probably never were. The people of Maʿan are today on the losing end of selective investments in infrastructures and industries that link profit-rendering spaces with global markets. Roads are poor, schools are short of funds, development projects few and far between, shortages denounced in the sporadic yet recurring clashes between local residents and the police. But still, notwithstanding the discontinuous presence of state actors in the city, certain institutions continuously reach into the town with just enough consistency and intensity to generate the state effect.

Thirty-six bakeries operate in the Maʿan governorate, twenty of them in the supposedly lawless town center. The efforts made to ensure the timely arrival of subsidized flour and the production of subsidized bread are nothing short of remarkable and constitute a stark contrast to the Jordanian government's withdrawal or disengagement from other tasks. Twice a week, trucks arrive with flour produced in mills located on the outskirts of Amman. Every two weeks, Health Ministry and MOITS officials conduct random inspections. Most bakeries open six days a week, some seven, for anywhere from eight to eighteen hours a day. Despite the state apparatus's inability to police petty crime, provide consistent electricity, or tax the vast majority of local businesses, subsidized bread was neither absent nor insufficient in Ma'an on any day during my twenty months in Jordan. When I asked one bakery owner about the surprising efficiency of state institutions in this regard, he remarked cynically: "The government is not stupid. They can fail on many things, but they know there would be problems if bread was not available." He then went on to detail, at length, the array of regulations and supervisory measures undertaken by MOITS at his bakery.

> The ministry makes this business very difficult. Inspection teams come at least once every two weeks, sometimes more. They check my workers' nails and hair for length and cleanliness. Then, they test our flour to make sure the extraction rate is correct. If anything is wrong, we get shut down immediately. The bakery is cleaner than a hospital. No business is more regulated than bread.

My surprise at the ministry's exertions, at the visible way in which it managed to actively intervene in Ma'an bakeries, elicited further remarks from one of the workers rolling out dough: "It's different than the situation with the police. Bread is an essential material for us. People know the flour trucks and recognize the inspection teams—and they let them do their job."

Local officials are hardly blind to the importance of certain state performances. Ma'an's mayor at the time of my first visit knew very well that town residents felt estranged from the organs of the state. "Given the poverty and lack of development, should we be that surprised that there are protests, that Ma'an is 'in crisis'?" he asked in an interview.[71] "Many in the city feel the state does not care about local residents except when we protest." Like his constituents, the mayor portrayed the Jordanian state as remote and unsympathetic, failing to fulfill the tasks many had come to expect of it. And it was precisely this lack that was worsening the lives of his constituents: "The state does not seem to have the tools to solve the problems in the city. They tell us that we need to respect the authority of the state. We value this authority, but not at the expense of the dignity of citizens." Placed in the impossible position of meeting local demands without much in the way of financial support, the mayor toed a fine line in expressing Ma'an's grievances while asserting his allegiance to the Hashemite monarchy and the Jordanian state. The manner in which he negotiated these tensions made clear the centrality of bread. "The youth need jobs. We [Ma'anis] need a new hospital, a lot of our streets need to

be rebuilt, but bread is untouchable. The ministry cannot stop providing it,"
he stressed. "Thank God our king understands this," he continued. "Bread is
indispensable to every house. Rich or poor, we cannot live without it." While
cautious in conveying popular outrage, the mayor effectively made clear that
state power, local allegiances, and bread provision were one flammable fabric.

The Hashemite regime's close attention to subsidized bread provision was
not lost on local residents. Most Ma'anis I queried acknowledged that, when
it was in their interest, the state and those at its helm could be incredibly
effective. One resident, employed as a teacher in a local public school, noted
while waiting for a fresh batch of *khubz 'arabi* how the bakery demonstrates
the state's capacity to provide public services. He contrasted its efficiency in
this regard with its lack of "ability or will" to improve public education at his
place of employment: "If they can provide bread, why is it so hard to provide
books, desks, or just pencils?" Similar remarks were repeatedly made during
my time in Ma'an, whose failing schools, lack of primary healthcare services,
and crumbling infrastructure were among the most frequent grievances aired
by residents. Many described the town's marginalization as a matter of effort
and attentiveness. "If the state was as good at promoting development or building hospitals as it is at flour distribution, Ma'an would be paradise," said one
bakery owner, whose qualms about the central government were wide-ranging
but did not extend to the bread subsidy. "The state prefers to spend its money
on other places and fancy projects. Ma'an is forgotten. We only get bread and
police," he told me. At the margins, longings for a benevolent state capable of
providing for its constituents often coexist with discourses of citizenship that
work to denounce marginalization and disempowerment. These sentiments
are frequently unstable, rooted in the mercurial ambiguities that permeate
popular attachments to the state.[72]

ENVY, DISCONNECTION, AND REDEMPTION

I returned to Ma'an in August of 2019, eager to see how the city had changed.
Police were now traversing the city limits and could be seen occasionally
driving through the downtown. At the municipality, most officials were keen
to emphasize improvements in Ma'an's relationship with the central government. Protests had died down over the previous three years, and instances
of police violence and armed confrontations with local residents were less

frequent than they had been from 2013 to 2015. Yet unemployment remained high, and the municipality was mired in debt; its main buildings had recently had their power cut off by Jordan's Electricity Distribution Company due to nonpayment. The downturn in oil prices (2016) had also hit the city in ways I had not expected, as Ma'anis who worked in Saudi Arabia had been forced to return when their contracts were not renewed. Life for local residents was perhaps calmer, but not appreciably better. I wondered what those charged with administering the city thought of these developments. When I spoke with the head of the municipality's planning department, he thought the source of Ma'an's problems was obvious:

> There are not as many opportunities here as in Aqaba or Amman. In those cities, the state offers investments, infrastructure, serious money. People gain experience and then the industries advance, the cities develop. Here we get no money and very brief investment. The only opportunities are in the bureaucracy or in very small businesses. That's why when you need a job, you ask your cousin, you use your influence (*wasta*). There is no other way.[73]

As Raed Shuwaikh, the deputy mayor of Ma'an, put it: "The state has stopped supporting people in Ma'an in the ways it used to. We have very high rates of unemployment, little investment. No one in the government listens when we tell them our problems, only the king. It's easier to call us lazy or criminal."[74] Echoing many other criticisms I heard in Ma'an, the deputy mayor bemoaned the shortcomings in a number of basic services. While he recognized how budget cuts had reduced government expenditures throughout the Hashemite Kingdom, he repeatedly pointed to the gaping difference between Ma'an and other cities. In the north, proximity to Amman meant that "capital moves much more easily; Irbid and Mafraq and their industrial zones get much more support than Ma'an. Support for industrialists is strong there because they are closer to Amman and all that the capital city offers." It was not just proximity to the capital that mattered, but the extent to which the state apparatus could benefit from intervening in certain places. "There is no comparison between Aqaba and Ma'an, everything is different. The state cares about Aqaba because it has the potential for serious investment and profits. Here, we get much less. It is not fair. The municipality doesn't even get the chance to make things better."

Shuwaikh's comparisons were not aggressive or disparaging. They were, however, tinged with a note of envy. In her exploration of *Ugly Feelings*, Sianne Ngai argues that envy is too often portrayed as a "static sign of deficiency rather than an active affective state."[75] Feminized, classed, and, I would add, spatialized, envious subjects are deemed hysterical and distraught. There is a resonance here with portrayals of Maʿan in the Jordanian media, which depicts its residents as outdated tribalists—lazy, angry, and lacking in the skills needed to compete in the country's rapidly changing economy. But as Ngai points out, envy need not be petty, unjustified, or effete. Instead, envy can be polemical, a recognition of and response to pervasive forms of inequality. "If we got half the funding that Aqaba gets, we could do so much," the deputy mayor speculated. "Maʿan has been forgotten. All we ask for is the same support as everyone else." Over the following month, comparisons with Aqaba and Amman regularly popped up in conversations. "The municipality is always trying to attract investment, but there is no plan. Companies come for a few months, but they always leave for Aqaba or Amman. You have real commerce there, connections to big foreign companies and markets," said one occasional NGO consultant, who had worked with USAID on several initiatives.[76] He portrayed the city's marginalization as an outcome of distance, which he sought to collapse. "Foreign NGOs used to be scared of working in Maʿan, but now many of them come and set up projects. They realize this is not a scary place, just one that is poor and neglected, very far from the central government and its resources. We have to bring these NGOs and the state closer, and make sure we collaborate productively with them." Others were less diplomatic.

Jalal frequently held court outside the storefront of his bakery. He would sit and chat with anyone who would join him at the plastic table set out by one of his employees every morning. His clothes were eclectic but he always wore dapper shoes—cleaned and polished every evening, as he liked to remind me after glancing down at my run-down pair of Nikes. Jalal always spoke in a hurry, as if conversation were a shield against feeling. "I've lived in Amman, and it wasn't easy," he reminisced one day. "But there you have opportunities. There are jobs if you want them. Here there is very little, only some small businesses that sell people's everyday needs."

I often asked Jalal about the past. Nearing his sixtieth birthday, he had been born and raised in Maʿan and spent most of his life there, aside from a few yearlong stints in Amman and Riyadh. "When I was growing up, everyone wanted to be a truck driver," he told me. "Maybe 75% of people in the area were involved in that sector. It was booming, especially during Iraq's war with Iran. Ma'an was connected to the Middle East; we were transporting goods everywhere. The state helped us." Connections were plentiful, distance easily erased. "Then, after the economic collapse and *habbet niyysan* (April 1989 uprising), everything changed," he recalled. "Locals went out to protest because so many of the reforms were hitting Ma'an the hardest, especially the cut in fuel subsidies. The state came in and clamped down, it repressed everyone. Nothing has been the same since. We are far from everywhere now, the city and its people are very isolated." Ma'an had become disconnected from the very places and networks that once assured its prosperity.[77]

"The state no longer works to improve things," Jalal continued. "It doesn't care about Ma'an, it's not present here. Things were better in the past."

Others nodded along. Most were eager to outline the various ways in which Ma'an had become detached, severed from those places and institutions to which it was once tied and through which it had once prospered. Public demonstrations were not their preferred way of expressing themselves, many told me. But they were the only way these citizens felt they could make themselves visible as loyal subjects demanding state care. Indeed, their loyalty to the Jordanian state was frequently emphasized; few, if any, were calling for the downfall of the regime.[78] Cognizant of their increasing remoteness from the levers of power, Ma'anis were instead calling for the state to come closer, to offer them the attention and resources they deserved as loyal citizens. Rather than engendering a desire for its overthrow, the shortcomings in public services seemed to elicit a desire for the state's redemption, its reappearance in what was perceived as its proper form.

When Jalal spoke, the clamor of conversation quickly gave way. He rarely smiled, and the hard lines of his jaw and swollen bags under his eyes gave him a forlorn appearance:

> The state does a bad job in Ma'an and so it's easier to blame us. They want us to be in awe of the state (*bidhum haybat ad-dawla*), to respect it. But respect is earned, not forced. In the past, we had good public services, the streets were clean and paved. If you needed a job or help starting a business, a ministry

would hire you or give you a loan. Government policies helped us survive. This
stopped thirty years ago. Now we are far from the state.

Ma'an's remoteness was not physical but relational. Local residents wanted the
state, at least in its provisionary capacity, to be closer, to erase a physical void, to
not be so far away. The absent here had "just as much of an effect upon relations
as recognizable forms of presence have."[79] I found it particularly striking that
these assessments were voiced by a bakery owner, whose business relied so
heavily on the competence of certain ministries. Nevertheless, perceptions of
state absence did not correlate in any neat way with wealth, political position,
or employment. Sometimes they emerged from contrasts with other cities.
Other times, they arose through comparisons with the past, when political
representation was minimal, to be sure, but public services were far more munificent. "The state does not care about Ma'an. In the past it was different, we
had lots of help and got plenty of attention. Now, we can all die tomorrow, the
city can collapse, and the state still will not care," Jalal lamented. Care here
entails the deployment of resources and the conferral of opportunities, two
things most Ma'anis agreed were sorely lacking in the city. Amid this void,
Anne Marie Baylouny has documented just some of the ways Jordanians have
worked to care for each other and combat dispossession and deprivation, supporting and sustaining themselves when public infrastructures fail to deliver.[80]
But still, Ma'anis like the ones who sat to chat outside Jalal's bakery expected
and yearned for a state that protected and provided. By poking at the state's
neglect, they "claimed the right to care by asserting its violation."[81] Viewed
from the prism of government planning, the abdication of responsibilities to
the market and the self-care of citizens appeared necessary, a compulsory set
of measures on the way to improved governance, reduced budget deficits, and
economic growth. For Ma'anis, such policies were lived as abandonment, the
withdrawal of gestures of care, which triggered a persistent sense of exclusion
and mistreatment. In this context, desires and pleas for state presence and the
infrastructures and services with which it is associated are a demand, a claim
on material equality in a deeply unequal country. They are also generative of
the state effect and of the processes of subjection upon which it relies.

Municipal officials, local activists, and ordinary citizens were at pains to
point out in various interviews and discussions that demands for improvements

do not indicate opposition to Hashemite rule or to the state as such. Rather, they work to denounce the retraction of certain programs and practices that citizens associate with the state's materialization in the city.[82] Some Ma'anis suspect that the state is actively vicious or violent. Others think it is simply negligent and inattentive. Yet still the fantasy endures that if somehow the state could recapture its role in protecting and providing for citizens, life would improve. In this respect, Ma'anis are similar to Michelle Obeid's interlocutors in the Lebanese town of Arsal, who seek the "ideal face of the state," one that has welfare and fairness, rather than force and punishment, at its core.[83] And their search transpires in particular ways, often through longings that judge the present versus a far more prosperous past or through envious comparisons with other cities. But in either case, Ma'anis who complain that the state is not present simultaneously affirm their yearning for exactly the type of resources and justice they believe it can provide.[84] That is, they keep faith in a state that so often lets them down, maintaining attachments to and thereby reproducing precisely the forces that injure them.[85]

Today, Ma'an exhibits extreme levels of infrastructural deprivation. A quick walk around town reveals broken sidewalks, infrequent lighting, and random garbage collection, what Braun and McCarthy characterize as the material dimensions of state abandonment.[86] Despite various ventures meant to lure investors, most infamously a 170-million-dollar glass factory and a failed industrial zone, employment in the armed forces and informal sector remain the main sources of livelihood for residents. State performances are largely transient, fleeting moments of staged authority that seek, but often fail, to claim permanence. Traffic regulations are laxly enforced and housing is unevenly codified. Healthcare services lack funds, and educational institutions are underserved. Electoral campaigns, Ramadan festivities, police raids, and royal visits bring a slight uptick in the presence of public officials, but their very garishness points to their infrequency. Faced with this marginalization, many Ma'anis often blame the state for their economic deprivation, poverty, and unemployment. Deficient public services are frequently portrayed as a form of punishment for past unrest, and the austerity measures have only exacerbated such sentiments. But, to my surprise, there is hope for the state, not just hope against it.[87] The bakery is crucial to maintaining this paradox. As the site of a popular welfare program, the bread-maker not only makes the state materially tangible, it reanimates it as an ideal and is crucial to its affective rendering. Under conditions where the state's presence is variable and lacking a stable ground, it is the repetition of flour deliveries, the reiteration of ministerial inspections, and the consistency of bread provision that allow the Hashemite regime to "act like a state," one with benevolence rather than coercion at its core.[88] This helps explain the seemingly contradictory feeling many local residents have towards the state—its ambivalent appeal.

CONCLUSION

State power manifests itself across Jordanian territory, but it does not encompass or cover contiguous geographic space. Rather, it jumps from point to point, and huge areas are routinely bypassed. The omnipresence of coercive agencies coincides with special economic zones bereft of manifest governmental interventions; intensely regulated commercial spaces stand next to informal housing settlements and untaxed businesses. State power does not flow smoothly from Ramtha in the north to Aqaba in the south; governmental practices neither covet nor are they capable of uncomplicated reach across national territory.[89] Instead, state power leaps and hops. It assembles selectively, is exercised and experienced erratically, an unstable product of negotiations and relationships between a host of people and things that cut across proximity and distance.[90] The resulting entanglements are shifting, transitory, and tenuous—open-ended encounters that reproduce the state, even if differently.[91] In this respect, a topological approach draws attention to more intricate institutional arrangements as well as to the shifting ties, connections, and relationships through which the state is composed. More crucially, it helps illuminate the textured patterns through which political authority echoes, reaches, and acquires presence. In both Aqaba and Ma'an, the state apparatus is discontinuous, a disjointed specter in most people's lives. In the former, it claims a minimal appearance; its light regulatory touch seeks to attract foreign investment. In the latter, legacies of violent repression, minimal investment opportunities, and irregular patronage practices are some of the reasons people decry its shortcomings. Yet even in these two cities, where the forms and functions of government have changed dramatically over the past thirty years, citizens remain witness to particular practices through which the state is performed. Crucial in this respect is the universal subsidy of *khubz 'arabi*, a governmental practice enacted with just enough regularity to reproduce relationships of power. Of course, Ma'anis, like Aqabawis, have day-to-day encounters with schools and health services, both of which contribute to their impressions of how and for whom state institutions operate. But it is also during their trips to the bakery, a routine vital to the survival of many residents, that the state "permeates everyday life in ways that go without saying."[92]

I began this chapter with Basel because of how often he spoke of the state as a tangible thing. Usually it was to criticize; at other times it was to mock and, very occasionally, to praise. Longing and fear, desire and condemnation were all entangled in a "relation of misrecognition" from which he simply could not, and probably did not want to, be extricated.[93] For besides his fondness for cold beer, Basel was also a notorious lover of falafel sandwiches, wrapped exclusively in subsidized *khubz 'arabi*. I would beg and plead for a dietary shift, maybe an occasional rice dish, perhaps some fish. Very rarely would I win him over. Basel adored what he termed *kebab al-fuqara* (kebab of the poor) and would go out of his way to find those sandwich makers who used handmade subsidized bread. As the end of our weekend visit in Aqaba approached, we needed to make two final stops, Basel told me. "First we get beer for home," he declared, "and then falafel sandwiches for the road." As we left, once we had crossed the customs checkpoint and set out on the long drive back to Amman, I told Basel how much I had enjoyed the weekend and hoped that we would come back more often. "Aqaba is great, I love it," he responded. "If only the rest of the country were like this." I asked him what he meant. "The police treats you with respect. The state doesn't tax you. It gives you cheap beer and bread. What else do you need?" Presence and absence; approval and critique. The spatial, moral, and historical grounds that underpin these encounters and appeals vary, but all work to constitute the state in some shape or form. Representations have productive effects—they echo. Citizens may relate to the state through compromises, complicity, cynicism, or sincere appeal, but they do not cease to reproduce the state as the great enframer of their lives.

Chapter 5

TACTICS AT THE BAKERY

AT FOUR THIRTY IN THE MORNING, Hani ambles down the hill from his house in Jabal B, a poor neighborhood in East Amman. A five-minute walk takes him to his bakery. He turns on the lights, takes a quick glance at some paperwork, jump-starts the flour mixer, and fires up the oven. By five, all of his workers have joined him. They drop their coats and belongings in the backroom as they arrive, and then begin the day's labor. The same six men will work until nine at night, rotating among different tasks throughout the day, and breaking up their long workday with a two-hour lunch break (see chapter 3). Hani spends most of the day at the cash register, chain-smoking. From his perch, he greets customers, barks orders to his employees, and sorts out the minutiae that make the business run: ordering salt, paying electricity bills, sorting out the payroll, and procuring discounted flour. It is the last of these tasks that consumes much of his time and causes the majority of his unease.

Three bakeries operate in Jabal B. One is smaller than Hani's, with just two employees. The other closes at three in the afternoon, following the lunch rush. For local residents, many of whom work in the wealthier neighborhoods of West Amman, Hani's outlet is therefore the closest place where they can buy bread for dinner. For others, it is the easiest place to obtain provisions for an early breakfast. The bakery's proximity to the neighborhood mosque also contributes to its popularity. Hani sells only subsidized *khubz 'arabi*. He prefers not to prepare any of the other, nonsubsidized wheat-based products from which other baker-ies derive most of their profits. His business practices target the local customer base: "Most families in this neighborhood are very poor. They may eat lamb or chicken once a week, they buy sweets in the *balad* (downtown) for holidays, but they eat bread with almost every meal," he reasons. Since 2012, Jabal B has witnessed a substantial influx of Syrian refugees, drawn by cheap rents and the neighborhood's proximity to a major public transportation hub.[1] Hani estimates that his customer base has grown by 15,000 people, yet his bakery has not been given a commensurate increase in its flour quota. This does not endanger his business—profits on subsidized bread sold from his quota remain steady at 7%—but it does threaten the routines, rhythms, and subsistence of his customers. Under his current flour allocation, subsidized bread would be scarce by three or four in the afternoon, he estimates. Faced with this conundrum, Hani commits a crime. Once a week, he meets a ministerial employee and pays him a bribe that ensures supplementary deliveries of discounted flour. Why? To what end? Although arrangements such as these are frequently called corruption, nepotism, or a failure of governance, I argue that they are better understood as *tactics* through which Jordanians negotiate and reorganize state power. Discrepancies between ambitions and outcomes traverse landscapes of rule; intended outcomes are never guaranteed. And sometimes, on occasion, these discrepancies favor the governed, rather than the forces that rule them.

In the process of providing bread to the country's residents, MOITS must construct, calculate, and rationalize that which it distributes and those who receive it. To render this arena of intervention both technical and improvable, humans and things must be bounded, mapped, classified, and documented.[2] Reference grids, censuses, and inspection forms seek to construct an abstract field of observation through which the governmental gaze can travel without impediment.[3] By reducing the messiness of place and practice, these "inscrip-tion devices"[4] make information both knowable and quantifiable, so as to make governance easier. Yet as numerous examples throughout this book have already shown, the bakery is a lively domain not easily made amenable to calculation or oversight.

Henri Lefebvre's work is useful for examining how and why divergences may occur. Lefebvre posits that during the transition to capitalist modernity, government institutions produce and disseminate a new form of socio-spatial organization. Lefebvre terms this "abstract space," a conceptualization that sees space as a solid, measurable substance, "an objectified, reified *thing*."[5] Planners, economists, developers, and bureaucrats of all stripes are crucial to the circulation of abstract space. By codifying and partitioning everyday life into calculable grids and clearly delineated jurisdictions, abstract space seeks to entrench capitalist modes of calculation in the realms of production and exchange, along with more comprehensive forms of control in the realm of statecraft.[6] MOITS's meticulous set of calculative practices offers an example. The ministry's data gathering and regulatory efforts mold what is dynamic and vibrant into a tangible, measurable microcosm, circulating the state's logic of socio-spatial control over humans and things.[7] Lefebvre was hardly a proponent of the dissemination of abstract space and remained sharply critical of the apolitical veneer through which it was deployed. He often contended that such efforts rarely accomplish that which they set out to achieve.[8] Whether it be humans, objects, environments, or practices, this "obdurate terrain" presents important constraints on that which governmental interventions seek to bring about.[9] And it is the spontaneity of everyday life that Lefebvre advances as a primary arena for prospective disruption, "the starting point for the realization of the possible."[10]

Michel de Certeau shares with Lefebvre an enduring interest in the everyday, although he is less convinced of its revolutionary potential.[11] In *The Practice of Everyday Life*, de Certeau dissects the ways in which subjects play with the powerful by using the very products and tools imposed on them, neither submitting to the demands of hegemonic forces nor confronting them head-on. He examines how people talk, walk, cook, and dwell, illustrating how citizens, by way of their ordinary actions, creatively manipulate strategies that entrench order. He calls these ruses "tactics."[12] While de Certeau tends to obscure the implication of citizens in power and overstates the coherence of governmental strategies, he nevertheless extends the domain of politics beyond formal institutions and collective action to the diverse ways of operating within everyday life. Frequently mythologized as the mundane, or the repository of passivity, it is everyday life that "harbors the most elusive depths, obscure corners, transient corridors that evade political grids and controls."[13] However, de Certeau's story is not one of revolution or grand upheaval but of stubbornness, obstinacy, and creativity. Throughout his work, he stresses the innumerable constraints and confined objectives of tactics. When "order is tricked by an art," it is often done without any illusion that this order will change anytime soon: it is a maneuver "within an enemy's field of vision" and "within enemy territory."[14] Tactics may deflect power, evade it, or redirect its strategies, but they do so always within its field of operation.

I find de Certeau's concept to be productive because it allows us to examine actions undertaken at the bakery not merely as reactive survival measures or modes of straightforward resistance to austerity or authoritarianism. His work, like that of Lefebvre, helps elucidate the diffuse and ingenious ways in which individuals caught up in governmental strategies enact ways of living that do not respond to singular causes and effects. Although a corpus of research on the politics of everyday life, largely inspired by James Scott,[15] has drawn our attention to the various mechanisms through which subaltern classes engage with their socioeconomic circumstances, these works far too frequently rely on dichotomous categories of domination and resistance. In the Middle East, such practices have frequently been portrayed as defensive coping mechanisms or acts of routine defiance that function as the building blocks of popular mobilization.[16] While the recent Arab uprisings do seem to indicate that these practices have the potential to "become infrastructures of action—foundations upon which resistance in the form of collective action can be built,"[17] their importance is not exhausted by such possibilities. Time in the field allowed me to observe actions that exhibit discontent but rely on calculated accommodation, that escape government suppression while also making use of public resources. They are neither revolutionary nor an indication of passivity. Of course, subversion is sometimes involved, but so too are improvisation, negotiation with authorities, and forms of "quiet encroachment"[18] through which ordinary people attempt to subsist and improve their lives. By attending to these compromised practices, this chapter, without succumbing to the "romance of resistance"[19] or sanitizing the politics of the subaltern,[20] will analyze just some of the ways in which citizens navigate the warrens of capitalist exchange and the grids of authoritarian rule. Melding Lefebvre's meditations on abstract space with de Certeau's notion of tactics, and drawing upon their shared concern with the quotidian, I contend that, at the bakery, Jordanians confound MOITS's classificatory grids and regulatory strategies while establishing alternative modes of togetherness that make precarity livable. Although the politics of these actions may be unclear, their tactical nature is familiar, recognizable, and, most importantly, effective.

Foregrounding them in this analysis seeks not only to problematize prevalent dichotomies (state/society, legal/illegal, corruption/transparency) but to illuminate some of the ways in which citizens appropriate public resources and refashion their lives amid the neoliberal and authoritarian logics that pervade the everyday in Jordan. And all while being entangled with the state—subversively, creatively, but inescapably.

JABAL B: BRIBING FOR SUBSISTENCE

During the day, the air in Jabal B was always thick and hazy. I would hope for a breeze, but it rarely arrived. Strong gusts would come instead, sweeping dust up off the ground and making me quickly regret having wished for a draft in the first place. Garbage was seldom collected; small fires to diminish the overflow were frequent. In the winter, sewage often seeped onto the smaller side streets, which were tightly packed with refuse to begin with. Water arrived twice a week. Electricity had moods—better not to ask or expect. Most residents of Jabal B were under- or informally employed.[21] Young men who were not employed at all would walk downtown for a stroll, while others simply sat on the stoop or street corner and hung out. Prosperous futures are not even promised here, so as not to raise anyone's hopes. The suffering is what Elizabeth Povinelli terms "ordinary, chronic and cruddy rather than catastrophic, crisis-laden and sublime."[22] Few can plan; instead, most search constantly among what is available to make ends meet. People strive, but mainly to persevere, a goal in and of itself. The ruling elite expects exhaustion and dejection in Jabal B. They probably assume that investments in public infrastructure would be wasted here. Neglect is easier and less costly. Those who want to make it out can put in some effort and swim against the tide. Others, well, they have to just tough it out or be swept away.

Apart from Fridays, when Hani's bakery only opened after the weekly prayer, the routine at the bakery was unwavering. Lunch plans varied. Friends or spouses occasionally came by for brief conversations. Government inspections every two weeks triggered a brief stoppage. But during work hours, the rhythms rarely fluctuated. The exception was Saturdays between four and five in the afternoon. At this hour, one of the bakery's rare downtimes, an acquaintance whom I did not initially recognize would arrive without fail.[23] During my first weeks working at Hani's, his weekly stopover caused an unease I could not grasp. Around thirty minutes before the man's expected arrival,

Hani would take the old cigarette carton that functioned as the bakery's cash register into the backroom. He would emerge edgy and apprehensive and pace around nervously until the man appeared. The visitor skillfully managed the entire episode. He would come in quietly, nod to Hani, and disappear into the backroom with him, where they spent a few minutes whispering together out of earshot. In less than five minutes he would be gone again, folded bills tucked away into his pocket. Fahed, I finally realized, was one of the several MOITS inspectors charged with overseeing bakeries in East Amman. Following his fifth consecutive Saturday visit, I put it together, though the casual *dishdasha* (caftan) he wore at these times formed a stark contrast to his workweek attire of slacks and a buttoned-down shirt. I had seen him during the routine inspections that MOITS staff undertook at this bakery twice a month. After eight weeks at Hani's, I decided to ask some of the workers about the purpose of his visit. "Corruption (*fasad*)," one worker told me; "there is no alternative (*ma fesh ghayru*)." I asked the workers to explain but they demurred, probably uneager to share their employer's business with an outsider whose presence they found puzzling. A month later, the routine still unchanged, I asked Hani about Fahed's visits. "Pay to play (*Al-dafʿa qabel al-rafʿa*),"[24] he stated jokingly, brushing my inquiry off. But after work ended that evening, Hani asked me to stay and offered to discuss my question.

Broadly popular and consistently defended, the bread subsidy undergirds one of the most consequential and recurring encounters of Jabal B's residents with the state apparatus, which seeks to meticulously control the production, distribution, and consumption of *khubz ʿarabi*. Yet this very monopoly periodically engenders inequitable outcomes, including neighborhoods where demand outstrips supply or vice versa. "As you can tell, we barely have enough bread for all our customers," Hani told me after a few pleasantries, "and this has only gotten worse over the past three years." I nodded in agreement as he went on to detail the various occasions on which he had requested an increase in his flour quota from MOITS, to no avail. "Every time, they [the ministry] say no. The bakery either does not have the baking capacity, or enough customers, or some other excuse." Hani then detailed how, for many of the neighborhood's residents, survival or modest levels of subsistence would not be possible without the subsidized foodstuff they were able to purchase at his bakery, a reality that drove him to take the steps I had witnessed. "My customers rely on me," he said, shrugging. "They know that at this bakery you can always find *khubz 'arabi* whenever we are open. Fahed helps me with this." Hani then expounded on the bribe itself, describing Fahed as an "old friend with a pure heart (*qalbu abyad*)," who understood "the situation," as he lived in a nearby neighborhood. Irritated by the ministry's intransigence, Hani had asked Fahed to arrange for supplementary deliveries of subsidized flour. He bought it at black market rates that left him minimal profits but made sure he had enough flour to stay open thirteen hours a day. Hani was quite cognizant of MOITS's ineffectiveness, although he was careful to distinguish between its "good" and "bad" employees. He openly acknowledged the imperfections in the temporary work-around he had found, suspecting that an optimal solution was far off. "I have no other choice," he averred. "The neighborhood depends on this bakery. We give it life (*'ayish* [literally life, figuratively bread])."

Hani claimed to run his business in accordance with Islamic precepts, practicing commerce through a higher order of ethics characterized by modesty, thriftiness, and abstention from superfluous profits. These traits were exemplified in his decision to pay higher wages to his workers and sell only subsidized bread, made strictly from discounted flour. During the lengthy workdays, he would often cite a *hadith* (prophetic saying): "He is not a believer whose stomach is filled while his neighbor goes hungry." These commitments superseded other prisms through which this bribe might have been assessed, immersed as this bakery owner was in what Amira Mittermaier terms "a divine order and in concrete material contexts."[25]

Local residents did not openly acknowledge Hani's black-market purchases, but implicitly, they gave them their imprimatur. "We appreciate this place," said one technician from a nearby garage who always purchased provisions for lunch. "We are thankful the owner does what he must to make our subsistence possible." His younger assistant echoed this sentiment: "Everyone needs help in this neighborhood. Sometimes you call a friend or a family member who works in the public sector and they do what they can. The state does little here [in Jabal B]; we have to protect and help each other. Hani does this. We all do."

Lacking the clout to change laws or policies, residents of Jabal B often work with street-level bureaucrats to access resources. Sometimes they do so using money, and other times they mobilize sympathies and notions of justice that are hard for public officials to deny. Making life livable matters far more than the legality of such practices. Diane Singerman and Salwa Ismail document similar dynamics in two different popular quarters of Cairo, where suspicion of the state fosters tax evasion and extralegal investments that are both common and seen as legitimate in the eyes of the community.[26] Similarly, negative experiences with state power foster a sense of shared conviviality and complicity among Jabal B's residents. Although I suspect that many residents knew of or could guess the extent of the black-market operations that made Hani's extensive opening hours possible, his noble aims, coupled with widespread distrust of the state, not only precluded disapproval but actively garnered praise among his customers.[27] The condition of generalized corruption appeared to justify lesser illegalities. There were few other pathways through which to surmount structural denials. Ultimately, Hani's success was judged neither by profit margins nor by victories in a normative political sphere but, rather, by his deft management of what was still an extralegal arrangement but that was not, despite its criminalization, necessarily considered illicit by local residents.[28] Reducing such exchanges to a normative breakdown of governance or a corruption of public programs places them far outside the context within which they were interpreted by the residents of Jabal B.

When describing his business, Hani portrayed the bakery as more than simply a workplace, profit source, or dispenser of public goods, preferring to identify it as a site of moral and effective economic action, a principled alternative to what he deemed a nationally compromised state of affairs. "The bakery feeds people, and at a just price," he was fond of saying. "Elsewhere, it is about profits and earnings. Politicians and the wealthy take advantage of ordinary citizens. Here [at the bakery] it is about people and bread, not profits." Local residents similarly described the bakery as a place somehow removed from the vicissitudes of the free market. "I feel safe at Hani's," one regular customer explained. "The prices do not change. It is the one time in the day when I purchase something without thinking about my budget or the difficulties of making ends meet." Another frequent customer, an employee at a nearby sandwich shop, also affirmed his attachments to this place: "Hani makes money," he reasoned, "but his bakery is not a regular business only concerned with profit. We all feel like it is a fixed part of our neighborhood. The owner cares for the customers, who rely on his bread to live." The language of neighborly interdependence here signals a profoundly different conception of the bakery than the language of impartial provision deployed in MOITS documents. Bread-makers and consumers coexist in Jabal B—proximity and subsistence mean they do far more than exchange bread for money. They do not flirt, but live a protracted romance, marked by a shared set of expectations that are manifested in the things that they simply cannot refuse each other—a cigarette, help dodging the police, or a loaf of bread.

Jabal B's residents were under no illusions about how or for whom the city "worked." Their feelings of estrangement emerged, in part, from a sense that those in power were working from a different set of values than their own, that they were dedicated to profit-seeking machinations rather than the public needs of Amman's inhabitants. It was no secret to these city-dwellers that political elites cared far more for the welfare of business than the business of welfare. Nevertheless, when faced with the slow erosion of their livelihoods—a lack of steady employment, a dearth of public services, the inequities of informal labor markets—Hani and his customers did not invoke the terms of revolution or resistance. In the main, they drew on vocabularies of connection and mutual dependence. They criticized the unjust structures and abuses that ensured their dispossession, of course. They knew that the poverty they suffered was the result far more of governmental priorities than of a lack of public resources. But at the same time, they made constant gestures of support—lending a few dinars, inviting a hungry neighbor for dinner, offering childcare when work suddenly appeared. Hani's business practices avowed such positionings, as he evaded the strict logics of the market while promoting an "ethics of care" for the community.[29] The commercial bakery may have commodified food production previously relegated to the home (when it was largely undertaken by unpaid female labor), but even in this alienated form, it still held out the possibility, for many, that forms of commerce might work differently, more justly, slightly less oppressively. No one in Jabal B simply imbibed abstract space, or the marketized forms of exchange that came with it. Their daily lives and routines were infused with alternative rules and conventions.

Hani's business practices, especially his extensive opening hours and disregard for other retail trades (sweets, expensive varieties of bread), were widely commended by local residents. Many described him as an exemplary business owner and generous man (*rajul karim*), appreciative that his bakery defied the logics of "capital surplus absorption" that increasingly prevailed in Amman.[30]

Most of those I spoke to acknowledged that making public resources flow to the neighborhood was highly contingent on connections, influence, and, failing that, cash. In occasional moments of conversation after work, Hani would assert that government neglect was a product of Jabal B's poverty, majority-Palestinian population, and support for Islamists. To overcome these impediments, Hani worked with a member of MOITS to claim access to a public resource. He asserted a speculative right to subsistence while paying a bribe to ensure its fulfillment. MOITS has developed strategies to try and make such kickbacks visible, but these cannot account for the solidarities and alliances that can (occasionally) subvert regimes of classification.[31] In this respect, Hani's tactic is a commonplace way those in Jabal B work against their marginalization, aided by what Michael Herzfeld terms "the tangled skeins of complicity"[32] among agents of the state, business owners, and ordinary citizens. Street-level bureaucrats may assent to certain rules on paper but undermine them in practice, or they may scheme with those they are meant to oversee out of sympathy or personal gain. As Johan Mathew argues in relation to the arms trade in the Arabian Sea, "Not only was the distinction between state and society ambiguous, but the officials responsible for parsing this distinction were not always motivated to keep these categories distinct."[33] Welfare services are complicated by the fleeting alignments of those charged with their implementation and oversight.

At the same time, Hani's actions were not about resistance to domination but about the preservation of place-based practices that relied upon the tenuous reappropriation of public resources. Of course, his self-recognized ability to circumvent regulations did not mean that he had overcome the system or secured his long-term interests in perpetuity. Hani remained open to harassment, enforced closure, or onerous fines, realities he acknowledged with shrugs and wariness. Nor was the point to aggrandize bureaucratic negotiability as if it were a panacea for all of Jordan's residents, when in fact it usually worked in favor of the wealthy. What Hani's business practices illustrated was how any welfare service inevitably encounters a landscape entangled with social relations, urban livelihoods, and moral economies that shape how they are perceived, navigated, and enacted. Ideas and expectations of reciprocity, obligation, and appropriate conduct often outweigh the strictures of the law. Corruption and illegality had little purchase on Hani's tactics; no one I spoke to accused him of either. Many of them shared stories of pilfering public resources, which were far easier to capture for alternative uses than those that had been privatized. Like Hani's engagement with state power, such actions are not necessarily visible, spectacular, or direct. They bear more of a resemblance to Foucault's concept of counter-conduct, "a struggle against the processes implemented for conducting others," exertions made "not to be governed like that."[34] Far from transcending the state or seeking its downfall, these tactics were intimately tied to, even relied on, its strategies of rule. Hani's purposeful navigation of government regulations, here seen in the unofficial purchase of subsidized flour from a ministerial employee, and the world of relations that gave meaning to such practices, constituted the terms by which this baker disrupted and reordered state performances without outright challenging the order they sought to enshrine. To ensure that his bakery met his own high standards, Hani had to cultivate social relations not only with local residents but also with ministry officials. He had to negotiate fields of power as well as precise combinations of flour, water, and yeast.

JABAL C: SWEETENING LIVES

Jabal C is a lower-middle-class neighborhood in Amman. It covers an area of 4 square kilometers and houses approximately 55,000 residents. The quarter began as an extension of a nearby Palestinian refugee camp in the early 1950s. Over the following two decades, it expanded steadily. As with a few other sections of East Amman established near urban refugee camps, the quarter was slowly integrated into the capital's urban sprawl and increasingly came to resemble other low-to-middle-income neighborhoods in the city.[35] Jabal C is now a bustling commercial district. Local inhabitants work predominantly in the service sector. Small shopping malls, independent clothing shops, medical clinics, and restaurants are scattered throughout the neighborhood. While some families in the community are poor, most are lower middle class. In spite of the disposable income and savings that many possess, their economic well-being is far from secure. Rising food and real estate prices are a source of constant worry and anxious conversation. I spent much of my time in Jabal C at *al-Rif,* one of six bakeries in this subdistrict of Amman. As I outlined in chapter 3, when I described my apprenticeship at this bakery, *al-Rif* produces mechanized *khubz 'arabi.* It also sells nonsubsidized *khubz ash-shrak*,[36] a key ingredient in *mansaf,* Jordan's national dish.[37] The bakery also produces an array of sweet biscuits (*ka'k*) that are usually dipped in tea (see figure 10). The

FIGURE 10. Varieties of kaʿk.

latter, which come in various shapes, sizes, and flavors, sold very poorly, a constant source of frustration for the bakery's owner. Confident of the quality of his *kaʿk*, Hamza blamed dubious machinations at Samir's, one of three nearby bakeries, for his bad luck.

After leaving *al-Rif*, I would usually wander around the neighborhood, shop for household supplies, or join friends for coffee. One day, my curiosity piqued, I went to examine Samir's baked goods. The reason for his success at selling biscuits quickly became apparent. Samir's *kaʿk* cost, on average, around half the price of its equivalents at other bakeries. Hamza, the owner of *al-Rif*, was wholly unsurprised by my findings. He explained how this drastic markdown was achieved: Hamza presumed that Samir made private use of a public resource, concealing its subsidized origins. He did so by shrewdly mixing discounted flour (*muwwahad*) with the nondiscounted Zero variety typically used for biscuits (see figures 11 and 12).[38] Because the discounted floor cost one-tenth as much as the nondiscounted variety, Samir could sell *kaʿk* at a dramatically lower price than his competitors, all while retaining a considerable

FIGURE 11. Subsidized flour (*muwwahad*).

FIGURE 12. Nonsubsidized flour (Zero).

profit margin.[39] *Al-Rif*'s owner accused Samir of "fraud," of cheating both the government and his customers, who either could not tell the difference or, given the price, did not care. Hamza's protestations to ministerial officials were frequent and heated. On more than one occasion I heard him lodge accusations over the phone. I was told that, partly due to such complaints, Samir's bakery had been shut down on various occasions. But it always reopened the next day, a product of his connections at the ministry, *al-Rif*'s owner inferred. It turned out, however, that the story was more complex.

I eventually met Samir through a mutual friend at the Bakery Owners Association (BOA). He proved a stark contrast to the scheming caricature that had been described to me at *al-Rif*. Exuberant and cheerful, Samir had infectious energy and a smile that was never too far from his face. His public self-presentation was that of a devout, God-fearing businessman, traits reflected in his place of business. Samir's bakery was filled with Qur'anic *suras*, and a sign behind his cash register read: "The importance of bread derives from Islam." The place was always bustling, packed full with customers purchasing an array of baked goods throughout the day. Samir supplemented these retail transactions with a thriving wholesale trade with nearby hotels and restaurants. In explaining his success, which positioned him in the upper echelons of Jordan's small middle class, Samir emphasized the social networks he had forged and accumulated. He had built connections with other merchants through activities such as fundraising for local charities. On three separate evenings during Ramadan, I witnessed Samir and his business associates organize *Mawa'id al-rahman* (banquets of the Merciful), public meals during which the poor are given food to break their fast, just outside of his bakery. In addition to accumulating valuable symbolic capital, the social dimension of such acts helped to develop ties between benefactors and recipients, which Samir would draw upon in key moments. Customers whom I asked or interviewed spoke of him highly, as did neighboring business owners, who appreciated the foot traffic his bakery generated. And when I eventually asked him about his *ka'k* prices, Samir was surprisingly forthcoming. Before 2007, every variety of flour had been universally subsidized, he noted (accurately). But new legislation then caused a huge price rise in all wheat-based goods except for *khubz 'arabi*, which became the only product that MOITS supported with discounted flour.[40] While Samir saw no reason why croissants or fancy baguettes should receive government support, *ka'k* was different. "Cheap *ka'k* to dip in tea is hardly a luxury," he insisted. "Enjoying these little pleasures offers a moment of respite during the long workday, or a small indulgence for poor families who could afford little else." Crucially, his customers agreed.

During my time living in Amman, Samir's bakery was closed on two occasions. Following complaints from anonymous members of the public, MOITS officials would arrive and inspect the extraction rate of various flour sacks and the quality of his baked goods. When inconsistencies were suspected, officials would meticulously catalogue their findings on the appropriate inspection forms. After the ministry's biweekly meeting to discuss violations across the country, a committee would decree a temporary suspension of subsidized flour deliveries to Samir and issue him a modest fine. His response to these government interventions was neither rebellious nor compliant but tactical. He would shut his shop the same afternoon the decision was issued and post a placard outside his business blaming the ministry for the bakery's closure. That evening, he would mobilize friends and acquaintances for a protest outside the bakery. The following day, a crowd would gather on the street and sidewalks, chanting various slogans revolving around bread. Hawkers, restaurant workers, and off-duty construction personnel in the vicinity were the main participants in the two such protests I witnessed. The traffic police, who had been notified of the gathering ahead of time, casually stood among the protesters. I watched uncomfortably as Samir approached them. He listed his complaints and explained the reasons for the protest. His remarks emphasized bread's importance to the community and how the penalties endangered local residents' access to a key subsistence good: "Our survival is at stake" and "our existence is in danger" were phrases he used repeatedly. Samir concluded by animating the crowd, which was now energetically waving loaves of bread.

To my surprise, the police were apathetic; two officers were holding back smiles. Notwithstanding the public spectacle, their interactions with the protesters were affable, even affectionate. The conversation that followed Samir's remarks made it clear that the police's concern was not with the substance of the bakery owner's demands but with the logistics of the demonstration. The policeman explained that their job was to avoid traffic buildups and violence. Like the hawker pickets that Jonathan Anjaria documents in Mumbai, the demonstrations outside Samir's bakery were "no dramatic challenge to authority but a cordial encounter."[41] This was neither a spontaneous expression of communal anger nor a typical opposition-led political rally; it was instead a tactical medium used to communicate local grievances. Samir did not seek to contest the Hashemite regime, which he openly supports and praises, but to marshal the state apparatus to serve particular ends.

Once the press arrived, the gathering quickly dissipated. The demonstrators dispersed and Samir huddled for a round of press interviews, some of which appeared on the nightly news. As Samir recounted, by seven or eight the same evening he would receive a phone call from a ministry official, who would duly inform him that the penalties imposed had been rescinded. "For the ministry, it is not worth the bother," he told me with a smile. "Their job is to stay out of the news, and they must have received twenty angry phone calls from powerful people yesterday." Knowing this, Samir would choreograph a protest to try to produce a desired outcome: he would notify not only the police but also the press, who would make an appearance and transmit to the broader public the complaints aired in Jabal C. Due to his astute cultivation of communal networks, this baker never became the object of collective rancor; he was viewed as the victim rather than the instigator of the bakery's closure. Fearful of social unrest or of appearing indifferent to popular demands, anonymous ministry officials would respond by annulling the monetary fine as well as the suspension of discounted flour. Samir's approach to his bakery's closure, as well as the reaction of his customers and friends, shows how rarely the state is experienced as a unitary entity; instead, it is seen as something far more disconnected and fragmentary. As in Ma'an and Aqaba, opposing one mode of intervention does not mean opposing the state as such. Samir's success, and the informal functioning of government that it seems to indicate, do not mark a complete absence of rules or laws. Rather, they illuminate how the intermittent exercise of government control, the murkiness of the law, and the negotiations around it suffuse everyday life.

I was struck by this event because of what it revealed about the possible kinds of engagements citizens have with state institutions. Through his mobilization of local networks and clever use of crowd action, Samir mobilized communal passions to convey local complaints. These distressed public authorities, who were concerned about unrest. Yet neither his maneuver nor the protest outside his bakery qualifies as a straightforward moment of resistance. Far from contesting the sovereignty of the state or seeking its downfall, Samir's actions recognized the state's authority and its ability to adjudicate discounted flour and impose penalties. He strove instead to manage ministerial interventions, to shape the relationship between the law and its application at the bakery. While the criminalization of his business practices might seem to have closed off certain possibilities, his use of shrewd tactics allowed this bakery owner to defy governmental regulations in a fashion that was awkward for the Hashemite regime to suppress, given its commitment to "the Jordanian people." Samir knew well that the state's presence is often bought at the cost of dispersed power and muddled outcomes. Even though his *ka'k* remained illegal, his response to MOITS's penalties produced extralegal recognitions of his baking practices, which were provisionally recognized through unofficial compromise. It is here, in this interstice, that the possibility of counterfeit *ka'k* was determined. Samir's success illustrates how navigating MOITS's regulations involves managing extraction rates and subsidized flour quotas but also proficiency in "negotiating dense (and equally opaque) networks of mediation" that include ministry officials, elected politicians, members of the media, and loyal customers.[42] In this respect, Jordan's bakers do not navigate a political sphere of rights-bearing citizens or the rational machinery of an anonymous bureaucracy. Rather, they operate within a supple terrain of (il)legalities where success means neither revolution nor social upheaval but, as Samir put it, the ability to "sweeten [people's] lives."

Widely denounced by government officials as fraud that jeopardizes the bread subsidy's future, Hani's awkward Saturday payoff and Samir's purposeful closure are much more than a perversion of how this welfare program ought to work. While the payment of bribes and the selective enforcement of regulations seem to point to the presence of a predatory state, the relationships and practices that emerge from such encounters also serve to open up possibilities. "Corruption" here does not work only to alienate or disenfranchise citizens, as is so often surmised. More concretely, the selective enforcement of regulations enables substantive rights to bread to be negotiated and maintained, outside the proceduralist realm of the law. For those with little or no access to governmental bodies, it offers one of the few levers through which to demand services or material improvements. Such dynamics also make clear that policemen, ministerial employees, bakers, and ordinary citizens are not autonomous agents of the state, business, and society but are likewise entangled in ongoing relations of kinship, friendship, and community that engulf the governmental grids and analytic binaries that seek to carve them up. Simple dichotomies between resistance and domination, corruption and transparency, state and society cannot capture the generative and productive nature of these relationships that, in a practical sense, offer avenues through which to negotiate welfare provisions that otherwise may very well go undelivered. Notwithstanding efforts to codify the bakery through ordered diagrams and governable grids, people strive to create, preserve, and expand places of social reproduction in ways that do not neatly correspond to abstract space's classificatory logic.[43] Laws and constitutionally defined rights matter little in Jabal B and C. More important are the transient, contextual, and erratic arrangements arrived at through direct negotiations.[44] Compromises, bargains, and tensions characterize the citizenry's everyday encounters with the state apparatus—a contingent formation whose apparent unity always condenses contradictions.

JABAL D: BREAD FOR FREE

I want to further sift through some of these contradictions by way of a third ethnographic example. *Jawharat Amman* (The Jewel of Amman) is an emporium of baked products. In addition to *khubz ʿarabi*, it sells a bewildering collection of wheat-based goods, ranging from Western-style cakes to Arabic sweets (*baklava, harisa, basbusa*) and more expensive varieties of bread (baguette, *khubz tanur, khubz saj*). Located in Jabal D, a rapidly expanding wealthy neighborhood of Amman, its offerings target an affluent clientele. However, the bakery's proximity to a working-class housing settlement, coupled with the presence of day laborers and a nearby factory, mean that it cannot eschew the sale of subsidized *khubz ʿarabi*. This bakery's production patterns, like those of Hani's bakery in Jabal B, have been affected by the influx of Syrian refugees, many of whom work informally in the area. Nevertheless, the owner's response to his growing customer base has been far different. Khaled, the bakery's owner, has an extensive business empire. In addition to three bakeries scattered throughout the city, he owns four restaurants and is involved in various event-planning enterprises. Khaled scoffed at the idea of bribing ministry officials; the risk was simply not worth the paltry reward, although he was far from unaware of the problems that plagued bread provision: "The current subsidy mechanism is impossible to police. Corruption can arise from so many different directions . . . It is also very hard for bakers," he noted. "If we want to temporarily increase production to serve new customers, or decrease it to avoid wastage, it is impossible to change our flour quota when we need to. So we just produce as always, and have months, for instance in the summer and during Ramadan, when less *khubz ʿarabi* is consumed and much of it is wasted."[45] I asked Khaled what happened to the leftover bread, mentioning other cases where bakers sold their surplus to farmers, who would use it as animal feed. "I used to give it away," he said. "But now we have the campaign."

Two months before I began working at *Jawharat*, the bakery had signed on to a novel initiative founded by two Jordanians unconnected in any way to the bread industry. Christened the "Bread for Free Campaign," the project partners with receptive bakeries to provide subsidized bread free of charge. It does so through an ingenious set of practices that neither escape government regulations nor subvert them, but instead navigate them tactically. First, the project's founders, a lawyer and a fashion entrepreneur, contact bakery owners and explain their project. If the establishment's proprietor agrees, they begin by providing him or her with 30 JD per month. In exchange, the baker must use these funds for the purchase of subsidized bread, which is placed on a shelf or counter in the bakery's retail space that displays the campaign's sign. The latter reads: "This bread is free, for those who cannot afford it" (see figure 13). The initiative then encourages customers to buy subsidized bread and leave it on the designated shelf where those in need can find it, so that the founders' monthly contribution eventually becomes unnecessary. In *Jawharat*, the campaign had proceeded largely as expected. When they saw the sign, customers would ask a staff member about the campaign, which was quickly explained. Many would then buy a few extra kilograms of subsidized bread and deposit them on the designated shelf, while others preferred to pay the cashier an extra amount that they would ask to have directed towards the initiative.

According to the campaign's founders, the project was inspired by the existing practices of Amman's bakery owners, many of whom already quietly offered free bread to the indigent and unemployed. Since the campaign's launch in 2012, its founders had refused large donations and kept an intentional distance from the media and government "in an effort to ensure our purity," as

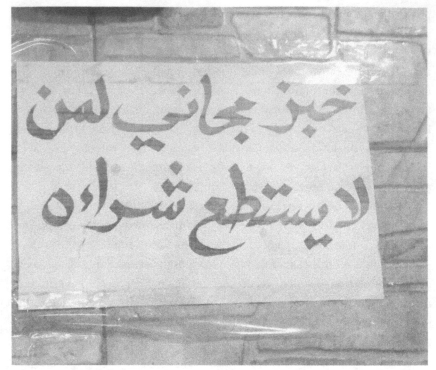

FIGURE 13. Sign in an Ammani bakery: "This bread is free, for those who cannot afford it."

one of them stated, because "they would only interrupt our work and harm its effectiveness." The campaign's approach was shaped by its originators' view of the state, which was largely negative. They portrayed MOITS as a bureaucratic monster, "infiltrated by personal interests and political considerations." In addition, they critiqued social welfare policies more broadly as inefficient, doing little to help those in need. The inadequacy of government interventions means that it is up to ordinary citizens such as themselves to devise innovative solutions. "The state does not do enough. It leaves it to citizens to solve most problems," they told me. The campaign's founders argued that Bread for Free sought to reawaken civic consciousness and avoid acute deprivation through a highly localized initiative that reinforced the symbolism of bread. The campaign's self-declared goal was to create connections between people "in a very direct way, to help individuals help each other without government interference."⁴⁶ And while the two founders criticized institutionalized welfare for failing to assist the needy efficiently or comprehensively, they did not see their initiative as charity, either. They were actively seeking to avoid denigrating or institutionalizing their beneficiaries and preferred the anonymity of a shelf filled with bread over the kind of very visible occasions where prominent individuals donate food to the poor. By doing away with distinctions between donors and recipients, Bread for Free sought to disrupt the paternalist logics that accompany charitable initiatives, while conjuring a momentary collectivity inflected by relations of interdependence.

Despite their relative wealth, the campaign's founders portrayed themselves as "estranged citizens."⁴⁷ They lacked both the wealth to influence policy on a macro scale and the knowledge of street-level collusions through which bakers ensure access to subsidized bread. The campaign's two founders felt excluded from both the politics of the elite and the informal machinations of the poor and well-connected. Despite longings for more effective forms of governance, they recognized the pervasiveness of bureaucratic inertia and negotiated legalities. Yet rather than engage with these gray areas directly, they preferred to navigate around them. Bread for Free sought to offer a discreet but direct form of assistance that, while technically illegal, tendered disinterested succor and much-needed food to Jordanians. Like cast-off bread, which is almost always left outside rather than thrown away, the campaign performed "public gestures of consideration for others in need even if those gestures neither are based on, nor create, long-term relationships with these others."⁴⁸ But as the founders of Bread for Free insisted, their goals were far from insurrectionary. Mutual aid, the prevention of food waste, and disinterested assistance could all be viewed as trenchant critiques of the capitalist consumer culture that increasingly dominated everyday life in Amman. The campaign also implicitly pointed to drastic shortcomings in governance in a country where not everyone had enough to eat. Yet Bread for Free sought neither to overturn class distinctions, overthrow the monarchy, nor bring about significant structural change. The campaign's self-proclaimed objective was limited to relieving the poor and refugees without creating either dependency or institutionalized entitlement.

The view from MOITS was very different. As one ministerial official cynically put it: "The campaign works because it lets bakers profit from and get rid of supplies they would otherwise throw away. It's a great business strategy. More people come to the bakery and what would have gone unsold, is sold."[49] While the initiative had proven too popular to be curtailed, its distortion of governmental grids was foremost in the mind of this official. "We have no relationship with this campaign," he relayed. "We give discounted flour quotas based on our own criteria, and while we do not think our calculations have been too affected by the initiative, the ministry worries that it only further undermines the sustainability of the bread subsidy."[50] For this bureaucrat, the campaign only served to drain funds from a welfare program already under harsh financial scrutiny.

Others at MOITS were slightly more sympathetic. They described the program as an emergency-induced measure that filled a crucial niche in the face of the Syrian refugee influx. This attitude was especially on display among the more senior officials in the bureaucratic hierarchy. Because the campaign was premised on the illegal use of subsidized bread, they could not openly support it. Yet they could not ignore it either. Distortions notwithstanding, most senior officials seemed to acknowledge that the campaign fostered subsistence, which they saw as the primary task of the bread subsidy.[51] As a result, they dealt with the campaign not as a group of citizens or a legal civil society initiative but as an expedient instrument for the administration of welfare to marginal groups. So long as social stability was maintained, self-help activities and legal infractions could more easily be overlooked. Although such technically illegal solutions were not openly acknowledged, perhaps the fact that they were tacitly tolerated was felt to be a reasonable compensation for the broader withdrawal of social services. Whatever the reasons, at MOITS, calculations of political expediency, concerns about popular unrest, and a perceived obligation to look after the poor precluded efforts to eliminate the Bread for Free Campaign.

Meanwhile, at *Jawharat*, few cared about the ministry's disapproval. Throughout my stay there, a steady and varied stream of people would retrieve bread from the campaign's shelf, which was rarely empty. Many stopped to thank the employees, who took great pride in the initiative's success at their workplace.[52] Khaled, *Jawharat's* owner, saw it as an incredibly effective way to both combat starvation and prevent bread wastage, but also as much more than that. Like the female volunteers in the Jordanian Islamic charities surveyed by Jung and Petersen,[53] he presented his engagement with the campaign as a way not of changing society or politics but of fulfilling his individual religious duty. Helping to feed the poor by recirculating bread was a way of serving God. It was a disinterested gift to the divine that made its way to anonymous others, helping Khaled cultivate an ethical self.[54] The campaign's success was intimately tied to its ambiguity in this respect. While some of Khaled's employees saw it as a way of overcoming MOITS's inertia, others described it as an individualized form of pious behavior. No one described it as an overtly political act. The head baker with whom I most often coincided on my work shift styled it as a simple acknowledgment of interdependency among humans, a particular mode of togetherness in the present. "Who knows when you or I will be in need? The campaign recognizes that we all must live together. Hunger and poverty undermine this." By espousing neither explicitly religious vocabularies nor political goals, Bread for Free allowed Jordanians to infuse their actions at the bakery with whatever ethical or political positionings they saw fit. Equally important, no one involved was forced into either an oppositional stance or open compliance with the political order.

Bread for Free suggests a response to state power that is very different from public mobilization against price increases or organized lobbying that seeks to reform policy. It is also not the type of politically motivated Islamist service provision frequently studied in the Middle East. The campaign stands outside the binaries that so often inflect discussions of state and society, resistance and domination, offering an alternative set of practices whose politics are unclear. The entire initiative was based on tactically manipulating a well-regarded social welfare program, yet its impact was not systematically positive. By draining public coffers through the increased consumption of subsidized bread that it fostered, the campaign may have put the bread subsidy, long under the microscope of international financial institutions, in further peril. At the same time, the campaign offered a direct avenue through which Jordanians could assist their neighbors and help feed anonymous others. Yet in doing so, it may very well have been preventing the types of unrest that might have emerged were it not for such remedies. Recirculating what would have been wasted bread could offer a model for non-capitalist modes of exchange, but it was also easy for the campaign to be absorbed by horizons of capital and authoritarian rule that see such initiatives as a way of preventing starvation and unrest. Of course, Bread for Free, like the tactics explored earlier, established limits on the penetration of abstract space, while also demonstrating what alternative economic practices could look like. But in offering poor citizens another way of getting by, the campaign may have decreased the demand for organizations with explicit political agendas that pursue programmatic change. This is why de Certeau emphasizes the flagrant ambivalence of tactics; they can be both "expansively inclusive and oppressively exclusive," and need not come in emancipatory forms.[55] What is clear, however, is that governmental practices allow for unforeseen reconfigurations, enmeshed as they are in sedimented landscapes that shape their reach. Statistics can (possibly) grasp the extent and impact of these tactics—but not their form. Performing the state is a process continually in motion, one that is shaped by the exigencies of both rulers and ruled.

STATELY ENTANGLEMENTS AND RECONFIGURATIONS

MOITS maps bakeries, standardizes baking practices, and regulates consumption patterns throughout Jordan. But these classificatory schemes, and the socio-spatial conceptualizations of the world that they circulate, are not simply reflections of the world; they are models for it. To work, they must render humans and things legible, part and parcel of a process of standardization that seeks to make categories stick to a recalcitrant reality. But as Rose and Miller argue, "We do not live in a governed world so much as a world traversed by the 'will to govern,' fueled by the constant registration of 'failure,' the discrepancy between ambition and outcome."[56] Like all welfare services, the subsidized bread program must negotiate its conditions of possibility "on the ground." And its daily enactment allows for creative possibilities, for its reappropriation by the very people it is meant to categorize and control. These tactics can take several forms, and I have sought to highlight in the examples above just some of the ways in which ordinary people engage with the governmental strategies that seek to organize their lives. But the point I wish to emphasize here is how such negotiations, disruptions, and compromises do not interrupt or overcome the state, but may indeed help to consolidate it. In his excellent *Hydraulic City*, Nikhil Anand argues that leakages in Mumbai's water distribution infrastructure "trouble the form and formation of government," as they "interrupt performances of the authoritative, knowing state."[57] He claims that frictions, whether social, material, or political, "compromise projects to consolidate political authority."[58] I disagree, and contend that even amid cases of "failure," when intended outcomes are not achieved, welfare services and infrastructures continue to work on the social body. Of course, tactics at the bakery may derail the documentary regime through which the bread subsidy is administered. They can jeopardize the reputation of a bakery owner or ministry official, maybe even the welfare program itself. Yet still, the bread subsidy buoys the state, it gives it a certain matter-of-factness by virtue of its ability to lay claim to certain functions and serve as a site of address among citizens.[59] By learning the intricacies of the subsidy system, appealing to the bureaucracy for a remedy to shortages, or manipulating bread provision to further certain outcomes, tactics work to reinscribe the state in everyday life, even while opposing its logics of control.

This is where de Certeau and his notion of tactics may fall short. Unlike Bourdieu, he holds in high esteem the creativity and nimbleness of the powerless, as well as their dynamism and volition, rather than docility. However, de Certeau does not quite offer us the tools to think through the ways tactics relate to strategies, and the structures seen to uphold them. Jordanians can divert materials from their original uses, reinvent their modes of coexistence, and foster modes of social stabilization amid a ruthlessly unequal set of possibilities. Citizens can negotiate, outfox, and circumnavigate abstract space, but only once they accept, even if tacitly, the structures that govern them. Agency begins here, after citizens have met the requirements of subjection, a recognition that matters far more than obeying any one law or ordinance. The fact that regulations are violated or protocols not enforced does not mean that they fail to fulfill a purpose or have an effect. Individuals and communities may object to certain laws and conventions, they may even reconfigure government regulations or welfare programs in the process, but the form of their objections works to consolidate that which they take as given. Both the daily routines that ensure bread provision and the tactical distortions of this welfare program position the state in what Stuart Halls calls the "horizon of the taken-for-granted."[60] Tactics are intelligible, even successful, because they work through the same set of practices through which the state effect operates; they accept its form, if not necessarily its contents. This affords an insight into modes of rule that rely far less on governing populations legibly or exercising a monopoly on the legitimate use of force than on producing the very conditions through which reappropriations and dislocations occur. Although they may redirect it, tactics do not precede power. Not only are tactics reliant upon but, through routine entanglements, they reproduce the very political order in which they take place.

CONCLUSION

Amman's bakers epitomize many contradictions: cherished providers, despised competitors, and legitimized lawbreakers. Their practices defy easy characterization and their relationship with government institutions is complex, including predatory extortion, occasional collaboration, and uneasy compromise. Or consider the bakery itself. While planners and policy makers see it through the prism of abstract space—diagrams, grids, and statistics, all with objective properties—ordinary citizens and bread-makers imbue the bakery with meaning and adjust their practices accordingly. Inspectors are hardly unsympathetic to such attachments. They do not operate in a realm separate from the worlds they seek to regulate. Unauthorized arrangements between low-level ministry officials and bakers reflect relational histories and subtle negotiations that occur in a shared social milieu. These actors inhabit intersecting worlds, consume similar goods, and experience analogous forms of alienation from Amman's new sites of luxury consumption. Hierarchies of class, gender, and age undoubtedly inflect their modes of interaction, but these do not preclude certain forms of arbitration and compromise. Affinities are multiple and dense; few are unencumbered.

This does not mean we should be inattentive to the vast and enduring asymmetries of power that shape the exchanges among citizens, bakery owners, and agents of the state apparatus. I do not seek to idealize the bakery as a subaltern venue for service provision nor as an informal avenue of participation. Nor do I wish to posit the bakery as an insurrectionary site of resistance, offering some coherent alternative to the dominant order that can somehow stand in for radical ideological action.[61] Indeed, I aim to warn against romanticizing the precarious condition that bakeries such as Samir's and Hani's inhabit. Their practices situate them outside the law, and both bakers emphasized how, despite their contacts, their businesses remained insecure and their livelihoods precarious. Additionally, other bakers are not necessarily as successful in negotiating the fine lines between pragmatism, necessity, resourcefulness, and bribes. Some are caught between government regulations and uncodified norms, unable or unwilling to navigate this volatile terrain. Others face selective enforcement, repeated closures, and the relentless pressure of government prosecution. In spite of how successful their own tactics were, Samir and Hani went to great lengths to stress that the state maintains ultimate control over a basic subsistence good essential to the citizenry. What their actions do bring to the fore is the paucity of concepts through which such engagements with state power can be understood. Tactics might be seen as evidence for arguments about state weakness in Jordan. They could also be used to confirm frequently repeated narratives about bureaucratic inertia, cronyism, or deficiencies in the rule of law in the Middle East. I want to push against these facile interpretations and draw on ethnography to strike out in other directions—to push political scientists to be more attentive to the ways in which people operate in everyday life. If the arrangements through which the bread subsidy are enacted blur the boundaries between state and civil society, legality and illegality, corruption and transparency, it may very well be because these categories are descriptively incapable of capturing the lived realities they seek to portray. Perhaps politics worthy of study occurs outside formal institutions and social movements, where less visible stances of defiance and compromised positionings reign supreme. There is an art to governing, of course, but there is an art to being governed as well.

Notwithstanding government efforts to discipline and systematize distribution at the bakery, to objectify the citizenry by standardizing its rhythms and routines of bread consumption, Jordanians manipulate their objectified status through a repertoire of tactics. These take on a multiplicity of localized forms. Some work consistently. Others are more makeshift. Yet all seek, in some way or another, to alter the conditions of communal existence, to help people get by. I find de Certeau's concept of tactics productive because it offers a less loaded view of people's reluctance, refusal, and compromise in the face of power and a more ambiguous, less decisive, less ideologically driven lens through which to analyze the many ways in which citizens inhabit their subjection. The payment of bribes to ensure subsidized flour, the stubborn use of crowd action to safeguard illegal sweets, and the free provision of discounted bread through mutual assistance are not oriented against an abstract authoritarian regime or a unitary state but are far more situated—enmeshed in "contingent constellations of practice, milieu and materiality."[62] Born of necessity and perpetuated by cooperation and compromise, these actions lay claim to a specific terrain through direct, purposeful actions that shrewdly negotiate cross-cutting fields of power, taking place in their blind spots. Tactics at the bakery illustrate forms of agency that emerge from within power's terms, its unpredictable deviations. They are less about rebellion than about a calculated reappropriation that seeks to make precarity and interdependence livable. Too often, we ignore the ambivalence of such activities, which are more easily categorized as resistance. But as Saba Mahmood argues, "While acts of resistance to relations of domination constitute one modality of action, they certainly do not exhaust the field of human action."[63] That is to say, agentic capacity is operative not only in those practices that contest domination, but also in the various ways in which people inhabit power. Yet we continue to define political agency far too restrictively, as an active stance of defiance or opposition that takes place within a demarcated public sphere, or an intentionally concealed form of resistance in need of detection. In doing so, we not only foreclose certain questions about the workings of power but impose norms of hypervisibility and liberal politics on communities that have different ways of making community and eluding control.[64] To grasp this is to recognize the conundrums of those who live and labor in authoritarian settings and to appreciate the vast political terrain that lies between quiescence and revolt. It is also to embed the politics of place in everyday life, not as simple sites of subaltern resistance nor as part of a governmental apparatus of acquiescence. In the Hashemite Kingdom, bakeries are so much more.

Chapter 6

LEAVENED APPREHENSIONS

I WAS STUCK. No way out. I had jumped into a taxi early, at seven thirty in the morning, with the hopes of beating traffic. But the driver had decided to transit right through Shmeisani, Amman's aging business district, rather than around it. We didn't stand a chance. I was fuming, partly because I was going to be late, but mainly because I still had not mastered Amman's traffic patterns after more than a year living in the city. My groan was unambiguous. The driver probably detected my frustration. As we surveyed the gridlocked scene in front of us, he stretched out his spindly legs as best he could in the cramped sedan. He looked over at me and knitted his fingers before clasping his hands behind his head and leaning gently back into his seat. "Traffic," he sighed. "Relax, let's listen to al-Wakeel."

His proposal brought some relief, if only temporary. I liked *Birnamaj al-Wakeel*, a morning call-in show presented by one of Jordan's most prominent radio hosts. In its own way, it reminded me of my childhood, when my mother would tune in to similar programs on our way home from school. Citizens from all walks of life would call in and relay their grievances and complaints to the host, ranging from the deadly serious (medical malpractice) to the salacious (a senator's sex life). Sometimes they would ask for help or mediation in dealing with a government agency. Other times, callers just shared their thoughts or divulged their opinions on newsworthy topics.[1]

Mohammad al-Wakeel's booming voice had become a ubiquitous part of more commutes than I can remember. The radio host always sounded like he could be sitting right in your living room, coffee cups jangling away as he chatted and joked with callers. Today, the show was about a half an hour in. Al-Wakeel was already engrossed in a discussion about bread subsidy reform. Christine Lagarde, the IMF's managing director, had been in a public spat with Jordan's prime minister the day before. At an international conference held in an Amman hotel, Lagarde had argued for increased discipline in public finance and the restriction of consumer supports to only the poorest citizens. In an agitated tone, while carefully making reference to no one in particular, Abdullah Ensour, the prime minister, criticized rigid fiscal prescriptions and called for international financial institutions to more closely consider local contexts when recommending reforms. The prime minister was tired of being told what to do by experts who were accountable to no one. We had tuned in at a fortuitous moment. "The matter is far larger than this," al-Wakeel bellowed in response to a caller. "It is bread we are talking about here" (*al-shaghla shaghla-t-khubz*).

After a brief commercial break, the radio host fielded a call from Mustafa, who identified himself as a hospitality manager at an unnamed luxury hotel. Formulaic greetings were exchanged. Mustafa then came to Lagarde's defense. "The honorable lady is correct," he declared. "Any subsidy should be only for the poor." Al-Wakeel sounded surprised, and after clarifying the caller's position, he asked Mustafa to elaborate. "Well, take my hotel," the caller replied. "We charge something like 250 dinars (US$353) a night, so the people staying here are usually quite wealthy. And what do we serve at the breakfast buffet? Nice fruits and eggs and jams and honey. Expensive items," he pointed out, "but also, subsidized bread." Mustafa went on, "It is not just. Someone needs to explain to me why the wealthy corporation that owns my hotel feeds its rich customers *khubz 'arabi*. No sir. We should only give assistance to the poor, the people who really need it."

Next, al-Wakeel read aloud a message he had received through his Facebook page, one of the other methods through which listeners could get in touch. After describing how much bread is wasted and thrown away in homes, restaurants, and fast-food outlets, this listener recommended an increase in price. "People do not value bread because it is so cheap," al-Wakeel read out.

"If we eliminate the subsidy and charge the real price, people will begin to value it again." The radio host was skeptical, as was I, having heard the same argument from World Bankers any number of times. Only when prices were "real" would people consume bread efficiently, they claimed. I looked at the taxi driver, hoping for some indignation. He seemed hesitant, unwilling to opine, as I called bullshit.

The day was getting hotter by the minute. The lingering of pollutants and the deflection onto the pavement of heat left by the mid-May sun made the air dense and hazy. My driver was calm, but those around us were less so, and apparently all fully fledged members of the Amman honking school—with a strong inclination towards sustained, single-note blasts. After a brief musical interlude, two more callers were put on the air. Both were annoyed. The first, a car mechanic, quickly detailed his monthly budget—so much on produce, so much on clothes, this and that amount on public transportation and a mobile phone—before angrily asking his fellow listeners where exactly he was supposed to find the surplus cash if bread prices increased. He barely got by as is, he shouted. The state had a responsibility to provide bread, not out of charity but so people could survive, he told al-Wakeel. The radio host thanked him for his intervention and wished him good health.

Next, Malek from Sahab, a working-class district in southeast Amman, spoke at length about the importance of bread to his community. "Sorry, Mr. al-Wakeel," he began, "but I must say that no one is mentioning how important bread is to our society. Here in Sahab, everyone eats it, every household depends on bread." Yes, yes, this is important, added the radio host. The caller went on, "Bread is like water or electricity. It is crucial to us all. It also keeps everyone healthy and productive. No one in Jordan dies from starvation, Mr. al-Wakeel. We should be proud of this. I believe bread is a basic good that the state should provide."[2] "Message received, Brother Malek," the radio host responded.

Al-Wakeel then began one of his characteristic monologues. After summarizing the positions espoused by his callers and mockingly recalling the long history of failed IMF remedies in Jordan, the radio host criticized the project of subsidy reform. He briefly disparaged the Ministry of Industry, Trade, and Supply (MOITS) for not catching those who were exploiting the welfare program. Hotels and fancy restaurants should not benefit, he stressed. But for the

Jordanian people, *khubz 'arabi* is vital, its low price key. The foodstuff helps the poor survive and ensures social stability, he emphasized. There are citizens of the country who survive on just bread and tea (*khubz wa chai*), al-Wakeel thundered. Managing Director Lagarde should sit with these humble people and enlighten them as to the IMF's reform plan, perhaps over the plates of hummus that they all too rarely get to eat. I could not help myself and started to laugh as I imagined the scene. Lagarde crouched down, sipping some tea while trying to explain to a group of hungry citizens how consumer subsidies distort prices, thereby leading to fiscal imbalances and allocative inefficiencies.

The taxi driver abruptly shut the radio off. "Al-Wakeel is wrong," he said, looking me in the eye, ready to drive home his point. "The government shouldn't be involved in what we eat. This only breeds corruption. Let people make their own choices," he insisted. "Take me, I don't eat so much bread. I'd rather have the cash and spend it on fuel."

I sighed. "We must agree to disagree," I offered hesitantly, before repeating one of the stock phrases I had become fond of when describing my research: "Bread is life."

The driver cracked a smile: "Man, I want to spend my money as I please and as I desire. Bread is overrated" (*Ana ya 'ami bidi asraf masari 'ala mazaji wa zay ma bidi. mbaligh fil khubz*). We chuckled together. I wondered if he was right.

In August of 2012, the Jordanian government agreed to a 36-month, US$2.06 billion standby arrangement with the IMF. Cuts in government expenditure were pledged in exchange for the assistance. Soon after, two World Bank assessments concluded that Jordan's consumer subsidies were "poorly targeted and costly," one of the largest strains on the country's annual budget.[3] After fuel prices were liberalized in November of 2012, triggering a series of protests throughout the country,[4] rumors about bread subsidy reform began circulating. They persisted for nearly two years. In early 2013, government officials subtly but publicly began to disseminate a plan centered on an electronic smart card.[5] This card would give only Jordanian citizens with valid identity cards a monthly allowance, to compensate for the difference between the subsidized bread price (0.16 JD per kilogram) and the predicted free-market price (0.38 JD per kilogram). Discounted bread at the bakery would be replaced by financial compensation for eligible individuals. Immediate protests quickly ensued from trade unions and consumer protection groups. The proposal was widely satirized in the press. In response to the public outcry, different government spokesmen seemed to surface weekly to ensure weary Jordanians that there would be no real rise in bread prices. The changes would apply only to foreigners, went the message repeated *ad nauseam* by the prime minister at the time, Abdullah Ensour. "Bread [prices] will not increase 1 penny for citizens," he promised.[6] But despite the prime minister's guarantees, an array of bakers conveyed their incredulity, perplexed at the smart card proposal and the details surrounding its possible implementation.[7] Prominent members of the military and security services also voiced their opposition. They highlighted not only the threat to their own living standards but the potentially destabilizing effects that subsidy reform could have on the refugee populations they were in charge of disciplining and the poor neighborhoods they had often been tasked with repressing.

These apprehensions were not misplaced. Aided by the regional oil boom, Jordan's ministries emerged from 1974 having assumed new and expanded roles in employment, economic regulation, and social welfare. Like the expansion of water provision that Ilana Feldman traces in Egyptian-controlled Gaza, the bread subsidy in Jordan was part of a more general process that bound citizens to political authority, creating "bidirectional obligation, responsibility, and demand."[8] As early as 1978, a one-*piaster* (i.e. about a 1.4-cent) increase in the price of a kilogram of bread (from 7.5 to 8.5 piasters) caused widespread unrest throughout Jordan. Again in August of 1996, Jordanians took to the streets to protest an IMF-backed price rise.[9] In meetings with donors, the Palace has always had ample recourse to past unrest and the possibility of future turmoil to justify the preservation of the bread subsidy, despite the requirements of structural adjustment.[10] Citizens have come to expect that they will always have enough bread to eat and to consider the foodstuff's availability as indicative of a given government's commitment to the citizenry, as the abovementioned protests make clear. But in this chapter, I will not examine moments of popular mobilization, fascinating as they are. Rather than focus on the "visible coastline of politics," I will unpack "the continent that lies beyond."[11] I consider and seek to illuminate a less prominent politics of welfare—the rationalities and modes of reasoning through which subjects are produced and government reflected upon—in order to understand why so many Jordanians proclaimed that the bread subsidy was a "red line."

LEAVENED APPREHENSIONS

By the time I landed in the traffic jam that day and inadvertently came across al-Wakeel's segment, the bread subsidy had been discussed frequently and at length. No decision had been made when Lagarde, the IMF's managing director, made her preferences known in May of 2014, but uncertainty abounded. So I asked, and asked often, what bread signified and why its reform triggered anxieties unlike those that surrounded other policy debates, even though this welfare service involved a far smaller proportion of people's purchasing power than other programs that had been eliminated over the past twenty years. Yet to my chagrin, bread, and the welfare program that ensured its discounted provision, defied easy categorization. Some called it a right, others a blessing from God. A few portrayed the subsidy as a clever ruse, a more filling yet equally potent version of opium for the masses. A handful saw it as appropriate compensation for taxation. The virtues espoused in all these depictions are fragments that were "originally at home in larger totalities of theory and practice."[12] Those who supported the subsidy often associated the program with values such as care, solidarity, or mutual responsibility or with desired circumstances ranging from subsistence to social stability. Opponents spoke of personal responsibility, equity, or freedom and sought to overcome conditions of inefficiency, wastefulness, and corruption. Everyone mentioned justice.

After months of interviews and conversations, I realized that none of these interpretations were "wrong." The claims of my interlocutors were irresolvable, in ways we too seldom recognize. Despite my best attempts, I could not identify "paramount values" underlying a Jordanian "cultural order" through which a moral economy of bread could be determined, as some variants of structural anthropology attempt to do.[13] Instead, values that were circulated through Sunni Islam, Arab socialism, neoliberalism, and conservative royalism all appeared in peoples' descriptions of bread and its subsidy. Sometimes they appeared alongside characteristically liberal concepts such as rights or utility. At others, citizens combined a mixture of values, aims, and codes in what Samuli Schielke terms "a loose and unsystematic dialogue of different modalities, or registers, of normative action and speech."[14] And while examining the cultural values underpinning the moral economy of bread may very well be a worthwhile endeavor, I hesitate to attempt that here, unsure whether there are any conclusions we could reach or how exactly we could settle disparities between rival concepts of the good and the just.[15] Nevertheless, the argument that bread is a subsistence good, and that it should be sold at a price accessible to all, was a formidable one, an argument that resonated beyond any one moral code or value system in the Hashemite Kingdom.[16] That is to say, *khubz 'arabi* was a collective concern, with many meanings, but which allowed for overlapping commitments and shared expectations around which publics could align, if only partially and temporarily. Bread is multivocal and, as a result, symbolically malleable and potent.

So rather than examine the cultural values or moral codes underpinning bread's importance, I want to examine the debate surrounding subsidy reform as a terrain, a "discursive problem-space" in which certain political rationalities operate and resonate, while others do not.[17] To be clear, these political rationalities are not equivalent to an ideology conjured to mask class interests, nor are they the clear-cut product of economic creeds transposed onto the political. Rather, as Wendy Brown argues, they offer a "specific form of normative political reason organizing the political sphere, governance practices and citizenship" and regulating what is intelligible in these domains.[18] They have an epistemological character in that they represent the objects and subjects to be governed and set out particular ways of conceiving the state, economy, and society. Although it came late in his work, and he is inconsistent in its use, Foucault employs the term "political rationality" in his later lectures to explore how exactly neoliberalism becomes self-evident as a form of reasoning, part and parcel of a "regime of truth that is itself generative of power, yet not identical with its exercise."[19] Here I want to do something a bit different, to use some of Foucault's and Brown's tools to assess how two political rationalities contoured the bread subsidy debate, in the hopes of sketching out a useful theorization of Jordanian politics. Of particular interest are the truths to which policy debates must adhere and the types of questions and answers that can emerge within these truths. This does not mean that other factors are not crucial to the Palace's effectiveness in circulating certain understandings of the world. The Hashemite regime utilizes American and Gulf support to cultivate loyal security forces, exploit intra-elite antagonisms, censor the media, and inflame divisions among the opposition, all of which are important. But the very fact that so many citizens defend the regime or express themselves in the monarchy's vocabularies of choice—above and beyond those who derive an obvious material benefit from doing so—should force us to ponder why public debates take the forms that they do.

What I present here is intentionally schematic. I eschew a great deal of nuance in favor of a wider-ranging account of the disputes that the bread subsidy brought to the fore, and the questions I am interested in are the following: What modes of reasoning orient citizens, specify the conditions of their citizenship, and inflect policy appraisals? What kinds of subjectivities do certain rationalities presume and solidify and in relation to what forms of political authority? How are embodied knowledges of the Jordanian state transposed onto contemporary debates regarding the responsibilities this entity should undertake? Arguments over these questions structure the plot of this chapter, while the conclusion considers the effects of these representations—what they assume and what they entrench. Rumors of bread subsidy reform were a rising agent, leavening apprehensions and propagating uncertainties among more than a few. Many asked: If the state does not provide bread, what exactly is it supposed to do?

LOVERS OF THE INVISIBLE HAND

A friend of the free-market persuasion, an unabashed lover of the invisible hand, alerted me to the columns of Fahed Fanek. I quickly understood the appeal. His prose was unassuming and direct, the type of thing you could read swiftly on your smartphone or with your morning tea. Throughout 2013, Fanek, an economist and the former chairman of the Jordan Press Foundation, wrote a daily column for *al-Raʿi*, a government-owned newspaper. I made a habit of seeking his articles out, as he offered a cogent synopsis of views prevalent among the business-friendly (read: West Ammani) elite. Fanek's biggest bugaboos were populism and corruption. Champions of the bread subsidy were guilty of either or both, he told readers in two separate articles published while the reform debate was raging. Fanek was familiar with some of the challenges that plagued the subsidy program and was happy to parrot the government's rhetoric on leakage. The current system, Fanek asserted, fostered fraud and tampering by bakery owners, who made illegal use of discounted flour.[20] It also encouraged leakage because it incentivized farmers to use subsidized bread as animal feed. Corruption in the bread industry was both "blatant and costly," he argued. Subsidy supporters ignored these facts to further their own interests or score political points from bread's symbolic appeal.

Yet more galling than leakage, for Fanek, was how the bread subsidy encapsulated a misguided approach to government. He repeatedly emphasized the welfare program's impact on fiscal concerns. Given Jordan's lack of a budget surplus, universal subsidies were an "extravagance," as funding for them was dependent on loans from abroad.[21] Failure to lower the deficit would eventually hurt the "purchasing power of the dinar," the columnist argued, triggering a rise in the prices of all commodities.[22] Like the international financial institutions that were conferring with the Jordanian government, Fanek's position displayed a market-oriented bias, aggrandizing macroeconomic indicators and prioritizing them above all other concerns.[23] He assumed that ensuring the free flow of supply and demand, so that consumers could satisfy their individual preferences, was the only way to guarantee a just allocation of resources. Like the growing number of government officials who shared his outlook, Fanek justified unpopular reforms by ascribing their implementation to inescapable global forces.[24] He deemed popular opposition to subsidy reform uninformed or unimportant; changes must be driven by budgetary prudence and the undeniable realities of the market. King Abdullah II often championed this view. The monarch was fond of telling parliamentarians and citizens that the country must "modernize economic legislation to keep pace with international advancements and best practices" in order to offer an "improved environment for investors with better quality services."[25] Much like Fanek's assertions, although carrying far more heft, such statements divorce policy questions from public deliberation; economic reforms are rendered technical and politically neutral, and thereby necessary. As Fanek put it, rather incredibly, some months later, "The problem is that the IMF shows a lot of flexibility. It does not insist on reducing expenditures like subsidies, but accepts increasing revenues as a substitute."[26]

Implicit in Fanek's columns was, of course, a conceptualization of what the state is and ought to do—how it should govern. The truths and mode of reasoning forming his outlook are familiar and need little in the way of rehearsal: a belief in the efficacy of the invisible hand; a desire to replace bureaucrats with markets as regulators of economic activity; and a longing to remake government and citizens in the form of enterprise.[27] Competition cures all ills, he often proclaimed, especially the inefficiencies of planned economies. Universal entitlements and outdated safety nets should be replaced by flexible springboards, so that Jordanians could better calculate their needs and desires and spend their cash accordingly. Government programs that do not prompt a discernible market value were, for Fanek, simply not worthwhile. To this end, his columns consistently promoted the economization of what were once considered noneconomic spheres, in an attempt to disseminate market logics to new domains. For this to occur, citizens had to be disabused of what Fanek called "populist" doctrines and policy measures and be reconstituted as "individuated risk calculators."[28] We know where such positions lead, although the gendered implications are too rarely commented upon in the Jordanian context. Women remain overwhelmingly responsible for social reproduction and care in and outside of the household. They not only rely on the types of welfare programs that Fanek sought to dismantle but are also rendered as the "invisible infrastructure" sustaining the ostensibly liberated *homo economicus* that will allegedly emerge from reform.[29] The burdens placed upon them by patriarchy, poverty, and precarity are disavowed. Forsaken too in this rationalization of government is any anchoring of welfare in the goals or commitments of the past—solidarity, social responsibility, and development. Instead, welfare is undergirded by a minimalist conception of basic needs.

Clearly, Fanek's conception of government was far different from the political rationalities that undergirded public policy in the past. He was neither unique nor alone in espousing this position, yet I find him to be of consequence because of how succinctly he captured and concretized a shift that was underway in the Jordanian body politic. As will become clear in the sections to come, Fanek's rationalization of government was not yet hegemonic. But it was rapidly gaining ground. While only a handful of politicians were willing to espouse Fanek's position publicly at that point, the decoupling of welfare provision from a solidaristic notion of government was ascendant. Recipients of social spending were portrayed less and less as anonymous Jordanians warranting public services and more often as deprived individuals in need of assistance. And whereas welfare programs had previously been driven by the developmentalist telos of modernity, suggesting an obligation of the state to care for its citizens, foster well-being, and collectivize the risks of market failure, Fanek believed that they should be geared towards satisfying only the most rudimentary penuries. One "must govern for the market, rather than because of the market."[30] And while neoliberalism in the Jordanian context remains a political rationality formulated mainly by those working within the governmental milieu, reliance on IMF loans and external assistance gives it disproportionate influence there. Nevertheless, the bread subsidy was not so easily made to seem superfluous—especially when the specter of unrest loomed on the horizon.

CAUTIOUS DEVOTEES

Jordan's Finance Ministry, a drab modernist office block located just outside Amman's historic city center, looks more like the beating heart of a bloated bureaucracy than a sleek hub for business-friendly free marketeers. Yet during the last thirty years, the ministry has been at the center of Jordan's socio-economic transformation, the outpost of technocrats bent on implementing a comprehensive set of pro-market reforms. The finance minister, Umayya Toukan, received me in his office on the second day of Ramadan. It was June 30, 2014, and subsidy reform was once again in the news, not having ever really left since Christine Lagarde's spat with Ensour, the prime minister, in mid-May. Toukan began by offering a brief history of consumer subsidies in the region, noting that governments throughout the Middle East had strategically chosen to support specific commodities rather than targeting assistance to the poor during the heydays of Arab Socialism. Jordan adopted some of these measures but did so later than most, as unlike many of its neighbors, it had not experienced revolutionary upheavals. The inflationary spiral of 1974 was key in this respect, Toukan continued. It led the government to implement a host of consumer supports modeled after those in Egypt and Syria. Because remittances, foreign aid, and regional economies were growing exponentially, these subsidies were of little budgetary concern. If anything, they boosted the Hashemite regime's standing among citizens—no one lacked for food or fuel. But problems emerged for non–oil-producing countries whenever global prices in commodities spiked, as their inflexible subsidy systems put governments under fiscal duress. They were forced to spend in order to maintain the price of certain goods, and deficits were hard to predict and, in bad years, impossible to control. The stipulations that accompanied structural adjustment in 1989 brought these issues to the fore.

When asked about the current policy, the finance minister argued that universal subsidies inherently fostered perverse incentives: "Currently, flour is wasted, smuggled, and used illegally. Government interventions inevitably create market distortions."[31] While many defended the bread subsidy precisely because it defied the logics of the free market, this former head of Jordan's Central Bank described price controls as the source of "wasteful and inefficient outcomes." His stated preference for the free market was not solely based on macroeconomic considerations: "The inequality of outcomes is quite clear. The rich and highly profitable businesses benefit far more from subsidized goods than the poor, who do not get their fair share." Toukan's pro-market positioning was hardly amoral; he saw no gap between questions of justice and cold-blooded calculations of allocative efficiency. He reasoned that benefits from marketizing reforms would eventually trickle down to all Jordanians, who were only harmed by government interventions that compromised efficiency, the maximization of utility, and economic freedom. "Bread subsidy reform is not about hurting the poor, but rationalizing consumption," he insisted. "Why should we choose what foods people eat?" He went on to say that government should avoid arrogance and overreach. Only by treating bread like any other good could leakage and overconsumption be avoided, went the logic. Yet Toukan seemed to know that transforming modalities of valuation, at least in the case of bread, was hard work. "Bread is sensitive, I know. But our job at the ministry is to come up with good economic plans, which parliamentarians are free to reject. Politically, I don't know how to achieve subsidy reform," he told me, "but I know we should do it."

At the time of our interview, Finance Minister Toukan epitomized the neoliberal wing of the Hashemite regime, a loosely tied amalgamation of policy makers and technocrats who have populated the country's main economic decision-making bodies and ministries since King Abdullah II's ascent to the throne. Their speeches and public remarks are infused with emblematic tropes that emphasize efficiency, freedom to consume, and self-care as the path to economic liberty, individual productivity, and social justice. Ministerial documents and civic education textbooks circulate these truths. They emphasize the government's desire to ease regulatory controls and accelerate the privatization of public enterprises.[32] Inequality is best remedied through "cooperation with the private sector," which should take on "further social responsibilities," especially in the realms of "rehabilitation and training," the Ministry of Social Development declares.[33] Social progress is best achieved through market mechanisms; eliminating deprivation is simply a matter of fostering "income generation activities through welfare-to-work measures" and implementing "activation incentives," the country's Poverty Reduction Strategy proclaims. Precarity is not a result of structural inequalities, citizens are told, but "the difficulties of access to finance for poor and low-income Jordanians."[34] And welfare reforms have largely followed in the tracks of such pronouncements. Since 1989, most price controls, subsidies, and welfare entitlements have been eliminated or reduced. In their stead there are conditional poverty reduction programs and targeted interventions such as the National Aid Fund and the Enhanced Economic and Social Productivity Program. The rationales for welfare have shifted away from the principle of collective responsibility for the ills resulting from inflation and inequality. The burden is now placed on individuals to become industrious and reduce the burden they place on public resources. But bread subsidy reform was not so easy—it had not been and would not be. People were attached to bread; its true value escaped quantification. Despite his strong pro-reform inclinations, Toukan acknowledged these complications. His remarks on the topic were cautious: "The bread subsidy is an issue where politics and economics may not align with each other. Good policy may not be politically possible or desirable."[35]

In spite of their disapproval of universal subsidy systems, a number of my interviewees who shared Toukan's inclinations also emphasized that economic reforms should stop short of endangering social stability. The political context is key, they were fond of saying. Like others, Ibrahim Saif, then the minister of planning and international cooperation, expressed the government's concern with "the fraud and corruption that occurs in the current subsidy system. It is something we have failed to make clear to citizens."[36] But any changes to the bread policy needed to account for popular opinion. Confident that the subsidy "would eventually be changed," Saif described why reform was currently obstructed:

> There was no real consensus on the fuel subsidy before it was changed. For many of the poor who did not consume that much fuel, they said, "Yes, I do not own a car, it is the rich who benefit the most, why not increase the price." Bread is not the same. Even discussions of reform make it seem like we [the

government] do not have society's best interests at heart, like we are ruthlessly going after the poor. People are attached to bread, they call it life ('*ayish*) in Egypt for a reason. It is an extremely sensitive political issue. We cannot speak of stability and then make a decision that would surely destabilize the country.

While more attentive to popular opinion than Toukan, Saif was an eager critic of subsidies and the distortions they fostered. He shared with the finance minister a desire to cut the budget deficit, unshackle obstacles to capital accumulation, and make Jordan more attractive to foreign investment. Yet Saif was similarly hesitant about reforming the bread subsidy. He considered proposed alternatives to the policy problematic not because of the marketizing techniques they furthered but because their implementation could jeopardize the autocratic status quo. There are two seemingly contradictory rationalities at play here: one that promotes marketization and consumer choice, and another that emphasizes the importance of stability above all else. But what appears as an awkward combination can and does often come together, in a mode of reasoning akin to what Lisa Wedeen terms "neoliberal autocracy."[37] Pro-market reforms and capitalist norms are embraced, but only to the extent that they do not imperil authoritarian order, the crucial stand-in for what would otherwise be chaos. Cheap bread forestalls a possible breakdown. The finance minister, Toukan, expressed this sentiment succinctly towards the end of the interview: "The at-most 300 million JD spent on the bread subsidy is not so much, not as much as the symbolism bread gives to the life of the people." Hesitantly, suspiciously, unhappily, the ministers agreed that a concession or two to popular preferences might be necessary.[38] They all feared the potential repercussions of neoliberal consummation.

RELUCTANT REFORMERS

How can we understand the caution and concern expressed by the ministers above? More broadly, given the Jordanian government's recurring fiscal constraints, how are exceptions to economic reform rationalized? Since the country's independence in 1946, visions of government and citizenship have circulated primarily through an autocratic political rationality that seeks to minimize opposition and unrest but also to shape political life as a whole. This mode of reasoning has been consistently deployed by the Palace and circulated by many of its allies, and has been termed "conservative royalism"[39] or a "peculiar version of modern dynasticism."[40] Inflecting it through the analytic prism of nationalism, Stefanie Nanes dubs it Hashemitism, an "elite-led national identity that encompassed the people within the territory the Hashemite monarchy wished to govern."[41] The former Palace adviser Adnan Abu Odeh defines this royalist creed as standing for "the inherent equality of being above differences and sub-identities within Jordanian society . . . a single pan-Jordanian identity under the Hashemites."[42] But Hashemitism does more then interpellate people through nationalism. Instead, it offers the central ground from which modes of reasoning related to government and citizenship emerge in contemporary Jordan. While it is "fuzzy," and has been reworked in the face of key events in the country's history, such as the loss of the West Bank in 1967, Hashemitism has always prioritized and continues to prioritize the rule and reign of the current monarchy above all else.[43] It functions as a political rationality because it does not simply promote false consciousness, demarcate national identity, or legitimize the political status quo; it is productive and involves a "specific and consequential organization of the social, the subject, and the state."[44]

What truths lie at its core? Hashemitism promotes order, stability, national unity, and monarchical rule as the bases of Jordanian political life. Fearful of social unrest and regional instability, it seeks to realign conceptions of citizenship around a civic religion of sorts. Jordanians are figured not as scrupulously rational economic actors in every sphere of life, as they would be in neoliberalism, but rather as sacrificial subjects who must submit to authority so as to ensure order. Hashemitism actively eschews deliberation over public objectives and accountability for the solution of common problems in favor of distinctly autocratic formulations of national purpose. While internally diverse, this political rationality is animated by an explicit drive for power as well as anxieties linked to the supposed decay of civic pride. Much like neoconservatism in the United States as depicted by David Harvey and Wendy Brown, Hashemitism differs from its neoliberal counterpart in two important ways: first, in its concern for order before individual interests; and second, in its desire to impose an all-encompassing sense of obedience that can bring coherence to the body politic.[45] Where neoliberal rationality prefers to let self-interest run roughshod over the social body, transforming dependent citizens into hard-nosed entrepreneurs, Hashemitism seeks to fuse Jordanians together through a particular conception of government and citizenship, with the monarchy always positioned as the polity's unquestionable core.

There have been numerous notable attempts at disseminating and ingraining this autocratic political rationality. These range from government-led publicity campaigns (Jordan First, We Are All Jordan) to official pronouncements following the influx of Syrian refugees or the release of alleged Israeli plans to establish an alternative Palestinian homeland in Jordan.[46] Whatever the occasion, Hashemitism foregrounds national unity and loyalty, emphasizing the preeminence of Jordanian interests, as defined by the Palace, above all other considerations. For example, in a meeting with prominent intellectuals during the tumult of the Arab Spring, the king reminded those present of their responsibility to be "cautious and conscious in our political and intellectual discourse," eschewing debates that could "tear our society apart." Security and social stability are ascribed almost ethereal qualities. Euphemisms for rule premised on a compliant citizenry, they are portrayed as supreme values, both economically beneficial and politically necessary for a country ostensibly threatened by internal upheavals and external threats.[47] And it is precisely this dread of chaos, the constant nurturing of a vague possibility of impending violence and unrest, that the Palace has been able to cultivate. As the monarch puts it, "Without security and stability and the rule of law there can be no development, no modernization and no progress."[48] A willful political passivity and hollow patriotism are wrapped up together, all in the name of order, prosperity, and peace.

This rationality powerfully inflects how policy makers and bureaucrats think about government—its purposes, objectives, and mechanisms of rule. To my surprise, MOITS took the lead in promoting changes to the bread subsidy. When advocating for reform, ministry officials emphasized the disjunctures in a universal subsidy system that equally serves the poor and the rich, nationals and non-nationals, while fostering fraud among bakers and flour millers. The head of the ministry at the time said, "It is an injustice that bakers do not appropriately use all their flour allotment. They are taking from the poor and filling their pockets."[49] Although there are no reliable estimates of leakages, high-level MOITS officials discuss them constantly and cite them as a central impetus for reform. Yet in stark contrast to the finance minister, every MOITS official I spoke with prized the state's role in regulating markets; they simply sought to improve how it did so. As Samer Khouri, MOITS's director of market control, put it, "The ministry preserves social integrity through the subsidy, since bread is the food of the poor." The welfare program should be reformed, he and others at MOITS argued, but not to reflect market outcomes. Instead, changes should be beneficial to the needy citizens who were most reliant on government interventions. "Subsidized bread is crucial for the poor," Khouri reminded me. "Whenever prices have gone up, the country has experienced social unrest. We want to avoid such outcomes and find the way to get the subsidy to those who need it. We think the smart card is the best option."[50]

Dr. Essa al-Dmour, MOITS's director of internal audits, who holds the primary responsibility for bread-subsidy–related spending, similarly emphasized that "The subsidy mechanism must undoubtedly be changed. It disproportionately helps wealthy bakery and restaurant owners. Nevertheless, support for consumers must continue, it is our responsibility to the lives and well-being of the citizenry. Bread is the food of every house." For al-Dmour, as for his colleagues, the bread subsidy demonstrated the benevolence of the Hashemite regime, providing a necessary corrective to market outcomes and a key pillar of "social justice and governmental responsibility held sacred by all Jordanians." But that was not all it did. Without access to affordable bread, al-Dmour surmised, "It is very possible that chaos would ensue."[51] For these officials, the smart card proposal was simply a way to minimize corruption and save the treasury money without threatening people's livelihoods or unsettling society. They were all well aware that universal subsidies have uneven and in some cases regressive effects: restaurants, hotels, and other large enterprises, for instance, consume far more bread than your average household. They also knew all too well the difficulties of detecting leakage and fraud in the current system (see chapter 3). However, no one at MOITS ever suggested the wholesale elimination of consumer supports. Each official was careful to emphasize potential avenues for the targeted reimbursement of Jordanian citizens. Their remarks took aim not at the basic proposition that government institutions should guarantee subsistence, but at the mechanisms through which such principles were enacted. Ultimately, MOITS officials had no illusions about fashioning a free-market paradise or leaving bread provision to the invisible hand, even as they faced the constraints ordained by fiscal prudence. The question they wrestled with was how to structure consumer supports so as to safeguard social peace and assist those in need. But perhaps equally important here is that the predominant tenets of Hashemitism—social stability and national unity—colored these and other remarks I heard while conducting interviews and spending time at this ministry. While welfare provision was discussed less and less in terms of the logics of interdependence and solidarity, the limits placed on the complete marketization of bread were, always and without reservation, deemed judicious and necessary.

All the government officials I queried recognized bread's nutritional importance. No one disputed its symbolic appeal. Nevertheless, the political rationalities that were espoused, and the ways that these inflected policy positions vis-à-vis the bread subsidy, were far from similar.[52] Some emphasized attachments to efficiency, freedom, and competition, while others prized fairness, compassion, or solidarity. These divergent positions do not reflect only disagreements over current modes of welfare provision. They also make evident how the "social domain of speakable discourse" was configured in the Hashemite Kingdom.[53] What interests me here is not primarily who said what, but what constituted "the domain of the sayable," the limits and confines within which political speech operated.[54] One could embrace markets and individual responsibility, just as one could foreground loyalty, security, and patriotism as the primary criteria through which welfare was assessed. The coexistence of these vocabularies allowed different groups to espouse allegiance to the monarchical order while holding vastly dissimilar visions of how to govern. But to disavow social stability or Hashemite rule was, at least in the realm of policy debate, to move far outside the realm of speakability. Put differently, Hashemitism functions akin to what Alexei Yurchak describes as an "authoritative discourse," one that "employs a special script to demarcate itself from all other discourses with which it coexists; it cannot be changed by them but they must refer to it as a condition of their existence."[55] For a unified Jordanian nation to exist and prosper, it must be protected against not only outside threats but also internal challenges that could compromise national unity, communal cohesion, and the monarchy. Adherence to these tenets did not necessarily entail the need for redistributive measures or subsidies, but it did require that public policies not be seen to openly endanger social stability. Although such polyvalence, through its calculated inclusivity, aids the hegemony of the monarchy, it also allows certain tropes to be reappropriated and resignified by those it subjectifies. Hashemitism exceeds the interests of those most invested in constituting it as a field of truth.

RED LINES

Hashemitism operates across the religious and partisan proclivities that are usually used to explain political differences in Jordan. Sa'id, for one, described the bread subsidy in an Islamic register. "In the *hadith*, *khubz* embodies a responsibility of those in power. Today, the bread subsidy is how the regime demonstrates its commitment to fairness and compassion."[56] In our conversations, he would routinely emphasize bread's sanctity as well as the subsidy's connections to religious values he held dear, such as beneficence (*ihsan*) and almsgiving (*sadaqa*). He insisted throughout that his assertions were not political, but simply a matter of pointing out the obvious. "The state cannot let us starve, they cannot turn the petitioner away" (*wa amma al-saila fala tanhar*), he posited, using a Qur'anic turn of phrase.[57] "This whole smart card business can't be true," he told me one day after I had mentioned the well-publicized reform proposal. "People without access to this card could be left without bread. It is the state and the ruler's obligation to provide our basic needs, to ensure that no one goes hungry. It is a religious duty (*inu wajib dini*)."[58]

Sa'id was not alone in espousing such views. Throughout the subsidy debate, a wide array of individuals drew on religious idioms and precepts to both defend the bread subsidy and articulate what governmental practice should look like. Some prized the subsidy because it allowed for business practices that more closely corresponded to Islamic conceptions of property and trade. Others asserted that, in ensuring the timely distribution of flour, the state was combating the dissolution of the social bonds that give Islamic societies both meaning and order. Whatever the case, pious citizens valued subsidized bread not solely because of its caloric content but also because it fostered modes of conduct in accordance with a discursive tradition they held dear. While most, like Sa'id, avoided criticizing the Hashemite regime, they made clear that pro-market reforms were dissolving communal bonds and augmenting inequalities in ways inimical to Islamic precepts. Although King Abdullah II does not appeal to religious precepts as often as his father did, he does emphasize—as do the country's textbooks—Sunni Islam as a key pillar of

Hashemite legitimacy.[59] The monarchy's occasional recourse to this religious register is what makes the remarks above acceptable, potent, and subversive, all at the same time.

For Bashir, a student at the University of Jordan and a member of the country's small Communist Party, bread is a nutritional staple whose subsidy is a right achieved through social struggle: "The policy is hardly an expression of benevolence. The government knows it would face a backlash if it eliminated the subsidy," he told me. But Bashir's remarks forwent revolutionary demands and echoed instead a vision of government circulated by the Palace. For example, he stressed the Hashemite monarchy's emphasis on communal well-being and security when appraising potential subsidy reform:

> Bread is the fundamental element of every poor person's diet, which is why it is so important. Without it, we could not survive and would be left completely at the mercy of capitalism. There can be no justice, no security, stability, or survival if the people cannot eat. Bread makes life possible. This is why we defend it. The regime itself tells us it is a red line.

Similarly, the journalist Jumanah Ghnemiat (who later became the minister for media affairs) referred to the bread subsidy as "the last red line" in the dwindling social pact between the Hashemite regime and the citizenry.[60] With this phrase, which appeared time and again during the debate, she cogently expressed the attachments of many Jordanians to the more interventionist paradigm of rule that had prevailed until 1989 and the techniques for governing the social that had accompanied it. To call the subsidy a "red line" was to insist on the maintenance of a governing relationship with particular relations of obligation and reciprocity, ones that elites were not justified in ignoring.

Umm Hassan, a high school teacher and self-identified socialist, also clothed her critique in hegemonic dress: "Without bread we could not make do. Jordan would no longer be the country of safety and security (*balad al-amin wa-l-ayman*) those in power love to acclaim." Disinclined to countenance a free market for bread, she emphasized one of the regime's oft-parroted slogans to oppose subsidy reform, lending force to her pronouncement. She knew well what types of claims were possible, which were risky, and which were effective. "We have nothing (*ma'nash*)," Umm Hassan said. "Bread is what helps us survive.

Social stability depends on it. The king knows this. He won't let the state aban-
don us." Such views are indicative of the stake that many citizens continue to
have in retaining welfare provisions that operate under the emblem of the state.
Like others, Umm Hassan knew well that the bread subsidy did not solely affect
"me" but also "us," and spoke as if everyone else would understand the foodstuff
in similar terms.[61] When bread is framed as a public resource, which it almost
inevitably is, subsidy reform represents not only a threat to personal finances
but also a collective diminution of citizenship, a symbolically charged retreat of
the state from an obligation many hold to be sacred. These Jordanians are suspicious of the goals and ends that underpin subsidy reform and are unwilling to
reconstitute themselves as autonomous individuals who calculate risk and pay
for goods in discrete transactions. Their remarks demonstrate attachments to
competing modalities and traditions of social provisioning, ones that continue
to percolate through the Jordanian body politic.

In her exploration of an entrepreneurship and microcredit youth program
in Amman, Mayssoun Sukarieh similarly examines some of the obstacles faced
by projects of neoliberal subject-making. Her young interlocutors are unwilling
to understand themselves in or through the tenets of the microcredit training
program they attend, wedded as they are to a different set of values and preferences.[62] Their critiques of microcredit programs are driven by family, gender,
and religious identities, as well as a strong class awareness. While the lack
of viable economic alternatives keeps students coming back to the program,
what I want to emphasize here is an analogous reluctance to adopt neoliberal tenets. Sukarieh's interlocutors have little interest in becoming ruthless
entrepreneurs or seeing government run as a business. They remain devoted
to values such as collective care and solidarity and are happy to draw on
these when assessing public policy. Yet in contrast to Sukarieh, I want to posit
that these critiques are not linked only to class consciousness or to identity.
Instead, Hashemitism, through the malleability of its terms, offers resources
citizens can use to ground and voice their views.[63] Critiques of government
are possible, elites are easy to denigrate, but the terms through which citizens
can do so are not infinite, at least not in public. Hashemitism is both "a tool
and a liability for those who wield it."[64]

Over the course of the subsidy debate, bread was detached from its position
(always and already brimming with meaning) in everyday life and attached

to other framings, as the policy became a crucial index of government—an "implicit vessel of meaning of another particular sort."[65] Time and again, individuals, legislators, and political parties turned a material necessary for subsistence into a crucial emblem of the relationship between state and citizenry. Neoliberalism as a mode of political reasoning did not reverberate in the way that ministers and international financial institutions had anticipated or hoped. Other political rationalities continued to hold sway. But how much of the appeal to Hashemitism in public forums and remarks to a foreign researcher was pure prudence and formula? How much was heartfelt compliance? It is impossible to know. More important is how a diverse group of citizens deployed "conventions of personhood and collectivity,"[66] both to minimize the odds of repression and in order to voice certain claims. To mention social stability and national unity in the context of the subsidy debate was to mark a relationship between the citizenry to be sustained and those responsible for sustaining it. The obligation that this relationship entailed sometimes took the shape of a religious duty, sometimes that of a social contract or a paternalist mode of reciprocity. Whatever the case, Hashemitism offered Jordanians modes of appeal through which to contest policy proposals they believed to be inimical to their own interests as well as those of their fellow citizens. Citizens were Hashemitism's ever-vigilant wardens, rather than simply its prisoners. Entering realms of truth always comes with its own opportunities and impositions.

FORESEEABLE INCONGRUITIES

The Bakery Owners Association (BOA) offered what was probably the most intriguing policy position. During the debate, and against the wishes of its poorer constituents, the BOA promoted a three-year transitional period leading to the gradual elimination of the current subsidy system, maintaining that the government should avoid abrupt price shocks on the way to free market prices. At the same time, the BOA supported direct cash assistance for Jordanian citizens, disparaging the electronic smart card proposal as the impossible fantasy of a group of overeager ministerial technocrats. The BOA's president, Abdul Illah Hamawi, explained the group's position in a particularly strident interview in *al-Ra'i* in early 2014, which came on the heels of intense negotiations throughout 2013. Hamawi was treading a fine line between neoliberal suspicions of government involvement and Hashemitism's affirmation of social stability as a goal of supreme importance. He voiced the BOA's "support for the ministry's inspection campaign and supervision of the bakery sector," in theory, while attacking the "corruption, waste, and stealing" that accompanied government regulation in practice. Throughout the debate, Hamawi underscored the BOA's "commitment to bearing its national and moral responsibilities" while promoting direct cash assistance as the "best option for people as it preserves their dignity and achieves significant savings for the state treasury."[67] Crucially, Hamawi always placed the onus for affordable bread provision on the state, which was responsible for ensuring that Jordanians had relatively equal access to *khubz 'arabi*.

In defending the role of the bakery while underscoring the politico-nutritional importance of bread, Hamawi invoked certain tropes that were sure to appeal to government officials. The BOA president argued that, by "providing the strategic good of bread to the citizenry," bakers acted as loyal citizens. They dispensed a vital foodstuff while pursuing profits in responsible ways. In doing so, they fulfilled their "obligations to both the state and our customers." Yet the BOA was hardly immune to the pro-market penchants made commonplace by the circulation of a neoliberal political rationality. To improve the distribution of bread, the organization promoted a market-friendly technique: the freedom to produce and consume. It counterbalanced this proposal with one not strictly driven by market logics—direct cash subsidies for Jordanian citizens. The BOA wanted both relief from asphyxiating regulation and protection from a collapse in demand. The group's policy recommendation ultimately sought to minimize government interference in bakers' business practices while maintaining the purchasing power of the industry's consumers. "Our goal is to please both our customers and the government," Hamawi insisted matter-of-factly. "We all want to avoid the type of unrest and instability that occurs when bread is not available."[68] Tasked with representing the incredibly diverse number of bakery owners throughout the kingdom, the BOA articulated themes of social solidarity and cohesion, governmental ineptitude and state obligation, sensitivity to endemic poverty and potential class warfare.[69] Such tropes were deployed alongside pro-market rhetorics, ones usually associated with anti-welfare positions. Seemingly incoherent on the surface, the BOA's position illuminates the varied appeal and attraction of two very different ways of thinking about government. Incompatibilities need not always be resolved. Neoliberalism and Hashemitism overlap, lean on, and struggle with each other, without always offering a neat resolution. Crucially, the BOA's president framed the organization's position in ways that could effectively persuade both citizens and policy makers. The association's success in derailing the proposed smart card was intimately linked to this astute positioning.

Unsurprisingly, other groups were far more zealous in their rejection of subsidy reform. For many on Jordan's small but vocal left, unshackling bread prices was merely another sop to the foreign institutions that sought to rid the state of its provisionary responsibilities. A coalition of nationalist and leftist parties routinely criticized the government's adherence to IMF dictates, warning the prime minister of "the repercussions" of altering the bread subsidy, "a basic material in the lives of citizens . . . especially the poor."[70] Government efforts were alternately described as either a waste of time or, worse, a colossal mistake. The Islamic Action Front (IAF) also consistently questioned the wisdom of implementing pro-market measures, ascribing moral bankruptcy to economic policies that widened social inequality.[71] The Muslim Brotherhood's political arm described bread as a "necessary substance," the proposed smart card as "incompatible with Jordanian dignity, which cannot be touched."[72] For left-wing and Islamist currents, as well as several of the country's trade unions, the state's provisionary role was both sound economic policy and moral obligation. Many citizens agreed. The accelerated implementation of market-friendly measures under King Abdullah II has not eradicated these vociferous yet disparate forces, which have mobilized on various occasions in Jordan's recent history (1989, 1996, 1998, 2011, 2018) to denounce marketizing measures.[73] Yet beyond underscoring this long and composite tradition of opposition, what I want to do here is to outline how an autocratic political rationality structures so much of what is sayable in public forums. To make legible claims, one must speak in certain ways. And while each of the groups mentioned above was able to mobilize the presumptions of Hashemitism differently, Jordanian citizens were ensnared in a domain of truth that did not allow any simple escape.

Neoliberal and Hashemitist rationalities coincide in their de-democratizing effects, devaluing practices of participation and social equality in favor of market rule, on the one hand, and authoritarian power, on the other. Both take fright at the possibility of political mobilization by citizens, preferring the façade of democracy and market discipline to pacify, control, and contain. Neither is particularly interested in facts nor wrestles with critiques—monarchy and the market are true, right, and unquestionably good. Hence, in one speech, the king can claim that he sees "economic reform as a principal aspect of comprehensive reform" before adding that "national unity is a responsibility and one that hangs around the neck of each one of us."[74] Together, these formulations establish a contingent and conjunctural "relation of mutual reinforcement," whereby economic reform and authoritarian power can be legitimated as crucial to political order and development.[75] Yet the patriotic and self-sacrificing Hashemite subject does not overlap neatly with a neoliberal political rationality that scoffs at civic pride in favor of ruthless individualism.

Perhaps this is why opposition to bread subsidy reform was so common, and why it took the forms that it did. Ideological divisions, disputes over national belonging, and the intricacies of Jordan's class structure militated against collective action on most issues. The regime's institutional strategies, coupled with its shrewd links to tribal and economic elites, made the formation of any broad-based opposition coalition difficult. And while unified opposition to the country's electoral law, the privatization of public wealth, or the restriction of labor rights required elaborate organizational and framing efforts, most of which have failed, shared resolve regarding bread has been far easier to achieve. From Islamists to Marxists, conservative nationalists to Muslim Brothers, not one political organization of note publicly supported bread subsidy reform during the debate. Diverse, even contradictory, political commitments coalesced around *khubz 'arabi*. Astute critics tied the availability of subsidized bread to the dearth of disorder and social unrest, reminding policy makers that despite their pro-market inclinations: "Bread is neither caviar nor salmon."[76] During budgetary negotiations in November 2013, and again the following year, any and all changes to Jordan's bread policy were postponed. Various government sources indicated that, faced with leavened apprehensions, the king himself had intervened to put an end to subsidy reform. News reports consistently emphasized that the monarch also considered bread "a red line."[77] The social protections expected by citizens are precisely those obligations that the Palace appears to accept, answerable as it is to the very same representations of reality that fashion authoritarian monarchy, and the state, as common sense.

CONCLUSION

By forming subjectivities and circulating certain truths, a political rationality functions not as a mere epiphenomenal veneer but, rather, as a field of reason that shapes, organizes, and inculcates ways of governing and relating to government. Of course, welfare services do not proceed directly from these principles. But understandings of the real do inflect how people are governed. Like other programs of social assistance, the bread subsidy delineates specific modes of intervention, demarcates subjects deemed worthy of receiving assistance, and outlines how their needs should be met.[78] It is authorized through certain modes of reasoning and particular ways of understanding society, human nature, and authority. Describing welfare as "coercive distribution,"[79] as some political scientists are wont to do, occludes precisely how certain ways of thinking of and intervening in the social become capable of deployment—not to mention the attachments, dependencies, and subjectivities such interventions depend on and generate. The consequence is a feeble theory of power, one premised on a dichotomy between the ideological and material, where power works primarily through coercion rather than, in part, by producing subjects and the truths to which they must adhere.[80] And it is this ground—discursive, material, and, most of all, political—that I have sought to tease out at different levels in this chapter, demonstrating the work that Hashemitism does through the constraints and possibilities that each interlocutor intones and illuminates. I have attempted to contemplate the embodied knowledges through which power operates, precisely because it is impossible to separate the two.

To be sure, a distinctly neoliberal outlook has come to characterize monarchical rule over the past twenty years. The monarchy has sought to restructure governmental practices and subjectivities in order to conduct individual and collective bodies in accordance with market-friendly tenets. Yet to make citizens into consumers and entitlements into commodities requires not just reform and legislation, but the careful cultivation of novel ways of seeing and being in the world. Stately sensations are not easily transformed. Notwithstanding the Palace's avowed aspirations, the shift towards marketized policies has not been implemented uniformly nor in all sectors. To this day, no substantial cutbacks have been imposed on the military or bureaucracy, nor have aspirations to transform social policy along neoliberal templates been strictly applied. Unrest following welfare cuts or price increases has repeatedly allowed elites to negotiate the pace of restructuring with external donors, who fear the collapse of a consistent "Western" ally in what is considered an unstable region.[81] As a result, Jordan is far from a paragon of neoliberal dogmas. Rather, three decades of market-friendly reforms have worked to entrench a kleptocratic system characterized by a concerted emphasis on military prerogatives, the re-funneling of public expenditures towards large-scale private investments, and a labyrinthine system of patronage that extends from the Palace, through Parliament, down to the lowest levels of municipal administration. Neoliberalization has not eliminated government intervention in the economic realm; it has merely changed who is on the receiving end of its benefits.[82] Several scholars have pointed to these and other incongruities that characterize Jordan's economic reform process.[83] But rather than ascribing these inconsistencies to instrumental logics such as clientelism, corruption, rent-seeking, or the straightforward goal of regime maintenance, we should dwell a bit longer on the potency of conceptions of government that cannot countenance the wholesale subordination of welfare to the logic of the market. For the bread subsidy does not exist, or persist, "without a certain regime of rationality."[84]

Whether the opinions and critiques voiced above alter policy outcomes or shift public debates is perhaps beside the (main) point. No matter the result, these appraisals are as much a part of the process by which the state is made and remade as the routine distribution of bread at the neighborhood bakery. Whether they are accusing the state of shirking its responsibilities or of betraying its obligations, citizens are not undermining it but helping to render this abstract entity comprehensible—just by talking of it as a cohesive body that behaves in this or that way. This does not mean that we should dismiss the debates and disagreements examined herein. But it does mean we should be attentive to how even those who criticize the state or oppose one of its policies are in that very action invoking it and thereby rendering it intelligible. That is to say, these are practices of representing, ones with productive effects. When repeated and reiterated, they work to bring into being the reality they claim merely to describe. More simply, words and concepts do not depict pre-existing things. They are knowledge-making practices that are part and parcel of the phenomena we describe. What this chapter, and this book, have attempted to offer is precisely an alternative to representationalist modes of thinking and analysis, a way to ponder the state not as a structure to be measured, assessed, or assumed but by sifting through the material and discursive phenomena that give the state its appearance as an abstract truth.

CONCLUSION

ON FEBRUARY 1, 2018, the Jordanian government dramatically transformed the country's bread subsidy. Universal support via discounted *khubz 'arabi* at the point of sale was eliminated. Instead, the Ministry of Industry, Trade, and Supply (MOITS) would offer targeted assistance in the form of cash, based on a stringent set of considerations and only to Jordanian citizens. While MOITS would continue to set price caps for bread and serve as the primary importer of wheat into the country, it would no longer directly subsidize the *al-muwwahad* flour used for *khubz 'arabi*. For the first time since 1996, bread prices increased, doubling from 0.16 JD (US$0.23) to 0.32 JD (US$0.45) per kilogram.

This subsidy reform was neither unplanned nor inadvertent. It was part and parcel of a set of measures driven by the Jordanian government's need to meet the requirements of an agreement signed with the IMF in 2016, which included US$723 million in loans over a three-year period. In exchange, the IMF asked for the removal of budget distortions and the implementation of tax increases that would ameliorate Jordan's ballooning debt-to-GDP ratio, which had recently reached 95%. Unsurprisingly, the change to bread policy was accompanied by tax increases on cigarettes, jewelry, soft drinks, and fuel as well. Protests soon erupted. But public dissent, largely pre-empted by two factors, was more modest than it had been in the past. First, days before the price hike, the government had retracted what many considered the most ruthless tax increase, which would have raised the cost of all medicines, an onerous measure that was portrayed as callously targeting the poor and chronically infirm. And second, in an uncharacteristically savvy although xenophobic campaign, government spokespeople had spent months convincing Jordanians that discounted *khubz 'arabi* was being disproportionately consumed, and wasted, by migrants and refugees. Cash transfers would correct this discrepancy, citizens were told, as only eligible Jordanians under a certain income threshold would receive assistance. The new policy would reallocate governmental support, shifting it from the ostensibly inefficient subsidy of a foodstuff (bread) to the efficient dispersal of money to consumers. Most of my interlocutors regarded the promised cash transfers with suspicion, because in 2014, when the Jordanian government had made similar promises after removing fuel subsidies, the transfers lasted barely a year. What is more, fifteen days after the subsidy reform was implemented, the IMF publicly declared that it had cautioned against the measure, emphasizing its newfound belief that economic reforms should not unduly burden the poor. But the change stuck, the logic of universal welfare replaced by targeted cash.

On a sunny summer day, I arrived at the residence of the prime minister who had enacted the subsidy reform. It was August of 2019, more than a year after he had resigned from office in response to the sweeping protests that followed attempts to usher through changes to Jordan's income tax law. Swiftly ushered into the prime minister's home office by his housekeeper, I sat in what felt like the smallest of leather chairs, surrounded by shelves overflowing with honorary decorations and books. Hani Mulqi arrived, in a gray suit and black tie. I awkwardly stood up, fumbling with my pen and notepad. Mulqi shook my hand and briefly recalled our last conversation some five years earlier, before he had rescaled the heights of Jordanian political life. He then sat down, behind an intimidating wooden desk festooned with photographs of his father and members of the royal family, and quickly lit a cigar.

Mulqi knew of my interest in *khubz 'arabi* and was eager to tell his side of the story. "I wanted to make sure government support went to those who needed it," he told me. "You have to understand that bread is a basic food. For me. For Arabs. For Jordanians. But with the previous system, so much of it was being wasted." He went on to outline how much *khubz 'arabi* was consumed by Egyptian laborers and Syrian refugees. As the sunlight crept through the window and reflected back onto his face, a sternness fell across his compact features. "There was also tons of waste. Bakers profiting illegally. Bread thrown away and sold as animal feed. Any product that is artificially underpriced, people will misuse and over-consume it." Mulqi looked both warn out and unyielding, tired of repeating the same arguments he found so resounding.

And so I asked whether the targeted disbursements would indeed reach all those who needed it. "Yes," he assured me. "The system for subsidized bread is different now and so much better. We give people money and they buy what they want. We used to spend 170 million JD on the subsidy, and now we give that money directly to Jordanians," the former prime minister declared confidently.

I was skeptical, but Mulqi was not one to back down, nor cede an inch.

"Targeting the poor is a transparent process," he affirmed. "Government employees got the money deposited in their bank accounts, so too did retirees. Everyone else could register via a very simple process."

I asked about the popular reaction, the protests that had emerged in the aftermath of the reform, and whether cash could ever replace the comfort of the bakery.

"The bakery will surely become like any other store, with no more illegal profits or excessive consumption," he declared eagerly, averse to letting me get a word in. "Jordanians are too used to the government lying to them. I told them the truth, and those profiting from the previous system mobilized. When citizens see weakness, they abuse it. I wasn't going to back down. We have implemented policies of appeasement for too long," he affirmed with a scowl, indignation glowing in his eyes, the fury of a disillusioned man. "People know I'm hard, difficult. But they know I'm fair."

The civilizing undertones in Mulqi's narrative were palpable—ending the direct subsidy would teach citizens how to properly consume bread and further wean them off dependencies that should become a relic of the past. His comments acknowledged bread's symbolic importance but also reflected the increasing willingness to treat it as an economic good, one that would only be valued if it had a market-determined price. I disagreed, but wanted to probe further, enquiring whether Jordanians could trust those in power to maintain the targeted disbursement when other promises in the past had been so easily disavowed.

"Future governments will have to pay close attention to bread prices. The new system is flexible," Mulqi told me. "If wheat prices go up, bread prices need to also, and the government has to respond by giving citizens more cash."

It was precisely this kind of flexibility that had bedeviled Mulqi's successors. Because international wheat prices had risen since subsidy reform, bread prices should have increased as well. But they did not, because the government was unwilling to risk the popular backlash that a further price hike might have provoked. More astonishingly, subsidy reform had failed to produce the fiscal savings its proponents had promised for so long. The cash disbursed to Jordanian citizens consumed the equivalent of most of the previous subsidy budget, and rising wheat prices meant that the government had to step in once again to underwrite discounted flour. Subsidy reform was, even on its own terms, a qualified failure. But perhaps budgetary savings had never been the main goal.

"You have to ask yourself how society benefits from welfare policy," Mulqi concluded. "It's no use for migrant workers and refugees to have cheap food if our own people aren't doing well. Jordanians come first, second, and third. You'll see. They'll be happier with cash."

The proposal to shift bread subsidies to cash had many goals—to cut government expenditures, to reduce wastage, to prevent flour leakage. It was also, alongside a host of other policies, an attempt to further entrench novel mechanisms of rule that would work to create a new kind of political subject, one who relied less on public services and far more on private management as the path to self-realization. Mulqi, like most of those at the highest echelons of the Hashemite regime, urged Jordanian citizens to make themselves anew, as consumers, clients, and entrepreneurs. A very small minimum was offered to those facing drastically insufficient wages or unforeseen circumstances. But above that low threshold, everyone would have to provide for themselves. Of course, welfare was not completely eliminated, but it was increasingly sanctioned and justified in vastly disparate terms, and implemented via contrasting techniques.[1] In Jordan, welfare services no longer presuppose a world in which the government is responsible for ensuring subsistence and striving to maintain a modicum of collective well-being—which it never did all that well in the first place. They seek instead to fulfill only the most basic of needs, while remaining agnostic about welfare's ability to transform how citizens inhabit the world.

The day that subsidy reform was enacted, I had called Hani, the owner of *al-Khalil,* who appears frequently in the pages of this book. He sounded morose, despondent even. "I'm not sure how people will get by," he said to me quietly over the phone. "There are so many in the neighborhood who will not register or do not qualify."

I was hesitant to pick at an open wound, and decided instead to wish him my best. But the next time I saw him in person, his prognoses had, regrettably, come true. I visited *al-Khalil* the day after my interview with Mulqi, the former prime minister, intentionally arriving at the late afternoon rush hour in order to see the bakery in full swing. Fewer customers arrived than I remembered. Fewer kilos of bread were produced. Everyone was consuming less bread.

I stayed until late that evening, eager to chat once the hubbub of the work-day had eased. Never one to sulk, Hani was sad. "Bread is no longer something everyone can afford, something you know will be there when you have nothing else," he said.

The drastic reduction in the availability of black-market flour meant that Hani had to close at seven every night, rather than nine. Escalating diesel prices meant turning the oven on less frequently, resulting in less fresh bread. Two bakers had been laid off; there was not enough work to cover the outlay for their wages.

With the theoretical edifice of this book now ensconced in my mind, I asked about the state: whether it had disappeared, morphed, or improved, given the changes to the bread subsidy. Hani scanned my face. "Different per-haps," he offered, "but we are still governed, now it's just with cash."

I then inquired into the impact of the reforms on the neighborhood and our mutual friends. "The transfers overlook refugees and migrants, and all those who do not know how or do not want to register. Everyone is worse off; everyone can afford less and less," he answered. I asked how people made do, unable to imagine monthly budgets without subsidized bread.

"People do what they can, what they always have," Hani mumbled. I could hear his sadness. "This year it was bread; next year it will be water," he sighed, as we reached to pull down the shutters on *al-Khalil,* bringing an end to another day on which this bakery gave life through loaves of bread.

Hani turned to me, the furrows in his forehead accentuating his sorrow and distress. "The state takes and no longer gives back. It's just there to keep the powerful well-fed." I followed the path of his gaze and tried my best to absorb his desolation. A thick silence lingered. And then, with a sudden mischievous smile, Hani added: "But one day there will be nothing for the poor to eat—except for the rich."

We laughed together. I looked at his callused hands, the evidence of years of unremitting labor. I shifted my glance upwards to see Hani's wrinkles deepened by the last glimmers of the setting sun, dropping unevenly into the valley below.

"We'll see what the state does then."

*   *   *

The transformation of the bread subsidy into a direct cash disbursement is easily read as a further example of the global shift from regulatory strategies guided by Keynesian and socialist doctrines to those premised on market-friendly ones, a shift whose principles and techniques are extending more aggressive forms of capitalism across the globe. The reform illustrates how a governmental project seeking to safeguard the citizenry's subsistence through active intervention has been reimagined and restructured in order to cut public spending and foster individual discipline. But the bread subsidy was never just about providing food. *Khubz 'arabi* was a mode of address through which the Jordanian state both became, and subsisted, as a bearable object of people's imagination and a principle of bodily consensus. It was part and parcel of the ordinary terrain on which subjects congenial to the state effect were made and remade. And while the strategic defense of such programs should not blind us to the socioeconomic divisions, racial hierarchies, or structural violences they often either entrench or work to ameliorate, I want to speculate that if we are indeed to be governed, it may be more instructive and constructive to do so in polities where we regularly traverse life among others, where we experience routine occasions when we become part of something larger than any one person, community, or group. We are surely subsumed by forces of rule in the process, but do universal welfare programs not make life in their midst more bearable? Or at least slightly more just? Somewhat bloated and waste-prone perhaps, but is the bread subsidy, the bustling bakery, not far more nourishing than cash? Wherever one falls on these questions, welfare policies, as Hani well knows, have not ceased, and will continue, to be a topic of debate and disagreement. Along with other governmental practices, they will continue to form the fabric of experience within which political authority is produced. And while market-friendly modes of governance surely do transform this landscape, they hardly mark the end of the will to manage, regulate, and rule. So questions abound. What sensations and bodily dispositions will new welfare services produce? What knowledges will their enactment demand? What forms of reach will they require and what types of tactics will they induce? Most crucially, what subjectivities will they engender and what will these presume? Welfare—whether in the form of cash or food—is and will remain a source of the state's vitality, a key condition of its presence, a source of its astonishing ability to subsist and reproduce.

THE POLITICS OF PERFORMATIVITY

This book has sought to unravel some of the ways in which the state instantiates itself in the lives of Jordanian citizens. It has used bread, and the bakery, as a conduit for exploring the dynamics through which the preeminent source of political authority in the contemporary world is entrenched and felt as real. *States of Subsistence* has not been concerned with how the state coerces, distributes, or allocates, at least not as a singular institution that precedes the actions by which its seemingly unassailable unity is achieved. The burden of this book has been altogether different: to explore just some of the assemblages and entanglements through which that thing we call the state becomes tangible, thinkable, commonplace—a matter of course.

Performative accounts of political life can improve our analyses precisely because they denaturalize such givens. Without neglecting the enduring pull of those abstractions, such accounts can draw attention to the very mechanisms through which the powers that rule us come to seem fixed. *States of Subsistence* has done so in two parts. First, it has tracked key events, configurations of sensation, and modes of craft that allow the state to assemble in time and space. In the first three chapters, I suggested that the repetition of regulatory practices in the form of welfare leads to the materialization of the state in everyday life. That is, I showed the relationship between the state's coherence and just some of the varied sites and actors through which this coherence is made and remade. Whether in the oft-neglected realm of sensation or in the banal ways in which citizens negotiate the vibrancy of the human and nonhuman, the state effect transpires not just amid debate and discussion. It requires gatherings of people and things that produce the state as a palpable actor and allow it to be addressed as a tangible entity. For the state, like all patterns of rule, has conditions of possibility. Attention to their assembly is key.

The second half of this book focused less on realities effected than it did on realities represented and the productive effects of these representations. Here, gatherings of people and things were engulfed by debates and discussions regarding what exactly the state is and should do. In various sites associated with the bread subsidy, I explored the ideas, expectations, and encounters of Jordanian citizens with respect to practices of government, and the varied ways in which they described the state as a result. The point was not just to offer insights into how a diverse set of Jordanians imagined or portrayed the state, but to unpack how these situated depictions worked to enact the state as such. Put somewhat differently, knowledge-making practices are not neutral portrayals of a pre-existing reality. They are pungent condensations of our engagements with the world, and they contribute to the phenomena they describe. We cannot easily separate knower and known.

Throughout, I have unpacked the state as a performative project in an attempt to signal the contingencies of its making, taking what is often analyzed as a structural given and reframing it as a project of creation.[2] I have written about one very ordinary welfare service in Jordan in order to urge attention onto the people, things, and encounters that mediate relationships with political authority, not just in the Hashemite Kingdom but also in most other parts of the world. Rather than free governmental practices from local histories, contexts, and sociomaterial arrangements so that they can function as indicators, I am instead suggesting that we explore the political possibilities these practices open up and narrow down, the different ways in which welfare, taxation, or border control, for instance, exercise forms of rule and arrange subjects in relation to that rule. To forgo the unending search to identify a correspondence among descriptions, measurement, and reality and home in instead on the doings and actions that construct that reality in the first place; to focus less on the evidently given and more on the practices that produce the illusion of given-ness.

Surely, problematizing structures of rule may occasion a challenging loss of epistemological conviction. But it need not entail a paralyzing uncertainty. It may even disturb us into pondering new possibilities, shifts in our political thinking. For if the forces that govern us are not rigid apparatuses, then they rely on ongoing actions, encounters, and associations. The point is not simply that the state is performed through such intra-actions, but that their repetition is the mechanism through which that effect is enacted anew, time and again.[3] Slippages may be possible, disorderings too, but only after we acknowledge that we are implicated in that which we contest, formed and fashioned by the very same forces that underpin our agency. For now, we remain all too situated within the state's orbit, longing for its presence and consolation, decrying its abuses and mistreatments. Such are the ambivalences of political subjectivation. An escape might be required. But we have nowhere to go.

PREFACE

1. Sidney W. Mintz, *Sweetness and Power: The Place of Sugar in Modern History* (London: Penguin, 1986); Timothy Mitchell, *Carbon Democracy: Political Power in the Age of Oil* (New York: Verso Books, 2011).

INTRODUCTION

1. Ala al-Qiraleh, "Al-Hamawi: Iritfāʿa istihlāk al-khubz 15% muqārana mʿa al-ʿām al-māḍī" [Al-Hamawi: 15% rise in bread consumption compared to last year], *Al-Raʿi*, August 21, 2014, http://www.alrai.com/article/665039.html/. Because the subsidy is universal and non-exclusionary, only unreliable estimates exist for the amount of subsidized bread consumed by Jordanian citizens as opposed to all residents.

2. In these pockets, more than 80% of average monthly food expenditures go to cereals. World Food Programme, "Jordan Food Security Survey in the Poverty Pockets," August–September 2008, http://documents.wfp.org/stellent/groups/public/documents/ena/wfp204530.pdf/.

3. For more on how the colonial encounter introduced modes of governance radically at odds with the socio-ethical and political formations that had worked to form Muslim subjects beforehand, see Wael Hallaq, *The Impossible State: Islam, Politics and Modernity's Moral Predicament* (New York: Columbia University Press, 2013), 62–63; Wael Hallaq, *Restating Orientalism: A Critique of Modern Knowledge* (New

York: Columbia University Press, 2018), 79–84; Tamim Al-Barghouti, *The Umma and the Dawla: The Nation State and the Arab Middle East* (London: Pluto Press, 2008).

4. Melani Cammett and Lauren M. MacLean, "Introduction: The Political Consequences of Non-State Social Welfare in the Global South," *Studies in Comparative International Development* 46, no. 1 (2011): 4.

5. For examples of the former kind of framework, see Nita Rudra and Stephan Haggard, "Globalization, Democracy, and Effective Welfare Spending in the Developing World," *Comparative Political Studies* 38, no. 9 (2005): 1015–49; Brian Min, *Power and the Vote: Elections and Electricity in the Developing World* (Cambridge: Cambridge University Press, 2015); Madeline Baer, "Private Water, Public Good: Water Privatization and State Capacity in Chile," *Studies in Comparative International Development* 49, no. 2 (2014): 141–67; Simone Dietrich and Michael Bernhard, "State or Regime? The Impact of Institutions on Welfare Outcomes," *The European Journal of Development Research* 28, no. 2 (2016): 252–69; Jennifer Pribble, *Welfare and Party Politics in Latin America* (Cambridge: Cambridge University Press, 2013). For examples of the latter, see Melani Cammett, *Compassionate Communalism: Welfare and Sectarianism in Lebanon* (Ithaca: Cornell University Press, 2014); Jennifer Bussell, *Clients and Constituents: Political Responsiveness in Patronage Democracies* (Oxford: Oxford University Press, 2019); Adam Michael Auerbach, *Demanding Development: The Politics of Public Goods Provision in India's Urban Slums* (Cambridge: Cambridge University Press, 2019).

6. For two useful summaries, see Miriam Golden and Brian Min, "Distributive Politics around the World," *Annual Review of Political Science* 16 (2013): 73–99; Isabela Mares and Matthew E. Carnes, "Social Policy in Developing Countries," *Annual Review of Political Science* 12 (2009): 93–113.

7. Timothy Mitchell, "Everyday Metaphors of Power," *Theory and Society* 19, no. 5 (1990): 571.

8. See Friedrich Nietzsche, *The Birth of Tragedy and the Genealogy of Morals* (Garden City, NY: Doubleday, 1956), 178–79.

9. Judith Butler, *Bodies that Matter: On the Discursive Limits of Sex* (New York: Routledge, 2011), 59.

10. Butler, *Bodies that Matter*, xviii; Judith Butler, "Performative Agency," *Journal of Cultural Economy* 3, no. 2 (2010): 147–61.

11. Timothy Besley and Torsten Persson, "The Origins of State Capacity: Property Rights, Taxation, and Politics," *American Economic Review* 99, no. 4 (2009): 1218–44;

Richard Snyder and Ravi Bhavnani, "Diamonds, Blood, and Taxes: A Revenue-Centered Framework for Explaining Political Order," *Journal of Conflict Resolution* 49, no. 4 (2005): 563–97; Evan S. Lieberman, "Taxation Data as Indicators of State-Society Relations: Possibilities and Pitfalls in Cross-National Research," *Studies in Comparative International Development* 36, no. 4 (2002).

12. Carles Boix, "Economic Roots of Civil Wars and Revolutions in the Contemporary World," *World Politics* 60, no. 3 (2008): 390–437; Merete Bech Seeberg, "State Capacity and the Paradox of Authoritarian Elections," *Democratization* 21, no. 7 (2014): 1265–85.

13. Lauren M. MacLean, "State Retrenchment and the Exercise of Citizenship in Africa," *Comparative Political Studies* 44, no. 9 (2011): 1238–66; Zeynep Taydas and Dursun Peksen, "Can States Buy Peace? Social Welfare Spending and Civil Conflicts," *Journal of Peace Research* 49, no. 2 (2012): 273–87.

14. Hendrix argues that survey measures of bureaucratic quality and the tax-collecting capabilities of state institutions are the most theoretically and empirically justified measurements of state capacity. For a survey of this literature, which concludes by defending a multivariate approach to modeling state capacity, see Cullen S. Hendrix, "Measuring State Capacity: Theoretical and Empirical Implications for the Study of Civil Conflict," *Journal of Peace Research* 47, no. 3 (2010): 273–85.

15. Timothy Mitchell, *Colonising Egypt* (Berkeley: University of California Press, 1991), xii.

16. Timothy Mitchell, "The Limits of the State: Beyond Statist Approaches and Their Critics," *American Political Science Review* 85, no. 1 (1991): 93.

17. My reading here draws on Stephen Collier's interpretation of Foucault's later works. For more, see Stephen J. Collier, "Topologies of Power: Foucault's Analysis of Political Government beyond 'Governmentality,'" *Theory, Culture & Society* 26, no. 6 (2009): 78–108.

18. Collier, "Topologies of Power," 91.

19. Michel Foucault, *The Birth of Biopolitics: Lectures at the Collège de France, 1978–1979* (Basingstoke: Palgrave, 2010).

20. Mitchell, "Everyday Metaphors of Power," 567.

21. This is one of the reasons why Mitchell's insightful article has been interpreted and put to use in such vastly different ways. It may also be a result of Mitchell's reliance on the earlier works of Foucault, as the later parts of Foucault's *oeuvre* had not yet been translated.

22. For a useful summary, see James Loxley, *Performativity* (London: Routledge, 2007).

23. Stanley Fish, *Is There a Text in This Class?: The Authority of Interpretive Communities* (Cambridge: Harvard University Press, 1980), 198.

24. Judith Butler, *Excitable Speech: A Politics of the Performative* (London: Routledge, 1997), 155; Loxley, *Performativity*, 134.

25. Butler, *Excitable Speech*, 155; Judith Butler, *Notes Toward a Performative Theory of Assembly* (Cambridge: Harvard University Press, 2015), 163, 176. In political science, Cynthia Weber's work has drawn on Butler's insights and outlined a similar understanding of performativity with regard to sovereignty. Cynthia Weber, "Performative States," *Millennium* 27, no. 1 (1998): 77–95.

26. Butler more robustly acknowledges the role of the nonhuman in more recent works. See Butler, "Performative Agency," 147–61.

27. Karen Barad, *Meeting the Universe Halfway: Quantum Physics and the Entanglement of Matter and Meaning* (Durham, NC: Duke University Press, 2007), 33–34.

28. Karen Barad, "Posthumanist Performativity: Toward an Understanding of How Matter Comes to Matter," *Signs: Journal of Women in Culture and Society* 28, no. 3 (2003): 815.

29. Barad, "Posthumanist Performativity," 828.

30. Brett Christophers, "From Marx to Market and Back Again: Performing the Economy," *Geoforum* 57 (2014): 12–20.

31. John Law, "After ANT: Complexity, Naming and Topology," *The Sociological Review* 47, no. 1 (1999): 4, emphasis in original.

32. Michel Callon, ed., *The Laws of the Markets* (Oxford: Blackwell, 1998); Donald MacKenzie, "The Big, Bad Wolf and the Rational Market: Portfolio Insurance, the 1987 Crash and the Performativity of Economics," *Economy and Society* 33, no. 3 (2004): 303–34; Donald MacKenzie, "Is Economics Performative? Option Theory and the Construction of Derivatives Markets," *Journal of the History of Economic Thought* 28, no. 1 (2006): 29–55; Donald MacKenzie, *An Engine, Not a Camera: How Financial Models Shape Markets* (Cambridge: MIT Press, 2006).

33. For a fascinating account of how flawed material props (measuring chains, maps, iron rods) jeopardized the production of Egyptian markets in the late 19th and early 20th centuries, see Timothy Mitchell, *Rule of Experts: Egypt, Techno-Politics, Modernity* (Berkeley: University of California Press, 2002).

34. Lisa Wedeen, *Peripheral Visions: Publics, Power and Performance in Yemen* (Chicago: University of Chicago Press, 2009), 213.

35. Fiona McConnell, *Rehearsing the State: The Political Practices of the Tibetan Government-in-Exile* (Oxford: John Wiley & Sons, 2016); José Ciro Martínez and Brent Eng, "Struggling to Perform the State: The Politics of Bread in the Syrian Civil War," *International Political Sociology* 11, no. 2 (2017): 130–47; José Ciro Martínez and Brent Eng, "Stifling Stateness: The Assad Regime's Campaign against Rebel Governance," *Security Dialogue* 49, no. 4 (2018): 235–53.

36. For more on how extra-official ethnographic loci can offer insights into how the state takes shape among ordinary people, see Yael Navaro, *Faces of the State: Secularism and Public Life in Turkey* (Princeton: Princeton University Press, 2002); Begoña Aretxaga, "Maddening States," *Annual Review of Anthropology* 32, no. 1 (2003): 393–410; Noah Salomon, *For Love of the Prophet: An Ethnography of Sudan's Islamic State* (Princeton: Princeton University Press, 2016); Lisa Wedeen, *Ambiguities of Domination: Politics, Rhetoric, and Symbols in Contemporary Syria* (Chicago: The University of Chicago Press, 1999).

37. Navaro, *Faces of the State,* 179.

38. For more on this approach, see Loïc Wacquant, "The Body, the Ghetto and the Penal State," *Qualitative Sociology* 32, no. 1 (2009): 101–29.

39. Liam Stanley and Richard Jackson, "Introduction: Everyday Narratives in World Politics," *Politics* 36, no. 3 (2016): 224.

40. Nigel Ashton, *King Hussein of Jordan: A Political Life* (New Haven: Yale University Press, 2008); James D. Lunt, *Hussein of Jordan: Searching for a Just and Lasting Peace* (New York: William Morrow & Co., 1989); Curtis R. Ryan, *Jordan in Transition: From Hussein to Abdullah* (Boulder: Lynne Rienner Publishers, 2002); Peter John Snow, *Hussein: A Biography* (New York: RB Luce, 1972).

41. Betty S. Anderson, *Nationalist Voices in Jordan: The Street and the State* (Austin: University of Texas Press, 2005); Ellen Lust, "The Decline of Jordanian Political Parties: Myth or Reality?" *International Journal of Middle East Studies* 33, no. 4 (2001): 549–69; Ellen Lust, *Structuring Conflict in the Arab World: Incumbents, Opponents, and Institutions* (Cambridge: Cambridge University Press, 2005); Robert B. Satloff, *From Abdullah to Hussein: Jordan in Transition* (Oxford: Oxford University Press, 1994); Jillian Schwedler, *Faith in Moderation: Islamist Parties in Jordan and Yemen* (Cambridge: Cambridge University Press, 2006); Lawrence Tal, *Politics, the Military and National Security in Jordan, 1955–1967* (Basingstoke: Palgrave Macmillan, 2002).

42. Jamie Allinson, *The Struggle for the State in Jordan: The Social Origins of Alliances in the Middle East* (London: IB Tauris, 2016); Laurie Brand, *Jordan's Inter-Arab*

Relations: The Political Economy of Alliance-Making (New York: Columbia University Press, 1994); Curtis R. Ryan, "'Jordan First': Jordan's Inter-Arab Relations and Foreign Policy under King Abdullah II," *Arab Studies Quarterly* 26, no. 3 (2004).

43. For other examples in the genre, see Alex Jeffrey, *The Improvised State: Sovereignty, Performance and Agency in Dayton Bosnia* (Chichester, West Sussex: John Wiley & Sons, 2013); McConnell, *Rehearsing the State*; Alice Wilson, *Sovereignty in Exile: A Saharan Liberation Movement Governs* (Philadelphia: University of Pennsylvania Press, 2016); Akhil Gupta, *Red Tape: Bureaucracy, Structural Violence, and Poverty in India* (Durham, NC: Duke University Press, 2012); Thomas Blom Hansen and Finn Stepputat, eds., *States of Imagination: Ethnographic Explorations of the Postcolonial State* (Durham, NC: Duke University Press, 2001); Salomon, *For Love of the Prophet*; Madeleine Reeves, *Border Work: Spatial Lives of the State in Rural Central Asia* (Ithaca: Cornell University Press, 2014); Nayanika Mathur, *Paper Tiger: Law, Bureaucracy and the Developmental State in Himalayan India* (Cambridge: Cambridge University Press, 2016); Stuart Corbridge, Glyn Williams, René Véron, and Manoj Srivastava, *Seeing the State: Governance and Governmentality in India* (Cambridge: Cambridge University Press, 2005); Navaro, *Faces of the State*.

44. Anna Lowenhaupt Tsing, *The Mushroom at the End of the World: On the Possibility of Life in Capitalist Ruins* (Princeton: Princeton University Press, 2015), 22; Jane Bennett, *Vibrant Matter. A Political Ecology of Things* (Durham, NC: Duke University Press, 2010), 28; Tania Murray Li, "Beyond 'the State' and Failed Schemes," *American Anthropologist* 107, no. 3 (2005): 383–94.

45. Karen Barad, "Quantum Entanglements and Hauntological Relations of Inheritance: Dis/continuities, Spacetime Enfoldings, and Justice-to-Come," *Derrida Today* 3, no. 2 (2010): 259.

46. Donna Haraway, "Situated Knowledges: The Science Question in Feminism and the Privilege of Partial Perspective," *Feminist Studies* 14, no. 3 (1988): 575–99.

47. For more on the term's connotations, especially in reference to transient modes of dynastic rule, see Al-Barghouti, *The Umma and the Dawla*; Hallaq, *The Impossible State*.

48. Barad, *Meeting the Universe Halfway*, 49.

CHAPTER 1

1. The elite brigade had fought in the Golan Heights during the 1973 October War.

2. Associated Press, "Mutiny Reported at a Jordan Camp," *New York Times*, February 7, 1974.

3. Retrospective accounts of the mutiny by American diplomats also depict inflationary pressures as having been crucial. See Backchannel Message from the Deputy Director of Central Intelligence (Walters) to the President's Assistant for National Security Affairs (Kissinger), March 8, 1974, Kissinger Office Files, Box 139, Country Files, Middle East, Palestinians, Folder 1, Document 30, NSC Files, Nixon Presidential Materials, United States National Archives (hereafter USNA); "Memorandum for General Scowcroft from The Situation Room," September 27, 1976, CIA Library (hereafter CIALib), Freedom of Information Act Electronic Reading Room, https://www.cia.gov/library/readingroom/docs/LOC-HAK-542-7-3-9.pdf.

4. Personal interview with anonymous retired member of the Jordanian armed forces, October 8, 2016, Amman.

5. Mr. Fry, State RCI Operations Center to Mr. McCants, White House Situation Room, "Mutiny of Armored Brigade in Jordan," February 3, 1974, doc. no CIA-RDP78S01932A000100020008–8, CIALib, Freedom of Information Act Electronic Reading Room, www.cia.gov/library/readingroom/docs/CIA-RDP78S01932A000100020008-8.pdf.

6. Terence Smith, "Hussein Attempts to Quiet Soldiers," New York Times, February 8, 1974. Washington cited a postponement by "mutual agreement" to explain the deferment of the king's visit.

7. Personal interview with HE Jawad A. Anani, November 20, 2015.

8. Associated Press, "Mutiny Reported at a Jordan Camp."

9. Warwick Knowles, Jordan Since 1989: A Study in Political Economy. (London: IB Tauris, 2005), 62.

10. Personal interview with HE Marwin al-Qasim, August 1, 2019.

11. Pete W. Moore, Doing Business in the Middle East: Politics and Economic Crisis in Jordan and Kuwait (Cambridge: Cambridge University Press, 2004), 101–2. The ESC was tasked with improving the country's economic situation, as the 1970–71 conflict with the PLO had virtually shut down commerce and closed various trade routes, reducing GDP by 15% for the year.

12. Many of the policies adopted after Prime Minister Wasfi al-Tal's assassination were quite different from the ones that had been dreamt up by his associates on the ESC. In particular, al-Tal had sought to boost irrigation in the Badia and the side valleys rather than the Jordan Valley, while shifting the direction of urbanization eastwards into the steppe rather than to the agriculturally fertile parts of what is now West Amman. I thank Tariq Tell for reminding me of this.

13. For more on the drivers of the dramatic increase in world grain prices, see Yahya M. Sadowski, *Political Vegetables? Businessmen and Bureaucrats in the Development of Egyptian Agriculture* (Washington DC: Brookings Institution, 1991), 32–33; Bill Winders, "The Vanishing Free Market: The Formation and Spread of the British and US Food Regimes," *Journal of Agrarian Change* 9, no. 3 (2009): 315–44.

14. Personal interview with HE Jawad A. Anani, November 20 2015, Amman. In Egypt, which had previously enacted subsidies for bread, the budget for food imports grew from 3 to 10% of GDP between 1972 and 1974. As in Jordan, these imports were largely financed through foreign aid from the Gulf and a growing volume of US assistance, including Public Law 480 grain shipments. Sadowski, *Political Vegetables?*, 33, 168.

15. Quoted in Smith, "Hussein Attempts to Quiet Soldiers."

16. Michel Foucault, "Governmentality," in *The Foucault Effect: Studies in Governmentality*, eds. Graham Burchell, Colin Gordon, and Peter Miller (Chicago: University of Chicago Press, 1991), 103.

17. Mitchell Dean, *Governmentality: Power and Rule in Modern Society* (London: Sage, 2010), 2. For more on whether governmentality should be seen as solely a state practice, see Fiona McConnell, "Governmentality to Practise the State? Constructing a Tibetan Population in Exile," *Environment and Planning D: Society and Space* 30, no. 1 (2012): 78–95; Donald S. Moore, *Suffering for Territory: Race, Place, and Power in Zimbabwe* (Durham, NC: Duke University Press, 2005).

18. Nikolas Rose, *Powers of Freedom: Reframing Political Thought* (Cambridge: Cambridge University Press, 1999), 18, 52.

19. Ariel I. Ahram and Ellen Lust, "The Decline and Fall of the Arab State," *Survival* 58, no. 2 (2016): 7–34; Nazih N. Ayubi, *Over-Stating the Arab State: Politics and Society in the Middle East* (London: IB Tauris, 1995); Steven Heydemann, "Social Pacts and the Persistence of Authoritarianism in the Middle East," in *Debating Authoritarianism: Dynamics and Durability in Non-Democratic Regimes*, ed. Oliver Schlumberger (Stanford, CA: Stanford University Press, 2007), 21–38; Larbi Sadiki, "Towards Arab Liberal Governance: From the Democracy of Bread to the Democracy of the Vote," *Third World Quarterly* 18, no. 1 (1997): 127–48; Eckhart Woertz, *Oil for Food: The Global Food Crisis and the Middle East* (New York: Oxford University Press, 2013).

20. Bradley Louis Glasser, *Economic Development and Political Reform: The Impact of External Capital on the Middle East* (Cheltenham: Edward Elgar Publishing, 2001); Ghassan Salamé, "The Middle East: Elusive Security, Indefinable Region," *Security*

Dialogue 25, no. 1 (1994): 17–35; Larbi Sadiki, "Popular Uprisings and Arab Democratization," *International Journal of Middle East Studies* 32, no. 1 (2000): 71–95; John Waterbury, "From Social Contracts to Extraction Contracts," in *Islam, Democracy, and the State in North Africa,* ed. John Entelis (Bloomington: Indiana University Press, 1997), 141–76.

21. Salwa Ismail, *Political Life in Cairo's New Quarters: Encountering the Everyday State* (Minneapolis: University of Minnesota Press, 2006), 68.

22. Foucault, "Governmentality," 11.

23. Joseph Massad, *Colonial Effects: The Making of National Identity in Jordan* (New York: Columbia University Press, 2001), 102; Eugene L. Rogan, "Bringing the State Back: The Limits of Ottoman Rule in Jordan 1840–1910," in *Village, Steppe and State: The Social Origins of Modern Jordan,* eds. Eugene L. Rogan and Tariq Tell (London: British Academic Press, 1994), 32–57; Eugene L. Rogan, *Frontiers of the State in the Late Ottoman Empire: Transjordan, 1850–1921* (Cambridge: Cambridge University Press, 2002).

24. Rogan, "Bringing the State Back," 37–39. Eugen Rogan describes this law as one of the more effective pieces of *Tanzimat* legislation.

25. Most notably the collapse (1873) of Ottoman rule in the *sanjak* of Ma'an, a fortified oasis town along the pilgrimage route to Mecca.

26. Rogan, "Bringing the State Back," 44.

27. Rogan, "Bringing the State Back," 52.

28. The lure of cheap grain was crucial, as Syrian and Palestinian merchants sought out new ways to invest their capital after the European Great Depression (1873–90). For more, see Rogan, *Frontiers of the State,* 100.

29. For more on the decline and reemergence of flour mills in the Ottoman period, and the various ways these related to administrative expansion, see Eugene Rogan, "Reconstructing Water Mills in Late Ottoman Transjordan," *Studies in the History and Archaeology of Jordan* 5 (1995): 753–56.

30. Imperial domains in the north of contemporary Jordan (Salt, Ajlun) were and continued to be more receptive to centralized rule, as they were far more integrated into the Ottoman administrative apparatus. For more, see Rogan, *Frontiers of the State,* 44–94 and 184–217.

31. Tariq Tell, *The Social and Economic Origins of Monarchy in Jordan* (London: Palgrave, 2013), 41–72.

32. Tell, *The Social and Economic Origins,* 73.

33. Massad, *Colonial Effects,* 159; See also Jamie Allinson, *The Struggle for the State*

in Jordan: The Social Origins of Alliances in the Middle East (London: IB Tauris, 2016), 68–93.

34. Riccardo Bocco and Tariq Tell, "Pax Britannica in the Steppe: British Policy and the Transjordanian Bedouin," in *Village, Steppe and State: The Social Origins of Modern Jordan*, eds. Eugene L. Rogan and Tariq Tell (London: IB Tauris, 1994), 127.

35. John Bagot Glubb, "The Economic Situation of the Trans-Jordan Tribes," *Journal of the Royal Central Asian Society* 25, no. 3 (1938): 448–59.

36. For more on land reforms and land registration during the Ottoman period, see Martha Mundy, "Village Land and Individual Title: Musha' and Ottoman Land Registration in 'Ajlun District," in *Village, Steppe and State: The Social Origins of Modern Jordan*, eds. Eugene Rogan and Tariq Tell (London: British Academic Press, 1994), 58–80. For more on the British period, and the shift towards privatized land ownership, see Michael R. Fischbach, *State, Society, and Land in Jordan* (Leiden: Brill, 2000).

37. Administrative costs consumed around 75% of budget allocations between 1924 and 1944. See Tariq Tell, "The Politics of Rural Policy in East Jordan 1920–1989," in *The Transformation of Nomadic Society in the Arab East*, eds. Martha Mundy and Basim Musallam (Cambridge: Cambridge University Press, 2000): 90–98; Tell, *The Social and Economic Origins*, 66.

38. Tariq Tell, ed., *The Resilience of the Hashemite Rule: Politics and State in Jordan, 1946–1947 (Amman: CERMOC, 2001)*, 95; See also Vartan M. Amadouny, "Infrastructural Development under the British Mandate," in *Village, Steppe and State: The Social Origins of Modern Jordan*, eds. Eugene Rogan and Tariq Tell (London: British Academic Press, 1994), 128–61.

39. Fischbach, *State, Society, and Land in Jordan*, makes this argument most forcefully.

40. Paul Kingston, "Rationalizing Patrimonialism: Wasfi al-Tal and Economic Reform in Jordan, 1962–67," in *The Resilience of the Hashemite Rule: Politics and the State in Jordan, 1946–67*, ed. Tariq Tell (Amman: CERMOC, 2001), 115–44.

41. For more on the role of the school system in producing the "British-imagined Transjordanian," see Massad, *Colonial Effects*, 150–52.

42. Michel Foucault, *Security, Territory, Population. Lectures at the Collège de France, 1977–1978 (Basingstoke: Palgrave, 2009)*, 65.

43. Although social services were scarce, few lacked employment and almost all had enough to eat, as Transjordan was self-sufficient in the production of fruits, vegetables, and cereals, even producing enough for export in certain years. Sugar, tea, and coffee were the only widely consumed goods that were imported during this period. Abla

Amawi, "The Consolidation of the Merchant Class in Transjordan during the Second World War," in *Village, Steppe and State: The Social Origins of Modern Jordan*, eds. Eugene Rogan and Tariq Tell (London: British Academic Press, 1994), 162–86; Timothy J. Piro, *The Political Economy of Market Reform in Jordan* (London: Rowman & Littlefield, 1998), 25–26; Amadouny, "Infrastructural Development under the British Mandate."

44. E. M. H. Lloyd, *Food and Inflation in the Middle East, 1940–1945* (Stanford, CA: Stanford University Press, 1956); George Kirk, *The Middle East in the War* (London: Oxford University Press, 1952), 180.

45. Eric Schewe, "How War Shaped Egypt's National Bread Loaf," *Comparative Studies of South Asia, Africa and the Middle East* 37, no. 1 (2017): 54. For a sense of British policy in the colonies and on cereals, see Visit of Mr. T. W. Davies to Middle East: Report on Import and Consumption Control in Colonial Territories, 1942, CO/852/490/7, United Kingdom National Archives (henceforth UKNA); Cereals, CO/852/489/10, UKNA.

46. Sherene Seikaly, *Men of Capital: Scarcity and Economy in Mandate Palestine* (Stanford, CA: Stanford University Press, 2015), 82.

47. Martin W. Wilmington, *The Middle East Supply Centre* (Albany: State University of New York Press, 1971). For more on the MESC's impact on the region, see Steven Heydemann and Robert Vitalis, "War, Keynesianism, and Colonialism: Explaining State-Market Relations in the Postwar Middle East," in *War, Institutions, and Social Change in the Middle East,* ed. Steven Heydemann (Berkeley: University of California Press, 2000): 100–146.

48. Moore, *Doing Business in the Middle East,* 64–66; Fischbach, *State, Society and Land in Jordan*, 155; Amawi, "The Consolidation of the Merchant Class," 168–70.

49. Abla Amawi, *"State and Class in Transjordan: A Study of State Autonomy"* (PhD diss., Georgetown University, 1992), 480.

50. Seikaly, *Men of Capital*, 2–3.

51. For an interesting example of bakery regulation in Palestine, see Food Control Report for Quarter Ending 30 September 1942, FO/922/163, UKNA. For an excellent discussion, see Seikaly, *Men of Capital*, 82–86.

52. Heydemann and Vitalis, "War, Keynesianism, and Colonialism."

53. Tell, *The Social and Economic Origins*, 75, 111–12.

54. By the end of 1948, there were approximately 458,000 refugees in the newly expanded Hashemite Kingdom, which now included territories on the West Bank of the Jordan River. See Philip Robins, *A History of Jordan* (New York: Cambridge University Press, 2004), 84.

55. For more on how Palestine came to depend on these imports, see Riyad Mousa, "The Dispossession of the Peasantry: Colonial Policies, Settler Capitalism and Rural Change, 1918–1948," (PhD diss., University of Utah, 2006).

56. International Bank for Reconstruction and Development (IBRD), *The Economic Development of Jordan* (Baltimore: Johns Hopkins Press, 1957), 4.

57. This included not only Palestinians but also Bedouins and inhabitants of villages near the Israeli border. IBRD, *The Economic Development of Jordan*, 70.

58. Robert B. Satloff, *From Abdullah to Hussein: Jordan in Transition* (Oxford: Oxford University Press, 1994).

59. Betty S. Anderson, *Nationalist Voices in Jordan: The Street and the State* (Austin: University of Texas Press, 2005); Uriel Dann, *King Hussein and the Challenge of Arab Radicalism: Jordan, 1955–1967* (Oxford: Oxford University Press, 1989); Fawaz Gerges, "In the Shadow of Nasser: Jordan in the Arab Cold War, 1955–1967," in *The Resilience of the Hashemite Rule: Politics and State in Jordan, 1946–1967*, ed. Tariq Tell (Amman: CERMOC, 2001); Massad, *Colonial Effects*, 163–221; Tell, *The Resilience of the Hashemite Rule;* Lawrence Tal, *Politics, the Military and National Security in Jordan, 1955–1967* (Basingstoke: Palgrave Macmillan, 2002).

60. Kimberly Katz, *Jordanian Jerusalem: Holy Places and National Spaces* (Gainesville: University Press of Florida, 2005); Massad, *Colonial Effects;* Marc Lynch, *State Interests and Public Spheres: The International Politics of Jordan's Identity* (New York: Columbia University Press, 1999).

61. Nigel Ashton, "A 'Special Relationship' Sometimes in Spite of Ourselves: Britain and Jordan, 1957–73," *The Journal of Imperial and Commonwealth History* 33, no. 2 (2005): 221–44; Douglas Little, "A Puppet in Search of a Puppeteer? The United States, King Hussein, and Jordan, 1953–1970," *The International History Review* 17, no. 3 (1995): 512–44; Salim Yaqub, *Containing Arab Nationalism: The Eisenhower Doctrine and the Middle East* (Chapel Hill: UNC Press Books, 2004).

62. Kingston, "Rationalizing Patrimonialism," 120–21; Paul Kingston, "Breaking the Patterns of Mandate: Economic Nationalism and State Formation in Jordan, 1951–57," in *Village, Steppe and State*, eds. Eugene Rogan and Tariq Tell (London: British Academic Press, 1994), 187–216.

63. IBRD, *The Economic Development of Jordan,* 22; Anne Marie Baylouny, "Militarizing Welfare: Neo-Liberalism and Jordanian Policy," *The Middle East Journal* 62, no. 2 (2008): 284.

64. Moore, *Doing Business in the Middle East,* 69–70.

65. Not only was the number of enlisted personnel increased, but the income of soldiers and officers was also increased, as part of the Palace's attempts to ensure loyalty after the 1958 Iraqi revolution. Panayiotis Vatikiotis, *Politics and the Military in Jordan: A Study of the Arab Legion, 1921–1957* (London: Routledge, 1967); Massad, *Colonial Effects*, 210.

66. Anne Marie Baylouny, *Privatizing Welfare in the Middle East: Kin Mutual Aid Associations in Jordan and Lebanon* (Bloomington: Indiana University Press, 2010), 53.

67. Tell, "The Politics of Rural Policy in East Jordan 1920–1989," 96.

68. IBRD, *The Economic Development of Jordan,* 27.

69. IBRD, *The Economic Development of Jordan,* 29.

70. US Embassy Amman, "US Policy Objectives in Jordan," June 24, 1958, Jordan Subject Files (1953–60), Box 14, Record Group 469, USNA; See Letter, F. Hill to Hugh Walker, July 1, 1959, Grant File/59–229, Ford Foundation Archives (hereafter FFA), New York.

71. Robins, *A History of Jordan,* 108.

72. Kingston, "Rationalizing Patrimonialism," 120.

73. The plan was later re-launched as the seven-year plan for 1964–70 due to changes in US aid receipts. Government of Jordan, *Five-Year Program for Economic Development, 1962–1967* (Amman: Jordan Development Board, 1962).

74. Support for the planning division came from the American Point Four Program and a team of Ford Foundation economists. During the 1950s, the JDB had no economic planning staff. The only economic planning group in the country at a ministerial level was the Economic Planning Division in the Ministry of Economy. IBRD, *The Economic Development of Jordan,* 426.

75. Robins, *A History of Jordan,* 112.

76. Hazim Nuseibeh, *Dhikrayat Muqaddasiyya* [Sacred memories] (Beirut: Rayyes, 2010); Letter, Benjamin Lewis to Hugh Walker, June 22, 1959, Grant file/59–229, FFA.

77. Many of these shifts drew on the legacy of the Jordanian National Movement and Hamad Farhan's tenure at the Ministry of Finance. I thank Tariq Tell for reminding me of these links.

78. The Central Bank quickly became the primary compiler of domestic economic data and producer of research on the local marketplace. Prior to this period, the Department of Statistics in the Ministry of National Economy had produced some economic data, but it was deemed "ambiguous and unreliable" due to a lack of staff

monitoring the country's monetary and fiscal situation. IBRD, *The Economic Development of Jordan*, 32–33.

79. See Letter, F. Hill to Hugh Walker, December 9, 1958, Grant file/59–229, FFA, New York; Letter, Hugh Walker to Champion Ward, Beirut, July 1, 1959, Grant file/59–229, FFA; US Embassy, "Ford Foundation," September 18, 1959, reel 7, Jordan 1955–59, CSDCF, Record Group/59, USNA.

80. While I find that he overestimates the impact of the JDB on Jordan's economic planning, as well as the government's ability to put forth a coherent development policy, Cyrus Schayegh offers some fascinating details on the shifts in the Jordanian planning regime at the time. Cyrus Schayegh, "1958 Reconsidered: State Formation and the Cold War in the Early Postcolonial Arab Middle East," *International Journal of Middle East Studies* 45, no. 3 (2013): 421–43.

81. Iran saw similar attempts to promote industrial growth and modernization through five-year plans during this period. For more, see Kevan Harris, *A Social Revolution: Politics and the Welfare State in Iran* (Oakland: University of California Press, 2017), 60–62.

82. *Filastin*, February 14, 1965, 1. Al-Tal sought to carry out this mission by explicitly rejecting the numerous left-wing revolutionary ideologies of the day, which he saw as hostile to the private sector and foreign capital, in favor of an ambiguous Arabism with Islamic hues. In public pronouncements, al-Tal often emphasized Jordan as a "Muslim, Arab country in everything related to the teachings of Islam and the heritage of Arabism," while highlighting the monarchy's links to the family of the Prophet Muhammad. See *Filastin*, May 2, 1965, 3.

83. Before al-Tal's electrification drive, electric power was poorly supplied throughout the country. Of a population of 1.4 million, approximately 500,000 residents had electricity in 1958. Supply was also unevenly distributed, heavily tilted towards the capital, Amman, which accounted for 45% of the total capacity. IBRD, *The Economic Development of Jordan*, 348–49. Over the next twenty years, the share of urban homes supplied with electricity improved, from 39% in 1961 to 78% in 1979. Eric Verdeil, "The Energy of Revolts in Arab Cities: The Case of Jordan and Tunisia," *Built Environment* 40, no. 1 (2014): 128–39.

84. Unsurprisingly, many of al-Tal's rural development proposals had military add-ons.

85. For more on the Jordanian government's efforts to integrate the West Bank, albeit in a subordinate position, see Jamil Hilal, *Al-ḍiffa al-gharbiyya, al-tarkīb al-ijtim*

āʿi wa al-Iqtiṣādī (1948–1974) [The West Bank: its social and economic composition, 1948–1974] (Beirut: Markaz al-Abḥath, Munazzamat al-Tahr īr al-Filastīniyya, 1975), 77–176; Massad, *Colonial Effects*, 235–36.

86. Stephen J. Collier, *Post-Soviet Social: Neoliberalism, Social Modernity, Biopolitics* (Princeton: Princeton University Press, 2011), 61–62.

87. For one example detailing this viewpoint, see Wadi Sharamiya, *Al-tanmiyya al-īqtiṣādiyya fi al-ūrdun* [Economic development in Jordan] (Cairo: Center for Arab Research and Studies, 1967).

88. Kingston, "Rationalizing Patrimonialism," 121; Asher Susser, *On Both Banks of the Jordan: A Political Biography of Wasfi al-Tall* (London: Routledge, 1994), 37.

89. Michael P. Mazur, *Economic Growth and Development in Jordan* (Boulder: Westview Press, 1979), 27.

90. Kingston, "Rationalizing Patrimonialism," 128. The successes that al-Tal achieved were eventually almost entirely destroyed by the General Intelligence Directorate (GID). For more, see Pete W. Moore, "A Political-Economic History of Jordan's General Intelligence Directorate: Authoritarian State-Building and Fiscal Crisis," *The Middle East Journal* 73, no. 2 (2019): 242–62.

91. Government of Jordan (GoJ), *Five-Year Program for Economic Development, 1962–1967* (Amman: Jordan Development Board, 1962); Government of Jordan (GoJ), *Investment Opportunities in Jordan* (Amman: Jordan Development Board, 1964).

92. Samir A. Mutawi, *Jordan in the 1967 War* (Cambridge: Cambridge University Press, 2002); Avi Raz, *The Bride and the Dowry: Israel, Jordan, and the Palestinians in the Aftermath of the June 1967 War* (New Haven: Yale University Press, 2012).

93. Robins, *A History of Jordan*, 124–25.

94. Paul Lalor, *"Black September 1970: The Palestinian Resistance Movement in Jordan, 1967–1971"* (PhD diss., University of Oxford, 1992).

95. I use the words "convoluted" and "ostensibly" because the loyalties of Jordan's inhabitants did not break down along strictly national lines. The case of Palestinian business elites and the Amman Chamber of Commerce, which they dominated, offers one such instance. The desire for a calm investment climate and fears of the PLO's communist sympathies led the majority to support the Hashemite regime over the PLO. For the most extensive empirical account of the civil war, see Lalor, *"Black September 1970."*

96. Massad, *Colonial Effects*.

97. In order for this consolidation to occur, the military's loyalty was indispensable.

Before his assassination in November, 1971, al-Tal orchestrated the dismissal of a large number of Palestinian officers and bureaucrats, as well as East Bankers whose loyalty was in doubt. At the same time, a major recruitment campaign targeting monarchists, for all branches of the military as well as the GID, was introduced. These security organs were to be the base on which Hashemite supremacy would be built. The loyalty of its members had to be blind, their devotion to the monarchy steadfast. For more on this period see Massad, *Colonial Effects*, 204–16 and 240–57.

98. Yezid Sayigh traces an overlap between a general shift in regional attitudes towards King Hussein and the allegiance of Palestinian Jordanians following Black September. After the conflict, he argues, the "question of legitimacy ceased to be an active threat to the throne's stability and continuity." Yezid Sayigh, "Jordan in the 1980s: Legitimacy, Entity and Identity," in *Politics and the Economy in Jordan*, ed. Rodney Wilson (London: Routledge, 1991), 170.

99. Michel Foucault, *Society Must Be Defended* (London: Allen Lane, 2003), 216.

100. This shift is analogous to that traced by Foucault in his 1976 lectures, *Society Must Be Defended*, in which he traces how "internal racism" aimed at domestic subversives lies at the epicenter of many modern welfare institutions. Foucault argues that this shift can only occur when a monopoly on legitimate violence is achieved, after which the state's suppression of internal enemies through bureaucratic means can become more finely meshed. Foucault, *Society Must Be Defended*, 258–63; Mitchell Dean and Kaspar Villadsen, *State Phobia and Civil Society: The Political Legacy of Michel Foucault* (Stanford, CA: Stanford University Press, 2016), 81–83 and 97.

101. Smith, "Hussein Attempts to Quiet Soldiers."

102. "Hussein āmar bitaḥsīn al-āwḍā li-m'ayisha lil-quwāt al-museliḥa" [Hussein orders an improvement in the living conditions of the armed forces], *Al-Dustur*, February 8, 1974, 1.

103. Personal interview with HE Jawad A. Anani, November 20, 2015, Amman; "King Hussein's Statement," FCO 93/416/92–93, UKNA.

104. "King Hussein's Statement," FCO 93/416/93, UKNA.

105. "ā'lan al-Hussein inshā' wizāra lil-tamwīn [Hussein announces establishment of the Ministry of Supply], *Al-Dustur*, February 15, 1974, 1. For the British assessment, see "King Hussein," February 15, 1974, FCO 93/416/95, UKNA. FCO 93/416/88–96 contains a wealth of information on the mutiny and its aftermath.

106. For a summary of the speech from the perspective of American diplomats, see "King Hussein's Response to Zarqa Incident," From Amman Embassy to Department

of State, February 16, 1974, in WikiLeaks: https://wikileaks.org/plusd/cables/1974AM-MAN00820_b.html.

107. "ā'lan al-Hussein inshā' wizāra lil-tamwīn [Hussein announces establishment of the Ministry of Supply], *Al-Dustur*, February 15, 1974, 1.

108. "mas'ūliyāt muqtaraḥa li-wizāra al-tamwīn [Proposed responsibilities for the Ministry of Supply], *Al-Dustur*, February 16, 1974, 1.

109. Dean, *Governmentality*, 134.

110. "ā'lan al-Hussein inshā' wizāra lil-tamwīn [Hussein announces establishment of the Ministry of Supply], *Al-Dustur*, February 15 1974, 1.

111. Mitchell Dean, "What Is Society? Social Thought and the Arts of Government," *The British Journal of Sociology* 61, no. 4 (2010): 681.

112. Knowles, *Jordan Since 1989;* Moore, *Doing Business in the Middle East;* Piro, *The Political Economy of Market Reform in Jordan;* Robins, *A History of Jordan.*

113. The delineation and production of economic knowledge, as Mitchell points out in a different context, contributed to the "parallel effect of the economy as an object separate from the state that operated as a visible mechanism independent of the processes of government." Timothy Mitchell, "Economentality: How the Future Entered Government," *Critical Inquiry* 40, no. 4 (2014): 479–507.

114. Michel Foucault, *The History of Sexuality, Volume 1: Introduction*, trans. Robert Hurley (New York: Penguin, 1991), 142–43.

115. "mas'ūliyāt muqtaraḥa li-wizāra al-tamwīn [Proposed responsibilities for the Ministry of Supply]," *Al-Dustur*, February 16, 1974, 1.

116. Z. J. Sha'sha, "The Role of the Private Sector in Jordan's Economy," in *Politics and the Economy in Jordan*, ed. Rodney Wilson (London: Routledge, 1991), 89. As Prince Hassan put it in a speech to the Second Jordan Development Conference, "the development process in Jordan has been deprived of the benefit of continuity which is a basic requirement for accelerated growth." His Royal Highness Crown Prince Hassan, "Remarks to the Second Jordan Development Conference, Amman, Jordan, May 1976," in Government of Jordan, National Planning Council, *Five-Year Plan for Economic and Social Development 1976–1980* (Amman: Royal Scientific Society Press, 1976).

117. "fī muwwtamr ṣaḥafī li-wizāra al-tamwīn [Press conference for the Ministry of Supply]," *Al-R'ai*, March 4, 1974.

118. From 1956 to 1966, the United States provided nearly half of Jordan's external revenue. In the period from 1973 to 1985, other Arab countries, mainly Saudi Arabia

and Kuwait, provided more than 80% of foreign aid. Moore, *Doing Business in the Middle East*, 67.

119. For more on the geopolitics of wheat during this period, see Sébastien Abis, *Géopolitique du blé: Un produit vital pour la securité mondiale* (Paris: IRIS, 2015), 74–78.

120. Nikolas Rose and Peter Miller, "Political Power Beyond the State: Problematics of Government," *British Journal of Sociology* 43, no. 2 (1992): 182.

121. Government of Jordan, *Five-Year Plan 1976–1980*, 386–87.

122. Dean, *Governmentality*, 30; Tania Murray Li, *The Will to Improve: Governmentality, Development, and the Practice of Politics* (Durham, NC: Duke University Press, 2007), 126.

123. While there is no automatic or causal link between the availability of data and an expansion in welfare, it seems reasonable to conclude that the enactment of social policies is far more likely when statistics about the habits and health of the population are available. Theda Skocpol and Dietrich Rueschemeyer, *States, Social Knowledge, and the Origins of Modern Social Policies* (New York and Princeton: Russell Sage Foundation and Princeton University Press, 1996), 3–14.

124. Patrick Joyce, *The State of Freedom: A Social History of the British State since 1800* (Cambridge: Cambridge University Press, 2013), 55; Rose and Miller, "Political Power Beyond the State," 181.

125. James C. Scott, *Seeing Like a State: How Certain Schemes to Improve the Human Condition Have Failed* (New Haven: Yale University Press, 1998), 82.

126. Personal interview with anonymous retired official, Ministry of Supply, December 2, 2015, Amman.

127. Matthew G. Hannah, *Governmentality and the Mastery of Territory in Nineteenth-Century America* (Cambridge: Cambridge University Press, 2000), 115.

128. Alice Wilson, *Sovereignty in Exile: A Saharan Liberation Movement Governs* (Philadelphia: University of Pennsylvania Press, 2016), 125; Scott, *Seeing Like a State*.

129. Moore, *Doing Business in the Middle East*, 102–3. Total foreign aid increased more than 1000% between 1963 and 1985. Fawzi Khatib, "Foreign Aid and Economic Development in Jordan: An Empirical Investigation," in *Politics and the Economy in Jordan*, ed. Rodney Wilson (London: Routledge, 1991), 65. Saudi Arabian grants were particularly important and soon became the "cornerstone of Jordanian budget security." Brand, *Jordan's Inter-Arab Relations*, 105.

130. Employment in the bureaucracy increased by nearly 70% between 1971 and 1975. Mazur, *Economic Growth and Development in Jordan*, 108–15. Public investments

in capital-intensive projects also grew dramatically, especially around the country's phosphate and potash deposits as well as its infrastructure, including roads, an international airport, and electricity generation.

131. Jordan was hardly alone in responding to the inflationary spiral in this manner. A range of *ad hoc* measures were similarly enacted in Kuwait in both 1972 and 1974, for example. The government froze retail prices on many consumer staples. And similarly to what happened in Jordan, the following years saw Kuwait's state apparatus take over the import and subsidy of basic commodities. Moore, *Doing Business in the Middle East*, 95.

132. Price controls placed on food and rent were codified first in the Egyptian constitution of 1956 and again following the ostensibly socialist revolution of 1961. Mine Ener, *Managing Egypt's Poor and the Politics of Benevolence, 1800–1952* (Princeton: Princeton University Press, 2003), 133; Schewe, "How War Shaped Egypt's National Bread Loaf."

133. Jawad Anani, "Adjustment and Development: The Case of Jordan," in *Adjustment Policies and Development Strategies in the Arab World*, ed. S. El-Nagger, Papers presented at a seminar held in Abu Dhabu, UAE, February 16–18, 1987 (IMF), 127.

134. Abraham W. Ata, "Jordan," in *Social Welfare in the Middle East*, ed. John Dixon (London: Croon Helm, 1987), 72; "mas'ūliyāt muqtaraḥa li-wizāra al-tamwīn [Proposed responsibilities for the Ministry of Supply], *Al-Dustur*, February 16, 1974, 1.

135. Moore, *Doing Business in the Middle East*, 108.

136. "mas'ūliyāt muqtaraḥa li-wizāra al-tamwīn [Proposed responsibilities for the Ministry of Supply], *Al-Dustur*, February 16, 1974, 1.

137. For the full text of the law that established the Ministry of Supply, see Al-Jaridah al-Rasmiyyah [The Official Gazette] no. 2486 (April 16, 1974). Decree #23, "The Regulation and Administration of the Ministry of Supply, issued in accordance with Article 120 of the Constitution."

138. Personal interview with HE Jawad A. Anani, November 20, 2015, Amman.

139. Knowles, *Jordan Since 1989*, 62. For categories of goods not under strict control, such as car parts and curtains, the MOS developed a formula through which it established set prices, publishing them in local newspapers.

140. Moore, *Doing Business in the Middle East*, 180.

141. Anani, "Adjustment and Development: The Case of Jordan," 13.

142. Baylouny, "Militarizing Welfare," 291.

143. Mazur, *Economic Growth and Development in Jordan*, 234; Jawad Anani,

"Falsafat al-iqtisad al-Urduni bayna al-fikr wa al-tatbiq khilala nisf al-qarn al-madi"
[Philosophy of the Jordanian economy between theory and practice during the last
half century], in *al-Iqtisad al-Urduni: al-mushkilat wa al-afaq [The Jordanian economy: problems and future]*, ed. Mustafa al-Hamarneh (Amman: Center for Strategic
Studies, 1994).

144. Personal interview with HE Jawad A. Anani, November 20, 2015, Amman.
In the late 1970s, the government had to pay for more and more of its imports with
cash, as subsidies and grants of wheat from the United States' PL 480 program were
drastically reduced.

145. Personal interview with HE Jawad A. Anani, November 20, 2015, Amman.

146. Sha'sha, "The Role of the Private Sector in Jordan's Economy," 86–94.

147. Personal interview with the engineer Musa H. Maaytah, former minister of
political development and current senator, April 27, 2014.

148. The Grain Office merely moderated the very considerable influence that was
exercised over wheat prices by a small number of merchants, who were also the owners
of the country's modern flour mills. IBRD, *The Economic Development of Jordan*, 120–22;
Mohamed Haitham Mahmoud El-Hurani, "Economic Analysis of the Development of
the Wheat Subsector of Jordan" (PhD diss., Iowa State University, 1975).

149. Until the late 1950s, wheat was the main crop grown in Jordan, providing
nearly 30% of the gross value of all agricultural production. Wheat was produced in
Amman, Balqa, Karak, Ma'an, and Irbid, the latter being by far the most important
governorate in terms of production. There were also some small-scale farms in the
Jordan Valley. In 1970, the United States government donated 110,000 tons of wheat
to the Jordanian government so as to avoid bread shortages during the conflict with
the PLO. During the preceding decade, Jordan had also drawn on PL 480 Title II assistance from the United States, which permits the government to apply for relief in
drought years and under emergency conditions. The government used this support
to keep bread prices low in urban areas. The result of American assistance, combined
with the massive influx of refugees and the urbanization of fertile agricultural lands
in and around Amman, eventually moved the country from a position of near self-
sufficiency to one in which it had to import the bulk of its basic foodstuffs. From 1970
to 1982, for example, the sufficiency ratio for wheat averaged 22% (ranging from 68%
of domestic consumption in 1974, a wet year, to 5% in 1979, a dry year). El-Hurani,
"Economic Analysis," 3, 34, and 48.

150. Collier, *Post-Soviet Social*, 100, 111.

151. Katharina Lenner, "Policy-Shaping and Its Limits: The Politics of Poverty Alleviation and Local Development in Jordan" (PhD diss., Freie Universität Berlin, 2014), 111.

152. Baylouny, *Privatizing Welfare,* 54; Massoud Karshenas and Valentine M. Moghadam, "Social Policy in the Middle East: Introduction and Overview," in *Social Policy in the Middle East*, eds. Massoud Karshenas and Valentine M. Moghadam (Houndmills: Palgrave Macmillan, 2006), 1–30; Moore, *Doing Business in the Middle East,* 104.

153. Lenner, "Policy-Shaping and Its Limits," 117–19.

154. Harris, *A Social Revolution;* Maurizio Ferrera, "The 'Southern Model' of Welfare in Social Europe," *Journal of European Social Policy* 6, no. 1 (1996): 17–37; Evelyne Huber, "Options for Social Policy in Latin America: Neoliberal versus Social Democratic Models," in *Welfare States in Transition: National Adaptations in Global Economies*, ed. Gøsta Esping-Andersen (Thousand Oaks, CA: SAGE Publications, 1996): 141–91.

155. Tell, "The Politics of Rural Policy," 97.

156. Lenner, "Policy-Shaping and Its Limits," 122; Robins, *A History of Jordan,* 142–43.

157. Sayigh, "Jordan in the 1980s," 179.

158. Navaro, *Faces of the State*, 165.

159. Sayigh, "Jordan in the 1980s," 167–83.

160. Foucault, *Security, Territory, Population,* 107–8.

161. Mitchell, "The Limits of the State," 92; Thomas Lemke, *Foucault, Governmentality and Critique* (Boulder: Paradigm Publishers, 2015), 31; Thomas Lemke, *Foucault's Analysis of Modern Governmentality: A Critique of Political Reason* (New York: Verso Books, 2019), 372.

CHAPTER 2

1. Benedict Anderson, *Imagined Communities: Reflections on the Origin and Spread of Nationalism* (New York: Verso Books, 2006).

2. David Sutton, "Whole Foods: Revitalization through Everyday Synesthetic Experience," *Anthropology and Humanism* 25, no. 2 (2000): 120–30.

3. Lars Buur, "The South African Truth and Reconciliation Commission: A Technique of Nation-State Formation," in *States of Imagination: Ethnographic Explorations of the Postcolonial State*, eds. Thomas Blom Hansen and Finn Stepputat (Durham, NC: Duke University Press, 2001), 149–81; Veena Das, "Sexual Violence, Discursive Formations and the State," *Economic and Political Weekly* (1996): 2411–23; Akhil Gupta, "Narratives of Corruption: Anthropological and Fictional Accounts of the Indian

State," *Ethnography* 6, no. 1 (2005): 5–34; Jyoti Puri, *Sexual States: Governance and the Struggle over the Antisodomy Law in India* (Durham, NC: Duke University Press, 2016).

4. Thomas Blom Hansen and Finn Stepputat, eds., *States of Imagination: Ethnographic Explorations of the Postcolonial State* (Durham, NC: Duke University Press, 2001), 5.

5. Hansen and Stepputat, *States of Imagination*, 5.

6. Davide Panagia, *The Political Life of Sensation* (Durham, NC: Duke University Press, 2009), 2.

7. Jacques Rancière, "Contemporary Art and the Politics of Aesthetics," in *Communities of Sense: Rethinking Aesthetics and Politics*, eds. Beth Hinderliter and Vered Maimon (Durham, NC: Duke University Press, 2009), 31.

8. Nikhil Anand, Akhil Gupta, and Hannah Appel, eds. *The Promise of Infrastructure* (Durham, NC: Duke University Press, 2018); Stephen Graham and Colin McFarlane, eds. *Infrastructural Lives: Urban Infrastructure in Context* (London: Routledge, 2014); Brian Larkin, *Signal and Noise: Media, Infrastructure, and Urban Culture in Nigeria* (Durham, NC: Duke University Press, 2008); Rudolf Mrázek, *Engineers of Happy Land: Technology and Nationalism in a Colony* (Princeton: Princeton University Press, 2018); Chandra Mukerji, *Impossible Engineering: Technology and Territoriality on the Canal du Midi* (Princeton: Princeton University Press, 2015); Wolfgang Schivelbusch, *The Railway Journey: The Industrialization of Time and Space in the Nineteenth Century* (Berkeley: University of California Press, 1986).

9. Noah Salomon, *For Love of the Prophet: An Ethnography of Sudan's Islamic State* (Princeton: Princeton University Press, 2016), 133.

10. Birgit Meyer and Jojada Verrips, "Aesthetics," in *Key Words in Religion, Media, and Culture,* ed. David Morgan (London: Routledge, 2008), 20–30; Brian Larkin, "Promising Forms: The Political Aesthetics of Infrastructure," in *The Promise of Infrastructure*, eds. Nikhil Anand, Akhil Gupta, and Hannah Appel (Durham, NC: Duke University Press, 2008), 175–222. For a fantastic introduction to debates concerning Aristotle's use of the term *aesthesis* that are still relevant today, see David W. Hamlyn, "Aristotle's Account of Aesthesis in the De Anima," *The Classical Quarterly* 9, no. 1 (1959): 6–16.

11. Terry Eagleton, *The Ideology of the Aesthetic* (Blackwell: Oxford, 1990), 13.

12. Larkin, "Promising Forms,"188.

13. A larger flatbread, traditionally baked in a clay oven similar to a tandoor.

14. Jacques Donzelot, "The Promotion of the Social," *Economy and Society* 17, no. 3 (1988): 395–427.

15. Antina von Schnitzler, *Democracy's Infrastructure: Techno-Politics and Protest after Apartheid* (Princeton: Princeton University Press, 2016), 12.

16. For an exploration of just some of the foodways, as well as social and kinship relations, in which bread was tied up prior to 1974, see Gustav Dalman, "Khubz" [Bread], trans. Yunus al-Tamimi, in *al-fanūn al-sha'biyya* no. 4 (November 1974), 40–45.

17. This refers to rain-fed agriculture, the predominant farming practice in the semi-arid landscape of Jordan's northern governorates.

18. Beginning in the mid-1960s, commercial millers had been steadily reducing their purchases of local wheat, which was usually priced higher than government imports, mainly donations by the United States. The Hashemite regime did eventually recognize the problems that came with such dependence and begin to purchase wheat from local farmers at higher prices so as to re-incentivize domestic production. Nevertheless, the 1967–77 period saw a drastic decline in local wheat yields, as wheat production was increasingly limited to rural, non-irrigated areas, where residents produced their own bread or used it as feed for livestock. For a detailed discussion of these measures and their impact, see Mohamed Haitham Mahmoud El-Hurani, "Economic Analysis of the Development of the Wheat Subsector of Jordan" (PhD diss., Iowa State University, 1975), 34–46 and 358–82.

19. For more on these practices, see Carol Palmer, "'Following the Plough': The Agricultural Environment of Northern Jordan," *Levant* 30, no. 1 (1998): 129–65.

20. For a detailed account of how the shift away from wheat occurred in one particular locale, as well as its long-term impact, see Shaker Jarrar and Yazan Malham, "raf'a al-ghaṭā 'an al-mujtam'a: ṭarīq liwāa dībān ila al-faqir wa al-baṭāla" [Lifting the lid on society: the Dhiban District's road to poverty and unemployment], *7iber,* March 10, 2019, https://www.7iber.com/society/theeban-road-to-poverty-and-unemployment/?fbclid=IwAR1s3s2ZVXEL4aGUrNz95MN1EgV7RqyeaIBeQ20O-HFD2Lf-JqWX1riY-ac.

21. For more on earlier milling practices, and the role of the flour mills as social foci, see Carol Palmer, "Milk and Cereals: Identifying Food and Food Identity among Fallāhīn and Bedouin in Jordan," *Levant* 34, no. 1 (2002): 176–77.

22. Tawfīq Canaan, "Superstition and Folklore about Bread," *Bulletin of the American Schools of Oriental Research* 167, no. 1 (1962): 42.

23. For a brief but fascinating exploration of the silo as symbol and infrastructure of modernity, see Ateya Khorakiwala, "Silo as System: Infrastructural Interventions into the Political Economy of Wheat," *Engagement Blog,* https://aesengagement.wordpress.

com/2016/04/12/silo-as-system-infrastructural-interventions-into-the-political-econ-omy-of-wheat/.

24. Crucial here as well was how British land settlement in the 1930s transferred communal shareholding to individual ownership, altering the calculus of farmers and landowners in northern Jordan. For more on this process, which is closely tied to how tree crops had become more profitable than cereals by the time the bread subsidy emerged, see Palmer, "Following the Plough," 157.

25. For more on how this shift in production patterns altered women's influence on household provisioning, see Palmer, "Milk and Cereals," 192.

26. Canaan, "Superstition and Folklore about Bread," 42.

27. Abd al-Rahman Munif, *Story of a City: A Childhood in Amman*, trans. Samira Kawar (London: Quartet Books, 1996), 84. Munif recounts that those who bought this Western bread "used it as one would use a dip, wrapping it in thin home-made bread and eating it, because it had been made out of white Zero-brand flour." He surmised that "This new kind of bread did not have a bright future."

28. Munif, *Story of a City, 84.*

29. There have been several reasons put forward for the lack of commercial bak-eries prior to the establishment of bread subsidies across the region. Canaan argues that bread sold in the market was not seen as blessed because of the many eyes that had been laid upon it, especially those of the needy and hungry. Canaan, "Superstition and Folklore about Bread," 45. Kanafani-Zahar's study of Lebanon posits that bread produced in commercial bakeries was perceived differently because of the flours used as well as the hearth ovens fueled with gasoline used in its production, both of which affected its taste. Aïda Kanafani-Zahar, "'Whoever Eats You Is No Longer Hungry, Whoever Sees You Becomes Humble': Bread and Identity in Lebanon," *Food and Foodways* 7.1 (1997): 45–71.

30. Palmer, "Milk and Cereals," 192.

31. Carole M. Counihan, "Bread as World: Food Habits and Social Relations in Modernizing Sardinia," *Anthropological Quarterly* 57, no. 2 (1984): 47.

32. Ben Anderson, *Encountering Affect: Capacities, Apparatuses, Conditions* (London: Routledge, 2017), 47. For more on how "new bodily habituations" emerged with the agricultural tempos of perennial irrigation in Egypt, see Jennifer L. Derr, *The Lived Nile: Environment, Disease, and Material Colonial Economy in Egypt* (Stanford, CA: Stanford University Press, 2019), 114.

33. Personal interview with anonymous retired baker, November 12, 2015, Amman.

34. For more on how the state apparatus can deploy cuisine to shape publics and expand the state's imbrication with sensory experience, albeit in a very different context, see Camille Bégin, *Taste of the Nation: The New Deal Search for America's Food* (Urbana: University of Illinois Press, 2016).

35. This standardization of bread's taste, size, and texture has parallels with what Schewe finds in the case of the *raghif watani* (national loaf) that was instituted by the Egyptian government during World War II. Eric Schewe, "How War Shaped Egypt's National Bread Loaf," *Comparative Studies of South Asia, Africa and the Middle East* 37, no. 1 (2017): 49–63.

36. Panagia, *The Political Life of Sensation*, 138.

37. Joseph Massad, *Colonial Effects: The Making of National Identity in Jordan* (New York: Columbia University Press, 2001), 76.

38. Ziad Fahmy, "Coming to Our Senses: Historicizing Sound and Noise in the Middle East," *History Compass* 11, no. 4 (2013): 305–15.

39. Ann Laura Stoler, *Carnal Knowledge and Imperial Power: Race and the Intimate in Colonial Rule* (Berkeley: University of California Press, 2010), 198.

40. Katherine Verdery, *What Was Socialism, and What Comes Next?* (Princeton: Princeton University Press, 1996).

41. Verdery, *What Was Socialism?*, 46.

42. For a related argument that illuminates temporal shifts among urban workers and peasants in colonial Egypt, see On Barak, *On Time: Technology and Temporality in Modern Egypt* (Berkeley: University of California Press, 2013).

43. Sara Pursley, *Familiar Futures: Time, Selfhood, and Sovereignty in Iraq* (Stanford, CA: Stanford University Press, 2019), 59.

44. Pierre Bourdieu, *Pascalian Meditations* (Cambridge: Polity Press, 2000), 135, italics in original; Pierre Bourdieu, "Rethinking the State: Genesis and Structure of the Bureaucratic Field," in *Practical Reason* (Cambridge: Polity Press, 1998), 54–55.

45. Panagia, *The Political Life of Sensation*, 3.

46. Karen Barad, *Meeting the Universe Halfway: Quantum Physics and the Entanglement of Matter and Meaning* (Durham, NC: Duke University Press, 2007), 65.

47. Here it is worth quoting Merleau Ponty at length: "The body is the vehicle of being in the world, and having a body is, for a living creature, to be involved in a definite environment, to identify oneself with certain projects and be continually committed to them." Maurice Merleau Ponty, *Phenomenology of Perception*, trans. Colin Smith (London: Routledge, 2002), 94.

48. Foucault, *History of Sexuality*, 151–52.

49. Personal interview with HE Jawad A. Anani, November 20, 2015.

50. Personal interview with HE Marwan al-Qasim, August 1, 2019.

51. Salomon, *For Love of the Prophet*, 147.

52. Salomon, *For Love of the Prophet*, 129.

53. Catherine Fennell, "'Project Heat' and Sensory Politics in Redeveloping Chicago Public Housing," *Ethnography* 12, no. 1 (2011): 40–64.

54. Jacques Rancière, *The Politics of Aesthetics: The Distribution of the Sensible*, trans. Gabriel Rockhill (London: Bloomsbury, 2004), 12

55. Undoubtedly, discerning and unpacking a process of the "redistribution of the sensible" involves "some concentrated gleaning, which depends upon being able to pull together diverse sources and indicators." Nigel Thrift, *Non-Representational Theory: Space, Politics, Affect* (London: Routledge, 2008), 32.

56. Wolfgang Schivelbusch, *Disenchanted Night: The Industrialization of Light in the Nineteenth Century* (Berkeley: University of California Press, 1995); Stephen Graham and Simon Marvin. *Splintering Urbanism: Networked Infrastructures, Technological Mobilities and the Urban Condition* (London: Routledge, 2001), 39–90.

57. Hallaq, *The Impossible State*, 101.

58. Mitchell, "Everyday Metaphors of Power," 567.

59. Joyce, *The State of Freedom*, 50.

60. Rancière, "Contemporary Art," 80.

61. Joyce, *The State of Freedom*, 121.

62. Eagleton, *The Ideology of the Aesthetic*, 13.

63. Yael Navaro, *The Make-Believe Space: Affective Geography in a Postwar Polity* (Durham, NC: Duke University Press, 2012), 20. See also Thomas J. Csordas, "Embodiment as a Paradigm for Anthropology," *Ethos* 18, no. 1 (1990): 5–47; Thomas J. Csordas, "Somatic Modes of Attention," *Cultural Anthropology* 8, no. 2 (1993): 135–56.

64. Saba Mahmood, *Politics of Piety: The Islamic Revival and the Feminist Subject* (Princeton: Princeton University Press, 2005), 194.

65. Nigel Thrift, "Understanding the Material Practices of Glamour," in *The Affect Theory Reader*, eds. M. Gregg and G. J. Seigworth (London: Duke University Press, 2010), 289–308.

66. For an interesting assessment of how, in Lebanon, "honor, generosity, hospitality, and cooperation thus begin with bread," see Kanafani-Zahar, "'Whoever Eats You,'" 48–71.

67. Warren Belasco, "Why Food Matters," *Culture & Agriculture* 21, no. 1 (1999): 27–34.

68. Kathleen Stewart, *Ordinary Affects* (Durham, NC: Duke University Press, 2007), 27.

69. Charles Hirschkind, *The Ethical Soundscape: Cassette Sermons and Islamic Counterpublics* (New York: Columbia University Press, 2006), 123.

70. Reeves, *Border Work,* 187.

71. Panagia, *The Political Life of Sensation,* 73.

72. Rancière, *The Politics of Aesthetics,* 44–45; Davide Panagia, *Rancière's Sentiments* (Durham, NC: Duke University Press, 2018), 51.

73. Birgit Meyer, "Aesthetics of Persuasion: Global Christianity and Pentecostalism's Sensational Forms," *South Atlantic Quarterly* 109, no. 4 (2010): 749.

74. Christina Schwenkel, "Sense," Theorizing the Contemporary, *Fieldsights,* September 24, 2015. https://culanth.org/fieldsights/sense. To be clear, I do not mean to argue that the senses are a stable foundation upon which some unassailable truth can be erected, nor that stately sensations reside in any one organ of perception. Rather, I am positing that perception is intersensory and that perceived objects such as bread and the bakery can take on a determinant but contingent form in particular moments.

75. Hirschkind, *The Ethical Soundscape,* 101; Birgit Meyer, "Introduction: From Imagined Communities to Aesthetic Formations: Religious Mediations, Sensational Forms, and Styles of Binding," in *Aesthetic Formations: Media, Religion, and the Senses,* ed. Birgit Meyer (New York: Palgrave Macmillan, 2009), 1–28.

76. Jacques Rancière, *Dissensus: On Politics and Aesthetics,* ed. and trans. Steven Corcoran (London: Bloomsbury Publishing, 2015), 152.

77. "The embodied experience of place is inevitably relational," and it differs drastically between residents and tourists, researchers and informants. I do not ascribe these differences to cognitive schemata or cultural models but to the way in which bodily training shapes how people become attuned to the landscape that surrounds them. Rivke Jaffe et al., "What Does Poverty Feel Like? Urban Inequality and the Politics of Sensation," *Urban Studies* 57, no. 5 (2020): 1015–31.

78. Lauren Berlant, *Cruel Optimism* (Durham, NC: Duke University Press, 2011), 72.

79. Asef Bayat, "Un-Civil Society: The Politics of the 'Informal People,'" *Third World Quarterly* 18, no. 1 (1997): 53–72.

80. For more on how the non-rich navigate the bakery and practice casual care

towards bread, see Jessica Barnes and Mariam Taher, "Care and Conveyance: Buying Baladi Bread in Cairo," *Cultural Anthropology* 34, no. 3 (2019): 417–43.

81. Berlant, *Cruel Optimism*, 15.

82. Ash Amin, "Animated Space," *Public Culture* 27, no. 2 (2015): 244.

83. Gesa Helms, Marina Vishmidt, and Lauren Berlant, "Affect & the Politics of Austerity. An Interview Exchange with Lauren Berlant," *Variant*, 39–40, August 5, 2012, http://www.variant.org.uk/39_40texts/berlant39_40.html.

84. Hirschkind, *The Ethical Soundscape*.

85. José Ciro Martínez and Omar Sirri, "Of Bakeries and Checkpoints: Stately Affects in Amman and Baghdad," *Environment and Planning D: Society and Space* 38, no. 5 (2020): 849–66.

86. Paul Cloke, Jon May, and Sarah Johnsen, "Performativity and Affect in the Homeless City," *Environment and Planning D: Society and Space* 26, no. 2 (2008): 260.

87. Birgit Meyer, *Sensational Movies: Video, Vision, and Christianity in Ghana* (Berkeley: University of California Press, 2015), 150.

88. D. Asher Ghertner, *Rule by Aesthetics: World-Class City-Making in Delhi* (Oxford: Oxford University Press), 126.

89. Hirschkind, *The Ethical Soundscape*, 2.

CHAPTER 3

1. This phrase is attributed to Karl Marx, but also appears in several chronicles of 18th- and 19th-century Paris. For more, see Steven Laurence Kaplan, *The Bakers of Paris and the Bread Question, 1700–1775* (Durham, NC: Duke University Press, 1996); Samuel Fromartz, *In Search of the Perfect Loaf: A Home Baker's Odyssey* (New York: Penguin Books, 2015), 19.

2. Ash Amin, "Lively Infrastructure," *Theory, Culture & Society* 31, no. 7–8 (2014): 146.

3. AbdouMaliq Simone, "People as Infrastructure: Intersecting Fragments in Johannesburg," *Public Culture* 16, no. 3 (2004): 407.

4. Hannah C. Appel, Nikhil Anand, and Akhil Gupta, "Introduction: Temporality, Politics and the Promise of Infrastructure," in *The Promise of Infrastructure*, eds. Nikhil Anand, Akhil Gupta, and Hannah Appel (Durham, NC: Duke University Press, 2018), 12–13; Timothy Mitchell, *Carbon Democracy: Political Power in the Age of Oil* (New York: Verso Books, 2011).

5. Colin McFarlane, "Urban Shadows: Materiality, the 'Southern City' and Urban Theory," *Geography Compass* 2, no. 2 (2008): 340–58; Amin, "Lively Infrastructure."

6. For more on the relation of *metis* to the state, see Tania Murray Li, "Beyond 'the State' and Failed Schemes," *American Anthropologist* 107, no. 3 (2005): 383–94.

7. Erin O'Connor, "Embodied Knowledge in Glassblowing: The Experience of Meaning and the Struggle Towards Proficiency," *The Sociological Review* 55 (2007): 135.

8. Richard Sennett, *The Craftsman* (New Haven: Yale University Press, 2008), 95; Peter Dormer, *The Art of the Maker: Skill & Its Meaning in Art, Craft & Design* (London: Thames and Hudson, 1994).

9. Matti Siemiatycki, Theresa Enright, and Mariana Valverde, "The Gendered Production of Infrastructure," *Progress in Human Geography* 44, no. 2 (2020): 297–314.

10. Diane Wolf, ed., *Feminist Dilemmas in Fieldwork* (Boulder: Westview Press, 1996); Loïc Wacquant, "Carnal Connections: On Embodiment, Apprenticeship, and Membership," *Qualitative Sociology* 28, no. 4 (2005): 463.

11. Wacquant, "Carnal Connections," 463.

12. Wacquant, "Carnal Connections," 465.

13. For more on how apprenticeship can illuminate components of the corporeal intelligence that guides social agents, often below the plane of language or propositional reasoning, see Loïc Wacquant, *Body and Soul* (New York: Oxford University Press, 2004); Wacquant, "Carnal Connections"; O'Connor, "Embodied Knowledge."

14. L. A. Suchman and R. H. Trigg, "Artificial Intelligence as Craftwork," in *Understanding Practice: Perspectives on Activity and Context*, eds. S. Chaiklin and J. Lave (Cambridge: Cambridge University Press, 1993), 173.

15. For an excellent attempt to center the role of embodied labor in infrastructural systems, see Rosalind Fredericks, *Garbage Citizenship: Vital Infrastructures of Labor in Dakar, Senegal* (Durham, NC: Duke University Press, 2018).

16. Every silo has an analogous unit that manages storage, which is administratively connected to the ministry.

17. USAID donations are notorious for being at or very close to the lowest protein percentage possible (8%).

18. Wheat imported for purposes of reexportation, mainly to Iraq and Syria, is not regulated by MOITS. It cannot, however, be distributed locally.

19. Larger bakeries, which almost always make sweets and other types of bread, are forced to have at least 10% of their total purchase be nonsubsidized flour, in order

to ensure that they can only divert so much of their subsidized flour allocation to other, illegal usages.

20. James C. Scott, *Seeing Like a State: How Certain Schemes to Improve the Human Condition Have Failed* (New Haven: Yale University Press, 1998), 1.

21. Nikolas Rose, *Powers of Freedom: Reframing Political Thought* (Cambridge: Cambridge University Press, 1999), 36, 198; see also Peter Burke, *Social History of Knowledge: From Gutenberg to Diderot* (Cambridge: Polity Press, 2000).

22. Some of this data is produced by Jordan's Department of Statistics, which confronts an entirely different set of measurement conundrums.

23. Nikhil Anand, *Hydraulic City: Water and the Infrastructures of Citizenship in Mumbai* (Durham, NC: Duke University Press, 2017), 161–62.

24. Matthew S. Hull, *Government of Paper: The Materiality of Bureaucracy in Urban Pakistan* (Berkeley: University of California Press, 2012), 167.

25. Penny Harvey and Hannah Knox, *Roads: An Anthropology of Infrastructure and Expertise* (Ithaca: Cornell University Press, 2015), 83, 100; see also Bruno Latour, *Reassembling the Social. An Introduction to Actor-Network-Theory* (Oxford: Oxford University Press, 2005).

26. For an interesting parallel in police work, see Ilana Feldman, *Police Encounters: Security and Surveillance in Gaza under Egyptian Rule* (Stanford, CA: Stanford University Press, 2015), 69, 76.

27. Bernardo Zacka, *When the State Meets the Street: Public Service and Moral Agency* (Cambridge: Harvard University Press, 2017), 85.

28. Max Weber, *Essays in Sociology*, trans. and ed. H. H. Gerth and C. Wright Mills (New York: Oxford University Press, 1946), 233–34.

29. James Ferguson, *The Anti-Politics Machine: "Development," Depoliticization, and Bureaucratic Power in Lesotho* (Minneapolis: University of Minnesota Press, 1994).

30. Timothy Mitchell, *Rule of Experts: Egypt, Techno-Politics, Modernity* (Berkeley: University of California Press, 2002).

31. Andrew S. Mathews, *Instituting Nature: Authority, Expertise, and Power in Mexican Forests* (Cambridge: MIT Press, 2011), 175.

32. David Jackson, Sarah Tobin, and Jennifer Philippa Eggert, "Capacity Building for Politicians in Contexts of Systemic Corruption: Countering 'Wasta' in Jordan," *U-4 Anti-Corruption Resource Centre* 9 (2019); Aseel Al-Ramahi, "Wasta in Jordan: A Distinct Feature of (and Benefit for) Middle Eastern Society," *Arab Law Quarterly* (2008): 35–62.

33. Zacka, *When the State Meets the Street*, 34.

34. Michael Lipsky, *Street-Level Bureaucracy: The Dilemmas of the Individual in Public Service* (New York: Russell Sage, 1980).

35. Zacka, *When the State Meets the Street*, 34; Celeste Watkins-Hayes, *The New Welfare Bureaucrats: Entanglements of Race, Class, and Policy Reform* (Chicago: University of Chicago Press, 2009), 4.

36. Hans Vaihinger, *The Philosophy of 'As If,' A System of the Theoretical, Practical and Religious Fictions of Mankind*, trans. C. K. Ogden (New York: Harcourt, Brace & Company, 1924), quoted in Harvey and Knox, *Roads*, 89.

37. Anand, *Hydraulic City*, 105.

38. Zacka, *When the State Meets the Street*, 58.

39. Bruno Latour and Steve Woolgar. *Laboratory Life: The Construction of Scientific Facts* (Princeton: Princeton University Press, 1979), 51–52.

40. Julia Elyachar, "Before (and After) Neoliberalism: Tacit Knowledge, Secrets of the Trade, and the Public Sector in Egypt," *Cultural Anthropology* 27, no. 1 (2012): 78.

41. For surprising similarities in patterns of knowledge transmission among those working on gravitational radiation in physics, see Harry Collins, *Gravity's Shadow: The Search for Gravitational Waves* (Chicago: University of Chicago Press, 2004).

42. David Graeber, *The Utopia of Rules: On Technology, Stupidity, and the Secret Joys of Bureaucracy* (London: Melville House Publishing, 2015), 75.

43. Paulina B. Lewicka, "Twelve Thousand Cooks and a Muhtasib. Some Remarks on Food Business in Medieval Cairo," *Studia Arabistyczne I Islamistyczne* 10 (2002): 7–19.

44. The *muhtasib* relied on a host of assistants with knowledge of particular professions to prevent business owners from defrauding their customers, so as to implement the Qur'anic injunction and general duty of "ordering good and forbidding evil." For more on the terms *hisba* and *ihtisab*, and their frequent association with the notion of "reckoning" or "accounting," see Abdul Rahman I. Doi, "Hisbah," in *The Oxford Encyclopedia of the Islamic World*, 1st ed., ed. John L. Esposito (New York: Oxford University Press, 2009).

45. Lewicka ("Twelve Thousand Cooks," 12) cites the fact that "the majority of records referring to the implementation of penalties on fraudulent food dealers mentioned in chronicles concern grain dealers, millers or bakers," as evidence of this. See also Boaz Shoshan, "Grain Riots and the 'Moral Economy': Cairo, 1350–1517," *The Journal of Interdisciplinary History* 10, no. 3 (1980): 459–78.

46. Lewicka, "Twelve Thousand Cooks," 11.

47. Ground chickpeas or broad beans and turmeric were the medieval Cairo baker's

mixers of choice. For more on how bakers sought to maximize their profits, see R. P. Buckley, "The Muhtasib," *Arabica* 39, no. 1 (1992): 59–117.

48. Amalia Levanoni, "Food and Cooking during the Mamluk Era: Social and Political Implications," *Mamluk Studies Review* 9, no. 2 (2005): 210.

49. Harvey and Knox, *Roads*, 94.

50. For a fascinating account of the French baking industry's shift to mechanized kneading, see Steven Laurence Kaplan, *Good Bread Is Back: A Contemporary History of French Bread, the Way It Is Made, and the People Who Make It* (Durham, NC: Duke University Press, 2006), 34.

51. Sennett, *The Craftsman*, 54.

52. Trevor H. J. Marchand, "Making Knowledge: Explorations of the Indissoluble Relation between Minds, Bodies, and Environment," *Journal of the Royal Anthropological Institute* 16 (2010): S9.

53. Karen Barad, *Meeting the Universe Halfway: Quantum Physics and the Entanglement of Matter and Meaning* (Durham, NC: Duke University Press, 2007), 33.

54. Pierre Bourdieu, *The Logic of Practice*, trans. Richard Nice (Cambridge: Polity Press, 1990), 66.

55. Michael Polanyi, *Personal Knowledge: Towards a Post-Critical Philosophy* (Chicago: University of Chicago Press, 1962), 55.

56. O'Connor, "Embodied Knowledge," 187.

57. Tim Ingold, *Making: Anthropology, Archaeology, Art and Architecture* (London: Routledge, 2013), 115–16.

58. Bourdieu, *The Logic of Practice*, 73.

59. O'Connor, "Embodied Knowledge," 134; Heather Paxson, *The Life of Cheese: Crafting Food and Value in America* (Berkeley: University of California Press, 2013).

60. Jean-Pierre Warnier, "A Praxeological Approach to Subjectivation in a Material World," *Journal of Material Culture* 6, no. 1 (2001): 7.

61. Maurice Merleau Ponty, *Phenomenology of Perception*, trans. Colin Smith (London: Routledge, 2002), 143.

62. O'Connor, "Embodied Knowledge," 189.

63. Ingold, *Making*, 415.

64. Wacquant, *Body and Soul*, 95.

65. Fromartz, *In Search*, 10.

66. Tim Ingold, "Toward an Ecology of Materials," *Annual Review of Anthropology* 41 (2012): 434.

67. Anand, *Hydraulic City*, 12

68. Jane Bennett, *Vibrant Matter. A Political Ecology of Things* (Durham, NC: Duke University Press, 2010), 24.

69. Barad, *Meeting the Universe Halfway*, 239.

70. Jessica Barnes, *Cultivating the Nile: The Everyday Politics of Water in Egypt* (Durham, NC: Duke University Press, 2014), x.

71. Tim Ingold, *The Perception of the Environment: Essays on Livelihood, Dwelling and Skill* (London: Routledge, 2000), 55.

CHAPTER 4

1. Areej Abuqudairi, "Jordan Reels from Week of Violence in Maan," *Al Jazeera*, April 28, 2014, https://www.aljazeera.com/news/middleeast/2014/04/jordan-reels-from-week-violence-maan-20144281256437277.html.

2. Ahmed Abdullah Suleiman al-Ajlouni, "ṣūra madīna Maʿan fī al- ṣaḥāfa al-ūrduniyya" [Portrait of the city of Maʿan in the Jordanian press], (master's thesis, Jordanian Media Institute, 2017).

3. Akhil Gupta, "Blurred Boundaries: The Discourse of Corruption, the Culture of Politics, and the Imagined State," *American Ethnologist* 22, no. 2 (1995): 375–402; Joe Painter, "Prosaic Geographies of Stateness," *Political Geography* 25, no. 7 (2006): 752–74; Anna J. Secor, "Between Longing and Despair: State, Space, and Subjectivity in Turkey," *Environment and Planning D: Society and Space* 25, no. 1 (2007): 33–52.

4. Secor, "Between Longing and Despair," 33.

5. International borders mark off the "foreign" from the "domestic" and establish the nation-state as the container of the social, historical, and political dynamics with which the subfield is primarily concerned. Certain observers emphasize its endorsement of methodological nationalism: Daniel Chernilo, *A Social Theory of the Nation-State: The Political Forms of Modernity beyond Methodological Nationalism* (London: Routledge, 2008); Andreas Wimmer and Nina Glick Schiller, "Methodological Nationalism and Beyond: Nation–State Building, Migration and the Social Sciences," *Global Networks* 2, no. 4 (2002): 301–34. Others have shown how static portrayals obscure the transnational relations in which state power is embedded, a critique that dates back to Theda Skocpol's review of Barrington Moore's *Social Origins of Dictatorship and Democracy* (1966), in which she highlights the need to switch from an "intra- to an intersocietal orientation." Theda Skocpol, "A Critical Review of Barrington Moore's *Social Origins of Dictatorship and Democracy*," *Politics & Society* 4, no. 1 (1973): 33.

6. For the most recent summary of the subnational as a strategy of social science inquiry, see Agustina Giraudy, Eduardo Moncada, and Richard Snyder, eds., *Inside Countries: Subnational Research in Comparative Politics* (Cambridge: Cambridge University Press, 2019).

7. Giraudy, Moncada, and Snyder, *Inside Countries*; Prerna Singh, *How Solidarity Works for Welfare: Subnationalism and Social Development in India* (Cambridge: Cambridge University Press, 2016); Hillel David Soifer, "Regionalism, Ethnic Diversity, and Variation in Public Good Provision by National States," *Comparative Political Studies* 49, no. 10 (2016): 1341–71. For one of the earliest examples, see Guillermo A. O'Donnell, *Counterpoints: Selected Essays on Authoritarianism and Democratization* (South Bend, IN: University of Notre Dame Press, 1999), 137–40.

8. David Bach and Abraham L. Newman, "Transgovernmental Networks and Domestic Policy Convergence: Evidence from Insider Trading Regulation," *International Organization* 64, no. 3 (2010): 505–28; Jacint Jordana, David Levi-Faur, and Xavier Fernández i Marín, "The Global Diffusion of Regulatory Agencies: Channels of Transfer and Stages of Diffusion," *Comparative Political Studies* 44, no. 10 (2011): 1343–69; Tanja A. Börzel and Thomas Risse, "Governance Without a State: Can It Work?" *Regulation & Governance* 4, no. 2 (2010): 113–34; Henry Farrell and Abraham L. Newman, "Domestic Institutions Beyond the Nation-State: Charting the New Interdependence Approach," *World Politics* 66, no. 2 (2014): 331–63.

9. John Allen, *Topologies of Power: Beyond Territory and Networks* (London: Routledge, 2016), 17.

10. Aradhana Sharma and Akhil Gupta, "Rethinking Theories of the State in an Age of Globalization," in *The Anthropology of the State: A Reader*, eds. Aradhana Sharma and Akhil Gupta (Oxford: Blackwell, 2009), 9.

11. John Allen, "Topological Twists: Power's Shifting Geographies," *Dialogues in Human Geography* 1, no. 3 (2011): 284.

12. John Allen and Allan Cochrane, "Assemblages of State Power: Topological Shifts in the Organization of Government and Politics," *Antipode* 42, no. 5 (2010): 1073.

13. For a noteworthy exception, see D. Asher Ghertner, "When Is the State? Topology, Temporality, and the Navigation of Everyday State Space in Delhi," *Annals of the American Association of Geographers* 107, no. 3 (2017): 731–50.

14. Begoña Aretxaga, "Maddening States," *Annual Review of Anthropology* 32, no. 1 (2003): 398; Michel Rolph Trouillot, "The Anthropology of the State in the Age of Globalization: Close Encounters of the Deceptive Kind," *Current Anthropology* 42, no. 1 (2001): 126.

15. Allen and Cochrane, "Assemblages of State Power," 1073, emphasis in the original.

16. Anne M. Peters and Pete W. Moore, "Beyond Boom and Bust: External Rents, Durable Authoritarianism, and Institutional Adaptation in the Hashemite Kingdom of Jordan," *Studies in Comparative International Development* 44, no. 3 (2009): 273.

17. Peters and Moore, "Beyond Boom and Bust," 274.

18. Christopher Parker, "Tunnel-Bypasses and Minarets of Capitalism: Amman as Neoliberal Assemblage," *Political Geography* 28, no. 2 (2009): 120.

19. Adam Hanieh, *Money, Markets, and Monarchies: The Gulf Cooperation Council and the Political Economy of the Contemporary Middle East* (Cambridge: Cambridge University Press, 2018).

20. Parker, "Tunnel-Bypasses and Minarets of Capitalism," 116; Najib Hourani, "Assembling Structure: Neoliberal Amman In Historical Perspective," *Urban Anthropology and Studies of Cultural Systems and World Economic Development* 45, no. 1/2 (2016): 1–62.

21. Aihwa Ong, *Neoliberalism as Exception: Mutations in Citizenship and Sovereignty* (Durham, NC: Duke University Press, 2006), 103.

22. Jillian Schwedler, "The Political Geography of Protest in Neoliberal Jordan," *Middle East Critique* 21, no. 3 (2012): 259–70; Parker, "Tunnel-Bypasses and Minarets of Capitalism;" Hourani, "Assembling Structure."

23. For an interesting discussion of the state's material presence in the former Soviet Union and the impact of its dismantling on Kazakhstan's capital, Astana, see Mateusz Laszczkowski, "State Building(s): Built Forms, Materiality and the State in Astana," in *Ethnographies of the State in Central Asia: Performing Politics*, eds. Madeleine Reeves, Johan Rasanayagam, and Judith Beyer (Bloomington: Indiana University Press, 2013), 151–68.

24. Department of Statistics Hashemite Kingdom of Jordan, "Employment Survey, for Establishments Engaging Five Persons or More" (Amman: Department of Statistics, 1992), Tables 8 and 9.

25. Anne Marie Baylouny, "Militarizing Welfare: Neo-Liberalism and Jordanian Policy," *The Middle East Journal* 62, no. 2 (2008): 277. For more on the historical origins of what one scholar terms the "Hashemite compact," see Tariq Tell, *The Social and Economic Origins of Monarchy in Jordan* (London: Palgrave, 2013).

26. Curtis R. Ryan, "Peace, Bread and Riots: Jordan and the International Monetary Fund," *Middle East Policy* 6, no. 2 (1998): 54–66; Katharina Lenner, "Projects of

Improvement, Continuities of Neglect: Re-Fragmenting the Periphery in Southern Rural Jordan," *Middle East—Topics & Arguments* 5, (2015): 81.

27. Allen, *Topologies of Power*, 55.

28. For more on the development strategies pursued in Aqaba in the 1970s and 1980s, see Pascal Debruyne, "Spatial Rearticulations of Statehood: Jordan's Geographies of Power under Globalization" (PhD diss., Ghent University, 2013), 167–73.

29. Its design, known as the Aqaba Master Plan, drew heavily on USAID projects in the Philippines and previous studies conducted by the Jordanian government with international consulting companies. Debruyne, "Spatial Rearticulations of Statehood," 169–71; Marwan Kardoosh, *The Aqaba Special Economic Zone, Jordan: A Case Study of Governance* (Bonn: ZEF Bonn Center for Development Research, 2005), 16.

30. Mathieu Alaime, "Aqaba an Extra-Territorial City," in *Atlas of Jordan: History, Territories and Society*, ed. Myriam Ababsa (Beirut: Presses de l'IFPO, 2013), 410.

31. It should be emphasized that plans to streamline Aqaba's bureaucracy so as to foster macroeconomic growth had long been in the making, although the original efforts were shaped by a very different set of governmental rationalities. In the country's 1976 development plan, policy makers were already pondering ways to minimize the "Multiplicity of official bodies responsible for the development of the Aqaba region in respect of port facilities, roads, water supply, and the development of the southern coast, free trade and industrial zones, and other services and facilities." While previous plans did not espouse the sorts of neoliberal vocabularies present in ASEZA documents, they did call for "a single authority to coordinate the development of the region and the implementation of projects on an integrated basis." Government of Jordan, National Planning Council (NPC), *Three-Year Development Plan, 1973–1975* (Amman: National Planning Council, 1973), 253.

32. This is ASEZA's mission statement.

33. For more see Debruyne, "Spatial Rearticulations of Statehood," 169, 171, 195.

34. Benjamin Schuetze, *Promoting Democracy, Reinforcing Authoritarianism* (Cambridge: Cambridge University Press, 2019), 154.

35. Schuetze, *Promoting Democracy*, 159.

36. Healthcare services are widely viewed by both foreign investors and local residents as far below the standard in the rest of the country. Public education is hampered by a lack of trained teachers at the K-12 level and of investment in the University of Jordan's Aqaba branch. For more, see Kimberly K. Cavanagh, "Shifting Landscapes:

The Social and Economic Development of Aqaba, Jordan" (PhD diss., University of South Carolina, 2013), 89–92.

37. The delineation of responsibilities was enacted in Law No. 32 of 2000.

38. Nikolas Rose, *Powers of Freedom: Reframing Political Thought* (Cambridge: Cambridge University Press, 1999), 74.

39. Bonnie Honig, *Public Things: Democracy in Disrepair* (New York: Fordham University Press, 2017).

40. Honig, *Public Things*, 5.

41. Honig, *Public Things*, 30.

42. Akhil Gupta, *Red Tape: Bureaucracy, Structural Violence, and Poverty in India* (Durham, NC: Duke University Press, 2012), 113; Lisa Björkman, *Pipe Politics, Contested Waters: Embedded Infrastructures of Millennial Mumbai* (Durham, NC: Duke University Press, 2015).

43. Sophia Stamatopoulou-Robbins, *Waste Siege: The Life of Infrastructure in Palestine* (Stanford, CA: Stanford University Press, 2019), 110.

44. Stamatopoulou-Robbins, *Waste Siege*, 137.

45. Sian Lazar, *El Alto, Rebel City: Self and Citizenship in Andean Bolivia* (Durham, NC: Duke University Press, 2008), 21; Gupta, *Red Tape*, 92, 100.

46. Timothy Mitchell, "Society, Economy, and the State Effect," in *State/Culture: State-Formation after the Cultural Turn*, ed. George Steinmetz (Ithaca: Cornell University Press, 1999), 77.

47. Personal interview with ASEZA commissioner, November 24, 2015.

48. Personal interview with ASEZA deputy commissioner, November 24, 2015.

49. Hannah C. Appel, "Walls and White Elephants: Oil Extraction, Responsibility, and Infrastructural Violence in Equatorial Guinea," *Ethnography* 13, no. 4 (2012): 461.

50. Allen, *Topologies of Power*, 105, emphasis in original.

51. Andrew Lakoff and Stephen J. Collier, "Infrastructure and Event: The Political Technology of Preparedness," in *Political Matter: Technoscience, Democracy, and Public Life*, eds. Bruce Braun and Sarah J. Whatmore (Minneapolis: University of Minnesota Press, 2010), 244.

52. Brenda Chalfin, *Neoliberal Frontiers: An Ethnography of Sovereignty in West Africa* (Chicago: University of Chicago Press, 2010), 229; Allen, *Topologies of Power*, 157.

53. Madeleine Reeves, *Border Work: Spatial Lives of the State in Rural Central Asia* (Ithaca: Cornell University Press, 2014), 238; James Ferguson and Akhil Gupta,

"Spatializing States: Toward an Ethnography of Neoliberal Governmentality," *American Ethnologist* 29, no. 4 (2002): 981–1002.

54. Nikhil Anand, *Hydraulic City: Water and the Infrastructures of Citizenship in Mumbai* (Durham, NC: Duke University Press, 2017), 6.

55. Hannah C. Appel, Nikhil Anand, and Akhil Gupta, "Introduction: Temporality, Politics and the Promise of Infrastructure," in *The Promise of Infrastructure*, eds. Nikhil Anand, Akhil Gupta, and Hannah Appel (Durham, NC: Duke University Press, 2018), 3.

56. Ferguson and Gupta, "Spatializing States," 984.

57. United Nations Development Programme (UNDP), "Poverty Reduction Strategy, 2013–2020," UNDP, 2013, http://www.jo.undp.org/content/dam/jordan/docs/Poverty/Jordanpovertyreductionstrategy.pdf.

58. Rana Husseini, "Sporadic Clashes Continue in Maan as Government Continues 'Limited' Hunt for Suspects," *Jordan Times,* April 26, 2014, http://www.jordantimes.com/news/local/sporadic-clashes-continue-maan-gov%E2%80%99t-continues-limited%E2%80%99-hunt-suspects; "al-āmin faraq tajam'an ghayr mashru'a fi m'ān" [Security forces disperse illegal gathering in Ma'an], *al-Ra'i,* August 25, 2012, http://alrai.com/article/532687/%D8%A7%D9%84%D8%B1%D8%A3%D9%8A/%.

59. Jean Aziz, "Islamic Extremism on Rise in Jordan," *Al-Monitor,* May 18, 2014, http://www.al-monitor.com/pulse/originals/2014/05/jordan-fears-syria-war-islamists.html.

60. Aida Alami, "Sympathy for ISIL Runs High in Jordan's Restive Maan," *Al Jazeera,* November 4, 2015, http://www.aljazeera.com/news/2015/11/sympathy-isil-runs-high-jordan-restive-maan-151104055011196.html.

61. Although the protests were eventually put down, they did force the monarchy down a path of political liberalization, the goal of which was not meaningful participation but stability and control. In return for the opposition's acceptance of the monarchy as the supreme arbiter of Jordanian politics, increased participation was permitted, an agreement formalized in the 1991 National Charter. Elections became a way to manage and channel popular discontent, while Parliament became an institutionalized forum through which to distribute patronage to loyal communities. They have played similar roles ever since. For more, see Russell E. Lucas, "Deliberalization in Jordan," *Journal of Democracy* 14, no. 1 (2003): 137–44; Glenn Robinson, "Defensive Democratization in Jordan," *International Journal of Middle East Studies* 30 (1998): 387–410; Quintan Wiktorowicz, "The Limits of Democracy in the Middle East: The Case of Jordan," *The Middle East Journal* 53, no. 4 (1999): 606–20.

62. Ellen Lust, "Competitive Clientelism in the Middle East," *Journal of Democracy* 20, no. 3 (2009): 122.

63. Anne Marie Baylouny, "Creating Kin: New Family Associations as Welfare Providers in Liberalizing Jordan," *International Journal of Middle East Studies* 38, no. 3 (2006): 353.

64. Anand, *Hydraulic City*, 202. See also Ellen Lust, "Elections under Authoritarianism: Preliminary Lessons from Jordan," *Democratization* 13, no. 3 (2006): 456–71; José Ciro Martínez, "Jordan's Self-Fulfilling Prophecy: The Production of Feeble Political Parties and the Perceived Perils of Democracy," *British Journal of Middle Eastern Studies* 44, no. 3 (2017): 356–72.

65. Bouziane finds a similar reliance on tribal linkages among the town's residents. Malika Bouziane, "The State from Below: Local Governance Practices in Jordan," *Journal of Economic and Social Research* 12, no. 1 (2010): 33–61.

66. Sean Yom, "The New Landscape of Jordanian Politics: Social Opposition, Fiscal Crisis, and the Arab Spring," *British Journal of Middle Eastern Studies* 42, no. 3 (2015): 284–300.

67. Jillian Schwedler, "Occupied Maan: Jordan's Closed Military Zone," *Middle East Report, Online* 3 (2002).

68. Bouziane, "The State from Below," 51.

69. These dynamics highlight the multiple ways in which state power is constantly negotiated, dependent as it is on the "informal sovereigns" who oversee daily movements in Maʻan. Cf. Thomas Blom Hansen, "Sovereigns Beyond the State: On Legality and Authority in Urban India," in *Sovereign Bodies: Citizens, Migrants, and States in the Postcolonial World,* eds. Thomas Blom Hansen and Finn Stepputat (Princeton: Princeton University Press, 2005), 191.

For more on the Jordanian state's imbrication with local forms of power that contradict Weberian ideals of statehood, see Bouziane, "The State from Below."

70. Melissa M. Lee, Gregor Walter-Drop, and John Wiesel, "Taking the State (Back) Out? Statehood and the Delivery of Collective Goods," *Governance* 27, no. 4 (2014): 635–54; Miguel A. Centeno, Atul Kohli, and Deborah J. Yashar. "Unpacking States in the Developing World: Capacity, Performance, and Politics," *States in the Developing World* (2017): 1–34.

71. Personal interview with Majed al-Sharari, mayor of Maʻan, October 25, 2015.

72. Janet Newman and John Clarke, "States of Imagination," *Soundings* 57, no. 57 (2014): 153–69.

73. Personal interview with the head of the planning department at the Maʻan Municipality, August 6, 2019.

74. Personal interview with Raed Shuwaikh, deputy mayor of Maʻan, August 6, 2019.

75. Sianne Ngai, *Ugly Feelings* (Cambridge: Harvard University Press, 2005), 127.

76. Personal interview with anonymous NGO consultant, August 12, 2019.

77. For more on how economic decline can engender feelings of disconnection, which are quite different from the feeling of never having been connected, see James Ferguson, *Expectations of Modernity: Myths and Meanings of Urban Life on the Zambian Copperbelt* (Berkeley: University of California Press, 1999).

78. In conversation, Maʻanis would often portray themselves as *abna' ad-dawla* (children of the state) before voicing their claims and criticisms. This phrase gestures towards a shared history, harkening back to the support Maʻanis offered to King Abdullah I upon his arrival in the city in November of 1920. For an interesting examination of Maʻan during the period preceding the Hashemite Amir's arrival, see Norig Neveu, "Repenser la Périphérie: Maʻān, Carrefour du Sud du *Bilād al-Shām* au tournant de la Première Guerre Mondiale," *Arabian Humanities* 6 (2016): doi: 10.4000/cy.3038.

79. Kevin Hetherington, "Secondhandedness: Consumption, Disposal, and Absent Presence," *Environment and Planning D: Society and Space* 22, no. 1 (2004): 157–73.

80. Baylouny, "Creating Kin," 349–68.

81. Stamatopoulou-Robbins, *Waste Siege*, 87.

82. Jean and John Comaroff term this "the paradox of presence and absence." Jean Comaroff and John L. Comaroff, *The Truth about Crime: Sovereignty, Knowledge, Social Order* (Chicago: University of Chicago Press, 2016), 37.

83. Michelle Obeid, "Searching for the 'Ideal Face of the State' in a Lebanese Border Town," *Journal of the Royal Anthropological Institute* 16, no. 2 (2010): 337.

84. Judith Beyer, "'There Is This Law': Performing the State in the Kyrgyz Courts of Elders," in *Ethnographies of the State in Central Asia: Performing Politics*, ed. Madeleine Reeves, Johan Rasanayagam, and Judith Beyer (Bloomington: Indiana University Press, 2013), 118; Michael Herzfeld, *The Social Production of Indifference: Exploring the Symbolic Roots of Western Bureaucracy* (Chicago: University of Chicago Press, 1992), 10.

85. Wendy Brown, "Wounded Attachments," *Political Theory* 21, no. 3 (1993): 390–410.

86. Bruce Braun and James McCarthy, "Hurricane Katrina and Abandoned Being," *Environment and Planning D: Society and Space* 23, no. 6 (2005): 802–9.

87. Stef Jansen, "Hope for/against the State: Gridding in a Besieged Sarajevo Suburb," *Ethnos* 79, no. 2 (2014): 238–60.

88. Lisa Wedeen, "Seeing Like a Citizen, Acting Like a State: Exemplary Events in Unified Yemen," *Comparative Studies in Society and History* 45, no. 4 (2003): 689.

89. Neil Brenner, *New State Spaces: Urban Governance and the Rescaling of Statehood* (Oxford: Oxford University Press, 2004), 111.

90. Allen, "Topological Twists," 284.

91. Anna Lowenhaupt Tsing, *The Mushroom at the End of the World: On the Possibility of Life in Capitalist Ruins* (Princeton: Princeton University Press, 2015), 83.

92. Yael Navaro, *Faces of the State: Secularism and Public Life in Turkey* (Princeton: Princeton University Press, 2002), 59.

93. Aretxaga, "Maddening States," 407.

CHAPTER 5

Parts of this chapter are based on José Ciro Martínez, "Site of Resistance or Apparatus of Acquiescence: Tactics at the Bakery," *Middle East Law and Governance* 10, no. 2 (2018): 160–84. Creative Commons License (CC-BY 4.0).

1. For more on how social welfare in Jordan intersects with emergency aid for Syrian refugees, see José Ciro Martínez, "Bread Is Life: The Intersection of Welfare and Emergency Aid in Jordan," *Middle East Report* 272, no. 44 (2014): 30–35.

2. Tania Murray Li, *The Will to Improve: Governmentality, Development, and the Practice of Politics* (Durham, NC: Duke University Press, 2007), 126.

3. Matthew G. Hannah, *Governmentality and the Mastery of Territory* (Cambridge: Cambridge University Press, 2000), 124; James C. Scott, *Seeing Like a State: How Certain Schemes to Improve the Human Condition Have Failed* (New Haven: Yale University Press, 1998).

4. Bruno Latour, "The Powers of Association," *The Sociological Review* 32, no. 1 (1984): 264–80.

5. Daniel Neep, "State-Space beyond Territory: Wormholes, Gravitational Fields, and Entanglement," *Journal of Historical Sociology* 30, no. 3 (2017): 475, emphasis in original.

6. Henri Lefebvre, *The Production of Space*, trans. Donald Nicholson-Smith (Oxford: Blackwell, 1991), 370.

7. Empirical studies have shown the variety of administrative, legal, and technical practices that further the state's dissemination of abstract space. These works

serve to illustrate how state space is not a given but rather an effect produced by particular technologies of power. For an excellent summary, see Neep, "State-Space beyond Territory."

8. Though cast through a familiar resistance/domination dichotomy, Lefebvre's *The Production of Space* makes clear that everyday life never neatly responds to the ordered diagrams and static distributions of the state apparatus.

9. Tania Murray Li, "Governmentality," *Anthropologica* 49, no. 2 (2007): 277; Tania Murray Li, "Fixing Non-Market Subjects: Governing Land and Population in the Global South," *Foucault Studies* 18, no. 2 (2014): 47.

10. Lefebvre, quoted in Andrew Merrifield, *Henri Lefebvre: A Critical Introduction* (New York: Routledge, 2006), 10.

11. For more on the connections between the work of these two authors and the ways in which de Certeau recognizes Lefebvre's work on the everyday as a key inspiration, see Michael Sheringham, *Everyday Life: Theories and Practices from Surrealism to the Present* (Oxford: Oxford University Press, 2006), 216–19.

12. Michel de Certeau, *The Practice of Everyday Life* (Berkeley: University of California Press, 1984).

For useful accounts of the difference between strategy and tactics, see Ian Buchanan, *Michel de Certeau: Cultural Theorist* (London: Sage, 2000), 86–108; Ben Highmore, *Everyday Life and Cultural Theory: An Introduction* (New York: Routledge, 2002), 145–74.

13. C. N. Seremetakis, "The Memory of the Senses, Part One: Marks of the Transitory," in *The Senses Still: Perception and Memory as Material Culture in Modernity*, ed. C. N. Seremetakis (Boulder, CO: Westview Press, 1994), 13.

14. de Certeau, *The Practice of Everyday Life*, 26, 37.

15. James C. Scott, *Domination and the Arts of Resistance: Hidden Transcripts* (New Haven: Yale University Press, 1990); James C. Scott, *Weapons of the Weak: Everyday Forms of Peasant Resistance* (New Haven: Yale University Press, 1985).

16. Reinoud Leenders and Steven Heydemann, "Popular Mobilization in Syria: Opportunity and Threat, and the Social Networks of the Early Risers," *Mediterranean Politics* 17, no. 2 (2012): 139–59; Charles Tripp, *The Power and the People: Paths of Resistance in the Middle East* (Cambridge: Cambridge University Press, 2013).

17. Salwa Ismail, *Political Life in Cairo's New Quarters: Encountering the Everyday State* (Minneapolis: University of Minnesota Press), 2006, xxiii.

18. Asef Bayat, *Life as Politics: How Ordinary People Change the Middle East* (Stanford, CA: Stanford University Press, 2010), 80.

19. Lila Abu-Lughod, "The Romance of Resistance: Tracing Transformations of Power through Bedouin Women," *American Ethnologist* 17, no. 1 (1990): 41–55.

20. Sherry B. Ortner, "Resistance and the Problem of Ethnographic Refusal," *Comparative Studies in Society and History* 37, no. 1 (1995): 173–93. For two inspiring examples, see Amira Mittermaier, "Bread, Freedom, Social Justice: The Egyptian Uprising and a Sufi Khidma," *Cultural Anthropology* 29, no. 1 (2014): 54–79; Laleh Khalili, "The Politics of Pleasure: Promenading on the Corniche and Beachgoing," *Environment and Planning D: Society and Space* 3, no. 3 (2016): 583–600.

21. For a dated, though very detailed, study of the informal sector and livelihoods in four marginalized neighborhoods of Amman, see Rebecca Miles Doan, "Class Differentiation and the Informal Sector in Amman, Jordan," *International Journal of Middle East Studies* 24, no. 1 (1992): 27–38.

22. Elizabeth Povinelli, *Economies of Abandonment: Social Belonging and Endurance in Late Liberalism* (Durham, NC: Duke University Press, 2011), 3.

23. In retrospect, I believe this time was chosen strategically. Saturday was the slowest day at Hani's. On the weekend, family meals usually center around rice, while the hummus stands and sandwich makers (major buyers of subsidized bread) that target commuters and local workers are either closed or operating far less briskly than usual.

24. Literally, this phrase means to "pay before you raise." What exactly is being raised is purposely left ambiguous. This phrase is used in various idiomatic sayings. One is common to public protests, in which demonstrators request payment (symbolic, or in the way of a material transfer) before price increases. In the context in which it is uttered here, it is analogous to a common vulgar expression I heard used by single young men, in which you must pay (al-dafʿa) before (qabal) raising (al-rafʿa) a woman's skirt (often used in reference to a prostitute). An alternative translation would be to pay in advance. I have chosen "pay to play" as I feel it is the most accurate rendition in this context.

25. Amira Mittermaier, *Giving to God: Islamic Charity in Revolutionary Times* (Berkeley: University of California Press, 2019), 69.

26. Diane Singerman, *Avenues of Participation: Family, Politics, and Networks in Urban Quarters of Cairo* (Princeton: Princeton University Press, 1995); Ismail, *Political Life in Cairo's New Quarters.*

27. Tacit knowledge of Hani's weekly bribe resembles what Michael Taussig describes as a "public secret," widely known but not spoken about publicly. Michael

T. Taussig, *Defacement: Public Secrecy and the Labor of the Negative* (Stanford, CA: Stanford University Press, 1999).

28. Jonathan S. Anjaria, "Ordinary States: Everyday Corruption and the Politics of Space in Mumbai," *American Ethnologist* 38, no. 1 (2011): 67.

29. Moya Kneafsey, Rosie Cox, Lewis Holloway, Elizabeth Dowler, Laura Venn, and Helena Tuomainen, *Reconnecting Consumers, Producers and Food: Exploring Alternatives* (Oxford: Berg, 2008).

30. David Harvey, *The Enigma of Capital, and the Crises of Capitalism* (London: Profile Books, 2010), 26.

31. The complicity of bureaucrats and ministerial officials in illegal practices is hardly restricted to Jordan. For other instances, see Jonathan S. Anjaria, *The Slow Boil: Street Food, Rights and Public Space in Mumbai* (Stanford, CA: Stanford University Press, 2016); Giorgio Blundo and Jean-Pierre Olivier de Sardan, *Everyday Corruption and the State: Citizens and Public Officials in Africa* (London: Zed Books, 2006).

32. Michael Herzfeld, *Cultural Intimacy: Social Poetics in the Nation-State* (New York: Routledge, 2005), 372; Brenda Chalfin, *Neoliberal Frontiers: An Ethnography of Sovereignty in West Africa* (Chicago: University of Chicago Press, 2010), 113.

33. Johan Mathew, *Margins of the Market: Trafficking and Capitalism Across the Arabian Sea* (Oakland: University of California Press, 2016), 111.

34. Michel Foucault, "What Is Critique?," in *The Politics of Truth*, ed. Sylvère Lotringer, trans. Lysa Hochroth and Catherine Porter (Los Angeles: Semiotext(e), 2007), 75; Helle Malmvig, "Free Us from Power: Governmentality, Counter-Conduct, and Simulation in European Democracy and Reform Promotion in the Arab World," *International Political Sociology* 8, no. 3 (2014): 293–310.

35. Luigi Achilli, *Palestinian Refugees and Identity: Nationalism, Politics and the Everyday* (London: IB Tauris, 2015).

36. A large sheet of unleavened bread, *khubz ash-shrak* is far thinner and more difficult to prepare than *khubz 'arabi*.

37. For more on *mansaf,* see Sally Howell, "Modernizing Mansaf: The Consuming Contexts of Jordan's National Dish," *Food & Foodways* 11, no. 4 (2003): 215–43; Joseph Massad, *Colonial Effects: The Making of National Identity in Jordan* (New York: Columbia University Press, 2001), 158–59.

38. Varieties of flour are distinguished by their extraction rate, the amount of bran and germ left in the flour after milling. *Muwwahad* has a 78% extraction rate, while other varieties typically lie somewhere between 55% and 68%.

39. During most of 2013, for example, subsidized flour cost Jordan's bakers 35 *JD* per ton (US$49), while the international market price hovered around 301.5 *JD* (US$426).

40. Samir's account is confirmed by various reports published at the time. For further details relating to the 2007 reform, see Ala' al-Furwati, " Darbake fī al-makhābiz wa ghaḍab fī al-shāri'a ba'd raf'a al-d'am 'an al-ṭahīn" [Chaos in the bakery and anger in the street after the removal of the flour subsidy], *Al-Sijil* 2, November 15, 2007, http://www.al-sijill.com/sijill_items/sitem86.htm.

41. Anjaria, *The Slow Boil,* 126.

42. Lisa Björkman, "The Ostentatious Crowd: Public Protest as Mass-Political Street Theatre in Mumbai," *Critique of Anthropology* 35, no. 2 (2015): 156.

43. Neil Brenner and Stuart Elden, "Henri Lefebvre on State, Space, Territory," *International Political Sociology* 3, no. 4 (2009): 367.

44. Partha Chatterjee, *The Politics of the Governed: Reflections on Popular Politics in Most of the World* (New York: Columbia University Press, 2004), 57.

45. Official figures reveal substantial declines in the consumption of subsidized bread during Ramadan and the summer months.

46. Personal interview with Ghassan Muammar, advocate (lawyer), of Muammar Law Firm, and Nadeen Ma'ayeh, CEO of Ecard Ltd, co-presidents of the Bread for Free Campaign, April 22, 2014, Amman.

47. Anjaria, *The Slow Boil,* 136.

48. Sophia Stamatopoulou-Robbins, *Waste Siege: The Life of Infrastructure in Palestine* (Stanford, CA: Stanford University Press, 2019), 170.

49. Personal interview with Atef Rashed Alawneh, employee in the Internal Audit Unit, Ministry of Industry, Trade, and Supply, May 7, 2014, Amman.

50. Personal interview with Atef Rashed Alawneh, employee in the Internal Audit Unit, Ministry of Industry, Trade, and Supply, May 7, 2014, Amman.

51. Personal interview with Samer Khouri, director of market control, Ministry of Industry, Trade, and Supply, April 7, 2014, Amman; personal interview with Dr. Essa al-Dmour, director of internal audits, Ministry of Industry, Trade, and Supply, April 8, 2014, Amman. Their counterparts in the security apparatus largely reaffirmed this view.

52. By the end of January 2016, the campaign had spread to approximately seventy bakeries and was garnering favorable coverage in the press.

53. Dietrich Jung and Marie Juul Petersen, "'We Think that This Job Pleases Allah':

Islamic Charity, Social Order, and the Construction of Modern Muslim Selfhoods in Jordan," *International Journal of Middle East Studies* 46, no. 2 (2014): 285–306.

54. Stamatopoulou-Robbins, *Waste Siege*, 162–65.

55. Ben Highmore, *Michel de Certeau: Analysing Culture* (London: Continuum, 2006), 114.

56. Nikolas Rose and Peter Miller, "Political Power Beyond the State: Problematics of Government," *British Journal of Sociology* 43, no. 2 (1992): 191.

57. Nikhil Anand, *Hydraulic City: Water and the Infrastructures of Citizenship in Mumbai* (Durham, NC: Duke University Press, 2017), 162.

58. Anand, *Hydraulic City*, 227.

59. Stamatopoulou-Robbins, *Waste Siege*, 146, 150.

60. Stuart Hall, "The Toad in the Garden: Thatcherism among the Theorists," in *Marxism and the Interpretation of Culture*, eds. Cary Nelson and Lawrence Grossberg (Urbana: University of Illinois Press, 1988), 44.

61. For more on the pragmatism-radicalism dialectic in the study of local politics that informs these two interpretations, see Paul Amar, "Beyond the 'Pragmatism-Radicalism Dialectic' in the Study of Local Politics," in *Local Politics and Contemporary Transformations in the Arab World*, eds. Malika Bouziane, Cilja Harders, and Anja Hoffman (London: Palgrave Macmillan, 2013), 65–90.

62. Donald S. Moore, *Suffering for Territory: Race, Place, and Power in Zimbabwe* (Durham, NC: Duke University Press, 2005), 44.

63. Saba Mahmood, *Politics of Piety: The Islamic Revival and the Feminist Subject* (Princeton: Princeton University Press, 2005), x.

64. Judith Butler, *Notes Toward a Performative Theory of Assembly* (Cambridge: Harvard University Press, 2015), 56; Mahmood, *Politics of Piety*, 9–14.

CHAPTER 6

Parts of this chapter draw on but also depart from two previously published articles. These are José Ciro Martínez, "Leavening Neoliberalization's Uneven Pathways: Bread, Governance and Political Rationalities in the Hashemite Kingdom of Jordan," *Mediterranean Politics* 22, no. 4 (2017): 464–83, https://www.tandfonline.com/toc/fmed20/current; José Ciro Martínez, "Leavened Apprehensions: Bread Subsidies and Moral Economies in Hashemite Jordan." *International Journal of Middle East Studies* 50, no. 2 (2018): 173–93. Creative Commons License (CC-BY 4.0).

1. For an excellent study of Jordanian talk radio and these particular "service programs," see Jona Fras, "Unifying Voices, Creating Publics: The Uses of Media Form in Contemporary Jordanian Radio," *British Journal of Middle Eastern Studies* 47, no. 2 (2018): 320–42.

2. All of these callers were men. For more on the "gendered soundscape" of Jordanian radio, see Salam Al-Mahadin, "Gendered Soundscapes on Jordanian Radio Stations," *Feminist Media Studies* 17, no. 1 (2016): 108–11.

3. World Bank, "Hashemite Kingdom of Jordan: Options for Immediate Fiscal Adjustment and Longer Term Consolidation," *Report No. 71979-JO* (Washington, DC: World Bank, 2012), 50–52; World Bank, *Hashemite Kingdom of Jordan—Development Policy Review: Improving Institutions, Fiscal Policies and Structural Reforms for Greater Growth Resilience and Sustained Job Creation (Vol. 1 of 2)* (Washington, DC: World Bank, 2012), https://openknowledge.worldbank.org/handle/10986/12302.

4. Hisham Bustani, "Lam yasquṭ hukum al-ṣandūq" [IMF rule does not fall], *7iber*, August 20, 2019, www.7iber.com/politics-economics/%D9%84%D9%85-%D9%8A%D8%B3%D9%82%D8%B7-%D8%AD%D9%83%D9%85-%D8%A7%D9%84%D8%B5%D9%86%D8%AF%D9%88%D9%82/; Ziad Abu-Rish, "Protests, Regime Stability, and State Formation in Jordan," in *Beyond the Arab Spring: The Evolving Ruling Bargain in the Middle East*, ed. K. Mehran (Oxford: Oxford University Press, 2014), 277–312.

5. Omar Obeidat, "Government Mulls Cash Transfers via Smart Cards for Fuel, Bread Subsidies," *Jordan Times*, September 18, 2013.

6. *Al-Dustur*, "lan tarfʿa saʿr al-khubz ʿala al-muwāṭin iṭlaqan" [Bread prices will never rise for citizens], November 28, 2014, p. 7.

7. Tarek al-Daʿjeh, "Al-makhābiz: taṭbīq al-biṭāqa al-dhakiya yatasabab bifawḍa wa yarbak al-muwaṭinīn" [Bakeries: the implementation of the smart card will cause chaos and confuse citizens], *Al-Ghad*, September 16, 2013. https://www.alghad.com/articles/576931.

8. Ilana Feldman, *Governing Gaza: Bureaucracy, Authority, and the Work of Rule, 1917–1967* (Durham, NC: Duke University Press, 2008), 165.

9. Driven in part by the dramatic rise in international wheat prices in 1995 (from US$155 to US$260 a ton), the IMF pushed the government of the prime minister Abdul Karim al-Kabariti to retract the subsidy in exchange for modest cash allowances for public-sector employees. For more, see Robin Bray, *Middle East Economic Digest* (MEED) 40 (1996): 35; Lamis Andoni and Jillian Schwedler, "Bread Riots in

Jordan," *Middle East Report* 201, no. 26 (1996): 40–42; Curtis R. Ryan, "Peace, Bread and Riots: Jordan and the International Monetary Fund," *Middle East Policy* 6, no. 2 (1998): 54–66.

10. Personal interview with Dr. Yusuf Mansur, CEO, ENconsult, former director general of the Telecom Regulatory Commission and economic adviser to the Prime Minister, May 19, 2014, Amman.

11. James C. Scott, *Domination and the Arts of Resistance: Hidden Transcripts* (New Haven: Yale University Press, 1990), 199.

12. Alasdair MacIntyre, *After Virtue* (London: Bloomsbury, 2013), 12.

13. Joel Robbins, *Becoming Sinners: Christianity and Moral Torment in a Papua New Guinea Society* (Berkeley: University of California Press, 2004), 12; Louis Dumont, *Homo Hierarchicus: The Caste System and Its Implications* (Chicago: University of Chicago Press, 1980). For my own messy attempt, see Martínez, "Leavened Apprehensions," 173–93.

14. Samuli Schielke, *Egypt in the Future Tense: Hope, Frustration, and Ambivalence before and after 2011* (Bloomington: Indiana University Press, 2015), 53.

15. My conclusions here rely on Alasdair MacIntyre's *After Virtue* in asserting the impossibility of moral consensus and the incommensurability of the claims through which concepts like justice are discussed in contemporary debates.

16. For more on how rulers in different contexts have been judged, often in moral terms, through the ways in which they fulfilled the obligation to feed their subjects, see Ellen Oxfeld, *Bitter and Sweet: Food, Meaning, and Modernity in Rural China* (Berkeley: University of California Press, 2017), 129; Stephanie Cronin, "Bread and Justice in Qajar Iran: The Moral Economy, the Free Market and the Hungry Poor," *Middle Eastern Studies* 54, no. 6 (2018): 843–77; Stacy E. Holden, *The Politics of Food in Modern Morocco* (Gainesville, University Press of Florida, 2014); Jonathan Fox, *The Politics of Food in Mexico: State Power and Social Mobilization* (Ithaca: Cornell University Press, 1993); Trevor Stack, *Knowing History in Mexico: An Ethnography of Citizenship* (Albuquerque: University of New Mexico Press, 2012).

17. Antina von Schnitzler, *Democracy's Infrastructure: Techno-Politics and Protest after Apartheid* (Princeton: Princeton University Press, 2016), 27n42; David Scott, *Conscripts of Modernity: The Tragedy of Colonial Enlightenment.* (Durham, NC: Duke University Press, 2004), 4.

18. Wendy Brown, "American Nightmare: Neoliberalism, Neoconservatism, and de-Democratization," *Political Theory* 34, no. 6 (2006): 693.

19. Wendy Brown, *Undoing the Demos: Neoliberalism's Stealth Revolution* (New York: Zone Books, 2015), 115.

20. Fahed Fanek, "Tanẓīm dʿam al-khubz" [The bread subsidy system], *al-Raʿi*, November 5, 2013. http://alrai.com/article/615305.html.

21. Fanek, "Tanẓīm dʿam al-khubz."

22. Fahed Fanek, "Siyāsa dʿam al-khubz tarak al-qadīm ʿala qadmuhu" [The old bread subsidy policy escapes on foot], *Al-Raʿi*, November 22, 2013, http://alrai.com/article/617925.html.

23. World Bank, "Hashemite Kingdom of Jordan: Options for Immediate Fiscal Adjustment."

24. Abdullah II, His Majesty King of Jordan, "Speech from the Throne Opening the First Ordinary Session of the 17th Parliament, Amman, Jordan, 3 November 2013," website of His Majesty King Abdullah II Ibn al Hussein King of the Hashemite Kingdom of Jordan, accessed August 4, 2016, https://kingabdullah.jo/en/speeches/opening-first-ordinary-session-17th-parliament.

25. Abdullah II, His Majesty King of Jordan, "Speech from the Throne Opening the Third Ordinary Session of the 17th Parliament, Amman, Jordan, 15 November 2015," website of His Majesty King Abdullah II Ibn al Hussein King of the Hashemite Kingdom of Jordan, accessed August 7, 2016, https://kingabdullah.jo/en/speeches/opening-third-ordinary-session-17th-parliament.

26. Fahed Fanek, "The Future of Subsidies," *Jordan Times*, March 6, 2016, http://jordantimes.com/opinion/fahed-fanek/future-subsidies.

27. Nikolas Rose and Peter Miller, *Governing the Present: Administering Economic, Social and Personal Life* (New York: John Wiley & Sons, 2013), 79.

28. Elizabeth Povinelli, *Economies of Abandonment: Social Belonging and Endurance in Late Liberalism* (Durham, NC: Duke University Press, 2011), 157.

29. Brown, *Undoing the Demos*, 106.

30. Foucault, *The Birth of Biopolitics*, 121.

31. Personal interview with Dr. Umayya Toukan, finance minister of the Hashemite Kingdom of Jordan, June 30, 2014, Amman.

32. Ahmed Khalif al-ʿAfif, Qaasim Muhammad Saʿleh, and Muhammad Khalil Al-Zaboon, *Al-Tarbiyya al-Wataniyya* [National education] (Amman: Dar Jarīr, 2013), 107; Ministry of Planning and International Cooperation (MOPIC), Hashemite Kingdom of Jordan, *Executive Development Program 2011–2013* (Amman: MOPIC, 2013).

33. Ministry of Social Development (MSD), Hashemite Kingdom of Jordan. *Policies of Social Development and the Evaluation of Government Effectiveness in Combating Poverty and Unemployment* (Amman: Royal Jordanian National Defense College, 2009).

34. Government of Jordan (GoJ) and United Nations Development Programme (UNDP), "Poverty Reduction Strategy, 2013–2020," UNDP, 2013, http://www.jo.undp.

org/content/dam/jordan/docs/Poverty/Jordanpovertyreductionstrategy.pdf, 10, 153, 154.

35. Personal interview with Dr. Umayya Toukan.

36. Personal interview with Dr. Ibrahim Saif, minister of planning and cooperation of the Hashemite Kingdom of Jordan, June 25, 2014, Amman.

37. Lisa Wedeen, *Authoritarian Apprehensions: Ideology, Judgment, and Mourning in Syria* (Chicago University of Chicago Press, 2019), 20.

38. Personal interview with Dr. Umayya Toukan; personal interview with Dr. Ibrahim Saif; personal interview with Dr. Hatem Halwani, minister of industry, trade, and supply of the Hashemite Kingdom of Jordan, June 5, 2014, Amman.

39. Curtis R. Ryan, "Political Opposition and Reform Coalitions in Jordan," *British Journal of Middle Eastern Studies* 38, no. 3 (2011): 367–90.

40. Andrew Shryock, "Dynastic Modernism and Its Contradictions: Testing the Limits of Pluralism, Tribalism, and King Hussein's Example in Hashemite Jordan," *Arab Studies Quarterly* 22, no. 3 (2000): 57–79.

41. Hillel Frisch, "Fuzzy Nationalism: The Case of Jordan," *Nationalism and Ethnic Politics* 8, no. 4 (2002): 86–103; Stefanie Nanes, "Hashemitism, Jordanian National Identity, and the Abu Odeh Episode," *Arab Studies Journal* 18, no. 1 (2010): 163.

42. Adnan Abu Odeh, *Jordanians, Palestinians, and the Hashemite Kingdom in the Middle East Peace Process* (Washington, DC: US Institute of Peace Press, 1999).

43. Nanes, "Hashemitism," 164

44. Brown, "American Nightmare," 693.

45. Brown, "American Nightmare," 693; David Harvey, *A Brief History of Neoliberalism* (New York: University Press, 2005), 82.

46. Ahmad El-Sharif, "Restoring Pride in Jordanian National Identity: Framing the Jordanian National Identity by the National Committee of Retired Army Veterans," *Studies in Literature and Language* 12, no. 5 (2016): 40–53; Stefanie Nanes, "Choice, Loyalty, and the Melting Pot: Citizenship and National Identity in Jordan," *Nationalism and Ethnic Politics* 14, no. 1 (2008): 85–116; Paul Maurice Esber, "Who Are the Jordanians? The Citizen-Subjects of Abdullah II" (PhD diss., University of Sydney, 2018).

47. For one example, see Hassan Abu Nimah, "Jordan Is Strong, Safe and Stable," *Jordan Times*, February 25, 2014, http://www.jordantimes.com/opinion/hasan-abu-nimah/jordan-strong-safe-and-stable.

48. His Majesty King of Jordan Abdullah II, "Remarks at the Celebration of Accession to the Throne, The Anniversary of the Great Arab Revolt and Army Day, Amman,

Jordan 8 June 2010," website of His Majesty King Abdullah II Ibn al Hussein King of the Hashemite Kingdom of Jordan, accessed September 10, 2017, https://rhc.jo/en/media/media-post/remarks-his-majesty-king-abdullah-ii-celebration-accession-throne-anniversary-great.

49. Personal interview with Dr. Hatem Halwani, minister of industry, trade, and supply of the Hashemite Kingdom of Jordan, June 5, 2014, Amman.

50. Personal interview with Samer Khouri, Ministry of Industry, Trade, and Supply, April 7, 2014, Amman.

51. Personal interview with Dr. Essa al-Dmour, director of internal audits, Ministry of Industry, Trade, and Supply, April 8, 2014, Amman.

52. For an excellent exposition of these and other viewpoints, see Dana Jibril, "Kayf waṣalnā ila rafʿa al-daʿm ʿan al-khubz wa silʿa āsāsiyya" [How did we arrive at the removal of subsidies on bread and basic goods?], 7iber, November 27, 2017, https://www.7iber.com/politics-economics/jordanian-government-lifts-subsidies-off-bread-basic-goods/.

53. Judith Butler, *Excitable Speech: A Politics of the Performative* (London: Routledge, 1997), 155; Loxley, *Performativity*, 133.

54. Butler, *Excitable Speech, 133.*

55. Alexei Yurchak, *Everything Was Forever, Until It Was No More: The Last Soviet Generation* (Princeton: Princeton University Press, 2005), 284.

56. The dearth of Qurʾanic references to bread contrasts quite clearly with their profusion in the *hadith*, in which bread appears nearly twenty times. One of the meanings ascribed to bread does coincide with Saʿid's remarks. Bread is mentioned on various occasions in al-Bukhari's compilation as the appropriate means of almsgiving during the life of the Prophet Muhammad.

57. Qurʾan 93:10.

58. There were other understandings of the bread subsidy that were also inflected by Islam. I found that interpretations of religious injunctions relating to trade and government owed as much to shifting manifestations of geography and social class as they did to any values defined as uniquely Islamic. For more, see Charles Tripp, *Islam and the Moral Economy: The Challenge of Capitalism* (Cambridge: Cambridge University Press, 2006); Lara Deeb and Mona Harb, *Leisurely Islam: Negotiating Geography and Morality in Shiʾite South Beirut* (Princeton: Princeton University Press, 2013).

59. al-ʿAfif, Saʿleh, and Al-Zaboon, *Al-Tarbiyya al-Wataniyya*; Elena Corbett, "Hashemite Antiquity and Modernity: Iconography in Neoliberal Jordan," *Studies in Ethnicity*

and Nationalism 11, no. 2 (2011): 163–93; Elena Corbett, *Competitive Archaeology in Jordan: Narrating Identity from the Ottomans to the Hashemites* (Austin: University of Texas Press, 2015); Joseph Massad, *Colonial Effects: The Making of National Identity in Jordan* (New York: Columbia University Press, 2001).

60. Jumanah Ghneimat, "ʿAyn Maqula 'Al-Khubz khṭ āḥmar'?!" [Where are they saying "bread is a red line"?!], *Al-Ghad*, September 17, 2013, http://www.alghad.com/ articles/524180.

61. Erica S. Simmons, *Meaningful Resistance: Market Reforms and the Roots of Social Protest in Latin America.* Cambridge: Cambridge University Press, 2016), 78–81; Erica S. Simmons, "Grievances Do Matter in Mobilization." *Theory and Society 43*, no. 5 (2014): 513–46.

62. Mayssoun Sukarieh, "On Class, Culture, and the Creation of the Neoliberal Subject: The Case of Jordan," *Anthropological Quarterly* (2016): 1213.

63. For interesting historical parallels in rural Egypt, see John Chalcraft, *Popular Politics in the Making of the Modern Middle East* (Cambridge: Cambridge University Press, 2016), 116–21.

64. Michael Herzfeld, *Cultural Intimacy: Social Poetics in the Nation-State* (New York: Routledge, 2005), 4.

65. Naor Ben-Yehoyada, *The Mediterranean Incarnate: Region Formation between Sicily and Tunisia since World War II* (Chicago: University of Chicago Press, 2017), 141.

66. Lisa Wedeen, *Peripheral Visions: Publics, Power and Performance in Yemen* (Chicago: University of Chicago Press, 2009), 219.

67. Saif al-Jenini, "Al-Hamawi: natāij kārithiyya l-āliyya dʿam al-khubz wa al-naqid al- mubāshir khiyāa maqbūl" [Hamawi: disastrous results for the bread subsidy mechanism, direct cash assistance an acceptable option], *Al-Raʿi*, January 23, 2014, http://www.alrai.com/article/628187.html.

68. Personal interview with Abdul Illah Hamawi, president of the BOA, November 5, 2013, Amman.

69. Of course, there were wide variations among the bakers in political views and policy preferences that the BOA's position did not and could not fully capture.

70. Jordanian Democratic People's Party (JDPP, HASHD [in Arabic]), "A statement issued by a coalition of nationalist and leftist parties," *Al-Ahali Weekly* 8, January 2014, http://www.hashahali.com/main/ahali/?p=21926#.VManJ45qE21.

71. Larbi Sadiki, "Popular Uprisings and Arab Democratization," *International Journal of Middle East Studies* 32, no. 1 (2000): 71–95.

72. Islamic Action Front, "'Islamic Action' Cautions against Bread Price Rise and Confirms Municipal Election Boycott," *Official Press Release*, 2013, http://www.ikh-wan-jor.com/Portals/Content/?info=YVdROU16UTBOaVp6YjNWeVkyVTlVM1ZpV-UdGblpTWjBlWEJsUFRFbSt1.ikhwan.

73. Sean Yom, "The New Landscape of Jordanian Politics: Social Opposition, Fiscal Crisis, and the Arab Spring," *British Journal of Middle Eastern Studies* 42, no. 3 (2015): 284–300.

74. Abdullah II, His Majesty King of Jordan, "Remarks at the Celebration of Accession to the Throne, The Anniversary of the Great Arab Revolt and Army Day, Amman, Jordan 8 June 2010," website of His Majesty King Abdullah II Ibn al Hussein King of the Hashemite Kingdom of Jordan, accessed September 10, 2017, https://rhc.jo/en/media/media-post/remarks-his-majesty-king-abdullah-ii-celebration-accession-throne-an-niversary-great.

75. Brown, "American Nightmare," 701.

76. George Barham, "Al-nāib al-Majali: al-Khubz laysa kāviār wala salmon" [MP Majali: Bread is neither caviar nor salmon], *Roya News*, May 21, 2015.

77. *Al-Sabeel*, "Takhawafāt sh'abiyya wa ḥizbiyya min raf'a sa'ar al-khubz" [People and parties fear rise in bread price], May 14, 2015, http://www.assabeel.net/local/item/109238-%D8%AA%D8%AE%D9%88%D9%81%D8%A7%D8%AA-%D8%B4%D8%B9%D8%A8%D9%8A%D8%A9-%D9%88%D8%AD%D8%B2%D8%A8%D9%8A%D8%A9-%D9%85%D9%86-%D8%B1%D9%81%D8%B9-%D8%B3%D8%B9%D8%B1-%D8%A7%D9%84%D8%AE%D8%A8%D8%B2.

78. The last two functions compose what feminist welfare state theory terms "distinct architectures of need." See Linda Haney, "'But We Are Still Mothers': Gender and the Construction of Need in Post-Socialist Hungary," *Social Politics* 4, no. 2 (1997): 210.

79. Michael Albertus, Sofia Fenner, and Dan Slater, *Coercive Distribution* (Cambridge: Cambridge University Press, 2018).

80. Timothy Mitchell, "Everyday Metaphors of Power," *Theory and Society* 19, no. 5 (1990): 545–77.

81. For more on the unprecedented amounts of foreign assistance that have entered regime coffers since the "Arab Spring," see Najib Hourani, "Neoliberal Urbanism and the Arab Uprisings: A View from Amman," *Journal of Urban Affairs* 36 (2014): 650–62; Yom, "The New Landscape."

82. Mitchell argues that the free-market program is more aptly portrayed "as a multi-layered political re-adjustment of rents, subsidies and control of resources."

See Timothy Mitchell, *Rule of Experts: Egypt, Techno-Politics, Modernity* (Berkeley: University of California Press, 2002).

83. Anne M. Peters and Pete W. Moore, "Beyond Boom and Bust: External Rents, Durable Authoritarianism, and Institutional Adaptation in the Hashemite Kingdom of Jordan," *Studies in Comparative International Development* 44, no. 3 (2009): 256–85; Eliana Abu-Hamdi, "Neoliberalism as a Site-Specific Process: The Aesthetics and Politics of Architecture in Amman, Jordan," *Cities* 60(A) (2017): 102–12; Pascal Debruyne, "Spatial Rearticulations of Statehood: Jordan's Geographies of Power under Globalization" (*PhD* diss., Ghent University, 2013); Katharina Lenner, "Policy-Shaping and Its Limits: The Politics of Poverty Alleviation and Local Development in Jordan" (PhD diss., Freie Universität Berlin, 2014).

84. Michel Foucault, "Governmentality," in *The Foucault Effect: Studies in Governmentality*, eds. Graham Burchell, Colin Gordon, and Peter Miller (Chicago: University of Chicago Press, 1991), 79.

CONCLUSION

1. Andrea Muehlebach, *The Moral Neoliberal: Welfare and Citizenship in Italy* (Chicago: University of Chicago Press, 2012); Antina von Schnitzler, *Democracy's Infrastructure: Techno-Politics and Protest after Apartheid* (Princeton: Princeton University Press, 2016); Stephen J. Collier, *Post-Soviet Social: Neoliberalism, Social Modernity, Biopolitics* (Princeton: Princeton University Press, 2011).

2. Julie Katherine Gibson-Graham, "Diverse Economies: Performative Practices for Other Worlds," *Progress in Human Geography* 32, no. 5 (2008): 613–32.

3. Judith Butler, "Performative Agency," *Journal of Cultural Economy* 3, no. 2 (2010): 148.

Bibliography

ARCHIVAL SOURCES: MANUSCRIPT COLLECTIONS

Al-Jaridah al-Rasmiyyah [The Official Gazette].

CIA Library, Freedom of Information Act Electronic Reading Room (CIALib).

Ford Foundation Archives, New York (FFA).

Ministry of Finance, Taxation Files, International Tender Files, Amman, Jordan.

Ministry of Industry, Trade, and Supply, Bakery Regulation Files, International Tender Files, Amman, Jordan.

National Library and Center for Documents and Documentation, Amman, Jordan.

St. Antony's College, Oxford University. Glubb Papers: Report on the Administration of the Deserts of Transjordan.

United Kingdom National Archives, London (UKNA).

United States National Archives, Washington DC, College Park, Maryland (USNA).

United States State Department Decimal Files.

University of Jordan, Center for Manuscripts and Documents, Amman.

Wikileaks.

NEWSPAPERS AND ONLINE NEWS SOURCES

7iber

Al-Ahali Weekly

Amman al-youm

Al-Bosala

Al-Dustur

Filastin

Al-Ghad

Al Jazeera

Joindependent

Jordan Times

Al-Nahar

New York Times

Al-Ra'i

Roya News

Al-Sabeel

Al-Sijil

PERSONAL INTERVIEWS

Alawneh, Atef Rashed, employee in the Internal Audit Unit, Ministry of Industry, Trade, and Supply, May 7, 2014 and December 2, 2015, Amman.

Anani, HE Jawad A., former minister of supply, minister of labor, deputy prime minister, foreign minister, director of social security corporation, and current senator, May 27, 2014 and November 20, 2015, Amman.

Anonymous NGO consultant, August 12, 2019, Aqaba.

Anonymous retired baker, November 12, 2015, Amman.

Anonymous retired member of the Jordanian armed forces, October 8, 2016, Amman.

Anonymous retired official, Ministry of Supply, December 2, 2015, Amman.

ASEZA commissioner, November 24, 2015, Aqaba.

ASEZA deputy commissioner, November 24, 2015, Aqaba.

al-Dmour, Dr. Essa, director of internal audits, Ministry of Industry, Trade, and Supply, April 8, 2014, Amman.

Halwani, Dr. Hatem, minister of industry, trade, and supply of the Hashemite Kingdom of Jordan, June 5, 2014, Amman.

Hamarneh, Dr. Mustafa, former member of Parliament, current head of the Economic and Social Research Council, September 11, 2019.

Hamawi, Abdul Illah, president of the BOA, November 5, 2013 and November 8, 2015, Amman.

Head of the planning department at the Ma'an Municipality, August 6, 2019, Ma'an.

al-Khouri, Riad, Jordanian economist, April 30, 2014, Amman.

Khouri, Samer, director of market control, Ministry of Industry, Trade, and Supply, April 7, 2014, Amman.

Maaytah, Engineer Musa H., former minister of political development and current senator, April 27, 2014, Amman, Jordan.

Mansur, Dr. Yusuf, CEO, ENconsult, former director general of the Telecom Regulatory Commission and economic adviser to the Prime Minister, May 19, 2014, Amman.

Muammar, Ghassan, advocate (lawyer), of Muammar Law Firm, and Nadeen Ma'ayeh, CEO of Ecard Ltd, co-presidents of the Bread for Free Campaign, April 22, 2014, Amman.

Mulqi, HE Hani, current prime minister, (then) senator, May 4, 2014 and August 29, 2019, Amman.

al-Qasim, HE Marwin, August 1, 2019, Amman.

Saif, Dr. Ibrahim, minister of planning and cooperation of the Hashemite Kingdom of Jordan, June 25, 2014, Amman.

al-Sharari, Majed, mayor of Ma'an, 25 October 2015, Ma'an.

Al-Shiyab, Suleiman, Islamic Action Front, July 9, 2014, Amman.

Shuwaikh, Raed, deputy mayor of Ma'an, August 6, 2019, Ma'an.

al-Tarawneh, Engineer Emad, Ministry of Industry, Trade, and Supply, May 14, 2014, Amman.

Toukan, Dr. Ummaya, finance minister of the Hashemite Kingdom of Jordan, June 30, 2014, Amman.

ARTICLES, BOOKS, REPORTS, AND DISSERTATIONS

Abdullah II, His Majesty King of Jordan. "Khitāb al-'arsh al-sāmī fī iftitāḥ al-dawra al-'ādiyya al-thāniyya li-majlis al-umma al-sāb'at ashir, Amman, Jordan, 2 November 2014." Website of His Majesty King Abdullah II Ibn al Hussein King of the Hashemite Kingdom of Jordan, accessed August 4, 2016. http://kingabdullah.jo/index.php/ar_JO/speeches/view/id/548/videoDisplay/0.html.

Abdullah II, His Majesty King of Jordan. "Remarks at the 9th World Islamic Economic Forum, London, United Kingdom, 29 October 2013." Website of His Majesty King Abdullah II Ibn al Hussein King of the Hashemite Kingdom of Jordan, accessed August 4, 2016. http://kingabdullah.jo/index.php/en_US/speeches/view/id/530/videoDisplay/0.html.

Abdullah II, His Majesty King of Jordan. "Remarks at the Celebration of Accession to the Throne, The Anniversary of the Great Arab Revolt and Army Day, Amman, Jordan 8 June 2010." Website of His Majesty King Abdullah II Ibn al Hussein King of the Hashemite Kingdom of Jordan, accessed September 10, 2017, https://rhc.jo/en/media/media-post/remarks-his-majesty-king-abdullah-ii-celebration-accession-throne-anniversary-great.

Abdullah II, His Majesty King of Jordan. "Speech from the Throne Opening the First Ordinary Session of the 17th Parliament, Amman, Jordan, 3 November 2013." Website of His Majesty King Abdullah II Ibn al Hussein King of the Hashemite Kingdom of Jordan. Accessed August 4, 2016. https://kingabdullah.jo/en/speeches/opening-first-ordinary-session-17th-parliament.

Abdullah II, His Majesty King of Jordan. "Speech from the Throne Opening the Third Ordinary Session of the 17th Parliament, Amman, Jordan, 15 November 2015." Accessed August 7, 2016. Website of His Majesty King Abdullah II Ibn al Hussein King of the Hashemite Kingdom of Jordan. https://kingabdullah.jo/en/speeches/opening-third-ordinary-session-17th-parliament.

Abis, Sébastien. *Géopolitique du blé: Un produit vital pour la sécurité mondiale.* Paris: IRIS, 2015.

Abu-Hamdi, Eliana. "Neoliberalism as a Site-Specific Process: The Aesthetics and Politics of Architecture in Amman, Jordan." *Cities* 60(A) (2017): 102–12.

Abu-Lughod, Lila. "The Romance of Resistance: Tracing Transformations of Power through Bedouin Women." *American Ethnologist* 17, no. 1 (1990): 41–55.

Abu Odeh, Adnan. *Jordanians, Palestinians, and the Hashemite Kingdom in the Middle East Peace Process.* Washington, DC: US Institute of Peace Press, 1999.

Abu-Rish, Ziad. "Protests, Regime Stability, and State Formation in Jordan." In *Beyond the Arab Spring: The Evolving Ruling Bargain in the Middle East.* Edited by K. Mehran, 277–312. Oxford: Oxford University Press, 2014.

Achilli, Luigi. "Becoming a Man in al-Wihdat: Masculine Performances in a Palestinian Refugee Camp in Jordan." *International Journal of Middle East Studies* 47, no. 2 (2015): 263–80.

Achilli, Luigi. *Palestinian Refugees and Identity: Nationalism, Politics and the Everyday.* London: IB Tauris, 2015.

al-'Afif, Ahmed Khalif, Qaasim Muhammad Sa'leh, and Muhammad Khalil Al-Zaboon. *Al-Tarbiyya al-Wataniyya* [National Education]. Amman: Dar Jarīr, 2013.

Agnew, John. "Sovereignty Regimes: Territoriality and State Authority in Contemporary World Politics." *Annals of the Association of American Geographers* 95, no. 2 (2005): 437–61.

Agnew, John. "The Territorial Trap: The Geographical Assumptions of International Relations Theory." *Review of International Political Economy* 1, no. 1 (1994): 53–80.

Ahram, Ariel I., and Ellen Lust. "The Decline and Fall of the Arab State." *Survival* 58, no. 2 (2016): 7–34.

al-Ajlouni, Ahmed Abdullah Suleiman. "ṣūra madīna Maʿan fī al- ṣaḥāfa al- ūrduniyya" [Portrait of the city of Maʿan in the Jordanian press]. Master's thesis, Jordanian Media Institute, 2017.

Akçali, Emel. "Introduction: Neoliberal Governmentality and the Future of the State in the Middle East and North Africa." In *Neoliberal Governmentality and the Future of the State in the Middle East and North Africa*. Edited by Emel Akçali, 1–14. New York: Palgrave Macmillan, 2016.

Alaime, Mathieu. "Aqaba an Extra-Territorial City." In *Atlas of Jordan: History, Territories and Society*. Edited by Myriam Ababsa. Beirut: Presses de l'IFPO, 2013.

Albertus, Michael, Sofia Fenner, and Dan Slater. *Coercive Distribution*. Cambridge: Cambridge University Press, 2018.

Allen, John. "Topological Twists: Power's Shifting Geographies." *Dialogues in Human Geography* 1, no. 3 (2011): 283–98.

Allen, John. *Topologies of Power: Beyond Territory and Networks*. London: Routledge, 2016.

Allen, John, and Allan Cochrane. "Assemblages of State Power: Topological Shifts in the Organization of Government and Politics." *Antipode* 42, no. 5 (2010): 1071–89.

Allinson, Jamie. *The Struggle for the State in Jordan: The Social Origins of Alliances in the Middle East*. London: IB Tauris, 2016.

Amadouny, Vartan M. "Infrastructural Development under the British Mandate." In *Village, Steppe and State: The Social Origins of Modern Jordan*. Edited by Eugene Rogan and Tariq Tell, 128–61. London: British Academic Press, 1994.

Amar, Paul. "Beyond the 'Pragmatism-Radicalism Dialectic' in the Study of Local Politics." In *Local Politics and Contemporary Transformations in the Arab World*. Edited by Malika Bouziane, Cilja Harders, and Anja Hoffman, 65–90. London: Palgrave Macmillan, 2013.

Amawi, Abla. "The Consolidation of the Merchant Class in Transjordan during the Second World War." In *Village, Steppe and State: The Social Origins of Modern Jordan*. Edited by Eugene Rogan and Tariq Tell, 162–86. London: British Academic Press, 1994.

Amawi, Abla. *State and Class in Transjordan: A Study of State Autonomy*. PhD diss., Georgetown University, 1992.

Amin, Ash. "Animated Space." *Public Culture* 27, no. 2 (2015): 239–58.

Amin, Ash. "Lively Infrastructure." *Theory, Culture & Society* 31, no. 7–8 (2014): 137–61.

Anand, Nikhil. *Hydraulic City: Water and the Infrastructures of Citizenship in Mumbai.* Durham, NC: Duke University Press, 2017.

Anand, Nikhil, Akhil Gupta, and Hannah Appel, eds. *The Promise of Infrastructure.* Durham, NC: Duke University Press, 2018.

Anani, Jawad. "Adjustment and Development: The Case of Jordan." In *Adjustment Policies and Development Strategies in the Arab World.* Edited by S. El-Nagger, 127–44. Papers presented at a seminar held in Abu Dhabu, UAE, February 16–18, 1987. IMF.

Anani, Jawad. *"Falsafat al-iqtisād al-Urdunī bayna al-fikr wa al-tatbīq khilala nisf al-qarn al-madī"* [Philosophy of the Jordanian economy between theory and practice during the last half century]. In *al-Iqtisad al-Urduni: al-mushkilat wa al-afaq [The Jordanian economy: problems and future].* Edited by Mustafa al-Hamarneh. Amman: Center for Strategic Studies, 1994.

Anderson, Ben. *Encountering Affect: Capacities, Apparatuses, Conditions.* London: Routledge, 2017.

Anderson, Benedict R. *Imagined Communities: Reflections on the Origin and Spread of Nationalism.* New York: Verso Books, 2006.

Anderson, Betty S. *Nationalist Voices in Jordan: The Street and the State.* Austin: University of Texas Press, 2005.

Andoni, Lamis, and Jillian Schwedler. "Bread Riots in Jordan." *Middle East Report* 201, no. 26 (1996): 40–42.

El-Anis, Imad. *Jordan and the United States: The Political Economy of Trade and Economic Reform in the Middle East.* London: IB Tauris, 2010.

Anjaria, Jonathan S. "Ordinary States: Everyday Corruption and the Politics of Space in Mumbai." *American Ethnologist* 38, no. 1 (2011): 58–72.

Anjaria, Jonathan S. *The Slow Boil: Street Food, Rights and Public Space in Mumbai.* Stanford, CA: Stanford University Press, 2016.

Appel, Hannah C. "Walls and White Elephants: Oil Extraction, Responsibility, and Infrastructural Violence in Equatorial Guinea." *Ethnography* 13, no. 4 (2012): 439–65.

Appel, Hannah C., Nikhil Anand, and Akhil Gupta. "Introduction: Temporality, Politics and the Promise of Infrastructure." In *The Promise of Infrastructure.* Edited by Nikhil Anand, Akhil Gupta, and Hannah Appel, 1–38. Durham, NC: Duke University Press, 2018.

Aretxaga, Begoña. "Maddening States." *Annual Review of Anthropology* 32, no. 1 (2003): 393–410.

Ashton, Nigel. *King Hussein of Jordan: A Political Life*. New Haven: Yale University Press, 2008.

Ashton, Nigel. "A 'Special Relationship' Sometimes in Spite of Ourselves: Britain and Jordan, 1957–73." *The Journal of Imperial and Commonwealth History* 33, no. 2 (2005): 221–44.

Ata, Abraham W. "Jordan." In *Social Welfare in the Middle East*. Edited by John Dixon. London: Croon Helm, 1987.

Auerbach, Adam Michael. *Demanding Development: The Politics of Public Goods Provision in India's Urban Slums*. Cambridge: Cambridge University Press, 2019.

Austin, J. L. *How to Do Things with Words*. Oxford: Clarendon Press, 1962.

Austin, J. L. *Philosophical Papers*. Edited by J. O. Urmson and G. J. Warnock. Oxford: Oxford University Press, 1979.

Ayubi, Nazih N. *Over-Stating the Arab State: Politics and Society in the Middle East*. London: IB Tauris, 1995.

Aziz, Jean. "Islamic Extremism on Rise in Jordan." *Al-Monitor*, May 18, 2014. http://www.al-monitor.com/pulse/originals/2014/05/jordan-fears-syria-war-islamists.html.

Bach, David, and Abraham L. Newman. "Transgovernmental Networks and Domestic Policy Convergence: Evidence from Insider Trading Regulation." *International Organization* 64, no. 3 (2010): 505–28.

Baer, Madeline. "Private Water, Public Good: Water Privatization and State Capacity in Chile." *Studies in Comparative International Development* 49, no. 2 (2014): 141–67.

Barad, Karen. *Meeting the Universe Halfway: Quantum Physics and the Entanglement of Matter and Meaning*. Durham, NC: Duke University Press, 2007.

Barad, Karen. "Posthumanist Performativity: Toward an Understanding of How Matter Comes to Matter." *Signs: Journal of Women in Culture and Society* 28, no. 3 (2003): 801–31.

Barad, Karen. "Quantum Entanglements and Hauntological Relations of Inheritance: Dis/continuities, Spacetime Enfoldings, and Justice-to-Come." *Derrida Today* 3, no. 2 (2010): 240–68.

Barak, On. *On Time: Technology and Temporality in Modern Egypt*. Berkeley: University of California Press, 2013.

Al-Barghouti, Tamim. *The Umma and the Dawla: The Nation State and the Arab Middle East*. London: Pluto Press, 2008.

Barnes, Jessica. *Cultivating the Nile: The Everyday Politics of Water in Egypt*. Durham, NC: Duke University Press, 2014.

Barnes, Jessica, and Mariam Taher. "Care and Conveyance: Buying Baladi Bread in Cairo." *Cultural Anthropology* 34, no. 3 (2019): 417–43.

Bartelson, Jens. *The Critique of the State*. Cambridge: Cambridge University Press, 2001.

Bayat, Asef. "Activism and Social Development in the Middle East." *International Journal of Middle East Studies* 34, no. 1 (2002): 1–28.

Bayat, Asef. *Life as Politics: How Ordinary People Change the Middle East*. Stanford, CA: Stanford University Press, 2010.

Bayat, Asef. "Un-Civil Society: The Politics of the 'Informal People.'" *Third World Quarterly* 18, no. 1 (1997): 53–72.

Baylouny, Anne Marie. "Creating Kin: New Family Associations as Welfare Providers in Liberalizing Jordan." *International Journal of Middle East Studies* 38, no. 3 (2006): 349–68.

Baylouny, Anne Marie. "Militarizing Welfare: Neo-Liberalism and Jordanian Policy." *The Middle East Journal* 62, no. 2 (2008): 277–303.

Baylouny, Anne Marie. *Privatizing Welfare in the Middle East: Kin Mutual Aid Associations in Jordan and Lebanon*. Bloomington: Indiana University Press, 2010.

Bégin, Camille. *Taste of the Nation: The New Deal Search for America's Food*. Urbana: University of Illinois Press, 2016.

Belasco, Warren. "Why Food Matters." *Culture & Agriculture* 21, no. 1 (1999): 27–34.

Bennett, Jane. *Vibrant Matter: A Political Ecology of Things*. Durham, NC: Duke University Press,   2010.

Ben-Yehoyada, Naor. *The Mediterranean Incarnate: Region Formation between Sicily and Tunisia since World War II*. Chicago: University of Chicago Press, 2017.

Berlant, Lauren. *Cruel Optimism*. Durham, NC: Duke University Press, 2011.

Besley, Timothy, and Torsten Persson. "The Origins of State Capacity: Property Rights, Taxation, and Politics." *American Economic Review* 99, no. 4 (2009): 1218–44.

Beyer, Judith. "'There Is This Law': Performing the State in the Kyrgyz Courts of Elders." In *Ethnographies of the State in Central Asia: Performing Politics*. Edited by Madeleine Reeves, Johan Rasanayagam, and Judith Beyer, 99–123. Bloomington: Indiana University Press, 2014.

Björkman, Lisa. "The Ostentatious Crowd: Public Protest as Mass-Political Street Theatre in Mumbai." *Critique of Anthropology* 35, no. 2 (2015): 142–65.

Björkman, Lisa. *Pipe Politics, Contested Waters: Embedded Infrastructures of Millennial Mumbai*. Durham, NC: Duke University Press, 2015.

Blundo, Giorgio, and Jean-Pierre Olivier de Sardan. *Everyday Corruption and the State: Citizens and Public Officials in Africa*. London: Zed Books, 2006.

Bocco, Riccardo. "Ingénieurs-agronomes et politiques de développement dans les steppes du sud Jordanien (1960–1985)." In *Bâtisseurs et bureaucrates: Ingénieurs et société au Maghreb et au Moyen-Orient*. Edited by Elisabeth Longuenesse, 255–79. Lyon: Maison de l'Orient, 1990.

Bocco, Riccardo, and Tariq Tell. "Pax Britannica in the Steppe: British Policy and the Transjordanian Bedouin." In *Village, Steppe and State: The Social Origins of Modern Jordan*. Edited by Eugene Rogan and Tariq Tell, 108–27. London: IB Tauris, 1994.

Boix, Carles. "Economic Roots of Civil Wars and Revolutions in the Contemporary World." *World Politics* 60, no. 3 (2008): 390–437.

Boltanski, Luc, and Laurent Thévenot. *On Justification: Economies of Worth*. Translated by Catherine Porter. Princeton: Princeton University Press, 2006.

Boone, Catherine. *Political Topographies of the African State: Territorial Authority and Institutional Choice*. Cambridge: Cambridge University Press, 2003.

Börzel, Tanja A., and Thomas Risse. "Governance Without a State: Can It Work?" *Regulation & Governance* 4, no. 2 (2010): 113–34.

Bourdieu, Pierre. *The Logic of Practice*. Translated by Richard Nice. Cambridge: Polity Press, 1990.

Bourdieu, Pierre. *On the State: Lectures at the Collège de France, 1989–1992*. Cambridge: Polity Press, 2014.

Bourdieu, Pierre. *Pascalian Meditations*. Cambridge: Polity Press, 2000.

Bourdieu, Pierre. "Rethinking the State: Genesis and Structure of the Bureaucratic Field." In *Practical Reason*. Cambridge: Polity Press, 1998.

Bouziane, Malika. "The State from Below: Local Governance Practices in Jordan." *Journal of Economic and Social Research* 12, no. 1 (2010): 33–61.

Brand, Laurie. *Jordan's Inter-Arab Relations: The Political Economy of Alliance-Making*. New York: Columbia University Press, 1994.

Braun, Bruce, and James McCarthy. "Hurricane Katrina and Abandoned Being." *Environment and Planning D: Society and Space* 23, no. 6 (2005): 802–9.

Bray, Robin. *Middle East Economic Digest* (MEED) 40 (1996): 35.

Brenner, Neil. *New State Spaces: Urban Governance and the Rescaling of Statehood*. Oxford: Oxford University Press, 2004.

Brenner, Neil, and Stuart Elden. "Henri Lefebvre on State, Space, Territory." *International Political Sociology* 3, no. 4 (2009): 353–77.

Brenner, Neil, Jamie Peck, and Nik Theodore. "Variegated Neoliberalization: Geographies, Modalities, Pathways." *Global Networks* 10, no. 2 (2010): 182–222.

Brown, Wendy. "American Nightmare: Neoliberalism, Neoconservatism, and De-Democratization." *Political Theory* 34, no. 6 (2006): 690–714.

Brown, Wendy. *Undoing the Demos: Neoliberalism's Stealth Revolution*. New York: Zone Books, 2015.

Brown, Wendy. "Wounded Attachments." *Political Theory* 21, no. 3 (1993): 390–410.

Buchanan, Ian. *Michel de Certeau: Cultural Theorist*. London: Sage, 2000.

Buckley, R. P. "The Muhtasib." *Arabica* 39, no. 1 (1992): 59–117.

Burke, Peter. *Social History of Knowledge: From Gutenberg to Diderot*. Cambridge: Polity Press, 2000.

Bussell, Jennifer. *Clients and Constituents: Political Responsiveness in Patronage Democracies*. Oxford: Oxford University Press, 2019.

Butler, Judith. *Bodies that Matter: On the Discursive Limits of Sex*. New York: Routledge, 2011.

Butler, Judith. *Excitable Speech: A Politics of the Performative*. London: Routledge, 1997.

Butler, Judith. *Notes Toward a Performative Theory of Assembly*. Cambridge: Harvard University Press, 2015.

Butler, Judith. "Performative Agency." *Journal of Cultural Economy* 3, no. 2 (2010): 147–61.

Buur, Lars. "The South African Truth and Reconciliation Commission: A Technique of Nation-State Formation." In *States of Imagination: Ethnographic Explorations of the Postcolonial State*. Edited by Thomas Blom Hansen and Finn Stepputat, 149–81. Durham, NC: Duke University Press, 2001.

Callon, Michel, ed. *The Laws of the Markets*. Oxford: Blackwell, 1998.

Callon, Michel. "What Does It Mean to Say that Economics Is Performative?" In *Do Economists Make Markets? On the Performativity of Economics. Edited* by Donald MacKenzie, Fabian Muniesa, and Lucia Siu, 311–57. Princeton: Princeton University Press, 2007.

Cammett, Melani. *Compassionate Communalism: Welfare and Sectarianism in Lebanon*. Ithaca: Cornell University Press, 2014.

Cammett, Melani, and Lauren M. MacLean. "Introduction: The Political Consequences of Non-State Social Welfare in the Global South." *Studies in Comparative International Development* 46, no. 1 (2011): 1–21.

Canaan, Tawfiq. "Superstition and Folklore about Bread." *Bulletin of the American Schools of Oriental Research* 167, no. 1 (1962): 36–47.

Cavanagh, Kimberly K. "Shifting Landscapes: The Social and Economic Development of Aqaba, Jordan." PhD diss., University of South Carolina, 2013.

Centeno, Miguel A., Atul Kohli, and Deborah J. Yashar. "Unpacking States in the Developing World: Capacity, Performance, and Politics." *States in the Developing World* (2017): 1–34.

Chalcraft, John. *Popular Politics in the Making of the Modern Middle East*. Cambridge: Cambridge University Press, 2016.

Chalfin, Brenda. *Neoliberal Frontiers: An Ethnography of Sovereignty in West Africa*. Chicago: University of Chicago Press, 2010.

Chatterjee, Partha. *The Politics of the Governed: Reflections on Popular Politics in Most of the World*. New York: Columbia University Press, 2004.

Chernilo, Daniel. *A Social Theory of the Nation-State: The Political Forms of Modernity beyond Methodological Nationalism*. London: Routledge, 2008.

Christophers, Brett. "From Marx to Market and Back Again: Performing the Economy." *Geoforum* 57 (2014): 12–20.

Cloke, Paul, Jon May, and Sarah Johnsen. "Performativity and Affect in the Homeless City." *Environment and Planning D: Society and Space* 26, no. 2 (2008): 241–63.

Collier, Stephen J. *Post-Soviet Social: Neoliberalism, Social Modernity, Biopolitics*. Princeton: Princeton University Press, 2011.

Collier, Stephen J. "Topologies of Power: Foucault's Analysis of Political Government beyond 'Governmentality.'" *Theory, Culture & Society* 26, no. 6 (2009): 78–108.

Collins, Harry. *Gravity's Shadow: The Search for Gravitational Waves*. Chicago: University of Chicago Press, 2004.

Comaroff, Jean, and John L. Comaroff. *The Truth about Crime: Sovereignty, Knowledge, Social Order*. Chicago: University of Chicago Press, 2016.

Corbett, Elena. *Competitive Archaeology in Jordan: Narrating Identity from the Ottomans to the Hashemites*. Austin: University of Texas Press, 2015.

Corbett, Elena. "Hashemite Antiquity and Modernity: Iconography in Neoliberal Jordan." *Studies in Ethnicity and Nationalism* 11, no. 2 (2011): 163–93.

Corbridge, Stuart, Glyn Williams, René Véron, and Manoj Srivastava. *Seeing the State: Governance and Governmentality in India*. Cambridge: Cambridge University Press, 2005.

Counihan, Carole M. "Bread as World: Food Habits and Social Relations in Modernizing Sardinia." *Anthropological Quarterly* 57, no. 2 (1984): 47–59.

Cronin, Stephanie. "Bread and Justice in Qajar Iran: The Moral Economy, the Free Market and the Hungry Poor." *Middle Eastern Studies* 54, no. 6 (2018): 843–77.

Csordas, Thomas J. "Embodiment as a Paradigm for Anthropology." *Ethos* 18, no. 1 (1990): 5–47.

Csordas, Thomas J. "Somatic Modes of Attention." *Cultural Anthropology* 8, no. 2 (1993): 135–56.

Dalman, Gustav. "Khubz" [Bread]. Translated by Yunus al-Tamīmī. In *al-fanūn al-shaʿbiyya* no. 4 (November 1974): 40–45.

Dann, Uriel. *King Hussein and the Challenge of Arab Radicalism: Jordan, 1955–1967.* Oxford: Oxford University Press, 1989.

Das, Veena. "Sexual Violence, Discursive Formations and the State." *Economic and Political Weekly* (1996): 2411–23.

Dean, Mitchell. *Governmentality: Power and Rule in Modern Society.* London: Sage, 2010.

Dean, Mitchell. "What Is Society? Social Thought and the Arts of Government." *The British Journal of Sociology* 61, no. 4 (2010): 677–95.

Dean, Mitchell, and Kaspar Villadsen. *State Phobia and Civil Society: The Political Legacy of Michel Foucault.* Stanford, CA: Stanford University Press, 2016.

Debruyne, Pascal. *"Spatial Rearticulations of Statehood: Jordan's Geographies of Power under Globalization."* PhD diss., Ghent University, 2013.

de Certeau, Michel. *The Practice of Everyday Life.* Berkeley: University of California Press, 1984.

Deeb, Lara, and Mona Harb. *Leisurely Islam: Negotiating Geography and Morality in Shiʿite South Beirut.* Princeton: Princeton University Press, 2013.

Department of Statistics Hashemite Kingdom of Jordan. "Employment Survey, For Establishments Engaging Five Persons or More." Amman: Department of Statistics, 1992.

Derr, Jennifer L. *The Lived Nile: Environment, Disease, and Material Colonial Economy in Egypt.* Stanford, CA: Stanford University Press, 2019.

Dietrich, Simone, and Michael Bernhard. "State or Regime? The Impact of Institutions on Welfare Outcomes." *The European Journal of Development Research* 28, no. 2 (2016): 252–69.

Doan, Rebecca Miles. "Class Differentiation and the Informal Sector in Amman, Jordan." *International Journal of Middle East Studies* 24, no. 1 (1992): 27–38.

Doi, Abdul Rahman I. "Hisbah." In *The Oxford Encyclopedia of the Islamic World*, 1st edition. Edited by John L. Esposito. New York: Oxford University Press, 2009.

Donzelot, Jacques. "The Promotion of the Social." *Economy and Society* 17, no. 3 (1988): 395–427.

Dormer, Peter. *The Art of the Maker: Skill & Its Meaning in Art, Craft & Design.* London: Thames and Hudson, 1994.

Dumont, Louis. *Homo Hierarchicus: The Caste System and Its Implications*. Chicago: University of Chicago Press, 1980.

Eagleton, Terry. *The Ideology of the Aesthetic*. Oxford: Blackwell, 1990.

Elyachar, Julia. "Before (and After) Neoliberalism: Tacit Knowledge, Secrets of the Trade, and the Public Sector in Egypt." *Cultural Anthropology* 27, no. 1 (2012): 76–96.

Elyachar, Julia. *Markets of Dispossession: NGOs, Economic Development, and the State in Cairo*. Durham, NC: Duke University Press, 2005.

Ener, Mine. *Managing Egypt's Poor and the Politics of Benevolence, 1800–1952*. Princeton: Princeton University Press, 2003.

Esber, Paul Maurice. "Who Are the Jordanians? The Citizen-Subjects of Abdullah II." PhD diss., University of Sydney, 2018.

Fahmy, Khaled. *All the Pasha's Men: Mehmed Ali, His Army and the Making of Modern Egypt*. Cambridge: Cambridge University Press, 1997.

Fahmy, Ziad. "Coming to Our Senses: Historicizing Sound and Noise in the Middle East." *History Compass* 11, no. 4 (2013): 305–15.

Farrell, Henry, and Abraham L. Newman. "Domestic Institutions Beyond the Nation-State: Charting the New Interdependence Approach." *World Politics* 66, no. 2 (2014): 331–63.

Feldman, Ilana. *Governing Gaza: Bureaucracy, Authority, and the Work of Rule, 1917–1967*. Durham, NC: Duke University Press, 2008.

Feldman, Ilana. *Police Encounters: Security and Surveillance in Gaza under Egyptian Rule*. Stanford, CA: Stanford University Press, 2015.

Fennell, Catherine. "'Project Heat' and Sensory Politics in Redeveloping Chicago Public Housing." *Ethnography* 12, no. 1 (2011): 40–64.

Ferguson, James. *The Anti-Politics Machine: "Development," Depoliticization and Bureaucratic Power in Lesotho*. Cambridge: Cambridge University Press, 1990.

Ferguson, James. *Expectations of Modernity: Myths and Meanings of Urban Life on the Zambian Copperbelt*. Berkeley: University of California Press, 1999.

Ferguson, James. *Give a Man a Fish: Reflections on the New Politics of Distribution*. Durham, NC: Duke University Press, 2015.

Ferguson, James, and Akhil Gupta. "Spatializing States: Toward an Ethnography of Neoliberal Governmentality." *American Ethnologist* 29, no. 4 (2002): 981–1002.

Ferrera, Maurizio. "The 'Southern Model' of Welfare in Social Europe." *Journal of European Social Policy* 6, no. 1 (1996): 17–37.

Fischbach, Michael R. *State, Society, and Land in Jordan*. Leiden: Brill, 2000.

Fish, Stanley. *Is There a Text in This Class?: The Authority of Interpretive Communities*. Cambridge: Harvard University Press, 1980.

Foucault, Michel. *The Birth of Biopolitics: Lectures at the Collège de France, 1978–1979*. Basingstoke: Palgrave, 2010.

Foucault, Michel. "Governmentality." In *The Foucault Effect: Studies in Governmentality*. *Edited* by Graham Burchell, Colin Gordon and Peter Miller, 87–104. Chicago: University of Chicago Press, 1991.

Foucault, Michel. *The History of Sexuality, Volume 1: Introduction*. Translated by Robert Hurley. New York: Penguin, 1991.

Foucault, Michel. *Security, Territory, Population. Lectures at the Collège de France, 1977–1978*. Basingstoke: Palgrave, 2009.

Foucault, Michel. *Society Must Be Defended*. London: Allen Lane, 2003.

Foucault, Michel. "What Is Critique?" In *The Politics of Truth*. Edited by Sylvère Lotringer, translated by Lysa Hochroth and Catherine Porter, 41–83. Los Angeles: Semiotext(e), 2007.

Fox, Jonathan. *The Politics of Food in Mexico: State Power and Social Mobilization*. Ithaca: Cornell University Press, 1993.

Fras, Jona. "Unifying Voices, Creating Publics: The Uses of Media Form in Contemporary Jordanian Radio." *British Journal of Middle Eastern Studies* 47, no. 2 (2018): 320–42.

Fredericks, Rosalind. *Garbage Citizenship: Vital Infrastructures of Labor in Dakar, Senegal*. Durham, NC: Duke University Press, 2018.

Frisch, Hillel. "Fuzzy Nationalism: The Case of Jordan." *Nationalism and Ethnic Politics* 8, no. 4 (2002): 86–103.

Fromartz, Samuel. *In Search of the Perfect Loaf: A Home Baker's Odyssey*. New York: Penguin Books, 2015.

Gerges, Fawaz. "In the Shadow of Nasser: Jordan in the Arab Cold War, 1955–1967." In *The Resilience of the Hashemite Rule: Politics and State in Jordan, 1946–1967*. Edited by Tariq Tell, 89–114. Amman: CERMOC, 2001.

Ghertner, D. Asher. *Rule by Aesthetics: World-Class City-Making in Delhi*. Oxford: Oxford University Press.

Ghertner, D. Asher. "When Is the State? Topology, Temporality, and the Navigation of Everyday State Space in Delhi." *Annals of the American Association of Geographers* 107, no. 3 (2017): 731–50.

Gibson-Graham, Julie Katherine. "Diverse Economies: Performative Practices for other Worlds." *Progress in Human Geography* 32, no. 5 (2008): 613–32.

Giraudy, Agustina, Eduardo Moncada, and Richard Snyder, eds. *Inside Countries: Subnational Research in Comparative Politics*. Cambridge: Cambridge University Press, 2019.

Glasser, Bradley Louis. *Economic Development and Political Reform: The Impact of External Capital on the Middle East*. Cheltenham: Edward Elgar Publishing, 2001.

Glubb, John Bagot. "The Economic Situation of the Trans-Jordan Tribes." *Journal of the Royal Central Asian Society* 25, no. 3 (1938): 448–59.

Glubb, John Bagot. *A Soldier with the Arabs*. London: Hodder & Stoughton, 1958.

Golden, Miriam, and Brian Min. "Distributive Politics around the World." *Annual Review of Political Science* 16 (2013): 73–99.

Government of Jordan (GoJ). *Five-Year Program for Economic Development, 1962–1967*. Amman: Jordan Development Board, 1962.

Government of Jordan (GoJ). *Investment Opportunities in Jordan*. Amman: Jordan Development Board, 1964.

Government of Jordan, National Planning Council, *Five-Year Plan for Economic and Social Development 1976–1980*. Amman: Royal Scientific Society Press, 1975.

Government of Jordan, National Planning Council (NPC). *Three-Year Development Plan, 1973–1975*. Amman: National Planning Council, 1973.

Government of Jordan (GoJ) and United Nations Development Programme (UNDP). "Poverty Reduction Strategy, 2013–2020." UNDP, 2013. http://www.jo.undp.org/content/dam/jordan/docs/Poverty/Jordanpovertyreductionstrategy.pdf.

Graeber, David. *The Utopia of Rules: On Technology, Stupidity, and the Secret Joys of Bureaucracy*. London: Melville House Publishing, 2015.

Graham, Stephen, and Simon Marvin. *Splintering Urbanism: Networked Infrastructures, Technological Mobilities and the Urban Condition*. London: Routledge, 2001.

Graham, Stephen, and Colin McFarlane, editors. *Infrastructural Lives: Urban Infrastructure in Context*. London: Routledge, 2014.

Gupta, Akhil. "Blurred Boundaries: The Discourse of Corruption, the Culture of Politics, and the Imagined State." *American Ethnologist* 22, no. 2 (1995): 375–402.

Gupta, Akhil. "Narratives of Corruption: Anthropological and Fictional Accounts of the Indian State." *Ethnography* 6, no. 1 (2005): 5–34.

Gupta, Akhil. *Red Tape: Bureaucracy, Structural Violence, and Poverty in India*. Durham, NC: Duke University Press, 2012.

Hall, Stuart. "The Toad in the Garden: Thatcherism among the Theorists." In *Marxism and the Interpretation of Culture*. Edited by Cary Nelson and Lawrence Grossberg, 35–73. Urbana: University of Illinois Press, 1988.

Hallaq, Wael. *The Impossible State: Islam, Politics and Modernity's Moral Predicament.* New York: Columbia University Press, 2013.

Hallaq, Wael. *Restating Orientalism: A Critique of Modern Knowledge.* New York: Columbia University Press, 2018.

Hamlyn, David W. "Aristotle's Account of Aesthesis in the De Anima." *The Classical Quarterly* 9, no. 1 (1959): 6–16.

Haney, Linda. "'But We Are Still Mothers': Gender and the Construction of Need in Post-Socialist Hungary." *Social Politics* 4, no. 2 (1997): 208–44.

Hanieh, Adam. *Money, Markets, and Monarchies: The Gulf Cooperation Council and the Political Economy of the Contemporary Middle East.* Cambridge: Cambridge University Press, 2018.

Hannah, Matthew G. *Governmentality and the Mastery of Territory in Nineteenth-Century America.* Cambridge: Cambridge University Press, 2000.

Hansen, Thomas Blom. "Sovereigns Beyond the State: On Legality and Authority in Urban India." In *Sovereign Bodies: Citizens, Migrants, and States in the Postcolonial World.* Edited by Thomas Blom Hansen and Finn Stepputat, 169–91. Princeton: Princeton University Press, 2005.

Hansen, Thomas Blom, and Finn Stepputat, eds. *States of Imagination: Ethnographic Explorations of the Postcolonial State.* Durham, NC: Duke University Press, 2001.

Haraway, Donna. "Situated Knowledges: The Science Question in Feminism and the Privilege of Partial Perspective." *Feminist Studies* 14, no. 3 (1988): 575–99.

Harris, Kevan. *A Social Revolution: Politics and the Welfare State in Iran.* Oakland: University of California Press, 2017.

Harvey, David. *A Brief History of Neoliberalism.* New York: Oxford University Press, 2005.

Harvey, David. *The Enigma of Capital, and the Crises of Capitalism.* London: Profile Books, 2010.

Harvey, Penny. "The Topological Quality of Infrastructural Relation: An Ethnographic Approach." *Theory, Culture & Society* 29, no. 4–5 (2012): 76–92.

Harvey, Penny, and Hannah Knox. *Roads: An Anthropology of Infrastructure and Expertise.* Ithaca: Cornell University Press, 2015.

Hassan, His Royal Highness Crown Prince. "Remarks to the Second Jordan Development Conference, Amman, Jordan, May 1976." In Government of Jordan, National Planning Council. *Five-Year Plan for Economic and Social Development 1976–1980.* Amman: Royal Scientific Society Press, 1976.

Helms, Gesa, Marina Vishmidt, and Lauren Berlant. "Affect & the Politics of Austerity. An Interview Exchange with Lauren Berlant." *Variant*, 39–40, August 5, 2012,
http://www.variant.org.uk/39_40texts/berlant39_40.html.

Hendrix, Cullen S. "Measuring State Capacity: Theoretical and Empirical Implications
for the Study of Civil Conflict." *Journal of Peace Research* 47, no. 3 (2010): 273–85.

Herzfeld, Michael. *Cultural Intimacy: Social Poetics in the Nation-State*. New York:
Routledge, 2005s.

Herzfeld, Michael. *The Social Production of Indifference: Exploring the Symbolic Roots
of Western Bureaucracy*. Chicago: University of Chicago Press, 1992.

Hetherington, Kevin. "Secondhandedness: Consumption, Disposal, and Absent
Presence." *Environment and Planning D: Society and Space* 22, no. 1 (2004):
157–73.

Heydemann, Steven. "Social Pacts and the Persistence of Authoritarianism in the
Middle East." In *Debating Authoritarianism: Dynamics and Durability in Non-
Democratic Regimes*. Edited by Oliver Schlumberger, 21–38. Stanford, CA: Stanford
University Press, 2007.

Heydemann, Steven, and Robert Vitalis. "War, Keynesianism, and Colonialism: Explaining State-Market Relations in the Postwar Middle East." In *War, Institutions,
and Social Change in the Middle East. Edited* by Steven Heydemann, 100–146. Berkeley: University of California Press, 2000.

Highmore, Ben. *Everyday Life and Cultural Theory: An Introduction*. New York: Routledge, 2002.

Highmore, Ben. *Michel de Certeau: Analysing Culture*. London: Continuum, 2006.

Hilal, Jamil. *Al-ḍiffa al-gharbiyya, al-tarkīb al-ijtim āʿi wa al-Iqtiṣādī (1948–1974)* [The
West Bank: its social and economic composition, 1948–1974]. Beirut: Markaz al-
Abḥath, Munazzamat al-Tahr īr al-Filastīniyya, 1975.

Hirschkind, Charles. *The Ethical Soundscape: Cassette Sermons and Islamic Counterpublics*. New York: Columbia University Press, 2006.

Holden, Stacy E. *The Politics of Food in Modern Morocco*. Gainesville: University Press
of Florida, 2014.

Honig, Bonnie. *Public Things: Democracy in Disrepair*. New York: Fordham University
Press, 2017.

Hourani, Najib. "Assembling Structure: Neoliberal Amman in Historical Perspective." *Urban Anthropology and Studies of Cultural Systems and World Economic
Development* 45, no. 1/2 (2016): 1–62.

Hourani, Najib. "Neoliberal Urbanism and the Arab Uprisings: A View from Amman." *Journal of Urban Affairs* 36 (2014): 650–62.

Howell, Sally. "Modernizing Mansaf: The Consuming Contexts of Jordan's National Dish." *Food & Foodways* 11, no. 4 (2003): 215–43.

Huber, Evelyne. "Options for Social Policy in Latin America: Neoliberal versus Social Democratic Models." In *Welfare States in Transition: National Adaptations in Global Economies*. Edited by Gøsta Esping-Andersen, 141–91. Thousand Oaks, CA: SAGE Publications, 1996.

Hull, Matthew S. *Government of Paper: The Materiality of Bureaucracy in Urban Pakistan*. Berkeley: University of California Press, 2012.

El-Hurani, Mohamed Haitham Mahmoud. "Economic Analysis of the Development of the Wheat Subsector of Jordan." PhD diss., Iowa State University, 1975.

Ingold, Tim. *Making: Anthropology, Archaeology, Art and Architecture*. London: Routledge, 2013.

Ingold, Tim. *The Perception of the Environment: Essays on Livelihood, Dwelling and Skill*. London: Routledge, 2000.

Ingold, Tim. "Toward an Ecology of Materials." *Annual Review of Anthropology* 41 (2012): 427–42.

International Bank for Reconstruction and Development (IBRD). *The Economic Development of Jordan*. Baltimore: Johns Hopkins Press, 1957.

Ismail, Salwa. *Political Life in Cairo's New Quarters: Encountering the Everyday State*. Minneapolis: University of Minnesota Press, 2006.

Itihād al-niqābāt, al-ʻamāliyya al-mustaqila. "taḥdir min rafʻa āsār al-khubz" [Declaration on bread price rise]. May 14, 2015. Accessed September 20, 2015. https://www.assawsana.com/portal/pages.php?newsid=216096.

Jackson, David, Sarah Tobin, and Jennifer Philippa Eggert. "Capacity Building for Politicians in Contexts of Systemic Corruption: Countering 'Wasta' in Jordan." *U-4 Anti-Corruption Resource Centre* 9 (2019).

Jaffe, Rivke, et al. "What Does Poverty Feel Like? Urban Inequality and the Politics of Sensation." *Urban Studies* 57, no. 5 (2020): 1015–31.

Jansen, Stef. "Hope for/against the State: Gridding in a Besieged Sarajevo Suburb." *Ethnos* 79, no. 2 (2014): 238–60.

Jeffrey, Alex. *The Improvised State: Sovereignty, Performance and Agency in Dayton Bosnia*. Chichester, West Sussex: John Wiley & Sons, 2013.

Jordana, Jacint, David Levi-Faur, and Xavier Fernández i Marín. "The Global Diffusion of Regulatory Agencies: Channels of Transfer and Stages of Diffusion." *Comparative Political Studies* 44, no. 10 (2011): 1343–69.

Joyce, Patrick. *The State of Freedom: A Social History of the British State since 1800.* Cambridge: Cambridge University Press, 2013.

Jung, Dietrich, and Marie Juul Petersen. "'We Think that This Job Pleases Allah': Islamic Charity, Social Order, and the Construction of Modern Muslim Selfhoods in Jordan." *International Journal of Middle East Studies* 46, no. 2 (2014): 285–306.

Kanafani-Zahar, Aïda. "'Whoever Eats You Is No Longer Hungry, Whoever Sees You Becomes Humble': Bread and Identity in Lebanon." *Food and Foodways* 7.1 (1997): 45–71.

Kaplan, Steven Laurence. *The Bakers of Paris and the Bread Question, 1700–1775.* Durham, NC: Duke University Press, 1996.

Kaplan, Steven Laurence. *Good Bread Is Back: A Contemporary History of French Bread, the Way It Is Made, and the People Who Make It.* Durham, NC: Duke University Press, 2006.

Kardoosh, Marwan. *The Aqaba Special Economic Zone, Jordan: A Case Study of Governance.* Bonn: ZEF Bonn Center for Development Research, 2005.

Karshenas, Massoud, and Valentine M. Moghadam. "Social Policy in the Middle East: Introduction and Overview." In *Social Policy in the Middle East.* Edited by Massoud Karshenas and Valentine M. Moghadam, 1–30. Houndmills: Palgrave Macmillan, 2006.

Katz, Kimberly. *Jordanian Jerusalem: Holy Places and National Spaces.* Gainesville: University Press of Florida, 2005.

Khalili, Laleh. "The Politics of Pleasure: Promenading on the Corniche and Beachgoing." *Environment and Planning D: Society and Space* 34, no. 4 (2016): 583–600.

Khatib, Fawzi. "Foreign Aid and Economic Development in Jordan: An Empirical Investigation." In *Politics and the Economy in Jordan.* Edited by Rodney Wilson, 60–70. London: Routledge, 1991.

Khorakiwala, Ateya. "Silo as System: Infrastructural Interventions into the Political Economy of Wheat." *Engagement Blog.* https://aesengagement.wordpress.com/2016/04/12/silo-as-system-infrastructural-interventions-into-the-political-economy-of-wheat/.

Kingston, Paul. "Breaking the Patterns of Mandate: Economic Nationalism and State Formation in Jordan, 1951–57." In *Village, Steppe and State.* Edited by Eugene Rogan and Tariq Tell, 187–216. London: British Academic Press, 1994.

Kingston, Paul. "Rationalizing Patrimonialism: Wasfi al-Tal and Economic Reform in Jordan, 1962–67." In *The Resilience of the Hashemite Rule: Politics and the State in Jordan, 1946–67.* Edited by Tariq Tell, 115–44. Amman: CERMOC, 2001.

Kirk, George. *The Middle East in the War.* London: Oxford University Press, 1952.

Kneafsey, Moya, Rosie Cox, Lewis Holloway, Elizabeth Dowler, Laura Venn, and Helena Tuomainen. *Reconnecting Consumers, Producers and Food: Exploring Alternatives.* Oxford: Berg, 2008.

Knowles, Warwick. *Jordan Since 1989: A Study in Political Economy.* London: IB Tauris, 2005.

Lakoff, Andrew, and Stephen J. Collier. "Infrastructure and Event: The Political Technology of Preparedness." In *Political Matter: Technoscience, Democracy, and Public Life.* Edited by Bruce Braun and Sarah J. Whatmore, 243–66. Minneapolis: University of Minnesota Press, 2010.

Lalor, Paul. "Black September 1970: The Palestinian Resistance Movement in Jordan, 1967–1971." PhD diss, University of Oxford, 1992.

Larkin, Brian. "Promising Forms: The Political Aesthetics of Infrastructure." In *The Promise of Infrastructure.* Edited by Nikhil Anand, Akhil Gupta, and Hannah Appel, 175–222. Durham, NC: Duke University Press, 2008.

Larkin, Brian. *Signal and Noise: Media, Infrastructure, and Urban Culture in Nigeria.* Durham, NC: Duke University Press, 2008.

Laszczkowski, Mateusz. "State Building(s): Built Forms, Materiality and the State in Astana." In *Ethnographies of the State in Central Asia: Performing Politics.* Edited by Madeleine Reeves, Johan Rasanayagam, and Judith Beyer, 149–72. Bloomington: Indiana University Press, 2013.

Latour, Bruno. "The Powers of Association." *The Sociological Review* 32, no. 1 (1984): 264–80.

Latour, Bruno. *Reassembling the Social. An Introduction to Actor-Network-Theory.* Oxford: Oxford University Press, 2005.

Latour, Bruno, and Steve Woolgar. *Laboratory Life: The Construction of Scientific Facts.* Princeton: Princeton University Press, 1979.

Law, John. "After ANT: Complexity, Naming and Topology." *The Sociological Review* 47, no. 1 (1999): 1–14.

Lazar, Sian. *El Alto, Rebel City: Self and Citizenship in Andean Bolivia.* Durham, NC: Duke University Press, 2008.

Lee, Melissa M., Gregor Walter-Drop, and John Wiesel. "Taking the State (Back) Out? Statehood and the Delivery of Collective Goods." *Governance* 27, no. 4 (2014): 635–54.

Leenders, Reinoud, and Steven Heydemann. "Popular Mobilization in Syria: Opportunity and Threat, and the Social Networks of the Early Risers." *Mediterranean Politics* 17, no. 2 (2012): 139–59.

Lefebvre, Henri. *The Production of Space*. Translated by Donald Nicholson-Smith. Oxford: Blackwell, 1991.

Lemke, Thomas. *Foucault, Governmentality and Critique*. Boulder: Paradigm Publishers, 2015.

Lemke, Thomas. *Foucault's Analysis of Modern Governmentality: A Critique of Political Reason*. New York: Verso Books, 2019.

Lenner, Katharina. "Policy-Shaping and Its Limits: The Politics of Poverty Alleviation and Local Development in Jordan." PhD diss., Freie Universität Berlin, 2014.

Lenner, Katharina. "Projects of Improvement, Continuities of Neglect: Re-Fragmenting the Periphery in Southern Rural Jordan." *Middle East—Topics & Arguments* 5 (2015): 77–88.

Levanoni, Amalia. "Food and Cooking during the Mamluk Era: Social and Political Implications." *Mamluk Studies Review* 9, no. 2 (2005): 201–22.

Lewicka, Paulina B. "Twelve Thousand Cooks and a Muhtasib. Some Remarks on Food Business in Medieval Cairo." *Studia Arabistyczne I Islamistyczne* 10 (2002): 7–19.

Lieberman, Evan S. "Taxation Data as Indicators of State-Society Relations: Possibilities and Pitfalls in Cross-National Research." *Studies in Comparative International Development* 36, no. 4 (2002): 89–115.

Lipsky, Michael. *Street-Level Bureaucracy: The Dilemmas of the Individual in Public Service*. New York: Russell Sage, 1980.

Little, Douglas. "A Puppet in Search of a Puppeteer? The United States, King Hussein, and Jordan, 1953–1970." *The International History Review* 17, no. 3 (1995): 512–44.

Lloyd, E. M. H. *Food and Inflation in the Middle East, 1940–1945*. Stanford, CA: Stanford University Press, 1956.

Loxley, James. *Performativity*. London: Routledge, 2007.

Lucas, Russell E. "Deliberalization in Jordan." *Journal of Democracy* 14, no. 1 (2003): 137–44.

Lunt, James D. *Hussein of Jordan: Searching for a Just and Lasting Peace*. New York: William Morrow & Co, 1989.

Lust, Ellen. "Competitive Clientelism in the Middle East." *Journal of Democracy* 20, no. 3 (2009): 122–35.

Lust, Ellen. "The Decline of Jordanian Political Parties: Myth or Reality?" *International Journal of Middle East Studies* 33, no. 4 (2001): 545–69.

Lust, Ellen. "Elections under Authoritarianism: Preliminary Lessons from Jordan." *Democratization* 13, no. 3 (2006): 456–71.

Lust, Ellen. *Structuring Conflict in the Arab World: Incumbents, Opponents, and Institutions.* Cambridge: Cambridge University Press, 2005.

Lynch, Marc. *State Interests and Public Spheres: The International Politics of Jordan's Identity.* New York: Columbia University Press, 1999.

MacIntyre, Alasdair. *After Virtue.* London: Bloomsbury, 2013.

MacKenzie, Donald. "The Big, Bad Wolf and the Rational Market: Portfolio Insurance, the 1987 Crash and the Performativity of Economics." *Economy and Society* 33, no. 3 (2004): 303–34.

MacKenzie, Donald. "Is Economics Performative? Option Theory and the Construction of Derivatives Markets." *Journal of the History of Economic Thought* 28, no. 1 (2006): 29–55.

MacKenzie, Donald. *An Engine, Not a Camera: How Financial Models Shape Markets.* Cambridge: MIT Press, 2006.

MacLean, Lauren M. "State Retrenchment and the Exercise of Citizenship in Africa." *Comparative Political Studies* 44, no. 9 (2011): 1238–66.

Al-Mahadin, Salam. "Gendered Soundscapes on Jordanian Radio Stations." *Feminist Media Studies* 17, no. 1 (2016): 108–11.

Mahmood, Saba. *Politics of Piety: The Islamic Revival and the Feminist Subject.* Princeton: Princeton University Press, 2005.

Malmvig, Helle. "Free Us from Power: Governmentality, Counter-Conduct, and Simulation in European Democracy and Reform Promotion in the Arab World." *International Political Sociology* 8, no. 3 (2014): 293–310.

Marchand, Trevor H. J. "Making Knowledge: Explorations of the Indissoluble Relation between Minds, Bodies, and Environment." *Journal of the Royal Anthropological Institute* 16 (2010): S1–S21.

Mares, Isabela, and Matthew E. Carnes. "Social Policy in Developing Countries." *Annual Review of Political Science* 12 (2009): 93–113.

Marks, Gary, Liesbet Hooghe, and Arjan H. Schakel. "Measuring Regional Authority." *Regional and Federal Studies* 18, no. 2–3 (2008): 111–21.

Martínez, José Ciro. "Bread Is Life: The Intersection of Welfare and Emergency Aid in Jordan." *Middle East Report* 272, no. 44 (2014): 30–35.

Martínez, José Ciro. "Jordan's Self-Fulfilling Prophecy: The Production of Feeble Political Parties and the Perceived Perils of Democracy." *British Journal of Middle Eastern Studies* 44, no. 3 (2017): 356–72.

Martínez, José Ciro. "Leavened Apprehensions: Bread Subsidies and Moral Economies in Hashemite Jordan." *International Journal of Middle East Studies* 50, no. 2 (2018): 173–93.

Martínez, José Ciro. "Leavening Neoliberalization's Uneven Pathways: Bread, Governance and Political Rationalities in the Hashemite Kingdom of Jordan." *Mediterranean Politics* 22, no. 4 (2017): 464–83.

Martínez, José Ciro. "Site of Resistance or Apparatus of Acquiescence? Tactics at the Bakery." *Middle East Law and Governance* 10, no. 2 (2018): 160–84.

Martínez, José Ciro. "Topological Twists in the Syrian Conflict: Re-Thinking Space through Bread." *Review of International Studies* 46, no. 1 (2020): 121–36.

Martínez, José Ciro, and Brent Eng. "Stifling Stateness: The Assad Regime's Campaign against Rebel Governance." *Security Dialogue* 49, no. 4 (2018): 235–53.

Martínez, José Ciro, and Brent Eng. "Struggling to Perform the State: The Politics of Bread in the Syrian Civil War." *International Political Sociology* 11, no. 2 (2017): 130–47.

Martínez, José Ciro, and Omar Sirri. "Of Bakeries and Checkpoints: Stately Affects in Amman and Baghdad." *Environment and Planning D: Society and Space* 38, no. 5 (2020): 849–66.

Massad, Joseph. *Colonial Effects: The Making of National Identity in Jordan.* New York: Columbia University Press, 2001.

Mathew, Johan. *Margins of the Market: Trafficking and Capitalism Across the Arabian Sea.* Oakland: University of California Press, 2016.

Mathews, Andrew S. *Instituting Nature: Authority, Expertise, and Power in Mexican Forests.* Cambridge: MIT Press, 2011.

Mazur, Michael P. *Economic Growth and Development in Jordan.* Boulder: Westview Press, 1979.

McConnell, Fiona. "Governmentality to Practise the State? Constructing a Tibetan Population in Exile." *Environment and Planning D: Society and Space* 30, no. 1 (2012): 78–95.

McConnell, Fiona. *Rehearsing the State: The Political Practices of the Tibetan Government-in-Exile.* Oxford: John Wiley & Sons, 2016.

McFarlane, Colin. "Urban Shadows: Materiality, the 'Southern City' and Urban Theory." *Geography Compass* 2, no. 2 (2008): 340–58.

Merleau-Ponty, Maurice. *Phenomenology of Perception*. Translated by Colin Smith. London: Routledge, 2002.

Merrifield, Andrew. *Henri Lefebvre: A Critical Introduction*. New York: Routledge, 2006.

Merrifield, Andrew. "Place and Space: A Lefebvrian Reconciliation." *Transactions of the Institute of British Geographers* 18, no. 4 (1993): 516–31.

Meyer, Birgit. "Aesthetics of Persuasion: Global Christianity and Pentecostalism's Sensational Forms." *South Atlantic Quarterly* 109, no. 4 (2010): 741–63.

Meyer, Birgit. "Introduction: From Imagined Communities to Aesthetic Formations: Religious Mediations, Sensational Forms, and Styles of Binding." In *Aesthetic Formations: Media, Religion, and the Senses*. Edited by Birgit Meyer, 1–28. New York: Palgrave Macmillan, 2009.

Meyer, Birgit. *Sensational Movies: Video, Vision, and Christianity in Ghana*. Berkeley: University of California Press, 2015.

Meyer, Birgit, and Jojada Verrips. "Aesthetics." In *Key Words in Religion, Media, and Culture*. Edited by David Morgan, 20–30. London: Routledge, 2008.

Miller, Peter, and Nikolas Rose. *Governing the Present: Administering Economic, Social and Personal Life*. New York: John Wiley & Sons, 2013.

Min, Brian. *Power and the Vote: Elections and Electricity in the Developing World*. Cambridge: Cambridge University Press, 2015.

Ministry of Planning and International Cooperation (MOPIC), Hashemite Kingdom of Jordan. *Executive Development Program 2011–2013*. Amman: MOPIC, 2013.

Ministry of Social Development (MSD), Hashemite Kingdom of Jordan. *Policies of Social Development and the Evaluation of Government Effectiveness in Combating Poverty and Unemployment*. Amman: Royal Jordanian National Defense College, 2009.

Mintz, Sidney W. *Sweetness and Power: The Place of Sugar in Modern History*. London: Penguin, 1986.

Mitchell, Lisa. "'To Stop Train Pull Chain': Writing Histories of Contemporary Political Practice." *Indian Economic & Social History Review* 48, no. 4 (2011): 469–95.

Mitchell, Timothy. *Carbon Democracy: Political Power in the Age of Oil*. New York: Verso Books, 2011.

Mitchell, Timothy. *Colonising Egypt*. Berkeley: University of California Press, 1991.

Mitchell, Timothy. "Economentality: How the Future Entered Government." *Critical Inquiry* 40, no. 4 (2014): 479–507.

Mitchell, Timothy. "Everyday Metaphors of Power." *Theory and Society* 19, no. 5 (1990): 545–77.

Mitchell, Timothy. "The Limits of the State: Beyond Statist Approaches and Their Critics." *American Political Science Review* 85, no. 1 (1991): 77–96.

Mitchell, Timothy. *Rule of Experts: Egypt, Techno-Politics, Modernity.* Berkeley: University of California Press, 2002.

Mitchell, Timothy. "Society, Economy, and the State Effect." In *State/Culture: State-Formation after the Cultural Turn.* Edited by George Steinmetz. Ithaca: Cornell University Press, 1999.

Mittermaier, Amira. "Bread, Freedom, Social Justice: The Egyptian Uprising and a Sufi Khidma." *Cultural Anthropology* 29, no. 1 (2014): 54–79.

Mittermaier, Amira. *Giving to God: Islamic Charity in Revolutionary Times.* Berkeley: University of California Press, 2019.

Moore, Donald S. *Suffering for Territory: Race, Place, and Power in Zimbabwe.* Durham, NC: Duke University Press, 2005.

Moore, Pete W. *Doing Business in the Middle East: Politics and Economic Crisis in Jordan and Kuwait.* Cambridge: Cambridge University Press, 2004.

Moore, Pete W. "A Political-Economic History of Jordan's General Intelligence Directorate: Authoritarian State-Building and Fiscal Crisis." *The Middle East Journal* 73, no. 2 (2019): 242–62.

Mousa, Riyad. "The Dispossession of the Peasantry: Colonial Policies, Settler Capitalism and Rural Change, 1918–1948." PhD diss., University of Utah, 2006.

Mrázek, Rudolf. *Engineers of Happy Land: Technology and Nationalism in a Colony.* Princeton: Princeton University Press, 2018.

Muehlebach, Andrea. *The Moral Neoliberal: Welfare and Citizenship in Italy.* Chicago: University of Chicago Press, 2012.

Mukerji, Chandra. *Impossible Engineering: Technology and Territoriality on the Canal du Midi.* Princeton: Princeton University Press, 2015.

Mundy, Martha. "Village Land and Individual Title: Musha' and Ottoman Land Registration in 'Ajlun District." In *Village, Steppe and State: The Social Origins of Modern Jordan.* Edited by Eugene Rogan and Tariq Tell, 58–80. London: British Academic Press, 1994.

Munif, Abd al-Rahman. *Story of a City: A Childhood in Amman.* Translated by Samira Kawar. London: Quartet Books, 1996.

Murray Li, Tania. "Beyond 'the State' and Failed Schemes." *American Anthropologist* 107, no. 3 (2005): 383–94.

Murray Li, Tania. "Fixing Non-Market Subjects: Governing Land and Population in the Global South." *Foucault Studies* 18, no. 2 (2014): 34–48.

Murray Li, Tania. "Governmentality." *Anthropologica* 49, no. 2 (2007): 275–81.

Murray Li, Tania. *The Will to Improve: Governmentality, Development, and the Practice of Politics*. Durham, NC: Duke University Press, 2007.

Mutawi, Samir A. *Jordan in the 1967 War*. Cambridge: Cambridge University Press, 2002.

Nanes, Stefanie. "Choice, Loyalty, and the Melting Pot: Citizenship and National Identity in Jordan." *Nationalism and Ethnic Politics* 14, no. 1 (2008): 85–116.

Nanes, Stefanie. "Hashemitism, Jordanian National Identity, and the Abu Odeh Episode." *Arab Studies Journal* 18, no. 1 (2010): 162–95.

Navaro, Yael. *Faces of the State: Secularism and Public Life in Turkey*. Princeton: Princeton University Press, 2002.

Navaro, Yael. *The Make-Believe Space: Affective Geography in a Postwar Polity*. Durham, NC: Duke University Press, 2012.

Nayanika, Mathur. *Paper Tiger: Law, Bureaucracy and the Developmental State in Himalayan India*. Cambridge: Cambridge University Press, 2016.

Neep, Daniel. "State-Space beyond Territory: Wormholes, Gravitational Fields, and Entanglement." *Journal of Historical Sociology* 30, no. 3 (2017): 466–95.

Neveu, Norig. "Repenser la Périphérie: Maʿān, Carrefour du Sud du *Bilād al-Shām* au tournant de la Première Guerre Mondiale." *Arabian Humanities* 6 (2016): doi: 10.4000/cy.3038.

Newman, Janet, and John Clarke. "States of Imagination." *Soundings* 57, no. 57 (2014): 153–69.

Ngai, Sianne. *Ugly Feelings*. Cambridge: Harvard University Press, 2005.

Nietzsche, Friedrich. *The Birth of Tragedy and the Genealogy of Morals*. Garden City, NY: Doubleday, 1956.

Nuseibeh, Hazim. *Dhikrayat Muqaddasiyya* [Sacred memories]. Beirut: Rayyes, 2010.

Obeid, Michelle. "Searching for the 'Ideal Face of the State' in a Lebanese Border Town." *Journal of the Royal Anthropological Institute* 16, no. 2 (2010): 330–46.

O'Connor, Erin. "Embodied Knowledge in Glassblowing: The Experience of Meaning and the Struggle Towards Proficiency." *The Sociological Review* 55 (2007): 126–41.

O'Donnell, Guillermo A. *Counterpoints: Selected Essays on Authoritarianism and Democratization*. South Bend, IN: University of Notre Dame Press, 1999.

Ohnuki-Tierney, Emiko. *Rice as Self: Japanese Identities through Time*. Princeton: Princeton University Press, 1994.

Ong, Aihwa. *Neoliberalism as Exception: Mutations in Citizenship and Sovereignty.* Durham, NC: Duke University Press, 2006.

Ortner, Sherry B. "Resistance and the Problem of Ethnographic Refusal." *Comparative Studies in Society and History* 37, no. 1 (1995): 173–93.

Oxfeld, Ellen. *Bitter and Sweet: Food, Meaning, and Modernity in Rural China.* Berkeley: University of California Press, 2017.

Painter, Joe. "Prosaic Geographies of Stateness." *Political Geography* 25, no. 7 (2006): 752–74.

Palmer, Carol. "'Following the Plough': The Agricultural Environment of Northern Jordan." *Levant* 30, no. 1 (1998): 129–65.

Palmer, Carol. "Milk and Cereals: Identifying Food and Food Identity among Fallāhīn and Bedouin in Jordan." *Levant* 34, no. 1 (2002): 173–95.

Panagia, Davide. *The Political Life of Sensation.* Durham, NC: Duke University Press, 2009.

Panagia, Davide. *Rancière's Sentiments.* Durham, NC: Duke University Press, 2018.

Parker, Christopher. "Tunnel-Bypasses and Minarets of Capitalism: Amman as Neo-liberal Assemblage." *Political Geography* 28, no. 2 (2009): 110–20.

Paxson, Heather. *The Life of Cheese: Crafting Food and Value in America.* Berkeley: University of California Press, 2013.

Peters, Anne M., and Pete W. Moore. "Beyond Boom and Bust: External Rents, Durable Authoritarianism, and Institutional Adaptation in the Hashemite Kingdom of Jordan." *Studies in Comparative International Development* 44, no. 3 (2009): 256–85.

Piro, Timothy J. *The Political Economy of Market Reform in Jordan.* London: Rowman & Littlefield, 1998.

Polanyi, Michael. *Personal Knowledge: Towards a Post-Critical Philosophy.* Chicago: University of Chicago Press, 1962.

Poulantzas, Nicos. *State, Power, Socialism.* London: Verso, 2014.

Povinelli, Elizabeth. *Economies of Abandonment: Social Belonging and Endurance in Late Liberalism.* Durham, NC: Duke University Press, 2011.

Pribble, Jennifer. *Welfare and Party Politics in Latin America.* Cambridge: Cambridge University Press, 2013.

Puri, Jyoti. *Sexual States: Governance and the Struggle over the Antisodomy Law in India.* Durham, NC: Duke University Press, 2016.

Pursley, Sara. *Familiar Futures: Time, Selfhood, and Sovereignty in Iraq.* Stanford, CA: Stanford University Press, 2019.

Al-Ramahi, Aseel. "Wasta in Jordan: A Distinct Feature of (and Benefit for) Middle Eastern Society." *Arab Law Quarterly* (2008): 35–62.

Rancière, Jacques. "Contemporary Art and the Politics of Aesthetics." In *Communities of Sense: Rethinking Aesthetics and Politics*. Edited by Beth Hinderliter and Vered Maimon, 31–50. Durham, NC: Duke University Press, 2009.

Rancière, Jacques. *Dissensus: On Politics and Aesthetics*. Edited and translated by Steven Corcoran. London: Bloomsbury Publishing, 2015.

Rancière, Jacques. *The Politics of Aesthetics: The Distribution of the Sensible*. Translated by Gabriel Rockhill. London: Bloomsbury, 2004.

Raz, Avi. *The Bride and the Dowry: Israel, Jordan, and the Palestinians in the Aftermath of the June 1967 War*. New Haven: Yale University Press, 2012.

Reeves, Madeleine. *Border Work: Spatial Lives of the State in Rural Central Asia*. Ithaca: Cornell University Press, 2014.

Robbins, Joel. *Becoming Sinners: Christianity and Moral Torment in a Papua New Guinea Society*. Berkeley: University of California Press, 2004.

Robins, Philip. *A History of Jordan*. New York: Cambridge University Press, 2004.

Robinson, Glenn. "Defensive Democratization in Jordan." *International Journal of Middle East Studies* 30 (1998): 387–410.

Rogan, Eugene L. "Bringing the State Back: The Limits of Ottoman Rule in Jordan 1840–1910." In *Village, Steppe and State: The Social Origins of Modern Jordan*. Edited by Eugene L. Rogan and Tariq Tell, 32–57. London: British Academic Press, 1994.

Rogan, Eugene L. *Frontiers of the State in the Late Ottoman Empire: Transjordan, 1850–1921*. Cambridge: Cambridge University Press, 2002.

Rogan, Eugene L. "Reconstructing Water Mills in Late Ottoman Transjordan." *Studies in the History and Archaeology of Jordan* 5 (1995): 753–56.

Rose, Nikolas. *Powers of Freedom: Reframing Political Thought*. Cambridge: Cambridge University Press, 1999.

Rose, Nikolas, and Peter Miller. "Political Power Beyond the State: Problematics of Government." *British Journal of Sociology* 43, no. 2 (1992): 173–205.

Rudra, Nita, and Stephan Haggard. "Globalization, Democracy, and Effective Welfare Spending in the Developing World." *Comparative Political Studies* 38, no. 9 (2005): 1015–49.

Ryan, Curtis R. "'Jordan First': Jordan's Inter-Arab Relations and Foreign Policy under King Abdullah II." *Arab Studies Quarterly* 26, no. 3 (2004): 43–62.

Ryan, Curtis R. *Jordan in Transition: From Hussein to Abdullah*. Boulder: Lynne Rienner Publishers, 2002.

Ryan, Curtis R. "Peace, Bread and Riots: Jordan and the International Monetary Fund." *Middle East Policy* 6, no. 2 (1998): 54–66.

Ryan, Curtis R. "Political Opposition and Reform Coalitions in Jordan." *British Journal of Middle Eastern Studies* 38, no. 3 (2011): 367–90.

Sadiki, Larbi. "Popular Uprisings and Arab Democratization." *International Journal of Middle East Studies* 32, no. 1 (2000): 71–95.

Sadiki, Larbi. "Towards Arab Liberal Governance: From the Democracy of Bread to the Democracy of the Vote." *Third World Quarterly* 18, no. 1 (1997): 127–48.

Sadowski, Yahya M. *Political Vegetables? Businessmen and Bureaucrats in the Development of Egyptian Agriculture*. Washington, DC: Brookings Institution, 1991.

Salamé, Ghassan. "The Middle East: Elusive Security, Indefinable Region." *Security Dialogue* 25, no. 1 (1994): 17–35.

Salomon, Noah. *For Love of the Prophet: An Ethnography of Sudan's Islamic State*. Princeton: Princeton University Press, 2016.

Satloff, Robert B. *From Abdullah to Hussein: Jordan in Transition*. Oxford: Oxford University Press, 1994.

Sayigh, Yezid. "Jordan in the 1980s: Legitimacy, Entity and Identity." In *Politics and the Economy in Jordan*. Edited by Rodney Wilson, 167–83. London: Routledge, 1991.

Schayegh, Cyrus. "1958 Reconsidered: State Formation and the Cold War in the Early Postcolonial Arab Middle East." *International Journal of Middle East Studies* 45, no. 3 (2013): 421–43.

Schewe, Eric. "How War Shaped Egypt's National Bread Loaf." *Comparative Studies of South Asia, Africa and the Middle East* 37, no. 1 (2017): 49–63.

Schielke, Samuli. *Egypt in the Future Tense: Hope, Frustration, and Ambivalence before and after 2011*. Bloomington: Indiana University Press, 2015.

Schivelbusch, Wolfgang. *Disenchanted Night: The Industrialization of Light in the Nineteenth Century*. Berkeley: University of California Press, 1995.

Schivelbusch, Wolfgang. *The Railway Journey: The Industrialization of Time and Space in the Nineteenth Century*. Berkeley: University of California Press, 1986.

Schuetze, Benjamin. *Promoting Democracy, Reinforcing Authoritarianism*. Cambridge: Cambridge University Press, 2019.

Schwedler, Jillian. *Faith in Moderation: Islamist Parties in Jordan and Yemen*. Cambridge: Cambridge University Press, 2006.

Schwedler, Jillian. "Occupied Maan: Jordan's Closed Military Zone." *Middle East Report*, Online 3 (2002).

Schwedler, Jillian. "The Political Geography of Protest in Neoliberal Jordan." *Middle East Critique* 21, no. 3 (2012): 259–70.

Schwenkel, Christina. "Sense." Theorizing the Contemporary, *Fieldsights*, September 24, 2015. https://culanth.org/fieldsights/sense.

Scott, David. *Conscripts of Modernity: The Tragedy of Colonial Enlightenment*. Durham, NC: Duke University Press, 2004.

Scott, James C. *Domination and the Arts of Resistance: Hidden Transcripts*. New Haven: Yale University Press, 1990.

Scott, James C. *Seeing Like a State: How Certain Schemes to Improve the Human Condition Have Failed*. New Haven: Yale University Press, 1998.

Scott, James C. *Weapons of the Weak: Everyday Forms of Peasant Resistance*. New Haven: Yale University Press, 1985.

Secor, Anna J. "Between Longing and Despair: State, Space, and Subjectivity in Turkey." *Environment and Planning D: Society and Space* 25, no. 1 (2007): 33–52.

Seeberg, Merete Bech. "State Capacity and the Paradox of Authoritarian Elections." *Democratization* 21, no. 7 (2014): 1265–85.

Seikaly, Sherene. *Men of Capital: Scarcity and Economy in Mandate Palestine*. Stanford, CA: Stanford University Press, 2015.

Sennett, Richard. *The Craftsman*. New Haven: Yale University Press, 2008.

Seremetakis, C. N. "The Memory of the Senses, Part One: Marks of the Transitory." In *The Senses Still: Perception and Memory as Material Culture in Modernity*. Edited by C. N. Seremetakis, 1–18. Boulder, CO: Westview Press, 1994.

El-Sharif, Ahmad. "Restoring Pride in Jordanian National Identity: Framing the Jordanian National Identity by the National Committee of Retired Army Veterans." *Studies in Literature and Language* 12, no. 5 (2016): 40–53.

Sharamiya, Wadi. *Al-tanmiyya al-īqtiṣādiyya fi al-ūrdun* [Economic development in Jordan]. Cairo: Center for Arab Research and Studies, 1967.

Sharma, Aradhana, and Akhil Gupta. "Rethinking Theories of the State in an Age of Globalization." In *The Anthropology of the State: A Reader*. Edited by Aradhana Sharma and Akhil Gupta, 1–41. Oxford: Blackwell, 2009.

Sha'sha, Z. J. "The Role of the Private Sector in Jordan's Economy." In *Politics and the Economy in Jordan*. Edited by Rodney Wilson, 86–94. London: Routledge, 1991.

Sheringham, Michael. *Everyday Life: Theories and Practices from Surrealism to the Present*. Oxford: Oxford University Press, 2006.

Shoshan, Boaz. "Grain Riots and the 'Moral Economy': Cairo, 1350–1517." *The Journal of Interdisciplinary History* 10, no. 3 (1980): 459–78.

Shryock, Andrew. "Dynastic Modernism and Its Contradictions: Testing the Limits of Pluralism, Tribalism, and King Hussein's Example in Hashemite Jordan." *Arab Studies Quarterly* 22, no. 3 (2000): 57–79.

Siemiatycki, Matti, Theresa Enright, and Mariana Valverde. "The Gendered Production of Infrastructure." *Progress in Human Geography* 44, no. 2 (2020): 297–314.

Simmons, Erica S. "Grievances Do Matter in Mobilization." *Theory and Society* 43, no. 5 (2014): 513–46.

Simmons, Erica S. *Meaningful Resistance: Market Reforms and the Roots of Social Protest in Latin America*. Cambridge: Cambridge University Press, 2016.

Simone, AbdouMaliq. "People as Infrastructure: Intersecting Fragments in Johannesburg." *Public Culture* 16, no. 3 (2004): 407–29.

Singerman, Diane. *Avenues of Participation: Family, Politics, and Networks in Urban Quarters of Cairo*. Princeton: Princeton University Press, 1995.

Singh, Prerna. *How Solidarity Works for Welfare: Subnationalism and Social Development in India*. Cambridge: Cambridge University Press, 2016.

Skocpol, Theda. "A Critical Review of Barrington Moore's *Social Origins of Dictatorship and Democracy*." *Politics & Society* 4, no. 1 (1973): 1–34.

Skocpol, Theda, and Dietrich Rueschemeyer. *States, Social Knowledge, and the Origins of Modern Social Policies*. New York and Princeton: Russell Sage Foundation and Princeton University Press, 1996.

Snow, Peter John. *Hussein: A Biography*. New York: RB Luce, 1972.

Snyder, Richard, and Ravi Bhavnani. "Diamonds, Blood, and Taxes: A Revenue-Centered Framework for Explaining Political Order." *Journal of Conflict Resolution* 49, no. 4 (2005): 563–97.

Soifer, Hillel David. "Regionalism, Ethnic Diversity, and Variation in Public Good Provision by National States." *Comparative Political Studies* 49, no. 10 (2016): 1341–71.

Springer, Simon. *The Discourse of Neoliberalism: An Anatomy of a Powerful Idea*. Lanham, MD: Rowman & Littlefield International, 2016.

Stack, Trevor. *Knowing History in Mexico: An Ethnography of Citizenship*. Albuquerque: University of New Mexico Press, 2012.

Stamatopoulou-Robbins, Sophia. *Waste Siege: The Life of Infrastructure in Palestine.* Stanford, CA: Stanford University Press, 2019.

Stanley, Liam, and Richard Jackson. "Introduction: Everyday Narratives in World Politics." *Politics* 36, no. 3 (2016): 223–35.

Stewart, Kathleen. *Ordinary Affects.* Durham, NC: Duke University Press, 2007.

Stoler, Ann Laura. *Carnal Knowledge and Imperial Power: Race and the Intimate in Colonial Rule.* Berkeley: University of California Press, 2010.

Suchman, L. A., and R. H. Trigg. "Artificial Intelligence as Craftwork." In *Understanding Practice: Perspectives on Activity and Context.* Edited by S. Chaiklin and J. Lave, 144–78. Cambridge: Cambridge University Press, 1993.

Sukarieh, Mayssoun. "On Class, Culture, and the Creation of the Neoliberal Subject: The Case of Jordan." *Anthropological Quarterly* (2016): 1201–55.

Susser, Asher. *On Both Banks of the Jordan: A Political Biography of Wasfi al-Tall.* London: Routledge, 1994.

Sutton, David. "Whole Foods: Revitalization through Everyday Synesthetic Experience." *Anthropology and Humanism* 25, no. 2 (2000): 120–30.

Tal, Lawrence. *Politics, the Military and National Security in Jordan, 1955–1967.* Basingstoke: Palgrave Macmillan, 2002.

Taussig, Michael T. *Defacement: Public Secrecy and the Labor of the Negative.* Stanford, CA: Stanford University Press, 1999.

Taussig, Michael T. *The Magic of the State.* London: Routledge, 1997.

Taydas, Zeynep, and Dursun Peksen. "Can States Buy Peace? Social Welfare Spending and Civil Conflicts." *Journal of Peace Research* 49, no. 2 (2002): 273–87.

Tell, Tariq. "The Politics of Rural Policy in East Jordan 1920–1989." In *The Transformation of Nomadic Society in the Arab East.* Edited by Martha Mundy and Basim Musallam, 90–98. Cambridge: Cambridge University Press, 2000.

Tell, Tariq, ed. *The Resilience of the Hashemite Rule: Politics and State in Jordan, 1946–1967.* Amman: CERMOC, 2001.

Tell, Tariq. *The Social and Economic Origins of Monarchy in Jordan.* London: Palgrave, 2013.

Thrift, Nigel. *Non-Representational Theory: Space, Politics, Affect.* London: Routledge, 2008.

Thrift, Nigel. "Understanding the Material Practices of Glamour." In *The Affect Theory Reader.* Edited by M. Gregg and G. J. Seigworth, 289–308. London: Duke University Press, 2010.

Tripp, Charles. *Islam and the Moral Economy: The Challenge of Capitalism*. Cambridge: Cambridge University Press, 2006.

Tripp, Charles. *The Power and the People: Paths of Resistance in the Middle East*. Cambridge: Cambridge University Press, 2013.

Trouillot, Michel Rolph. "The Anthropology of the State in the Age of Globalization: Close Encounters of the Deceptive Kind." *Current Anthropology* 42, no. 1 (2001): 125–38.

Tsing, Anna Lowenhaupt. *The Mushroom at the End of the World: On the Possibility of Life in Capitalist Ruins*. Princeton: Princeton University Press, 2015.

United Nations Development Programme (UNDP). "Poverty Reduction Strategy, 2013–2020." UNDP, 2013, http://www.jo.undp.org/content/dam/jordan/docs/Poverty/Jordanpovertyreductionstrategy.pdf.

Vaihinger, Hans. *The Philosophy of 'As If,' A System of the Theoretical, Practical and Religious Fictions of Mankind*. Translated by C. K. Ogden. New York: Harcourt, Brace & Company, 1924.

Vatikiotis, Panayiotis. *Politics and the Military in Jordan: A Study of the Arab Legion, 1921–1957*. London: Routledge, 1967.

Verdeil, Eric. "The Energy of Revolts in Arab Cities: The Case of Jordan and Tunisia." *Built Environment* 40, no. 1 (2014): 128–39.

Verdery, Katherine. *What Was Socialism, and What Comes Next?* Princeton: Princeton University Press, 1996.

von Schnitzler, Antina. *Democracy's Infrastructure: Techno-Politics and Protest after Apartheid*. Princeton: Princeton University Press, 2016.

Wacquant, Loïc. *Body and Soul*. New York: Oxford University Press, 2004.

Wacquant, Loïc. "The Body, the Ghetto and the Penal State." *Qualitative Sociology* 32, no. 1 (2009): 101–29.

Wacquant, Loïc. "Carnal Connections: On Embodiment, Apprenticeship, and Membership." *Qualitative Sociology* 28, no. 4 (2005): 445–74.

Warnier, Jean-Pierre. "A Praxeological Approach to Subjectivation in a Material World." *Journal of Material Culture* 6, no. 1 (2001): 5–24.

Waterbury, John. "From Social Contracts to Extraction Contracts." In *Islam, Democracy, and the State in North Africa*. Edited by John Entelis, 141–76. Bloomington: Indiana University Press, 1997.

Watkins-Hayes, Celeste. *The New Welfare Bureaucrats: Entanglements of Race, Class, and Policy Reform*. Chicago: University of Chicago Press, 2009.

Weber, Cynthia. "Performative States." *Millennium* 27, no. 1 (1998): 77–95.

Weber, Max. *Essays in Sociology*. Translated and edited by H. H. Gerth and C. Wright Mills. New York: Oxford University Press, 1946.

Wedeen, Lisa. *Ambiguities of Domination: Politics, Rhetoric, and Symbols in Contemporary Syria*. Chicago: The University of Chicago Press, 1999.

Wedeen, Lisa. *Authoritarian Apprehensions: Ideology, Judgment, and Mourning in Syria*. Chicago: University of Chicago Press, 2019.

Wedeen, Lisa. *Peripheral Visions: Publics, Power and Performance in Yemen*. Chicago: University of Chicago Press, 2009.

Wedeen, Lisa. "Seeing Like a Citizen, Acting Like a State: Exemplary Events in Unified Yemen." *Comparative Studies in Society and History* 45 (2003): 680–713.

Wiktorowicz, Quintan. "The Limits of Democracy in the Middle East: The Case of Jordan." *The Middle East Journal* 53, no. 4 (1999): 606–20.

Wilmington, Martin W. *The Middle East Supply Centre*. Albany: State University of New York Press, 1971.

Wilson, Alice. *Sovereignty in Exile: A Saharan Liberation Movement Governs*. Philadelphia: University of Pennsylvania Press, 2016.

Wimmer, Andreas, and Nina Glick Schiller. "Methodological Nationalism and Beyond: Nation–State Building, Migration and the Social Sciences." *Global Networks* 2, no. 4 (2002): 301–34.

Winders, Bill. "The Vanishing Free Market: The Formation and Spread of the British and US Food Regimes." *Journal of Agrarian Change* 9, no. 3 (2009): 315–44.

Woertz, Eckhart. *Oil for Food: The Global Food Crisis and the Middle East*. New York: Oxford University Press, 2013.

Wolf, Diane, ed. *Feminist Dilemmas in Fieldwork*. Boulder: Westview Press, 1996.

World Bank. *Hashemite Kingdom of Jordan—Development Policy Review: Improving Institutions, Fiscal Policies and Structural Reforms for Greater Growth Resilience and Sustained Job Creation*. Washington, DC: World Bank, 2012. https://openknowledge.worldbank.org/handle/10986/12302.

World Bank. "Hashemite Kingdom of Jordan: Options for Immediate Fiscal Adjustment and Longer Term Consolidation." In *Report No. 71979-JO*. Washington, DC: World Bank, 2012.

World Food Programme. "Jordan Food Security Survey in the Poverty Pockets, August-September 2008." http://documents.wfp.org/stellent/groups/public/documents/ena/wfp204530.pdf.

Yaqub, Salim. *Containing Arab Nationalism: The Eisenhower Doctrine and the Middle East.* Chapel Hill, NC: UNC Press Books, 2004.

Yom, Sean. "The New Landscape of Jordanian Politics: Social Opposition, Fiscal Crisis, and the Arab Spring." *British Journal of Middle Eastern Studies* 42, no. 3 (2015): 284–300.

Yurchak, Alexei. *Everything Was Forever, Until It Was No More: The Last Soviet Generation.* Princeton: Princeton University Press, 2005.

Zacka, Bernardo. *When the State Meets the Street: Public Service and Moral Agency.* Cambridge: Harvard University Press, 2017.

Stanford Studies in Middle Eastern
and Islamic Societies and Cultures

Joel Beinin and Laleh Khalili, editors

EDITORIAL BOARD
*Asef Bayat, Marilyn Booth, Laurie Brand, Timothy Mitchell, Jillian Schwedler,
Rebecca L. Stein, Max Weiss*

CPSIA information can be obtained
at www.ICGtesting.com
Printed in the USA
LVHW031456170323
741851LV00003B/412

9 781503 631328